New Insights into Interpreting Studies

STUDIES IN LANGUAGE, CULTURE AND SOCIETY

Edited by
Łucja Biel, Andrzej Kątny and Agnieszka Biernacka

VOLUME 18

PETER LANG

Berlin - Bruxelles - Chennai - Lausanne - New York - Oxford

Agnieszka Biernacka / Wojciech Figiel (eds.)

New Insights into Interpreting Studies

Technology, Society and Access

PETER LANG

Berlin - Bruxelles - Chennai - Lausanne - New York - Oxford

Bibliographic Information published by the Deutsche Nationalbibliothek
The Deutsche Nationalbibliothek lists this publication in the Deutsche Nationalbibliografie; detailed bibliographic data is available in the internet at http://dnb.d-nb.de.

Library of Congress Cataloging-in-Publication Data
A CIP catalog record for this book has been applied for at the Library of Congress.

This publication has been co-financed from the funds of the University of Warsaw within "Excellence Initiative – Research University" programme (microgrant BOB-661-791/2023).

This work has been reviewed by Łucja Biel (University of Warsaw).

ISSN 2195-7479
ISBN 978-3-631-88485-0 (Print)
E-ISBN 978-3-631-90712-2 (E-Book)
E-ISBN 978-3-631-90713-9 (EPDF)
DOI 10.3726/b21104

This publication has been peer reviewed.

www.peterlang.com

To Professor Małgorzata Tryuk for her contributions to Interpreting Studies.
For her enthusiasm and consistency in pursuing important and just causes in the academia and outside of it.
For being a person who makes a difference.

Contents

List of Contributors 9

Introduction 11

Franz Pöchhacker
Chapter 1 History, community, accessibility: Interpreting studies extended 15

Michaela Wolf
Chapter 2 Interpreting under threat: Nazi concentration camps as "non-places" 35

Sergey Tyulenev
Chapter 3 Interpreting and translation in military intelligence interrogations: A social-systemic perspective 55

Elisabet Tiselius
Chapter 4 Ethics of interpreting professions: One size fits all? 77

Agnieszka Biernacka
Chapter 5 Still *the Cinderella of interpretation*? Court interpreting in Poland revisited 93

Aleksandra Kalata-Zawłocka
Chapter 6 Preparation for interpreting in TV settings: Strategies employed by signed language interpreters across Europe 115

Heidi Salaets / Katalin Balogh
Chapter 7 Access to justice for vulnerable groups in society: Minors in Belgium as a case 141

Carmen Valero Garcés
Chapter 8 Exodus, refugees, and inclusion of the Afghan population in Spain. The project *Get To Know To Keep In Mind* 161

Alessandra Riccardi
Chapter 9 Interpreter training: A never-ending process 175

Danielle D'Hayer
Chapter 10 When a CoP mindset combined with hybrid pedagogy breaks silos to enhance interprofessional multilingual experiential learning and an inclusive participation of multiple communities. The case study of mock conferences for conference interpreting education at London Metropolitan University 189

Ivana Čeňková
Chapter 11 Artificial intelligence from the perspective of students and interpreters 221

Anna Jelec, Karol Bartkiewicz, Katarzyna Czarnocka and Joanna Ziobro-Strzępek
Chapter 12 Why not(es)? Automatic analysis of notes for consecutive interpreting training 243

Tomasz Korybski
Chapter 13 Hybrid and synchronous simultaneous interpreter training: Configurations, constraints, opportunities and perceptions 269

Wojciech Figiel
Chapter 14 Teaching simultaneous interpreting during the COVID-19 pandemic: Technology, society, access 289

List of Contributors

Katalin Balogh
KU Leuven Campus Antwerpen

Karol Bartkiewicz
Adam Mickiewicz University in Poznań

Agnieszka Biernacka
University of Warsaw

Katarzyna Czarnocka
University of Warsaw

Ivana Čeňková
Charles University, Prague

Danielle D'Hayer
London Metropolitan University

Wojciech Figiel
University of Warsaw

Anna Jelec
Adam Mickiewicz University in Poznań

Aleksandra Kalata-Zawłocka
University of Warsaw
Association of Polish Sign Language Interpreters (STPJM)

Tomasz Korybski
University of Surrey

Franz Pöchhacker
University of Vienna

Alessandra Riccardi
University of Trieste

Heidi Salaets
KU Leuven Campus Antwerpen

Elisabet Tiselius
Stockholm University

Sergey Tyulenev
Durham University

Carmen Valero-Garcés
University of Alcalá

Michaela Wolf
University of Graz

Joanna Ziobro-Strzępek
Krosno State College

Introduction

This volume, published in a series *Studies in Language, Culture and Society*, is a fruit of work of eminent researchers in the field of Interpreting Studies who kindly accepted our invitation to contribute with a chapter to a volume to celebrate the 70th birthday of Professor Małgorzata Tryuk.

Prof. dr hab. Małgorzata Tryuk is a worldwide known researcher in Interpreting Studies and author of publications on, among other topics, conference interpreting, community interpreting, interpreting history and interpreter training. She received Officier des Palmes académiques (2013) and 200th anniversary of the University of Warsaw (2016) awards. She represents the Institute of Applied Linguistics, University of Warsaw, in international organizations, such as CIUTI (Conférence Internationale Permanente d'Instituts Universitaires de Traducteurs et Interprètes) and EMT (European Masters in Translation) bringing together leading scholars and trainers in the field of Translation and Interpreting Studies. She is on the Board of AUPELF Réseau Lexicologie Traduction Terminologie, "Plejada" – Academic Association of Polish Romanists and is a member of the European Society for Translation Studies (EST). Her professional experience includes membership of the University of Warsaw Senate (1982–1985), the Faculty Council (1982–1984 and from 2004 on) and the Institute Council (1998–2002 and from 2004 on). She was Deputy Dean for Students' Affairs (2005–2008), Head of Interdisciplinary Postgraduate Studies in Translation and Interpreting (1999–2005) and Local Coordinator of European Masters in Conference Interpreting EMCI (2005–2020). The areas of her academic interest encompass not only Translation and Interpreting Studies, but also specialist languages, terminology and terminography. As far as her editorial activities are concerned, in the years 1978–1987 she was Secretary of "Kwartalnik Filologiczny", and has been a member of the editorial board of "Revue internationale d'Etudes en Langues modernes appliquées" since 2008 and "Lingua Legis". Moreover, she is a reviewer in national and international journals: *Między Oryginałem a Przekładem*, *Przekładaniec*, *Rocznik Przekładoznawczy*, *Across Languages and Cultures*, *Interpreters' Newsletter*, *RIELMA*, and *CLINA: An Interdisciplinary Journal of Translation, Interpreting and Intercultural Communication*. She is an experienced university teacher and a supervisor of dozens of MA theses.

The editors of the present volume owe Professor Małgorzata Tryuk special gratitude for supervising our doctoral dissertations. For us, not only has she been, and continues to be, mentor and role model in academic career, but colleague and collaborator who listens and supports in ideas and concerns we confide in her. True to the Polish denomination for supervisor ('*promotor*'), she has lost no opportunity to promote our professional achievements.

As editors of this volume, we are endlessly happy to present fourteen contributions written by eighteen researchers representing various sub-fields of Interpreting Studies. Although the subtitle of this book suggests a division into technology, society and access as three big topics covered by today's scholarly interests, we finally decided to abandon such a sharp setting of boundaries. This is due mainly to the fact that Interpreting Studies is nowadays a field that combines different disciplines and methodologies.

Therefore, Franz Pöchhacker in an opening chapter titled *History, community, accessibility: Interpreting studies extended* takes us on a journey back to the early 1990s and presents not only the chronological evolution of thought on interpreting, but also draws a picture of how Interpreting Studies has borrowed ideas from other fields of research.

New approaches to the research in the history of interpreting are presented in the following two chapters. Michaela Wolf in her text *Interpreting under threat: Nazi concentration camps as "non-places"* uses Marc Augé's concept of *non-place* to explore ambiguous, violent and aggressive communication patterns in concentration camps.

Sergey Tyulenev in his contribution entitled *Interpreting and translation in military intelligence interrogations: A social-systemic perspective* employs Niklas Luhmann's social systems theory to analyse a rarely studied aspect of history of translation and interpreting, namely the dynamics of interrelations in the military intelligence interrogation team.

Elisabet Tiselius invites to considering *Ethics of interpreting professions: One size fits all?* where she presents various perspectives on the professional ethics of interpreters, discusses the scope of ethical freedom in interpreting, as well as reflects on the similarities and differences in the ethics of different groups of interpreters.

The next chapter, prepared by Agnieszka Biernacka and titled *Still 'the Cinderella of interpretation'? Court interpreting in Poland revisited* follows in the footsteps of Professor Małgorzata Tryuk's research and reexamines the profession of court interpreters as both a separate type and the one having many features in common with community-based interpreting.

Aleksandra Kalata-Zawłocka presents her pioneer research in *Preparation for interpreting in TV settings: Strategies employed by signed language interpreters across Europe* conducted in the form of an online survey, the results of which are multidimensional as they are as important for the academia as for the interpreter community and deaf viewers.

In the next two chapters, the authors present outcomes of their research projects.

Heidi Salaets and Katalin Balogh in their text titled *Access to justice for vulnerable groups in society: Minors in Belgium as a case* not only present their research into the topic at hand, but also describe practical steps the authors have taken to make the project results sustainable and durable.

In a similar vein, Carmen Valero-Garcés in her text *Exodus, refugees, and inclusion of the Afghan population in Spain. The project 'Get To Know To Keep In Mind'* emphasises the need to integrate refugees and asylum seekers in hosting communities by recognizing their right to communicate in their languages (languages of lesser diffusion) as a valuable way to overcome language and cultural barriers.

A block of six contributions on pedagogical issues of interpreter training begins with a text *Interpreter training: A never-ending process* by Alessandra Riccardi who shows how a potential of a collective experience of interpreters as a profession embodied in memoirs of witnesses of the interpreting history can affect the interpreter training process.

Danielle D'Hayer contributes with the text *When a CoP mindset combined with hybrid pedagogy breaks silos to enhance interprofessional multilingual experiential` learning and an inclusive participation of multiple communities. The case study of mock conferences for conference interpreting education at London Metropolitan University*, in which advantages of building and maintaining a community of practice are explored. In this innovative approach students, educators and alumni are regarded as partners in revolutionizing the idea of mock conferences as a collaborative and inclusive effort that empowers learners.

Ivana Čeňková elaborates on *Artificial intelligence from the perspective of students and interpreters* and the extent to which it is able to change the interpreter training process and the profession itself. The article presents interesting insights from different stakeholders in interpreting (students, trainers) on what will probably exercise a decisive impact on the future of the profession to which Professor Tryuk has devoted most of her academic and professional life.

Anna Jelec, Karol Bartkiewicz, Katarzyna Czarnocka and Joanna Ziobro-Strzępek in their contribution *Why not(es)? Automatic analysis of notes for consecutive interpreting training* present the results of an empirical study on note-taking with a view to redesigning interpreter training curricula and assessment criteria of consecutive interpreting.

The final two contributions discuss the impact of the COVID-19 pandemic on teaching simultaneous interpreting.

In *Hybrid and synchronous simultaneous interpreter training: Configurations, constraints, opportunities and perceptions* Tomasz Korybski discusses advantages and disadvantages of hybrid mode of delivery of training in simultaneous interpreting and presents his empirical study on this topic.

The last contribution, entitled *Teaching simultaneous interpreting during the COVID-19 pandemic: Technology, society, access*, by Wojciech Figiel revisits the theme of this volume by providing an autoethnographical account of author's experiences with remote simultaneous interpreter training during the first few months of the COVID-19 pandemic. The author stresses the importance of support from disability activists in testing and adopting technical solutions accessible for all.

The themes of this volume, technological development in interpreting training and practice, access for all to interpreting and interpreter training, and socio-historical research on interpreter training and interpreting as a profession, have been the focus of Professor Małgorzata Tryuk's research and contributions to interpreting studies. We hope that the present volume will be a truly fitful commemoration of her 70th anniversary. When writing these words, we also hope for a future, in which everyone who needs it has access to services of highly qualified interpreters, the work of the latter is appreciated and transformative technologies contribute to well-being of both interpreters and their clients. And we are absolutely convinced that Professor Małgorzata Tryuk will continue to play an important role in achieving these ambitious goals.

As editors, we would like to extend our heartfelt thanks to all our authors – outstanding researchers in Interpreting Studies – who collaborated with us on this book with great commitment and understanding of tight deadlines. We thank them for the wonderful, enlightening and thought-provoking contributions based on their exceptional knowledge and expertise.

The Editors
Warsaw, October 2023

Franz Pöchhacker

Chapter 1 History, community, accessibility: Interpreting studies extended

Abstract: With reference to the contributions by Małgorzata Tryuk to the development of research on interpreting in Poland and beyond, this chapter reviews some of the major developments in the academic study of interpreting since the early 1990s, such as interpreting scholars' move to include historical as well as contemporary perspectives in their purview and to focus attention on interpreting practices beyond international conferences and organisations. Under the headings of 'history', 'community' and 'accessibility' I discuss how the scope of research on interpreting has come to be widened significantly since the mid-1990s and how individual efforts have contributed to these developments. The notion of access is used to frame the account of two ways in which interpreting studies has been extended beyond conference interpreting research, namely, the provision of community interpreting to ensure access to public services across barriers of language and culture, and the development of accessibility services to permit real-time access to communication in the media and live events. The latter implies some radical shifts that will be discussed with regard to the conceptualisation of interpreting as a social and professional practice.

Keywords: community interpreting, accessibility, respeaking, speech recognition, subtitling

1. Introduction

The study of interpreting as a social practice is a relatively recent academic pursuit, especially when compared to the study of law, medicine or the natural sciences. Depending on the chronology one may wish to adopt, it can be said to span about half a century or as many as seven decades. The timescale of 70 years – since the first more widely disseminated academic publications on interpreting (e.g. Herbert 1952; Thieme et al. 1956) – seems particularly appropriate in this case as it allows us to approach the evolution of interpreting studies on the scale of a human lifetime, and to relate a view of 'Interpreting Studies at 70' to the life and career of a scholar who has made significant contributions to this academic field. Małgorzata Tryuk, at 70, will be my reference point for this contribution to a volume paying tribute to her accomplishments. My theme, as indicated in the title, will be the notion of extension(s) – of ways in which the discipline, its research approaches and the concept of interpreting itself have been broadened, not least through some of the choices and initiatives of Małgorzata Tryuk. As will be seen, the link between the discipline and the scholar goes far beyond the coincidence that they share the same age; rather, my account of the development of interpreting studies, particularly in recent decades, will reveal important points of interface and multiple ways in which the trajectories of the discipline and the scholar are interrelated.

I will begin by looking back to the formative years of interpreting studies in the early 1990s, which correspond to the halfway point between Małgorzata Tryuk's PhD, in 1984, and the advanced doctorate (D.Litt.) she earned in 2004. A brief sketch of the field and its research approaches at the time will serve as a backdrop against which some major shifts and extensions in the development of the discipline can be highlighted. I will discuss these under the headings of 'history', 'community' and 'accessibility', first with regard to the discipline as such and then in relation to some of the scholarly as well as personal efforts of Małgorzata Tryuk.

2. History

In looking back on the formative years of interpreting studies as an academic (sub)discipline within the broader field of translation studies, the 'history' in question here is that of the field as such, and I will first offer a brief sketch of the scholarly community at the time, with special regard for its sociological make-up and its research priorities. The latter will then lead to a consideration of history in a different sense – that is, the history of interpreting, or historiography (Baigorri-Jalón 2015), as a topic of research in its own right, to which Małgorzata Tryuk has contributed in a particularly unique and memorable way.

2.1. Conference interpreting research

Thanks to the foundations laid in the 1970s by the 'Paris School' around Danica Seleskovitch at the École Supérieure d'Interprètes et de Traducteurs (Lederer 2015), the scholarly study of interpreting throughout the 1980s centred on professional interpreting in international conference settings. Efforts at elucidating its basic 'sense-based' technique mostly involved only the major European conference languages (English, French, German), and key publications were written in French, the original lingua franca of the conference interpreting profession. European still meant Western European, and the sporadic presence of scholars from the Soviet Union, most notably Ghelly Chernov, at international events (e.g. Chernov 1985) had only a very limited impact.

The community of interpreting scholars was still small and consisted of individuals dispersed in different countries, typically only one or two per university-level training program (see Pöchhacker 1995). Significantly, those engaged in the study of interpreting were generally individuals with experience in the professional practice of conference interpreting. In the case of Poland, such an individual was Andrzej Kopczyński, a contemporary of the Paris School (see Tryuk 2017). A few years after the fall of the Iron Curtain, he was a presenter at the Translation Studies Congress in Vienna in 1992, which was also where Daniel Gile (1994) used the label 'practisearcher' that was to gain such wide currency in later years.

With the exception of the long-dominant Paris School, the practisearcher profile could not easily be applied to entire institutions, and it was an institutional foundation that the field of 'conference interpreting research' was still lacking. One important exception was the 'Interpreter School' at the University of Trieste, where the scientific component of the institutional framework came mainly through interdisciplinary cooperation. The international conference organised at the University of Trieste in late 1986, while still devoted to the theme of interpreter training, marked a turning point toward internationalisation as well as institutionalisation (as depicted in Figure 1).

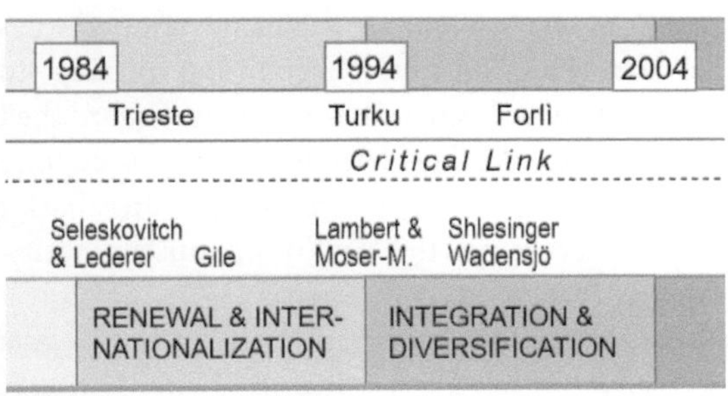

Figure 1. Formative decades of interpreting studies. (Adapted from Pöchhacker 2022: 50)

The 'Trieste era' of interpreting studies ushered in the dominance of English as the field's main medium of communication, which proved essential to broadening the field also geographically, particularly towards Asia, but also towards Eastern Europe. Having a more widely shared language in turn facilitated the institutionalisation of scholarly exchanges among the members of an increasingly global community. The launching of *The Interpreters' Newsletter* in the aftermath of the Trieste Conference gave the field its first platform for academic communication and became the first international journal for research on interpreting (preceded only by the *Journal of Interpretation* published by the US Registry of Interpreters for the Deaf). At the same time, Daniel Gile's closely related efforts to disseminate information on conference interpreting research throughout a network of international contacts (Gile 2015) gave the field its first database of bibliographic information.

Paradoxically, these significant developments in the fledgling discipline were not to the benefit of scholars like Małgorzata Tryuk at the time, who found their working languages, in this case mainly Polish and French, and their work marginalised. It is well worth noting that even a quarter-century later, Małgorzata Tryuk (2021a) showed her serious concern about this 'anglicization' of academia in a thorough bibliometric analysis of Polish scholars' publications in translation studies. While she herself went on to acquire an impressive level of proficiency in English, the example of her early days in the field shows how English-dominant internationalisation could also be experienced as a constraint on the formation of a linguistically diverse community of scholars. In this regard at least, interpreting scholars proficient in French would have been more comfortable in the era of the Paris School; in many others, however, the 'opening up' of the field, for which Gile (1994) pleaded in his plenary address at the 1992 Translation Studies Congress in Vienna, established new pathways and redressed the imbalance between center and periphery in interpreting studies. Whereas Gile's major concern may have been greater openness toward the theoretical and methodological approaches of other disciplines, such as cognitive psychology, his vision of a 'Renaissance' period in interpreting studies, harking back to role models such as David Gerver and the kind of interdisciplinarity in evidence at the 1977 Venice Symposium (Gerver & Sinaiko 1978), certainly accommodated a wider geographical scope and a greater diversity of working languages under study. Much less in evidence was an opening up of interpreting studies in terms of the diversity of research topics and objects of study. This happened only after the mid-1990s, along several lines, some of which can be related very closely to the work of Małgorzata Tryuk. These will be taken up in the sections below, in thematic rather than chronological order, beginning with work under the heading of 'history'.

Until the mid-1990s, interest in the history of interpreting was very limited. During the heyday of international conference interpreting in the decades after World War II, interpreting – in international conferences and organisations – was a newly developed profession that presumably did not have much of a past worth exploring. Even the origins of that profession in the early twentieth century were only poorly understood until Baigorri Jalón's (2000) seminal research on 'the birth of conference interpreting'. With few exceptions, other forms of interpreting as practiced throughout the millennial history of that activity were ignored, despite the solid foundations laid for historical scholarship in one of the field's earliest academic publications (Thieme et al. 1956). Though there had been some follow-up articles by Ingrid Kurz (e.g. 1985), it was not until the book chapter on 'Interpreters and the Making of History' by Margareta Bowen (1995) that the interpreting studies community was provided with a first comprehensive account of interpreting in the course of history. Nevertheless, history remained a marginal concern until well into the twenty-first century, when several new avenues of historical research emerged. One of the most innovative and significant contributions was made by Małgorzata Tryuk.

2.2. Interpreting in concentration camps

For decades, interpreting scholars' main points of reference to Hitler's German Reich were the Nuremberg Trial and the (often apologetic) memoirs of some leading interpreter personalities. And this focus on diplomacy and high-stakes tribunals would appear quite natural, given the field's dominant concern with high-level conference interpreting. What then did it take to discover that interpreting played an important role also in the most abysmal sites of human suffering that were brought into existence by the Nazi regime's murderous campaigns? Without much need to probe Małgorzata Tryuk's motivation to spend countless hours going through the recollections of former concentration camp inmates archived in the Auschwitz-Birkenau Memorial and Museum, one may assume that cultural proximity and human empathy and sensitivity must have been among the forces driving her immense labour of discovery. And her discoveries for the benefit of interpreting studies are striking: To begin with, Tryuk (2010a) makes clear that the Nazi concentration camps in Poland were sites of multilingualism, with prisoners from up to 40 different national or ethnic groups. The camp language (*Lagersprache*, also *Lagerszpracha*) that was created by the inmates from Polish, Yiddish, Silesian dialects and Hungarian (Tryuk 2010a: 128) was used for communication among themselves, but all official communication had to be in German. This necessitated the intervention of interpreters, and Tryuk's (2010a) research unravels the distinctions between different groups of interpreters and describes their recruitment, language combinations, duties, roles and techniques. She also portrays, even literally, several Polish camp interpreters (*Lagerdolmetscher*), who were drafted into that role because they had declared a knowledge of German.

Tryuk's (2010a) study on interpreting in concentration camps is a milestone with several important implications. Most obviously, it highlights the enormous interest and potential of studying interpreting activities in particular historical circumstances which allow for real discoveries – of unique practices and personalities alike. Such discoveries presuppose a keen awareness of potential sources of evidence, and the example of the Auschwitz-Birkenau archives can inspire further investigations in similar places. Another prerequisite is a broad view of interpreting as a communication-enabling activity, looking beyond the narrow confines of professional practice and status. Along these lines, the field of non-professional interpreting (and translation) has gained considerable momentum within interpreting studies. Furthermore, the extreme setting explored by Tryuk (2010a) serves as a paragon of research that looks at interpreting where it is most critically needed rather than where it commands the highest social esteem. Pertinent examples range from volunteers in international disaster relief operations and refugee crises to local recruits in warfare and occupation zones. As interpreting scholars are painfully aware, such interpreting in crisis situations has become increasingly frequent and has also attracted much greater attention from researchers in interpreting studies and beyond. This has given further prominence to some of the issues discussed by Tryuk (2010a) for interpreting 'under duress' – that is, the interpreter's role and ethical choices in situations of unequal power relations and oppression. Beyond the setting of her original study and related investigations (Tryuk 2016), Małgorzata Tryuk's (2015) monograph *On Ethics and Interpreters* aptly captures the broader themes of recent scholarship to which she made such an innovative contribution. What is more, she has herself extended the scope of her historical investigations beyond Nazi concentration camps and war crimes tribunals in Poland. Thus, recent handbook chapters offer a broader review of 'Translating and interpreting in conflict and crisis' (Tryuk 2020) and of 'Translation under Fascism and Nazism' (Tryuk 2021b), and the program of the 2022 Conference of the History and Translation Network in Tallinn featured her as one of the few presenters on interpreting with a paper on interpreting in the Spanish Civil War.

In summary, there can be no doubt that interpreting studies has seen its scope of research significantly broadened and extended into the past ever since it took shape as an international community of scholars (of conference interpreting) in the course of the 1990s. A serious concern with the history of interpreting is now an important component of the discipline, and Małgorzata Tryuk counts among those interpreting scholars who have given this strand of research a major impetus.

3. Community

Going back again to the formative years of interpreting studies as depicted in Figure 1, another major extension of the field can easily be discerned: the move beyond conference interpreting so as to include interpreting in community settings within the scope of the discipline. Once again, a brief sketch of this development will be given in general terms before some significant contributions are discussed.

3.1. From speeches to services

As suggested in the periodisation applied to interpreting studies in Figure 1, the year 1994 was an important marker, associated with an international conference, the publication of the first volume on interpreting in a recently launched book series, and the announcement of yet another international event. The first two can be said to mark a culmination point of the preceding period, labelled as 'renewal & internationalization', whereas the third marks a new beginning epitomised by the conference theme of interpreters in the community as 'the critical link'. I will briefly discuss these three developments in more detail below.

In an unprecedented effort at international collaboration, a team of scholars from Paris, Trieste and Turku organised a conference that was framed as the first opportunity after the 1977 Venice Symposium to take stock of the theoretical and methodological development of research on interpreting (Gile et al. 1997). Structured as a series of round-table sessions, the conference discussed such themes as research policy, training, methodology, quality and cognitive skills in (conference) interpreting, the latter being dealt with also in the plenary speech by a cognitive psychologist. In addition to these mainstream topics, there were sessions devoted to linguistics and discourse analysis, intercultural communication as well as media and court interpreting, along with a plenary by Per Linell (1997) with a focus on dialogue interpreting. Taken together, the parts of the program that were less closely linked to conference interpreting can be seen as pointing to interpreting in a greater diversity of settings, even though this is not reflected in the title of the proceedings volume (Gambier et al. 1997).

An even narrower focus on conference interpreting (i.e. on simultaneous interpreting) characterises the first volume on interpreting in John Benjamins' newly launched Benjamins Translation Library book series. The collection edited by Sylvie Lambert and Barbara Moser-Mercer (1994) includes reprints of earlier work as well as original papers, its contents supposedly ranging from pedagogical issues to topics in simultaneous interpreting and to neurological research. Whatever its merits, this stocktaking of empirical research contains no hint of the more diversified profile that research on interpreting was to develop in the course of the 1990s.

In the shadows of the new dynamics in research on conference interpreting in Europe and beyond, interpreting in different social settings had received a degree of scholarly attention in such countries as Australia, Canada and the UK in the 1980s, but it was only with the First International Conference on Interpreting in Legal, Health, and Social Service Settings, held in Orillia near Toronto in 1995, that 'interpreters in the community' gained greater visibility. In the announcement of that conference, community interpreting was defined as an activity that 'enables people who are not fluent speakers of the official language(s) of the country to communicate with the providers of public services' (Pöchhacker 2000: 37). Significantly, the definition does not refer to 'foreign' languages and therefore proved broad enough to accommodate also the communication needs of deaf persons in gaining 'full and equal access to legal, health, education, government, and social services'. This allowed the integration of signed language interpreting into the Critical Link community, which owed much of its strength at the time to its inclusive approach across linguistic modalities. At the same time, the reference in the definition to the (language of the) 'country' highlights one of the major constraints on community interpreting as a more or less professional service. Unlike international conference interpreting, which is practiced on a global scale, not least thanks to the efforts of AIIC, largely according to international standards, interpreting 'in the community' is by definition subject to the legal precepts and public policies and authorities of a given national context. This makes it indispensable for those engaged in 'research & development' of community interpreting services to work with, if not within, the framework of the relevant social institutions as well as the broader sociopolitical conditions of their country. This is precisely the path taken also by Małgorzata Tryuk in her efforts to extend scholarly work on interpreting to interpreting in the community.

3.2. New social and training needs

One of the first avenues of research in the newly emerging international scholarly community were studies designed to ascertain the status quo. Did such interpreting practices exist at all? If so, who was doing the interpreting, where, and under what conditions? Finding reliable answers to such questions proved an enormous task, given the great diversity of institutional settings and the general lack of explicit policies.

In her monograph on community interpreting, Małgorzata Tryuk (2004) consequently started out by laying the necessary foundations for an empirical exploration of the new field of practice. Following a review of early research to bring out the unique challenges of community interpreting as an object of study, she discussed the Polish sociopolitical context at the time of the enlargement of the European Union toward the East, after which issues surrounding migration and asylum would soon loom much larger. Engaging with key concepts in the emerging theorisation of community interpreting, she addressed the issue of norms, which also features in the title of her book, and the topic of the community interpreter's role, which dominated much scholarship in the early years of this new field of research.

In the empirical parts of her study, Tryuk (2004) adopted two different but equally productive methodological approaches: a questionnaire-based survey addressed to members of two Polish professional associations of (translators and) interpreters, and a discourse-based analysis of an asylum hearing in Warsaw, complemented by post-task interviews with the official conducting the hearing and two other employees of the institution acting as interpreters. Analysing the roles adopted by the two interpreters (taking turns) in the 90-minute encounter, Tryuk (2004: 234) finds that they frequently exceed their role of 'honest spokesperson' and adopt the stance of an active third party in the conversation. They do so, however, not on the strength of professional training as interpreters but by relying on their experience as employees of the institution with proficiency in the relevant language.

Tryuk's (2004) survey, developed in late 2002, was designed to draw up a professional profile of community-based interpreting in Poland. Out of the 300 questionnaires distributed, more than 90 responses were received and yielded quantitative as well as qualitative data relating to settings, working practices, norms and ethics. Legal settings (courts and police stations as well as border guard offices) emerged as the area where interpreters were in greatest demand, with healthcare settings accounting for a much smaller share of the work. In line with the respectable level of professionalisation achieved by the country's legal interpreting community, whose members formed part of the survey population, a large majority of the respondents felt well prepared for their work. Nevertheless, nearly thirty respondents felt that they lacked some of the necessary subject-matter knowledge and terminology and indicated a willingness to engage in further training (Tryuk 2004: 183). As brought out clearly in subsequent parts of the analysis, such training needs are even more pronounced when one accepts that professional standards of practice in community settings may need to differ from those established for international conference interpreting. Tryuk

(2004: 209–210) thus makes a strong case for developing standards of practice that respond to the requirements and constraints of specific institutional settings, and emphasises that the interpreter's role may need to be tailored to specific user needs. As she stated in her contribution to the Critical Link Conference held in Stockholm in 2004, 'behavior in each of the settings originates from a different tradition and is governed by a different set of rules. The needs of people assisted by interpreters also vary (…)' (Tryuk 2007: 103). Mindful of the need for professionalisation that also emerged very clearly from her survey findings, she concludes that 'the best and most justified solution would be to initiate training for community interpreters in institutions training translators and interpreters' (Tryuk 2007: 104).

The task thus formulated was and is perfectly clear; nevertheless, nearly two decades later, interpreter training institutions in many countries are still struggling to accomplish it. The reasons for such slow progress in the professionalisation of community interpreting are varied and must be expected to differ from one country to another. More critically still, one must assume considerable variability in the needs and expectations of particular institutions and groups of users. Here again, Małgorzata Tryuk worked to extend the body of research-based findings that are needed to inform realistic training practices and thus promote professionalisation.

Tryuk (2012) reports a series of questionnaire-based surveys designed to investigate the attitude of different communities of professional service providers to the role and work of interpreters in their particular setting. One study was devoted to the court setting, another one to immigration hearings, and a third to healthcare settings. In the survey addressed to 50 judges and attorneys in different courts in Warsaw, the 41 filled-in questionnaires reflected differences between the legal interpreters' codified role (i.e. what interpreters should do) and their actual behaviour, particularly when it comes to simplifying legal language and explaining cultural differences. On the whole, the study finds that there is room for further development of the legal interpreter's role beyond what it prescribed in the Polish code of practice for sworn translators and interpreters.

In the study devoted to the immigration setting, a mixed-method approach was adopted to elicit the views of officials as well as interpreters. In a first phase, questionnaires were completed by 16 officials and three interpreters regularly working for the Foreigners' Office. This was followed by semi-structured interviews conducted with ten immigration officers with experience in working with interpreters. Even more so than in the case of legal personnel, the results of the study reveal a highly contradictory pattern of expectations. On the one hand, immigration officials view interpreting as a strictly mechanistic task ('just interpret'); on the other hand, they expect interpreters to carry out a number of additional tasks that make it impossible for them to live up to idealised expectations of neutrality and impartiality.

Finally, interpreting in healthcare settings was the subject of a study involving a questionnaire as well as interviews and observations. More than fifty healthcare institutions were contacted to find out about the frequency of foreign-language-speaking patients, about arrangements for recruiting interpreters or ensuring communication by other means, and about communication to obtain informed consent before surgical interventions. While the findings indicated a non-negligible presence of non-Polish-speaking patients, the rate of interpreter utilisation was found to be very low. Interpreting needs were apparently met by doctors proficient in foreign languages and by family members or friends accompanying the patient. Informed consent forms were mainly in Polish, with only some in English. On the whole, the study concludes that 'medical interpreting is practically nonexistent' in public and private healthcare centres in Poland and that 'there is no academic training for medical interpreters' (Tryuk 2012: 135).

However sobering these findings may appear when viewed from the perspective of interpreting scholars aware of much more advanced practices in other countries, the studies reported by Tryuk (2012) – and presented in greater detail in a collective volume in Polish (Tryuk 2010b) – constitute essential groundwork for further initiatives to promote community interpreting in Polish public-sector institutions, where multilingual communication needs could be assumed to be on the rise even a decade ago and where the need for adequate training and service provision is as urgent as in many other countries.

What is also noteworthy about Tryuk's groundbreaking work in studying community interpreting in Poland is the fact that much of the empirical research was conducted by students under her supervision. This team effort, without which such comprehensive coverage of communication practices in legal, administrative and healthcare settings could hardly be envisaged, highlights Małgorzata Tryuk's role not only as a scholar but also as a research trainer and educator of future generations of practitioners and scholars of interpreting. It is this dimension of her academic work that also underlies the accomplishments to be described under the heading of 'accessibility', even though her pivotal role in these efforts is not necessarily conspicuous in published articles and books.

4. Accessibility

Until the turn of the millennium, the conceptualisation of translation and interpreting within the field of translation studies was typically expressed as bridging linguistic and cultural gaps or overcoming barriers of language and culture. These barriers were assumed to result from differences between languages, which essentially framed the 'problem' of translation as the problem of (overcoming) linguistic diversity. It was only in the early twenty-first century that a different kind of verbal imagery, centred on the notion of access, emerged on a broader scale in connection with translation and interpreting. The implications of this reconceptualisation for the theory and practice of interpreting and for interpreting studies are highly significant, as discussed below.

4.1. Barriers to access

As mentioned in an earlier section of this chapter, the notion of access first came to be used in interpreting studies in relation to community interpreting, the provision of which would allow persons with limited or no proficiency in the national language(s) to gain access to the services of relevant public institutions, especially in the areas of legal, healthcare and social services. Ensuring accessibility of this kind was still a matter of managing linguistic diversity, as the public services required would be offered in a national language of which potential service users speaking a different language had no sufficient command. In other words, it was 'language discordance' (Weng & Landes 2017) that created barriers to communication, which in turn amounted to barriers in accessing services.

This view of 'interpreting for access' in the context of multilingual communication in social institutions underpins the kind of research on community interpreting that was presented earlier as a major extension to the field of interpreting studies in general and as an area of groundbreaking research achievements by Małgorzata Tryuk. The present discussion will therefore take a different turn and sketch the development and increasing convergence of translation and accessibility as a backdrop to an account of recent proposals for a redefinition – and significant conceptual extension – of interpreting.

Considering its genesis in the late twentieth century and even some current theoretical positions, the notion of accessibility is entirely unrelated to translation. In an original and prototypical sense, it refers to physical access for persons with disabilities. Examples include barrier-free access to buildings or public transport facilities for wheelchair users. In addition to physical impairments, however, the concern with accessibility also relates to sensory and even cognitive impairments that may hinder a person's access to information and communication. All these major dimensions of accessibility are enshrined in the United Nations Convention on the Rights of Persons with Disabilities (United Nations 2006), which has been ratified and transformed into national legislation in many countries. Not surprisingly for the digital age, the dimension of access to information and communication, and not least to media services, has quickly moved centre-stage, accessible internet websites being a case in point. More consequential still from a societal perspective is access to media services like the news programs of public broadcasters. While some such access has been offered to hearing-impaired viewers via teletext services for quite some time, it has been thoroughly reshaped in recent decades with the advent of new digital technologies. The British national broadcaster, BBC, was among the leading institutions implementing closed captioning (subtitling) of television programs, and media companies in many other countries have followed suit. Similarly, audio description (AD) services have increasingly been implemented for visually impaired audiences.

On the face of it, this boom of media accessibility services in the early twenty-first century has nothing to do with translation. Nevertheless, it was scholars in the area of audiovisual translation (AVT), itself a booming subfield within translation studies (see Gambier 2004), who took charge of studying these new forms of media access services and designing training programs for future practitioners. The focus on subtitling may have served as a crucial interface, which allowed AVT scholars to bring their longstanding experience with interlingual subtitling to bear on the new intralingual variant referred to as subtitling for the deaf and hard of hearing (SDH). But great strides were also made in researching and teaching AD as a form of 'intersemiotic translation' (Jakobson 1959). AVT scholars embraced both intralingual and intermodal forms of translation as important extensions of their field of study (e.g. Orero 2004). More recently, though, media accessibility has increasingly been regarded as a field *sui generis*, overlapping with or even distinct from translation. This view, adopted most radically by Greco (2018), is reflected, for instance, in the title of the comprehensive *Palgrave Handbook* edited by Bogucki and Deckert (2020), where AVT and media accessibility are juxtaposed.

Against this background, Małgorzata Tryuk is once again found at the forefront of scholars shaping and extending the field of translation and interpreting studies. Questioning the name and nature of AVT, Tryuk (2008) makes the case for a broad conception of 'multimedia translation' inspired by Gambier's (2004) comprehensive vision. Most significantly for the purpose of the present discussion, she argues for an inclusive conceptualisation that incorporates intra- as well as interlingual translational processes in and between any semiotic modalities (Tryuk 2008: 38). Unlike other conceptions of AVT (e.g. Bogucki & Deckert 2020), this gives ample room to interpreting, and Tryuk (2008) makes explicit mention of spoken- and signed-language interpreting in the media and of processes involving written text, either as source material (text to speech) or as the resulting product (speech to text).

The proximity of interpreting and (audiovisual) translation in Tryuk's (2008) theoretically grounded integrative conception is mirrored rather strikingly in the internal structure of her academic home base at the University of Warsaw: the Institute of Applied Linguistics, which comprises six departments and five research groups, has a Department of Translation Studies separate from the Department of Interpreting Studies, but has 'Audiovisual Translation' attached to the latter. Not surprisingly, this is the unit headed by Małgorzata Tryuk.

This organisational choice can be read as a strong commitment to 'inter-subdisciplinarity' (Shlesinger 2004), which is indeed reflected in the Department's researcher profiles and research topics. One example is Wojciech Figiel, an expert in accessibility who completed his PhD research on translators and interpreters with visual impairments (Figiel 2017) under the supervision of Małgorzata Tryuk and with her strong support. Another is Łukasz Dutka, whose innovative research on live subtitling with respeaking (Dutka 2022) was initially promoted and supervised by Małgorzata Tryuk before the baton was passed to Agnieszka Szarkowska, the Department's specialist in AVT. It is the research on live subtitling, in particular, that epitomises the extension of interpreting studies beyond traditional boundaries and therefore merits special consideration as a capstone of this chapter.

4.2. From speech to text

Whereas the extension of interpreting research beyond the professional confines of conference interpreting had raised concerns about studying interpreting practices with lower standards of professionalism, or even no professional status at all, claiming live subtitling as an object of study for interpreting scholars has opened up a much more fundamental debate. Most superficially, traditionalists defending established professional positions would argue that interpreters produce spoken language (or signed output), so that a process designed to produce written text could not possibly come under the heading of interpreting. This position is in fact supported, or reflected, in current ISO standards, in which interpreting is defined as 'rendering spoken or signed information from a source language [...] to a target language [...] in oral or signed form' (ISO 2019).

It is worth noting that the ISO definition of translation takes a similar approach, based solely on linguistic modality, and hence misses the process-related distinction hinging on the immediacy or real-time nature of performance that has become widely adopted in interpreting studies (see Pöchhacker 2022: 11). But even if the ISO definition of interpreting could be extended to include the real-time or 'live' production of written text, the claim that live subtitling is a form of interpreting would still come up against the challenge that interpreting, whether professional or not, has always been an activity involving different languages. To some extent this argument can be overcome with reference to the interlingual form of live subtitling, which has also been gaining ground in some countries and communicative contexts and was the object of an international EU-funded project with a team of researchers in Małgorzata Tryuk's Department as key partners (ILSA 2020). Nevertheless, live subtitling as a media accessibility service for deaf and hard-of-hearing viewers largely remains an intralingual practice, typically sponsored by public broadcasters catering to their national audiences (see, e.g. Dutka 2022).

Admittedly, this issue is also clouded by terminological uncertainty among accessibility service providers. When such services for deaf and hard-of-hearing persons are performed at live events, such as conferences and lectures, the activity is often referred to as 'speech-to-text interpreting'. Therefore, the terms 'live subtitling' (or 'live captioning') and 'speech-to-text interpreting' are sometimes used to distinguish between different services (in media settings vs. live events), whereas either term is also used in a generic sense as including the other. (Semantically, this option is more easily justified for speech-to-text interpreting, which does not specify the format of the written output text.)

Whatever the terminological choices, however, considering intralingual live subtitling or speech-to-text interpreting as a form of interpreting has far-reaching implications for the interpreting profession and for interpreter education institutions alike. Even though there is increasing consensus that few individuals in this day and age can be considered monolingual, the professionalisation of intralingual speech-to-text interpreting would in fact imply that an interpreter need not have any bilingual competence; proficiency in a single working language – along with a high level of real-time content processing and multi-tasking skills – would suffice.

After a millennial tradition of viewing interpreters, first and foremost, as bilingually skilled individuals, it would indeed be a drastic move to extend the concept of interpreting to include monolingual communication access services. On the other hand, interpreting is not an end in itself but has always been a service rendered in response to communicative needs in a given scenario of human interaction. The strong (albeit rather recent) drive to achieve universal accessibility and social inclusion, aided by advances in digital technology (i.e. speech recognition) that have made efficient speech-to-text interpreting feasible and affordable, has created new social needs and new options for these needs to be met. In these new scenarios, the role of the interpreter – as an enabler of communication and real-time access to information – remains essentially unchanged. Where extensions to current assumptions and positions are needed is in the areas of theoretical conceptualisations, standards of practice and training models as well as professional boundaries. As this chapter has sought to show with reference to the highly successful efforts of Małgorzata Tryuk, major shifts and extensions in our understanding of interpreting as a social practice and an object of research are in fact possible; it only takes decades of great commitment and collaboration to bring them to fruition.

5. Conclusion

My aim for this chapter was to review some major shifts in the past and present development of interpreting studies, and to do so with reference to the work of a scholar with the same longevity as this discipline. Some of the ways in which interpreting researchers have extended the scope of their work and explored topics that were previously ignored or disregarded have been discussed under the headings of history, community and accessibility. In each case, the scholarly initiatives and achievements of Małgorzata Tryuk have served to illustrate what could be observed for the (sub)discipline of interpreting studies as a whole. As regards history, the field has seen unprecedented efforts since around the turn of the millennium to extend research interests into the past and to some unlikely settings on a global scale. Małgorzata Tryuk's pioneering work on interpreting in Nazi concentration camps in Poland stands out as a unique achievement, not only for illustrating what can be discovered through meticulous and persistent archival research but also, and particularly, for giving a voice to those individuals who practiced interpreting under cruelest circumstances as a matter of life and death for fellow prisoners or even themselves.

Another major extension of research and teaching interests in the field of interpreting studies was discussed under the heading of interpreting in the community. Limited to some dispersed efforts since the 1980s, scholarly interest in interpreting in legal, healthcare and social-service settings acquired great momentum toward the end of the twentieth century. As a practice that is by definition embedded in and governed by the national policies and institutional structures of a given society, research into community interpreting and the development of educational opportunities for its practitioners and users require a high degree of engagement with local practices and authorities. This is what Małgorzata Tryuk did with great commitment in Poland, paving the way for research into interpreting practices beyond business, diplomatic and conference settings, which also implies an openness toward non-professional interpreting in a variety of multilingual contact scenarios.

The most recent major extension of the field of interpreting studies was discussed under the heading of accessibility, a powerful notion that has its roots not in the area of languages and communication but in the philosophy of human rights and the equitable participation of all individuals in all areas of social life. Beyond physical barriers to access, policies focusing on sensory impairments hindering access to information and communication, particularly in the public media, have fueled the development of media accessibility services akin to some forms of audiovisual translation. Where such services are required and rendered 'live', the real-time processing skills of (simultaneous) interpreters are needed. Uncertainty persists, however, about the way such novel types of activity as live subtitling or speech-to-text interpreting are best conceptualised and designated, with even greater controversy about the professional implications of extending the concept of interpreting so as to include skilled practices involving written text production that do not necessarily require bilingual competence. Here again, the intellectual and organisational leadership of Małgorzata Tryuk in one of Poland's most prestigious centres of research and teaching in translation and interpreting has been shown to shift boundaries and prepare the ground for further extensions of the field of study. Having succeeded in shifting the focus toward access to services, as in efforts to professionalise interpreting in the community, yet another dynamic has been set in motion, shifting the focus toward media and communication access services. Interpreters would thus adapt their specialised language-processing skill set to new communicative needs and technological affordances, and yet remain as indispensable as ever in performing a reliable, user-oriented personal service allowing immediate access to information and communication.

References

Baigorri-Jalón, Jesús (2000). *La interpretación de conferencias: el nacimiento de una profesión, de París a Nuremberg*. Granada: Comares.

Baigorri-Jalón, Jesús (2015). History. In F. Pöchhacker (ed.), *Routledge Encyclopedia of Interpreting Studies*. London/New York: Routledge, 183–186.

Bogucki, Łukasz & Deckert, Mikołaj (eds.) (2020). *The Palgrave Handbook of Audiovisual Translation and Media Accessibility*. Cham: Palgrave Macmillan.

Bowen, Margareta (1995). Interpreters and the making of history. In J. Delisle & J. Woodsworth (eds.), *Translators through History*. Amsterdam: John Benjamins, 245–273.

Chernov, Ghelly V. (1985). Interpretation research in the Soviet Union: Results and prospects. In H. Bühler (ed.), *Xth World Congress of FIT. Proceedings: Translators and Their Position in Society*. Vienna: Wilhelm Braumüller, 169–177.

Dutka, Łukasz (2022). *Live Subtitling with Respeaking in Polish: Technology, User Expectations and Quality Assessment*. PhD thesis, University of Warsaw.

Figiel, Wojciech (2017). *Tożsamość i status tłumaczy z dysfunkcją wzroku*. PhD thesis, University of Warsaw.

Gambier, Yves (2004). La traduction audiovisuelle: un genre en expansion. *Meta* 49 (1), 1–11.

Gambier, Yves, Gile, Daniel & Taylor, Christopher (eds.) (1997). *Conference Interpreting: Current Trends in Research*. Amsterdam: John Benjamins.

Gerver, David & Sinaiko, H. Wallace (eds.) (1978). *Language Interpretation and Communication. Proceedings of the NATO Symposium, Venice, Italy, September 26–October 1, 1977*. New York/London: Plenum Press.

Gile, Daniel (1994). Opening up in interpretation studies. In M. Snell-Hornby, F. Pöchhacker & K. Kaindl (eds.), *Translation Studies – an Interdiscipline*. Amsterdam: John Benjamins, 149–158.

Gile, Daniel (2015). CIRIN Bulletin. In F. Pöchhacker (ed.), *Routledge Encyclopedia of Interpreting Studies*. London/New York: Routledge, 54–55.

Gile, Daniel, Gambier, Yves & Taylor, Christopher (1997). Foreword. In Y. Gambier, D. Gile & C. Taylor (eds.), *Conference Interpreting: Current Trends in Research*. Amsterdam: John Benjamins, 1–7.

Greco, Gian Maria (2018). The nature of accessibility studies. *Journal of Audiovisual Translation* 1 (1), 205–232.

Herbert, Jean (1952). *Manuel de l'interprète : comment on devient interprète de conférences*. Geneva: Georg.

ILSA (2020). ILSA Project: Interlingual Live Subtitling for Access. http://ka2-ilsa.webs.uvigo.es/project (accessed 12 January 2023).

ISO (2019). *ISO 20539:2019 Translation, Interpreting and Related Technology – Vocabulary*. Geneva: International Organization for Standardization.

Jakobson, Roman (1959). On linguistic aspects of translation. In R. A. Brower (ed.), *On Translation*. Cambridge, MA: Harvard University Press, 232–239.

Kurz, Ingrid (1985). The rock tombs of the Princes of Elephantine: Earliest references to interpretation in Pharaonic Egypt. *Babel* 31 (4), 213–218.

Lambert, Sylvie & Moser-Mercer, Barbara (eds.) (1994). *Bridging the Gap: Empirical Research in Simultaneous Interpretation*. Amsterdam: John Benjamins.

Lederer, Marianne (2015). Paris School. In F. Pöchhacker (ed.), *Routledge Encyclopedia of Interpreting Studies*. London/New York: Routledge, 295–297.

Linell, Per (1997). Interpreting as communication. In Y. Gambier, D. Gile & C. Taylor (eds.), *Conference Interpreting: Current Trends in Research*. Amsterdam: John Benjamins, 49–67.

Orero, Pilar (ed.) (2004). *Topics in Audiovisual Translation*. Amsterdam: John Benjamins.

Pöchhacker, Franz (1995). "Those who do…": A profile of research(ers) in interpreting. *Target* 7 (1), 47–64.

Pöchhacker, Franz (2000). *Dolmetschen. Konzeptuelle Grundlagen und deskriptive Untersuchungen*. Tübingen: Stauffenburg.

Pöchhacker, Franz (2022). *Introducing Interpreting Studies. Third Edition*. London/New York: Routledge.

Shlesinger, Miriam (2004). Inter-subdisciplinarity and beyond. In C. Schäffner (ed.), *Translation Research and Interpreting Research: Traditions, Gaps and Synergies*. Clevedon: Multilingual Matters, 116–123.

Thieme, Karl, Hermann, Alfred & Glässer, Edgar (1956). *Beiträge zur Geschichte des Dolmetschens*. München: Isar.

Tryuk, Małgorzata (2004). *L'interprétation communautaire: des normes et des rôles dans l'interprétation*. Warsaw: TEPIS.

Tryuk, Małgorzata (2007). Community interpreting in Poland. In C. Wadensjö, B. Englund Dimitrova & A.-L. Nilsson (eds.), *The Critical Link 4: Professionalisation of Interpreting in the Community*. Amsterdam: John Benjamins, 95–105.

Tryuk, Małgorzata (2008). Co to jest tłumaczenie audiowizualne? *Przekładaniec* 20, 26–39.

Tryuk, Małgorzata (2010a). Interpreting in Nazi concentration camps during World War II. *Interpreting* 12 (2), 125–145.

Tryuk, Małgorzata (ed.) (2010b). *O tłumaczach, prawnikach, lekarzach i urzędnikach: Teoria i praktyka tłumaczenia środowiskowego w Polsce*. Warsaw: Bel Studio.

Tryuk, Małgorzata (2012). The judge, the doctor, the immigration officer and the interpreter: Community interpreters' role perception – a Polish perspective. *The Interpreters' Newsletter* 17, 117–138.

Tryuk, Małgorzata (2015). *On Ethics and Interpreters*. Frankfurt: Peter Lang.

Tryuk, Małgorzata (2016). Interpreting and translating in Nazi concentration camps during World War II. *Linguistica Antverpiensia, New Series: Themes in Translation Studies* 15, 121–141.

Tryuk, Małgorzata (2017). Professor Andrzej Kopczyński – in memoriam. *Lingua Legis* 25, 7–8.

Tryuk, Małgorzata (2020). Translating and interpreting in conflict and crisis. In K. Koskinen & N. K. Pokorn (eds.), *The Routledge Handbook of Translation and Ethics*. London/New York: Routledge, 398–414.

Tryuk, Małgorzata (2021a). La traductologie polonaise en anglais? Du « centre » et de la « périphérie » de la recherche traductologique en Pologne. *Romanica Wratislaviensia* 68, 227–239.

Tryuk, Małgorzata (2021b). Translation under Fascism and Nazism. In C. Rundle (ed.), *The Routledge Handbook of Translation History*. London/New York: Routledge, 469–484.

United Nations (2006). *Convention on the Rights of Persons with Disabilities. Resolution 61/106 Adopted by the General Assembly.* New York: United Nations.

Weng, Suzie S. & Landes, Scott D. (2017). Culture and language discordance in the workplace: Evidence from the National Home Health Aide Survey. *Gerontologist* 57 (5), 900–909.

Michaela Wolf

Chapter 2 Interpreting under threat: Nazi concentration camps as *non-places*

Abstract: In this paper, I will focus on various features which made up the Nazi concentration camps, including ambiguity and some manifestations of violence, and which consequently had an impact on communication in the *lager*. To cast light on the context of these features, I will draw on Marc Augé's concept of *non-place* (1995). The thorough discussion of this concept will help better understand the kind of functioning of concentration camps and accordingly will help reveal the nature of the characteristics which shape communication in the camp.

By exploring the features which mould language in general and interpreting in more specific terms, I will mainly draw on reports written by survivors from various concentration camps. The analysis aims to enhance our understanding of the communication patterns adopted in the aggressive, brutal, deadly environment of the *lager*.

Keywords: Nazi concentration camps, interpreting, communication patterns, survivor accounts, Marc Augé, *non-place*

Studying the Shoah when you come from a land generally labelled as a land of perpetrators is certainly a task which requires even more responsibility and, additionally, needs a certain dose of self-reflexivity. I undertook this task in several steps, one of which was gathering sources, another one struggling with the concept of communication under extreme conditions, and yet another one defining my personal limits – until I came across Małgorzata's article "Interpreting in Nazi concentration camps during World War II" published in the international journal *Interpreting* (2010). The reading of the paper provoked the immense urge to contact her. It took a while until we could meet. Finally, in 2012, on my way to Lublin from where I undertook a trip to several concentration camps in today's eastern Poland, I stopped in Warsaw to meet Małgorzata. I must confess it was a most emotional encounter. While strolling through the campus of Warsaw University and the botanical garden on top of the University Library, watching eagerly learning students and researchers through the glass roof, our conversations immediately delved into the core of our research concerns related to the Shoah, and, especially, into the discussion of our fathers whose biographical itinerary could not be more diverse: hers, a survivor of several concentration camps, mine, a Wehrmacht soldier and member of the NSDAP.

I so well remember the naturalness in our conversations, the atmosphere of confidence and friendship from the very beginning.

This first encounter with Małgorzata left deep traces, both on a personal and an intellectual level. Actually, most of my subsequent research focussed on communication in Nazi concentration camps, and the corresponding refining of my research profile even allowed me to publish an article together with Małgorzata (Tryuk & Wolf 2015). The present contribution for Małgorzata's *Festschrift* is not only a yet another publication on "our" issue, but especially a proof of our friendship which, I am happy to say, in the meantime goes far beyond our research concerns.

1. Introduction

Communication in concentration and extermination camps of the Nazi regime is an under-researched field.[1] Also, whatever the state of the art of communication under conditions of terror might be, our perception of what we call "reality" in the camps is bound to remain opaque. In this chapter, I will focus on the features which made up the camp and which consequently had an impact on communication in the *lager*. These features are highly endowed with ambiguity as well as (alleged) neutrality, loneliness, temporariness, alienation, or extreme terror. To cast light on the context of some of these features, I will draw on Marc Augé's concept of *non-place* (1995) which, despite its original usage in the context of "supermodernity" – a term introduced by Augé to denominate a period within modernity characterised by excess – will help both to better characterise the nature of concentration camps and to closely shape the features which make up communication in the camps. The sources used in this chapter are scenes mainly retrieved from memoir accounts which depict language in more general terms and interpreting in more specific. When drawing on survivor reports of various concentration camps I am aware that these sources are exposed to arbitrariness and bias; however, in view of the lack of more "impartial" sources, I nevertheless decided to use this material.

2. Concentration camps as *non-places*

To describe the "society of terror" (Neurath 2005/2016) of concentration camps is not an easy task. There have been several attempts to portray and analyse social life in the camps, beginning with Hannah Arendt's early article (1948)

1 For a detailed literature report on this issue see e.g. Wolf (2016a).

"Concentration Camps", in which she resorted to a metaphor that instantly began to circulate amongst perpetrators, victims and observers alike: to illustrate the camps, she spoke of "factories of annihilation" (763), of "extermination factories" (762) and of "the corpse factories invented by the Nazis" (762); in *The Origins of Totalitarianism* she viewed the camps as "laboratories in the experiment of total domination" (1958: 436). Her attention did not focus on the murdering procedures, that is the mass gassing and the cremating of the corpses, but was rather directed towards the "tactical organizational measures" employed in the manufacturing of the "living dead" (1948: 746). Another attempt at depicting camp societies is Wolfgang Sofsky's *The Order of Terror* (1997). Yet, when he described the camp as an instrument of terror and mass killing, he did not analyse a "real" camp, but a constructed notion of a camp which is at the basis of his sociological model of a community defined by force. Another strand of describing concentration camps is represented by Giorgio Agamben who, equally to Sofsky, "denies any social quality with regard to prisoners and guards living together in the concentration camps and leans toward a vertical approach based on total power, reducing the prisoners to a collected mass" (Prenninger 2016: 26). Agamben tried to explain the camp as the bio-political paradigm of modernity and argues that "[t]he camp is merely the place in which the most absolute *conditio inhumana* that has ever existed on earth was realized" (Agamben 1998: 166, original emphasis). Against the backdrop of these and further approaches to describe concentration camps as a social arena, Alexander Prenninger in his concern to understand the functioning of a camp society, puts his focus on the inner world of the camps and the communal life of its components. He claims that to come closer to the understanding of social life, it is important to abandon the idea of perceiving social life in camps as based on a "closed system of suppressors and suppressed, ultimately dividing the actors int active perpetrators and passive victims" (Prenninger 2016: 39). Rather, the researchers' attention should be directed toward the phenomenon that many camps were characterised by multiple and often ambiguous relations between the various different individuals. Despite at times fierce conflicts between the prisoners, often related to perceived hierarchies between nations, antisemitism or antiziganism, social relations between prisoners and acts of mutual support existed to an astonishing extent and were an important part of everyday life. As Prenninger stresses, "[t]he camp society was thus perceived in a multitude of different ways according to each individual experience and might well be described as a polyphonic place of terror" (Prenninger 2016: 39–40).

Attempts at theoretically conceptualising concentration camps which also take account of their social component have highlighted Homi Bhabha's *third space* (see Bhabha 1990 and Tosoni 2015) or the trope of the *grey zone*, developed by Primo Levi (see Levi 1989 and Wolf 2020a, 2020b). In what follows I will discuss yet another concept which might allow for better understanding the social space of concentration camps: Marc Augé's *non-place*.

Augé elaborated the concept of *non-place* to respond to the phenomenon that more and more people in industrialised areas live in structures of accelerated circulation and spend more and more time in bus and train stations, interchanges and airports as well as large shopping centres, refugee camps, amusement parks, city parks etc. He defines *non-places* "in opposition to the sociological notion of place, associated by Mauss and a whole ethnological tradition with the idea of a culture localized in time and space" (Augé 1995: 34), stressing that *non-places* do not hold enough significance to be regarded as "places" in their anthropological definition. He makes a distinction between the "anthropological place" and the "non-place". While the former is associated with being relational and historical as well as concerned with identity, the latter is the exact opposite (77). "Anthropological places" could be both a concrete and symbolic construction of space, the layout of the house for instance, the configuration of public open spaces, or land distribution, and they "correspond for every individual to a system of possibilities, prescriptions and interdicts whose content is both spatial and social" (53). *Non-places*, on the other hand, are all places without history, lacking social interaction and identity. As a phenomenon of what Augé calls "supermodernity", they are characterised by lack of memory ("What reigns there is actuality, the urgency of the present moment", 104) and are spaces created for specific ends, such as commerce or transportation (94). In this context Mark Matienzo stresses that in a *non-place*, "the individual, in a sense, becomes invisible or indistinguishable from the masses of those who pass through it; everyone seemingly goes about their own business rather than being preoccupied with that of everyone else" (Matienzo 2004: 9). Another important feature which characterises the *non-place* is the presence of visible or invisible rules: "Sometimes these [instructions] are couched in more or less explicit and codified ideograms [...], sometimes in ordinary language" (Augé 1995: 96). As mentioned, Augé highlights that while places are characterised by history, *non-places* are determined by the provisional (103), so that history can no longer be read from them, triggering a loss of identity. This peculiarity is closely related to the *non-places* as being seen as transit zones: thus, when we talk about *non-places*, "we can contrast the realities of transit (transit camps or passengers in transit) with those of residence or dwelling; the interchange (where nobody crosses anyone else's path) with the crossroads (where people meet); the passenger (defined by his destination) with the traveller (who strolls along his route) [...]" (107). The idea of transit is associated with spaces which are born in connection with an emerging infrastructure (a petrol station, a travelling inn); spaces created for leisure and consumption (amusement parks, pubs); spaces where refugees are held (refugee camps, transit camps) (34, 78).[2]

Many of the features presented so far can be applied to aptly describing the space of a concentration camp. To begin, a *lager* can undoubtedly be seen as a transit space – with all characteristics involved, including the lack of history: concentration camps have no "history" in the traditional sense of the word, they were built for annihilation (see Hartmann 2020), for (in rare cases transitory) detention, at best for forced labour, and were closed and demolished when all prisoners were murdered or deported to other camps. Identity in concentration camps was a non-word, as upon the entrance of a person in the camp, the person's identity was wiped off by substituting her or his name with a number, by cutting the body hair, etc. The placelessness of the *non-place* even seems to present the most authentic trait of concentration camps, because the sense of placelessness is the "weakening of the identity of places to the point where they not only look alike but feel alike and offer the same bland possibilities for experience" (Relph 1976/2016: 90). Without identity, *non-places* also lack social interaction, a phenomenon which holds particularly true for concentration camps, where interhuman relations were immediately suppressed. As far as the absence of memory is concerned, the *lager* was the site par excellence where memory of the "outer world" was not only forbidden but a tabu – and memory in any form was only inscribed in the bodies of the prisoners, not in their mind. Augé's statement that *non-places* designate "spaces formed in relation to certain ends (transport, transit, commerce, leisure)" (Augé 1995: 94) is also applicable to concentration camps, their central function clearly being constituted in spreading terror and annihilation, in ceaselessly threatening with death, and in lethal forced labour. The genuine purpose of the *non-places* is self-explaining for its manner of functioning, which is mainly determined by the relations that individuals have with these spaces (94). These relations are enacted through words, texts, pictures[3], rules and codes, which are for immediate use and are not symbols in any sense. Another and more concrete link between

2 It would exceed the scope of this chapter to give room to the critical voices regarding Augé's concept of the *non-place*. See e.g. Weiß 2005: 34, 54, 61–62; Üngür 2012: 7.

3 "The link between individuals and their surroundings in the space of non-place is established through the mediation of words, or even texts", and the fact "that there are words which make […] images" (Augé 1995: 94–95).

individual and words or pictures in *non-places* is expressed in instructions (e.g. in the road traffic), in interdictions, or in explicit ideograms (on road signs or tourist guides). The initiators of these texts are always exclusively juristic persons or institutions such as ministries, municipalities and others. In concentration camps, such prohibitions, rules and regulations of all kinds abound, or more: it is this system of forceful instructions which is constitutive for the *lager*.

So, in which way does the concentration camp seen through the eyes of Marc Augé's concept of *non-place* have an impact on viewing the interpreting activity in the camp? Do the various features which make up the *non-place* give us a clue on the functioning mechanisms of the interpreting settings in concentration camps? Do the central traits of the *non-place*, once associated with some prototypical characteristics of (both the concentration camp and) the communication strategies inside the camp, enhance our understanding of the communication patterns adopted in the aggressive, brutal, deadly environment of the *lager*? To discuss these and further questions, the next section will explore the nature of a series of features which make up for communication in concentration camps by analysing various text passages drawn from camp survivors' memoir accounts.

3. Exploring communication in the *non-place* of the concentration camp

The activity of interpreting is mentioned in most accounts written by camp survivors, though to varying degrees. The close reading of approximately 450 memoir accounts, written in eight languages by ex-prisoners of about ten different concentration camps, reveal that interpreting, in its diverse forms, was a recurring concern for many prisoners. Drawing mainly on monographs and articles it was possible to retrace a great variety of interpreting situations that testify to the multiple attempts to tackle communication problems in the camp. The validity of these sources is of course questionable. In her study on *non-places* from a cultural anthropology perspective, Stephanie Weiß puts the question whether it was Marc Augé's intention to analyse *non-places* under empirical perspectives, or if he rather wanted to offer a conceptual construct. She stresses that a construct can be defined as a "gedankliche Hilfe" [mental help] to describe phenomena which are not accessible to direct observation; thus, a construct can be extrapolated only from other observable data and can therefore empirically tested only in an indirect way (Weiß 2005: 86). Without doubt this procedure is true for the case of the present corpus, as, understandably, no situation analysed in this chapter can claim authenticity.

The following analysis is structured according to some of the main features which make up the communication in Nazi concentration camps: ambiguity and manifestations of violence. In the examples it will be shown in which way the various factors which construct the communication inside the camps can be associated with the characteristics of the *non-place* discussed above. The central aim of the analysis is to augment our understanding of the typical components which make up the communication patterns in the camp.

3.1. Ambiguity

Generally speaking, ambiguity denominates a situation or statement that is unclear because it can be understood in more than one way and is thus open to various interpretations or explanations. Consequently, it can mean doubt, uncertainty or also vagueness. In the present context, ambiguity is one of the dimensions, which can be most frequently identified in concentration camps. It is perceptible in multifaceted forms, especially loss of identity and aspects of (linguistic) alienation, but also in the shape of its moral variant. The ambiguous role of interpreting can be primarily attributed to the enormous potentiality of manipulation inherent in any communication act: For the present context, interpreting in the camp always meant taking sides, there was no way in-between, no escape, no alternative. Robert Antelme in this well-known account *L'espèce humaine* (*The human race*) (1947) very clearly depicts the two types of interpreters:

> There were two types of interpreters. For Lucien the interpreter's task meant translating the SS and *Kapos*' orders, which he gradually adopted as his own. [...] He was always the interpreter for the SS and the *Kapos* and never for the prisoners. [...] Gilbert was the prisoners' interpreter, which means that he only used German to try to neutralize the SS, the *Kapos*, and the foremen. He [...] was brave enough to defend some comrades in front of the SS or to *excuse* them. He exercised his duty as political prisoner; he warned and shielded his comrades [...]. Through this behaviour Gilbert became an enemy of the *Kapos*. (Antelme 1947/2010: 176, my translation from the French original; original emphasis)

The moral ambiguity represented in this passage testifies to the interpreter's double role: the prisoners exhibit both mistrust and trust, revealing the ethically ambiguous and potentially powerful role ascribed to the interpreter. Disorientation and alienation are the most detectable ways to express ambiguity. Vereno Brugiatelli reminds us that the confrontation with the *non-place* – and, I would say, equally with the detention in a concentration camp – can provoke, or provokes, alienation, disorientation, and all kind of discomfort (Brugiatelli

2016: 60). In the camp, the total lack of communication prompted exactly these dimensions, as can be seen in the following example. In the scene Primo Levi (1919–1987) describes the *lager* as an appalling place, especially for the newcomers, for whom the first days were the hardest:

> It could happen, above all for those who did not understand German, that the prisoners did not even know in which part of Europe the Lager in which they were was situated [...]. They did not know about the existence of other Lagers [...]. They did not know for whom they worked. They did not understand the significance of certain sudden changes in conditions, and of the mass transfers. (Levi 1989: 6)

Such a situation could result in a disaster for the prisoners – not understanding the perpetrator's language meant isolation from what was happening in the camp, including the intrigues of SS personnel or the *Kapos*, which could bring about life-threatening situations at any time. A further disorientation was prompted by the procedures the prisoners had to undergo upon arrival at the camp. The confiscation of belongings, the total undressing, the tattooing of inmate numbers, and the shaving of all body hair contributed to intimidation and de-individualisation. This is elucidated in the following text passage by Vincenzo Pappalettera. Pappalettera (1919–1998), captured as a young antifascist and member of the Italian Resistance movement, was deported first to Mauthausen and then to St. Aegyd. His testimony, *Tu passerai per il camino. Vita a morte a Mauthausen* [*You Are Going Through the Chimney. Life and Death in Mauthausen*] (1965), was among the first survival accounts written in Italian. The following passage illustrates the moment of arrival at Mauthausen:

> Full of attention we listen to the interpreter who translates the order to undress naked; we can only keep shoes and belt. [...] I receive my first kick, because I expect to keep the photo of my Luigetto. They shout at me an avalanche of words that I don't understand, except *krematorium* repeated in the speech five or six times. (Pappalettera 1965/2006: 29, my translation from the Italian original; original emphasis)

The elimination of identity, achieved by substituting it with clothes symbolising homogeneity and with hierarchising classifications, culminated in eradicating the prisoner's name. The myriads of references to this traumatic procedure in the survivor reports testify to the enormous importance the prisoners ascribed to this phenomenon. Here are two more examples which illustrate this procedure:

> We then underwent a new identity check, or rather loss of identity, since, together with mismatched trousers and a jacket with a red triangle, which denominated political detainees, and the letter F, which meant French, we were given a number: 34534. [...] My name was abolished. I was supposed to no longer exist. I was nothing more than just a number, 34534. (Gouffault 2008: 72–73, my translation from the French original)

Similarly, Claude Antoine associates the loss of identity with the loss of his name:

> We definitely lost our identity, and we were nothing more than numbers that we had better learn by heart in German and Polish; 35.170, a number etched in my memory. (Antoine 1996: 141, my translation from the French original)

The horrifying rituals of the camps and the routine violence destroyed personal identity and social solidarity, so that daily life was reduced to a permanent struggle for survival. The consequent loss of identity of the detainees and additional intimidation allowed the SS officers to better control the prisoners and ensure that none of them dared to resist. The non-existing identity being one of the three major "realities" of the *non-place* – "non-relational, a-historical and not concerned with identity" (Augé 1995: 77) – in the context of concentration camps is certainly a key dimension. As Jan Schlosser tells us, "a loss of identity, both collective and individual, ignites in non-places. Functionalization as a passenger or customer seems total, while identity seems lost" (Schlosser 2016: 74).

It is the functionalization of the camp prisoners which is at the basis of another important aspect of ambiguity: alienation. The lack of communication without doubt results in different forms of alienation. Actually, any kind of communication decisively shaped the prisoners' life in the camp. This is understandable since the camp societies became more and more international over the years: in many camps there were prisoners of up to 40 different nationalities. Consequently, more differentiated mechanisms of communication were required and could only partially be managed by creating a camp *lingua franca*, often called *lagerszpracha*, *lagerjargon* or, with bitter irony, *crematorium Esperanto* (Jagoda et al. 1987). The *lagerszpracha* was a kind of communicative code based on German vocabulary adapted to the rules of mostly Polish grammar. Furthermore, nonverbal signs designated basic activities and events of the camp's daily life. A clear definition of the camp jargon is delivered by Kitty Hart-Moxon (born 1926), a young Jewish woman from Poland imprisoned in Auschwitz:

> I realised that the camp had its own language, and I was at an advantage because I could understand it. It was part German, part Yiddish, part Polish. You had to have the language to find your way around. And it had its own expressions: the most important was to "organize". This was a universal word for barter – to buy, to sell, to get food. (Hart-Moxon in Smith 2006: 173).

The importance of the *lagerszpracha* is also highlighted by Manuel Alfonso Ortells (1918–2017), deported to Mauthausen in 1940. He was a graphic designer and left a series of invaluable drawings of the camp to posterity (Deportados [2023]):

> And then the learning of our new way of life began, our new concentration camp language, which we had to learn by force with shouts and blows. (Alfonso Ortells 1966: 51, my translation from the Spanish original)

Primo Levi, too, refers to the *lagerszpracha* in various instances of his writings. In *The drowned and the saved* he associates it with military language on the one hand, and the brutal idiom of the SS, on the other, thus accentuating its violent character:

> But in the archipelago of German Lagers there had taken shape a sectorial language, a jargon, the "Lager jargon", subdivided into specific sub-jargons peculiar to each Lager and closely related to the old German of Prussian barracks and the new German of the SS. (Levi 1989: 76)

In a similar way, Éva Fahidi (born 1925 in Debrecen, Hungary) assigns the language she heard upon her arrival in Auschwitz, where her parents and sister were murdered, an utmost bizarreness full of brutality, fostered by the strangeness of the view of other prisoners:

> Undefinable figures welcome us, I can't classify them. They wear ugly grey-and-black striped pyjamas, and on their heads a strange seaman's cap made of the same striped fabric. They scream in a strange language that is reminiscent of German but isn't. (Fahidi 2011: 161, my translation from the German translation; original in Hungarian)

Alienation as one of the dimensions of ambiguity and foregrounded here primarily through the concentration camp's *lagerszpracha* is thus strongly associated with fear, violence, the growing erosion of the prisoners' own language and, as a most extreme manifestation, with the loss of their own mother tongue:

> We are unable to speak our language correctly, not even among compatriots, no matter how hard we try. We are so familiar with and used to the jargon of the lager, a concoction of dialects and languages from all over Europe, that the usual expressions come out spontaneously. (Pappalettera 1965/2006: 86, my translation from the Italian original)

This passage, besides the myriads of languages and dialects spoken by the detainees, also illustrates the co-existence of a great number of nationalities to which the prisoners belonged. Yet, the concentration camp universe was far from being a well-structured community – rather, due to all kinds of hardships they had to suffer – torture, exhausting forced labour, hunger, diseases, death – the prisoners felt to live in a kind of Babel, associating this biblical experience with the daily dreadful struggle for survival, with chaos, turmoil, confusion:

> In this demonic society, a promiscuity of races, peoples and nationalities, a veritable "Tower of Babel" where a crowd of grotesque beings is moving about […] (Antoine 1996: 155, my translation from the French original)

> The detainees understood that this kind of "Tower of Babel" made the confraternization between these components difficult. (Batiste Baila 1999/2001: 169, my translation from the Spanish original)

> The multitude of nationalities thrown together in this Tower of Babel was a source of misunderstanding and confrontation. (Arnould 1975: 186, my translation from the French original)

> Already, nationalities are mixed in the camps, so that the obstacle of languages and mentalities makes this multitude not a body, but a heterogeneous crowd incapable of cohesion and union. It is an immense Babel. (Carrouges 1958: 220, my translation from the French original)

All these aspects which shape the aftermath of Babel are constitutive for the concentration camp, and they are characteristic for the *non-place*: "The non-place is the opposite of utopia: it exists, and it does not contain any organic society" (Augé 1995: 111–112). Also, discussing places, Augé asserts that "when individuals come together, they engender the social and organize places" (111). In the *lager*, prisoners could not "organize places" in the sense that they created spaces filled with social life. If ever prisoners could establish bonds between each other, these remained temporary and were of an ephemeral nature. In addition, and primarily, they are no longer "individuals", but they were subjected to an enduring act of dehumanisation. Shortly after the arrival at Mauthausen, Roger Gouffault observes:

> Another thing struck me: the language. From then on, we only heard German. That was also hard. It added to the dehumanisation. French no longer existed, like us. (Gouffault 2008: 69)

Prisoners were not expected to communicate among each other, and less in their mother tongue. On the contrary, the SS officers did not like it and obviously found it highly ambiguous when prisoners communicated with each other and thus regained some humanity. This again illustrated the extreme process of dehumanisation and de-individualisation that went on in the camp to create isolation among the detainees.

3.2. Manifestations of violence

In the concentration camp, violence was practiced in the most variable ways. This issue was raised both by Tryuk (e.g. 2010, 2011, 2016a, 2016b) and Wolf (e.g. 2013, 2016b) in various contexts. However, when adopting Marc Augé's concept of *non-place* and the various features which shape it, a more differentiated view of violence in connection with interpreting, or language in more general terms, can be distinguished. Thus, in this sub-section a second set of examples drawn from survivor accounts will highlight various manifestations of violence.

Augé's claim that in *non-places* there exists a concrete connection between the individual and words/pictures which is primarily expressed through rules or codes (Augé 1995: 96; see above), in the concentration camp is enacted in a series of scenes, including the moments when entering the camp, a topos in most memorial accounts. In the following text passage, drawn from Imre Kertész's book *Sorstalanság*, 1975 (*Fateless*, 1992), after days of travelling, a transport from Hungary, packed with prisoners, arrives at Auschwitz concentration camp. The door of the train is pushed open and voices very similar to German sound from all sides. To ensure that all new arrivals without any knowledge of German also receive the information, inmates take on the task of interpreting:

> But already the news was circulating that the suitcases and parcels were to stay here. Later – it was explained, translated and passed on from mouth to mouth – everyone would of course get their property back. (Kertész 1973: 89, my translation from the German translation; original in Hungarian)

Imre Kertész describes this scene in a quite sober way, mirroring the situation realistically by obviously reproducing a regulation pronounced by a member of the SS personnel, therefore representing a situation known from most accounts written by camp survivors. In some of these reports the reader can realise that at the very moment of arrival, when confronting the universe of the *non-place* for the first time, the author still does not seem to have an idea of the terror he or she will be confronted with. In such a context, Pio Bigo (1924–2013)[4], who was 20 and a member of the Italian Resistenza when the SS arrested him in March 1944, tells us:

> Approaching our group, they asked us in German to hand over to them everything we had, money, gold, shoes, clothes, because once we were in there, we would be stripped of everything. Those of us who understood German translated their demands to us: no one wanted to agree, and the Kapos got angry, as if they wanted to strip us by force; but none of the comrades gave in. (Bigo 1998: 28–29, my translation from the Italian original)

The description of this scene creates discomfort and might be seen as foreshadowing more suffering, but it does not yet reflect the boundless fear that would become an everyday experience of terror in the later course of the presence in the concentration camp. With reference to the *non-place*, Jan

---

4 For more biographical information on Pio Bigo see Buchenwald [2023]. Bigo survived seven concentration camps.

Schlosser reminds us that "Augé's reflections show that encounters with places can trigger melancholy, while encounters with non-places can prompt decided unease" (Schlosser 2016: 76, my translation).

Very soon, however, every "newcomer" understood that they had passed the gate to hell. One of the Nazi regime's methods to demolish moral behaviour and to provoke a secure death was the dictum "death through work", which was a distinguishing motto for Mauthausen as the only concentration camp categorised as "camp level III". To bring about an early death, all imaginable and not imaginable kinds of hardships were adopted, beginning with the strategy that prisoners were given only the most primitive tools, and, whenever possible, they had to work with their bare hands. Actually, beyond direct murder through gassing or beating to death, "death through work" can be seen as the central function of concentration camps. Augé's argument that *non-places* mostly follow certain ends (Augé 1995: 94) can thus be directly referred to concentration camps. In the survivor reports, this key function is expressed primarily through excessive terror, often practiced with the help of the rubber truncheon, which especially in Mauthausen was called "interpreter". As reported in various accounts, this interpreter's language was understood by everyone:

> "You are a lawyer, and you are a professor? I am a criminal convicted of four robberies and one murder. Well, here I'm in charge. The world is upside down, do you understand? Or do you want the Dolmetscher – the interpreter?" And he showed his stick and struck them […]. (Albertinelli 1994: 179, my translation from the Italian original)[5]

Similarly, the "interpreter" is deployed when *kapos* play their games with the prisoners, provoking an atmosphere of fear and terror. In the following example the detainees are expected to learn orders in German language, "supported" by the employment of the rubber truncheon:

> The kapo and deputy kapo, the former armed with a large rubber stick and the latter with a strap, stand two metres away from the first line. The kapo wants to give us the first lesson in German. […] Hardly anyone understands the meaning of his commands, but the stick does wonders. In a short time, the main commands are executed to the point. (Fergnani 1945: 196, my translation from the Italian original)

Augé mentions yet another feature relevant for understanding the functioning of the *non-place*: solitude. When he says that the *non-place* "creates neither singular identity nor relations; only solitude, and similitude" (Augé 1995: 103),

5 These words were reported nearly verbatim by the brothers Vincenzo and Luigi Pappalettera 1970: 41.

this implies that the human being in the *non-place* is exposed to loneliness, silence, and uniformity in the most meaningless way (Schlosser 2016: 78). In the concentration camp, solitude became evident in a variety of situations. Some prisoners were pushed into a state of solitude when in the *lager* they were confronted not only with totally unknown conditions, but especially with foreign languages they did not understand. This is the case, among many others, in the following text passage, written by Viktor Frankl (1905–1997), the famous Viennese psychiatrist who founded the school of logotherapy:

> And so it went on a few times, after I had found myself among people from other countries, who all spoke foreign languages I didn't know. (Frankl 1977/2008: 90, my translation from the German original)

But more importantly, solitude pervaded the general condition and the dominant atmosphere in the camp, where total exhaustion was raging, where hunger increasingly threatened to dehumanise the camp society, and where violence was devastating any moral claims. These conditions pushed the prisoner into a frightening universe of solitude which sometimes was the limbo of becoming a muselmann[6]. The following individual experiences and perceptions speak for larger parts of the camp society:

> In this commando of Shahtbau with all the harshness that reigned there, I stayed about a year [...]. Very often, as the only Frenchman among prisoners of all nationalities, I had to overcome my despair and control myself very well. In this distress, I was quite isolated morally, except on Sundays when I was exempt from working in the mine and could get closer to the French prisoners in the camp. (Lainé 2003: 53, my translation from the French original)

Roger Lainé (1925–2012), detained in several concentration camps including Mauthausen and Melk, was liberated at the *lager* of Ebensee on 6 May 1945. His solitude was not only based on his despair of being the only Frenchman in his work crew, but also on the terrifying sufferings in the *lager*. Very similarly, Iakovos Kambanellis describes a scene at the camp of Mauthausen:

> Just as I sit in my corner, my head swaying back and forth from exhaustion, loneliness and tiredness, I hear a Serb who has come from outside telling a group of Spaniards in French what happened today at the river [...]. (Kambanellis 2010: 95, my translation from the German translation; original in Greek)

6 Muselmann was a term used amongst detainees in concentration camps. The term referred to persons suffering both from starvation and from resigning to their impending death.

Kambanellis (1921–2011) was a Greek writer who became particularly famous for his *Mauthausen Cantata*, a cycle of four songs with lyrics written by him, while the music was composed by his friend Mikis Theodorakis. The scene evokes an immeasurable exhaustion, a sense of being totally lost "in the stormy sea of not-understanding" (Levi 1989: 74), a solitude that is further enhanced by highlighting the picture of the author's crouching in "his corner" in the *lager*'s barrack, detached from the present time, but also from the past and the future. The description can be closely associated with Jan Schlosser's statement in the context of the characteristics which make up the *non-place* that "[l]iving in 'places' without a past triggers the feeling of being unhoused" (Schlosser 2016: 78).

4. Concluding remarks

The attempt to correlate Nazi concentration camps with Marc Augé's concept of *non-place* revealed that many of the central features which make up the *non-place* can be viewed as constitutive for a basic understanding of communication patterns in the camps. Under such a perspective, the role of language and language mediation in the *lager* becomes even more decisive. To test this claim, two sets of key factors were chosen which are particularly characteristic in moulding communication patterns in the *lager*: ambiguity and manifestations of violence.

The most evident factors to illustrate ambiguity were disorientation and alienation. In the analysis, they were carefully linked to the gradual loss of identity prompted, among others, by the increasing use of a *lagerszpracha*. As could be shown, the growing intensity of the impact of the *lagerszpracha* tended to augment the feeling of alienation of the prisoners. Moreover, the investigation of several examples drawn from survivor accounts under the perspective of various manifestations of violence showed that when adopting some of the features which shape the *non-place*, we can single out more differentiated views of violence in relation to communication. This relates particularly to detecting the gradual increase in identifying the various demonstrations of violent aggression, starting with different forms of discomfort in specific situations linked to the initial rituals at the entrance gate of the *lager*, up to sheer terror, here shown through the rubber stick, the interpreter, whose language was understood by everyone. Finally, following Augé's dictum that the *non-place* provokes, inter alia, solitude, helped to unfold this dimension in the context of the problems linked to language, language mediation and communication in the widest sense of the word.

Many of the most important – and here extensively discussed – characteristics of the *non-place* are clearly inscribed in the following quote from Roger Gouffault, which refers to his arrival at the Mauthausen concentration camp:

> At the top of the hill, on a kind of plateau, we saw a fortress, a sort of castle. As we approached, we could make out the impressive carved stone walls and the monumental entrance. "Ihr die hier eintretet, lasst alle Hoffnung fahren". "You who enter here, leave all hope". This was what was marked at the entrance, which we did not understand of course, and did not even see, because we were a herd of martyred beasts that advanced with their heads down, trying to avoid the blows. (Gouffault 2008: 68, my translation from the French original)

The concentration camp seen as a *non-place* – a view significantly enhanced in this text passage by Dante's dictum – opens up new perceptions and additional ways of interpretation which have yet a different impact on the communication patterns and their awareness in the *lager*. Eventually, it is true that "a place gets its meaning through the speaking or through the silence of those who know" (Gstettner 2002: 4).

References

Primary sources

Albertinelli, Lorenzo. 1994. *I Lager. Poema storico in sette canti*. Firenze: Giuntina.

Alfonso Ortells, Manuel. 1966. *De Barcelona a Mauthausen. Diez años de mi vida (1936–1945)*. Fuenlabrada: Editorial Queimada.

Antelme, Robert. 1947/2010. *L'espèce humaine*. Paris: Gallimard.

Antoine, Claude. 1996. *L'angoisse de l'aube. L'odyssée de Maurice Antoine pendant le Seconde Guerre Mondiale*. Montmélian: La Fontaine de Siloé.

Arnould, Roger. 1975. *Les témoins de la nuit*. Paris: F.N.D.I.R.P.

Batiste Baila, Francisco. 1999/2001. *El sol se extinguió en Mauthausen*. Vinaròs: Antinea.

Bigo, Pio. 1998. *Il triangolo di Gliwice. Memoria di sette Lager*. Alessandria: Edizioni dell'Orso.

Buchenwald. [2023]. "Pio Bigo", [online] https://www.buchenwald.de/1619/ [29 January 2023].

Carrouges, Michel. 1958. *Le Père Jacques*. Paris: Editions du Seuil.

Deportados. [2023]. "Manuel Alfonso Ortells", [online] http://deportados.es/alfonso_recuerdos [29 January 2023].

Fahidi, Éva. 2011. *Die Seele der Dinge*, trans. Doris Fischer. Berlin: Lukas Verlag.

Fergnani, Enea. 1945. *Un uomo e tre numeri*. Milano: Speroni.

Frankl, Viktor E. 1977/2008. *... trotzdem Ja zum Leben sagen. Ein Psychologe erlebt das Konzentrationslager*. München: dtv.

Gouffault, Roger. 2008. *Déporté à Mauthausen. Quand nous n'étions plus que des numéros....* Brive: Composition Cathy.

Kambanellis, Iakovos. 2010. *Die Freiheit kam im Mai*, trans. Elena Strubaki. Wien: Ephelant Verlag.

Kertész, Imre. 1973. *Roman eines Schicksallosen*, trans. Christina Viragh. Berlin: Rowohlt.

Lainé, Roger. 2003. *Journal de Roger Lainé*. Ermont: Imprimerie RPS.

Levi, Primo. 1989. *The Drowned and the Saved*, trans. Raymond Rosenthal. London: Abacus.

Pappalettera, Vincenzo. 1965/2006. *Tu passerai per il camino. Vita e morte a Mauthausen*. Milano: Mursia.

Pappalettera, Vincenzo & Luigi Pappalettera. 1970. *La parola agli aguzzini. Le SS e i kapò di Mauthausen svelano le leggi del Lager*. [Milano]: Mondadori.

Smith, Lyn. 2006. *Forgotten Voices of the Holocaust. True Stories of Survival – From Men, Women and Children Who Were There*. London: Ebury Press.

Secondary sources

Agamben, Giorgio. 1998. *Homo Sacer. Sovereign Power and Bare Life*, trans. Daniel Heller-Roazen. Stanford: Stanford University Press.

Arendt, Hannah. 1948. The Concentration Camps. *Partisan Review* 15(7), 743–763.

Arendt, Hannah. 1958. *The Origins of Totalitarianism*. Cleveland: Meridian Books.

Augé, Marc. 1995. *Non-Places. Introduction to an Anthropology of Supermodernity*, trans. John Howe. London: Verso.

Bhabha, Homi K. 1990. Interview with Homi Bhabha, in: Jonathan Rutherford (ed.), *Identity, Community, Culture, Difference*. London: Lawrence and Wishart, 207–221.

Brugiatelli, Vereno. 2016. For an Ethical and Integrated Way of Life: From Non-places to Places of Human Interaction. *Procedia. Social and Behavioral Sciences* 223, 58–61.

Gstettner, Peter. 2002. "Orte mit historischer Belastung. Zu einigen Schwierigkeiten der Gedenkarbeit an Tat-Orten. Referat bei der Tagung *Stigmatisierte Orte – Lernorte für die Zukunft*, Oberwart 23. März 2002", [online] https://kipdf.com/orte-mit-historischer-belastung-zu-einigen-schwierigkeiten-der-gedenkarbeit-an-t_5ab3acf81723dd369cf85259.html [29 January 2023].

Hartmann, Lars. 2020. "Deutsches Herz der Finsternis. Zur Befreiung von Auschwitz", in: *Glanz & Elend. Magazin für Literatur und Zeitkritik*, [online] https://www.glanzundelend.de/Red20/a-c-20/deutsches-herz-der-finsternis-zur-befreiung-von-auschwitz.htm [29 January 2023].

Jagoda, Zenon, Stanislaw Kłodziński & Jan Masłowski. 1987. "'bauernfuss, goldzupa, himmelautostrada'. Zum 'Krematoriumsesperanto' der Sprache polnischer KZ-Häftlinge", trans. Jochen August. *Die Auschwitz-Hefte* 2, 241–260.

Matienzo, Mark. 2004. "The Ethnology of Nowhere, Everywhere: Marc Augé's *Non-places* as an Analytical Tool for Supermodern Ahistory and Transience", [online] https://matienzo.org. [29 January 2023].

Neurath, Paul Martin. 2005/2016. *The Society of Terror. Inside the Dachau and Buchenwald Concentration Camps*. Edited by Christian Fleck and Nico Stehr. Abingdon: Routledge.

Prenninger, Alexander. 2016. The Camp Society: Approaches to Social Structure and Ordinary Life in Nazi Concentration Camps, in: Michaela Wolf (ed.), *Interpreting in Nazi Concentration Camps. With an Essay by Primo Levi*. New York: Bloomsbury, 25–42.

Relph, Edward. 1976/2016. *Place and Placelessness*. London: Sage Publications.

Schlosser, Jan T. 2016. "Orte und Nicht-Orte in Paul Celans *Engführung* (1959)". *Recherches germaniques* 46, 73–86, [online] http://journals.openedition.org/rg/315 [29 January 2023].

Sofsky, Wolfgang. 1997. *The Order of Terror: The Concentration Camp*, trans. William Templer. Princeton: Princeton University Press.

Tosoni, Lara Maria. 2015. *Primo Levi – der Zeuge und sein Zeugnis. Translation als Metapher für eine Grauzone zwischen Täter- und Opfersprache in* Ist das ein Mensch *von Primo Levi*. University of Graz: Master's thesis.

Tryuk, Małgorzata. 2010. Interpreting in Nazi Concentration Camps during World War II. *Interpreting* 12(2), 125–145.

Tryuk, Małgorzata. 2011. "You say nothing; I will interpret": Interpreting in the Auschwitz-Birkenau Concentration Camp, in: Dimitris Asimakoulas & Margaret Rogers (eds.), *Translation and Opposition*. Bristol: Multilingual Matters, 223–243.

Tryuk, Małgorzata. 2016a. Interpreters in the Concentration Camp of Majdanek, in: Michaela Wolf (ed.), *Interpreting in Nazi Concentration Camps. With an Essay by Primo Levi*. New York: Bloomsbury, 115–133.

Tryuk Małgorzata. 2016b. Interpreting and Translating in Nazi Concentration Camps during World War II. *Linguistica Antverpiensia* 15, 121–141.

Tryuk, Małgorzata & Michaela Wolf. 2015. Concentration Camps, in: Franz Pöchhacker, & Nadja Grbić, Peter Mead & Robin Sutton (eds.), *Routledge Encyclopedia of Interpreting Studies*. London: Routledge, 77–78.

Üngür, Erdem. 2012. "Contradiction and Ambiguity in Non-Place: Non-Place as a Transitional Spatial Concept", [online] http://www.academia.edu/2061331/Contradiction_and_Ambiguity_in_Non-Place_Non-Place_as_a_Transitional_Spatial_Concept [29 January 2023].

Weiß, Stephanie. 2005. *„Orte und Nicht-Orte": Kulturanthropologische Anmerkungen zu Marc Augé*. Mainz: Gesellschaft für Volkskunde in Rheinland-Pfalz e.V.

Wolf, Michaela. 2013. "German speakers, step forward!" Surviving Through Interpreting in Nazi Concentration Camps. *Translation and Interpreting* 8(1), 1–22.

Wolf, Michaela. 2016a. Introduction: Interpreting in Nazi Concentration Camps – Challenging the "Order of Terror"?, in: Michaela Wolf (ed.), *Interpreting in Nazi Concentration Camps. With an Essay by Primo Levi*. New York: Bloomsbury, 1–21.

Wolf, Michaela. 2016b. "Someone whispered the translation in 100 languages, like a Babel…": Interpreting in the Mauthausen Concentration Camp, in: Michaela Wolf (ed.), *Interpreting in Nazi Concentration Camps. With an Essay by Primo Levi*. New York: Bloomsbury, 95–113.

Wolf, Michaela. 2020a. Primo Levi's "Grey Zone" and the Ambiguity of Translation in Nazi Concentration Camps, in: Federico Italiano (ed.), *The Dark Side of Translation*. London: Routledge, 59–74.

Wolf, Michaela. 2020b. Primo Levi: „Wir können und müssen verstehen". Die Ambivalenz des Un_Übersetzten, in: Nadja Grbić, Susanne Korbel, Judith Laister, Rafael Y. Schögler, Olaf Terpitz & Michaela Wolf (eds.), *Übersetztes und Unübersetztes. Das Versprechen der Translation und ihre Schattenseiten*. Bielefeld: transcript, 181–202.

Sergey Tyulenev

Chapter 3 Interpreting and translation in military intelligence interrogations: A social-systemic perspective

Abstract: The chapter discusses the dynamics of interrelations in the military intelligence interrogation team from the socio-systemic point of view. It conceptualises military intelligence interrogation agency and translation agency as boundary phenomena, endo- and ectohomorous respectively. In the existing literature on military intelligence interrogation, translation is considered as present only when it is personified by interpreters and translators (also called "linguists"). The chapter argues that translation is always present in interlinguo-social military interrogation procedures, sometimes intrapersonally, sometimes in a personified fashion – as a third party mediating communication between the interrogator and the interrogatee. There are complex dynamics between these two boundary agencies and various scenarios of their interaction which are the subject of this discussion.

Keywords: social system, boundary phenomena, translation, interpreting, military intelligence, interrogation

1. Introduction

Asked what the role of the interpreter is in a military intelligence (MI) interrogation, a U.S.A. interrogator described metaphorically the interrogation team as a crew in the cockpit and the interpreter as the interrogator's "wingman" (Russano et al. 2014b: 842). The team's goal is to gain intelligence which can be used for planning and carrying out military operations. This goal can be achieved by crossing the linguo-socio-cultural boundary because the interaction is most of the time interlingual and inevitably inter-socio-cultural. The interrogator is responsible for obtaining the information, s/he leads interrogation, but s/he cannot function without translation, the only social agency that makes the crossing of linguo-socio-cultural boundaries possible. Translation can be done by the interrogator him/herself or an interpreter can be involved. In either case, there are complex dynamics between layers of the socio-systemic boundary. These dynamics are the focus of the present chapter.

2. Interrogation

Let us first look at interrogation. In dictionaries, interrogating is defined with modifiers which make it a very peculiar type of questioning. To interrogate is to ask "a lot of questions" and to ask them "formally and systematically" and "in a thorough and often forceful way" or "sometimes using threats or violence"; interrogations may last "for a long time"; and finally, the goal is "to get information."[1]

In the military literature, interrogating is defined more specifically: "Interrogation is […] responsible for MI [Military Intelligence] exploitation of enemy personnel and documents to answer the […] specific information requirements (SIR)" (*USArmyIIH 2005*: vii). It will be noted that while in the general dictionaries the object of interrogation is either not named or referred to vaguely as "someone," military interrogators see the interrogatee as their enemy. Also, the object of interrogation includes not only humans ("enemy personnel") but also the enemy documents. A document seized from the enemy is also part of the interrogation process: "The interrogator extracts intelligence from two primary sources: human sources and material sources (primarily CEDs [captured enemy documents])" (*USArmyIIH 2005*: 15). Translation is clearly recognised as a means of interrogating enemy's written sources:

> The DOCEX [document exploitation] section receives documents taken from captured personnel, battlefield casualties, and positions abandoned by the enemy. It processes captured documents; for example, screens for intelligence value, categorizes, and translates. It forwards translation reports on information of immediate tactical value. (*USArmyIIH 2005*: 35)

But translation as part of interrogating human sources is not always recognised as a means of gaining intelligence. It is seen only when it is personified by translators or interpreters. Yet it happens in every interlingual interrogation – sometimes in the form of interpreting and sometimes invisibly, in the interrogator's mind.

The goal of the MI interrogation is defined not just as getting information like in any other interrogation. Interrogation in military contexts can be used for different purposes, for instance to determine the measure of responsibility of a detainee in the enemy's hostile activities or to get a full picture of a military action. After WWII, high-ranking Nazi war criminals were interrogated in London with

1 https://dictionary.cambridge.org/dictionary/english/interrogate; https://www.merriam-webster.com/dictionary/interrogate; https://www.britannica.com/dictionary/interrogate (viewed 17 November, 2022).

the goal of "compiling evidence for the war crimes trials" (Fry 2017: 45). But the MI interrogation is after a specific type of information – the information that would answer the specific information requirements (SIR). These SIR responses must satisfy "the force commander's priority intelligence requirements (PIR) and intelligence requirements (IR)" (*USArmyIIH 2005*: vii). Interrogators in military intelligence contexts act "in support of the commander's intelligence needs" (*USArmyIIH 2005*: vii). The MI interrogation contributes "to the overall intelligence collection effort" (*USArmyIIH 2005*: vii).

What is noteworthy for the present discussion, the MI interrogation is a meeting point of the interacting parties which, in social-systemic terms, are representatives of two different social systems, each with its own linguo-socio-cultural properties. To achieve its goal – collection of intelligence, the MI interrogation should cross the social-systemic boundary, but the parties cannot interact directly, because they speak different languages and exist in different socio-cultural frameworks. For these two parties to interact across the boundary, another element is necessary – translation.

3. Translation and Interpreting in Interrogation Settings

There have been studies of interpreting and translation in a variety of extreme settings, such as trials of war criminals, concentration camps and military activities (Bowen and Bowen 1985; Gaiba 1998; Morris 1998; Snellman 2016; Tryuk 2016; Wolf 2016; Baigorri-Jalón 2021/2019, to name just a few). The focus of the present chapter is on interpreting and translation in yet another extreme modality in which the interpreter may find him/herself – the interrogation for gaining military intelligence.

Some research has been conducted into interpreting in interrogation-like settings (Pöllabauer 2005; Inghilleri 2012; Schumann 2020). To be sure, the military intelligence interrogation shares some properties with the other types of interrogation but it differs in what constitutes its goal – gaining information that would allow optimising war activities, and consequently, in the time constraints that are imposed on the interrogating team which frequently act under pressure to get "swift 'hot' information" (Fry 2017: 40). The interaction between the interrogator and the interpreter needs to be extremely efficient in order to obtain "timely, complete, clear, and accurate" intelligence as quickly as possible (*USArmyIIH 2005*: 8). MI interrogators should be specially trained even if they have had some other interrogation experience. Consequently, interpreting for MI must be different from other types of interpreting.

Sometimes the MI interrogation is carried out without an interpreter. Seemingly in such situations there is little for the translation scholar to discuss, but arguably translation is still there. It is not visible or personified, and therefore it falls outside the picture for both TIS and military professionals: interrogations are categorised as being either with or without interpreting.

The publications that discuss the role of interpreting in the process of gathering MI are rarely of a research nature such as Russano et al. 2014a and 2014b; rather they are of practical nature. Indeed, mostly, they are either instructions regarding the use of interpreting for interrogations in MI guidebooks and manuals, such as *USArmyIIH* 2005 and *HICO 2006*, or historiographical evidence gleaned from memoirs, such as Newbery 2015 and Fry 2017. In all these publications there has been little attempt to look at translation and its various modes as used in MI contexts with any scholarly depth; rather these publications are either historiographic, that is – describing history with some passages on interpreting/translation here and there, or efforts to disseminate the most efficient techniques of interrogation that includes interpreting, or straightforward instructions about the nuts and bolts of interrogation procedures when interpreting is involved.

The goal of the present chapter is different. This discussion is in line with my research into socio-systemic aspects of translation in general and my recent explorations of translation's interactions with a special body of socio-systemic formations called boundary phenomena (Tyulenev 2012, 2021, 2022).

4. Double-Layered Socio-Systemic Boundary

Viewed macro-sociologically, contemporary nation-states can be described as social systems (Luhmann 1995). They consist of subsystems, and each fulfils a particular function to meet a specific social need. For instance, the political subsystem is responsible for the distribution and handling of power in society; the economy provides everything needed for society's subsistence; education raises new generations of social agents etc. Translation can be viewed as one of the social function subsystems with its own primary function – to mediate across various types of boundary (Tyulenev 2012).

Some subsystems are responsible for fulfilling internal and some for the external functions of the system. Examples of the internal, or inward-oriented, subsystems are politics which is about handling power within the social system, or the economy dealing with material or other necessary supplies for the society and its members. But every social system is surrounded by other social systems, and therefore it needs structures which would enable it to interact with its social environment.

Translation is an example of such outward-oriented social structures: it allows the system to process the information coming into the system from its environment and the information the system projects into its environment. The external types of social structures are referred to as boundary phenomena. Besides translation, boundary phenomena include international trade relations, diplomacy, military actions, cultural exchange as well as espionage and its opposite – counterespionage. The boundary phenomena may be metaphorised as eyes or ears of the social system as they were by both Luhmann, the author of the term (1995: 197), and by intelligence gatherers, such as Admiral Nelson. Nelson called the frigates whose captains watched movements of ships in neutral ports in the Mediterranean "the eyes of the fleet" (cited in Deacon 1978: 28). Similarly but much earlier, in the fifth century B.C., Sun Tzu, a Chinese theorist of war, wrote that an army without spies is like a man without ears or eyes (cited in Scott 2015: 96).

The boundary of the social system is double-tiered (Tyulenev 2021). There are two layers: the internal, or endohomorous, and the external, or ectohomorous (from Greek "endon" meaning "inside", "ectos" meaning "outside" and "homoros"/ "horos" – "border"). The internal, endohomorous layer consists of social agencies which deal with foreign phenomena indirectly, not necessarily familiar with the foreign linguo-cultures. They act on the inside of their home socio-systemic boundary. For instance, diplomats pass on their governments' messages to the governments of the nations in they serve. They may or may not know the language of the other side, and even when they do, they are advised against the direct linguistic contact (Tyulenev 2022). The external, ectohomorous layer is made up of the agencies which are responsible for establishing a direct, unmediated contact with the foreign linguo-cultures. The external layer is most often (but not always) represented by translators and interpreters.

Let us once again consider a diplomat, who represents her/his country, but inevitably does that via translation. The diplomat may know the linguo-culture of the country in which s/he works but even when s/he is using her/his knowledge of the target linguo-culture, there will be translation taking place in his/her mind. When there is a translator/interpreter, translation is visible and personified; when the diplomat works without a translator/interpreter, translation is not visible, but it is still present – it is practiced intrapersonally. Thus, in either case, both endo- and ectohomorous boundary agencies are exercised. The boundary may only look one-layered: in fact, it is always double-layered.

5. Translation and Its Allomodes

Interlinguo-cultural translation as a type of social action has what can be termed as allomodes (compare allophones or allomorphs in linguistics), that is, various modes of its manifestation. Translation may be written or oral – the latter is usually (but not always and not by all) referred to as interpreting. These two allomodes of translation may be seen as two extremes of a continuum of various other mixed manifestations, for instance, a written source text may be translated orally. If we include sign language interpreting and kinetic translation (handling gestures, body language and facial expressions, Tyulenev 2018: 37–45), then it becomes clear how rich a repertoire of translation's allomodes is. In the present study, the focus will be on interpreting although the other allomodes will be touched upon as well because interrogations employ a range of translation allomodes.

Let us consider a WWII British interrogation report as an example. The report is a summary of a series of interrogations of survivors of a German U-boat, sunk by the British navy on the 5th April, 1941. The text is a result of mediation between German and English linguo-cultures which processed various pieces of military and industrial information. For example, the interrogated German officers' ranks (spelt with some variation in hyphenation) were supplied with English equivalents: "The Captain, Oberleutnant-zur-See (Lieutenant) Friedrich von Hippel […]" (*U 76 1941*: 5). Here, "Oberleutnant-zur-See" was rendered as "Lieutenant." These are examples of translating military information. One of the German officers, "the Junior Officer, Leutnant zur See (Sub-Lieutenant) Hans Peter Klages […] claimed that his father, Professor Dr. August Klages of Göttingen, had invented "Germisan" a germicide now manufactured by the Saccharine Factory of I.G. Farben in Magdeburg" (*U 76 1941*: 6). The interrogator recorded the information about Germisan with an explanation what it was and where it was manufactured. This is an example of industrial information that might turn out useful.

The information in the report is a reflection in writing of statements made orally: "'U 68' seems, from a statement made by a prisoner of war, to have been constructed […]"; "'U 69' was said to be available for active service" (*U 76 1941*: 12). From the description it is clear that some, but not all, German survivors could speak English. It was reported that "Von Hippel […] spoke some English" and even "was quite pleasant to talk to"; "The First Lieutenant, Oberleutnant-zur-See (Lieutenant) Hans Joachim Hagemann […] spoke English and French fairly well" (*U 76 1941*: 5–6). Thus, the report is a written document based on oral statements made by German speakers either in German (by those who did not speak English) or in English and possibly also in French.

In the same report there are examples of other allomodes of translation. In Appendix I of the report, there is a "translation of a broadcast in German for Germany on 2nd March, 1941, by Kapitänleutnant (Lieutenant-Commander) Heinrich Lehamann-Willenbrock" (*U 76 1941*: 26). It is a translation of an entire orally delivered text as opposed to the main body of the report discussed above which was a summarised written translation of a number of oral interrogations. These are two different allomodes – a gist translation of oral communication (in the report) and a written translation of an oral text.

In the translation there are traces of the anonymous translator's work. The following passage provides a few examples (the numbers in the square brackets mark the points which will be commented upon below):

> There were two single (or detached) [1] tankers. One was of 8,000 tons; it was the ('Kenya') [sic, 2], a beautiful, new, modern British tanker which we attacked on the surface -er- [3] which I attacked by day when submerged. One torpedo, which struck amidships, was enough. Is [sic] the heavy sea which was running the ship soon broke up. [4] We then surfaced and sank the two halves with our gun. (The gunner?) [5], who only seldom is able to use his weapon to advantage in a U-Boat, fired quite a number of rounds, and then she -er- [6] the two halves sank one after the other. (*U 76 1941*: 26)

In case [1], the translator hesitated how to render the German term: single or detached. In case [2], (s)he probably did not hear clearly enough the name of the sunk tanker. Cases [3] and [6] are the translator's attempts to render the oral nature of the source text. Case [4] is an example of an incorrect sentence which is clearly the translator's error: a typo "is" instead of "in" to read "in the heavy sea"; also English is not quite idiomatic: "the heavy sea which was running." Case [5] is a sign of the translator's hesitance perhaps caused by the imperfect sound quality. Later, there is an omission in the translation: "We then launched ourselves upon this (*one word omitted*)" (*U 76 1941*: 26, the italics are in the original). This translation offers a glimpse into the kind of English-German oral – less than perfect – interactions like those which must have happened during interrogations recorded in the analysed report, but those imperfections were edited out in the summarising translation-report while they were left in the appended translation of the radio transmission. The interrogation report shows that translation was always present even when the interrogators and the interrogatees spoke in one language, be it German or English. Even when there was not interpreter/ing, there was inevitably intrapersonal translation with imperfections. Both layers of the boundary were present, whether visibly or not.

Finally, in Appendix II of the report, there is an example of written-to-written translation mode. It is once again an anonymous translation. It is a translation of "a letter written in German by Steuermannsmaat Carl Becker of "U 76," on board H.M.S. "Arbutus," addressed to Frau Edith Becker, Wiesbaden, Wilhelnstrasse 81, dated Sunday, 6th April, 1941" (*U 76 1941*: 27). The translation is idiomatic and well-written, and in this sense, it is a stark contrast to the lower quality of the oral-to-written translation of the German broadcast in Appendix I.

The translations in Appendices I and II are materials added to the intelligence obtained in orally conducted interrogations. In the interrogations, translation as the ectohomorous layer of the boundary between the involved linguo-cultures was not personified by the interpreting agency, translation was exercised intrapersonally by those speaking English and German (and French?). However, in the appended translations, the ectohomorous agency of translation has manifested itself in plain sight – the appendices were even called translations. For the present discussion it is important to note that the quality of translation varied: the oral-to-written translation of the German broadcast in Appendix I is rather poor, while the written-to-written translation of the letter in Appendix II is considerably better written. It is legitimate to assume that the author of the translation in Appendix I must have been an unprofessional/untrained translator; it is likely that s/he was a non-native English speaker. The only professionally made translation (if fluency and absence of glaring errors can serve as criteria) is the translated letter in Appendix II.

It is safe to conclude that the interrogation was conducted drawing on linguistic capacities of the participants, interrogators and interrogatees, who were endohomorous agents – British interrogators and German military men. They were trained to act endohomorously, on the inside of their respective systemic boundary – between the United Kingdom and Germany. They tried or rather were forced by circumstances to act ectohomorously, that is, they crossed the external linguo-cultural side of the intersystemic boundary, although not always successfully. When the ectohomorous agent, a professional translator, took part in the interrogation process, there was an admittedly successful action. But perhaps the notion of success should be redefined for this type of interrogation: the point was to gain intelligence about the German U-boats and reflect it in a summarising translation-report for optimising further British military activities. A summarising translation based on the gist translation of German POWs' statements was sufficient, while the next-to-perfect translation in Appendix II looks almost a superfluity.

6. MI Interrogation and HUMINT

Military Intelligence consists of three parts. Signals intelligence (SIGINT) is obtained from radio-electronic emissions. Imagery intelligence (IMINT) is derived from radar and electro-optical imagery. Finally, human intelligence (HUMINT) is the information that is gained from human sources. Interrogation is part of gaining HUMINT.

HUMINT is a result of (direct) interhuman interactions. Any interhuman communication is complex because it takes place at the intersection of different psychological and sociocultural systems. HUMINT settings are usually connected with risk, danger and duress which add to the complexity of interhuman interactions. According to a WWII survey in the USA, despite all problems, 84% of all the HUMINT obtained was produced by interrogation and it was recognised as "the most valuable of all collection operations" (*USArmyIIH 2005*: 3).

To be valuable, MI should be timely (*USArmyIIH 2005*: 8). Time pressure affects interrogation which may be conducted at the tactical or strategic levels. As is clear from the terms, tactical interrogations aim at resolving immediate operational tasks while strategic interrogations are supposed to gain information for developing long-term counter-enemy plans. Tactical interrogations are especially time-sensitive and therefore, they are kept as brief as possible and they aim at obtaining a specific type of information – PIR (priority intelligence requirement). PIR-informed intelligence is supposed to inform military decision makers about the "size, activity, location, unit, time, equipment (SALUTE)" of the enemy forces (*USArmyIIH 2005*: 8). At the strategic level, there is more time and "a more expanded interrogation effort" is possible (*USArmyIIH 2005*: 8).

At the tactical level, the combination of endo- and ectohomorous agencies in one person is optimal because of the time and effort constraints. An example of MI interrogations conducted at the tactical level is the type of interrogation that happened in the London Cage, WWII prisoner-of-war facility for captured German military personnel. The goal there was to obtain "vital intelligence from prisoners as quickly as possible" (Fry 2017: 36). The urgency to gain hot intelligence was such that one of the London Cage interrogators, Randoll Coate, suggested to send interrogators with commando raids and, between 1940 and 1942, he himself participated in a number of them. Every time, "[o]n return to the home port, the main priority for Coate was to make sure he disembarked with the prisoners quickly, to avoid any delay in interrogation that could reduce the intelligence value of any material or prisoners captured" (Fry 2017: 41). In addition to POWs who were to be quickly interrogated, there could be materials such as seized documents or codes that needed to be processed as fast as possible to meet priority intelligence requirements (Fry 2017: 41). Coate, who was born in Switzerland to British parents and educated in Lausanne, was fluent in German, French, Dutch and Italian. He was an example of the interrogator-cum-translator who could combine endohomorous interrogator agency and ectohomorous translation agency in interrogating POWs and processing the captured documents. This combination of the two boundary agencies in one person was extremely useful when time and staff were limited.

At the strategic level, the interrogation is conducted on a different time scale and more personnel can be involved. For instance, intelligence gathered from interrogations of POWs at the London Cage was obtained over a longer period of time, with new POWs being constantly brought in. The goal was to identify not only key military targets, but also industrial ones in Germany that could be attacked or sabotaged (Fry 2017: 58). Information about factories that built component parts for aeroplanes, about work on the production of Tiger tanks, or about chemical works was obtained from interrogated prisoners. British intelligence gained a comprehensive understanding of the Nazi military industry of the time. The interrogations produced this intelligence a year before the invasion of Europe by the Allies in 1944. Thanks to this intelligence well before D-Day, already during 1943, the Allies could prepare for that decisive operation. The map of German industrial heartlands allowed focussed military planning and strategic bombing raids that crippled the enemy's war machine (Fry 2017: 61).

At the strategic level as exemplified by the London Cage operation, there was also a great deal of interrogators who, being bilingual in English and German, could act both endo- and ectohomorously. It is also clear from the memoirs and the historiography of the London Cage, that some interrogators who were exceptionally fluent in German and knowledgeable in the German culture acted not only as interrogators, but also as interpreters for other interrogators. For instance, Captain W. Kieser worked as a schoolmaster before WWII. In 1942, he was commissioned into the Intelligence Corps and specifically to the London Cage. One of his advantages was the "all-around knowledge of German" and, therefore, besides interrogating on his own, "his services [were] sought after as an interpreter" (Fry 2017: 40).

7. Translation and Interpreting in Different Stages of the MI Interrogation

The main sources of HUMINT are dialogues during MI interrogations between the interrogator and the prisoner. To elicit as much information from the interrogatee as possible, various other components of the interrogation are used. The MI interrogation may seem a point in time when the dialogue takes place but in fact it is a process. Translation and interpreting exercise their social ectohomorous agency with each stage in this process.

Captured documents may be confiscated from captured military personnel, and they may prove "a good starting point for interrogation" (Fry 2017: 53). Identity cards of German pilots interrogated at the London Cage gave information about the units to which they belonged, and their savings bank books with the records of last deposits of their pay made it possible to locate those units on the map. German officers carried notebooks with lists of their regiments and codes for all kinds of aircraft and notes of problems in their units. Such pieces of information leaked during an interrogation session gave the prisoners the impression that the interrogators were omniscient and there was no point in putting up resistance.

Of course, to equip the interrogator with the knowledge that could be obtained from the captured documents, the documents had to be read and translated, or translated and read, depending on the interrogator's expertise in the interrogatees' language (*USArmyIIH 2005*: 35). Translation could happen within the head of the bilingual interrogator. S/he might combine the endohomorous (interrogator) and ectohomorous (translator) agencies. Or translation could be done by a translator for an interrogator who prepared for an interrogation session. In that case the endo- and ectohomorous functions were responsibilities of different social agents. In any case, processing captured documents is a preparatory stage of an MI interrogation session, and translation, whether intra- or interpersonal, is indispensable.

Another source of information may be studying the interrogatee outside the interrogation sessions. For example, covert listening to conversations of detainees may be used as was the case with the British Forces in Aden, Yemen, in the mid-1960s:

> At Fort Morbut, monitoring equipment was installed so that conversations between detainees in the cells could be listened to remotely. It was learned that the presence of listening devices was suspected by detainees. Staff accordingly faked their departure for the night whilst secretly remaining behind to monitor conversations. The detainees were fooled and information was gained. (Newbery 2015: 40).

The recorded conversations would have made little sense unless they were translated for the British interrogators, especially because few of them understood Arabic. Interpreting made them accessible to the interrogators.

Little wonder translation and/or interpreting figure prominently whenever there is a discussion of interrogation, whether in the past or present, in the special literature. Translation and/or interpreting is inevitable because information to be elicited in interrogations had to be rendered "clear" (*USArmyIIH 2005*: 8). This implies crossing the intersystemic linguo-socio-cultural boundary, and there is only one social function subsystem which can do that – translation in its various allomodes and with its ability to render the required intelligence clear which otherwise would make little, if any, sense.

8. Agents

Since they work across the social-systemic boundary, military intelligence officers exercising their endohomorous function should, at least to an extent, be able to act ectohomorously. That is why they are required to have at least some knowledge of the interrogatees' language and culture – actually, the more the better. In other words, MI interrogators should be able at least to "peek" into the other linguo-socio-cultural system.

The notion of the linguo-socio-culture in this context includes familiarity with the mindset, behavioural patterns, ethics of the detainees to be interrogated. The interrogator should be conversant with the social, political, and economic aspects of the target country as well as its geography and history (*USArmyIIH 2005*: 18). Cultural aspects influence the interrogation process: interrogation methods "will differ based on the ethnic and cultural background of the enemy, and our failure to understand and adapt to this could hamper the collection effort" (*USArmyIIH 2005*: 7). The interrogator's knowledge of the interrogatee's culture may allow flexibility in the interrogation and make the difference between success and failure: a non-cooperative source may be willing to discuss nonmilitary topics and the interrogator "may gradually introduce significant topics into the discussion to gain insight about the conditions and attitudes in the target country" (*USArmyIIH 2005:* 18).

In addition to the knowledge of the general culture of the target country described above, the interrogator must know the military culture of the target country. S/he must know enemy materiel, armed forces uniforms and insignia (*USArmyIIH 2005*: 18). S/he is also required to know relevant international conventions and the order of battle – the current disposition of troops or ships participating in or prepared for combat.

Ultimately, the goal of the application of the interrogator's expertise in the target culture is twofold. On the one hand, it will help him/her in interrogation sessions and on the other, it will make his/her exploiting available sources, including captured documents, effective.

The interrogator is an endohomorous agent yet his/her ectohomorous proficiency, albeit inevitably more limited than that of a professional translator/interpreter who is an ectohomorous agent par excellence, is not only desirable but necessary. It is described in *USArmyIIH 2005* in the strongest possible modalities. For instance, "[t]he interrogator *must* be knowledgeable on a variety of subjects" which include the target language, the target country's culture, international agreements, enemy military structures and the order of battle (p. 17; highlighted by me). S/he "must" be proficient in foreign languages (*USArmyIIH 2005*: 17). This shows that the endohomorous agency cannot be exercised without at least some involvement with the ectohomorous side of the socio-systemic boundary.

Among the ectohomorous aspects of the endohomorous interrogator expertise, a paramount one is the interrogatee's language. A special section *USArmyIIH 2005* is devoted to the proficiency in the target language:

> The interrogator must be proficient in one or more foreign languages to exploit both human sources and C[aptured] E[nemy] D[ocument]s. According to the GPW [Geneva Convention Relative to the Treatment of Prisoners of War of August 12, 1949], a prisoner must be questioned in a language he understands. The more proficient an interrogator is with the target language, the better he will be able to develop rapport with his source, understand the nuances of the source's speech, and follow up on source leads to additional information. The skilled linguist will be able to translate CEDs quicker and more accurately than the interrogator who is merely familiar with the target language. (*USArmyIIH 2005*: 17–8)

It will be noted in the above citation that the line between the endohomorous agency ("the interrogator") and the ectohomorous agency ("the skilled linguist") is blurred. This interpenetration of the two socio-systemic boundary agencies is ideal and examples of such a combination are known in history of the MI interrogation and have already been mentioned above. But let us dwell on this point to appreciate it fully.

In the London Cage, fluency in German was a prerequisite for being employed as an interrogator. In the beginning of WWII, the British Directorate of Military Intelligence, Sector 9, published an advertisement in *The Times* in which people "fluent in languages" were invited to apply (Fry 2017: 41). Colonel Alexander Paterson Scotland, the head of the London Cage, "insisted that any good interrogator or intelligence officer had to have an intuitive understanding of the German mindset: understanding the psyche of the prisoner meant that information could be extracted from him" (Fry 2017: 37). In this case interrogators were supposed to act both endo- and ectohomorously. For instance,

Antony Terry, a London Cage interrogator, was born in London in 1913 but spent most of his life in pre-war Berlin where his father worked in the British Embassy. "This gave him an invaluable knowledge of pre-war Germany, as well as of the inner workings of the Nazi military and civilian regime" (Fry 2017: 44). He was described in British intelligence files as "bi-lingual German with good French" (Fry 2017: 44). Another officer, that is, Randoll Coate who worked in the London Cage, was mentioned above.

However, it is not always possible to find interrogators meeting such high requirements, or in socio-systemic terms – endohomorous agents capable of acting ectohomorously (sufficiently well). In such cases, there are two ways of solving this problem – to involve interpreters and/or to rely on the detainee's knowledge of the interrogator's language. For instance, in the 1960s, British interrogators in Aden did not speak Arabic well enough and that created "an occasional language barrier between detainee and interrogator" (Newbery 2015: 39). There were some "higher-grade [Arabic speaking] detainees" who spoke English; with the rest, interpreters had to be brought in. The same happened with US MI interrogators. Among "extreme challenges for interrogation operations" there may be "limited number of language-qualified interrogators," as was the case for the US forces in LIC [low-income] countries like Grenada and Panama (*USArmyIIH 2005*: 43).

Interrogators' proficiency in the language of the enemy is a problem to reckon with and it is taken into account in tactical planning:

> Interrogation element commanders often have to contend with a mismatch between language-qualified personnel assigned to the unit and languages needed to perform the mission. They overcome the mismatch by acquiring local national (LN) interpreter support throught the Assistant Chief of Staff, G1 (Personnel). They can also augment their interrogators by requesting other available linguists within the supported command to serve as interpreters. (*USArmyIIH 2005*: 7)

The endohomorous agency cannot be exercised without the ectohomorous agency, but even if the interrogator has some expertise in the interrogatee's language and culture, it is advisable, according to the modern MI requirements, that they rely on the interpreter. One of the US interrogators in a relatively recent interview said: "I am a member of a team, and without involving me as an interpreter and an expert on the culture, the interrogation might not bring about the desired result" (Russano et al. 2014b: 842). Unlike in the London Cage case, there is a realisation here that the two boundary agencies should be exercised by experts rather than combined in one person. No matter how proficient the endohomorous agent may be in the target language and culture, it is hard for them to compete with the ectohomorous agent. The two agencies interact but are still distinguishable from each other.

Moreover, the ectohomorous agency of the interpreter may have an added value for the endohomorous agency of the interrogator. The interpreter may flag up inconsistences in the behaviour of the interrogatee. For example, the interrogatee may claim to be an officer, but s/he uses excessive slang and profanity. The interpreter tells the interrogator about this discrepancy and the latter will be able to modify his/her assessment of the source (*USArmyIIH 2005*: 93). In other words, the ectohomorous agent may see finer details that the endohomorous agent may miss.

The interpreter may be asked to assist with preparing reports of interrogation sessions (*USArmyIIH 2005*: 93). The interpreter may help the interrogator "to fill in gaps and unclear areas in the interrogator's notes" (*USArmyIIH 2005*: 95). S/he may also do transliterating, translating, and explaining foreign terms.

Being ready to cooperate with the interpreter is a difference between a skilled and less skilled interrogator:

> A skilled interrogator might also develop a good rapport with the interpreter and brief the interpreter prior to the interrogation about the planned line of questioning, objectives and things for the interpreter to look for (e.g., based on cultural knowledge, body language, tone of voice and the choice of words, the interpreter might be able to advise if the target is avoiding the interrogator's question, buying for time, or outright lying). Without this insight, a less skilled interrogator may misunderstand the body language and arrive at a wrong conclusion. (Russano et al. 2014b: 842)

These are the words of another interviewed interrogator. Interestingly, he starts with describing what "a skilled interrogator" might do – seek the interpreter's expertise in the target culture. He finishes his answer by stating what the result of ignoring the interpreter's potential input into the interrogation might be, and ignoring the interpreter's role is the line between a "skilled" and a "less skilled" interrogator. In other words, the skilled interrogator knows his (endohomorous) limits and seeks assistance from the ectohomorous expert – the interpreter, the agent who would help him/her cross the socio-systemic boundary.

9. Rules of Interrogating with Interpreters

While involving interpreters may be inevitable, it has been viewed by interrogators as less desirable and "always unsatisfactory" (Newbery 2015: 39). The reasons for that are as follows:

(1) Interrogation with interpreting is time-consuming "because the interpreter must repeat everything said by the interrogator and source" (*USArmyIIH 2005*: 93). Interrogation via interpreters is "inevitably slower" (Newbery 2015: 39), and this is a problem "[i]n a fast-moving war, [when] a piece of intelligence one day [i]s history the next" (Fry 2017: 36). There is another aspect of the time concern. "The interrogator had to produce immediate results while a prisoner was still disoriented by the shock of capture" as there is always a risk that after the first shock, the prisoner may become "uncooperative" (Fry 2017: 37). Obviously when time is a key factor in military contexts, the combination of the endo- and ectohomorous agencies by means of intrapersonal translation, rather than personified interpreting is seen as preferable, although in real life, the complex interaction of the three parties involved – interrogator, interrogatee, interpreter – is more probable.

(2) Interpreting makes it harder for the interrogator to control and affect the emotional state of the detainee. Interpreting coming between a question and a response inevitably dampens the interrogator's push. Among the London Cage interrogators was Major Hans Kettler. Although in interrogations there was no physical torture, Kettler's interrogation style could be "a traumatic experience" (Fry 2017: 43). Kettler used psychological pressure and his treatment of interrogatees was described as "rough" in that sense (Fry 2017: 43). Physically, he was short and had a physically deformed body but a powerful mind and a great deal of energy, that is why the German prisoners nicknamed him *der Giftzwerg* (the poison-dwarf). It would be very hard for him to have the effect on his interrogatees that he did if he had to act via an interpreter.

Kettler's is an extreme case, but each interrogator tries to interact with the interrogatee taking into account and sometimes exploiting his/her psychological traits. Interpreting is inevitably an additional complicating element. The interrogator is recommended to have "[a] firm, deliberate, and businesslike manner of speech and attitude [which] may create a proper environment for a successful interrogation" (*USArmyIIH 2005*: 17). Ideally, this needs to be carried across in interpreting. But can this be guaranteed with all interpreters, especially with those who have not been specially trained or who are simply bilingual locals? Yet another scenario is when, in some situations, "the interrogator can deliberately portray a different (for example, casual or sloven) appearance and demeanour to obtain the cooperation of the source" (*USArmyIIH 2005:* 17). This kind of thespianism, ideally, should be rendered across interpreting. But once again, can that be guaranteed?

One of the solutions always discussed about interrogation interpreting, is sitting arrangement. It is not seen as a trivial matter, but as a way to let the interrogator stay in control: "Ideally, the interrogator and the source should face each other with the interpreter behind the source. This enhances interrogator control by allowing him to simultaneously observe the source and interpreter" (*USArmyIIH 2005*: 93). Obviously, it is only a partial solution.

(3) To solve the a-third - person-between - the-two problem, there are recommendations how the interrogator should work with the interpreter. In addition to preparing for the contact with the interrogatee, the interrogator must prepare for the contact with the interpreter. The interrogator "obtains information about his interpreter from the senior interrogator" and analyses it (*USArmyIIH 2005*: 93). S/he also talks with the interpreter before the interrogation session. One of the goals of this talk is to brief the interpreter (*USArmyIIH 2005*: 94) which includes the current tactical situation, the background information about the interrogatee, interrogation objectives and the method of interpreting. But there is also another goal – to learn more about the interpreter in order to choose, among other things, the method of interpreting – simultaneous or "alternate" (*USArmyIIH 2005*: 93). After the interrogation session, the interrogator is required to evaluate the interpreter. Thus, using interpreting/interpreter complicates for the interrogator not only the interrogation session but the entire process as a whole.

For the interpreter, interpreting in MI interrogations comes with its own specific requirements and complications as well. First of all, the psychological pressure is considerably higher than in many other types of interpreting. The MI interpretation is comparable with the most extreme interpreting modalities (compare Tryuk 2016; Wolf 2016). The interpreter is required to interpret "using the same content, tone of voice, inflection, and intent" (*USArmyIIH 2005*: 93). The interpreter is subjected to military discipline even if s/he does not have a military rank (compare Snellman 2016). The attitude of the interpreter is described in the strongest modalities: "The interpreter must not inject his own personality, ideas, or questions into the interrogation. The interpreter should inform the interrogator if there are any inconsistencies in the language used by the source" (*USArmyIIH 2005*: 93).

Overall, the interrogator and the interpreter are supposed to work and be seen by the interrogatee as working together – as a team. During the interrogation session, the interrogator may need to correct the interpreter if s/he violates any instructions on which s/he was briefed, for example, if the interpreter injects her/his own ideas into the dialogue between the interrogator and the interrogatee.

But corrections should be made “in a low-key manner” (*USArmyIIH 2005*: 94). The interrogator should not rebuke the interpreter “sternly or loudly while they are with the source” or argue with him/her “in the presence of the source” (*USArmyIIH 2005*: 94). If the interpreter cannot be corrected in a low-key manner, the interrogator and the interpreter are advised to leave the interrogation site and discuss the issue, but that can be done only when necessary.

I will finish with the following observation. The interpreter is instructed to behave as if s/he were not there:

> When the initial source contact is made, the interpreter must instruct him to maintain eye contact with the interrogator. Since rapport and control must be established, the interpreter should be able to closely imitate the attitude, behavior, and tone of voice used by the interrogator and source. The questioning phase is conducted in the same way it would be if no interpreter were used. During the termination phase, too, the interpreter’s ability to closely imitate the interrogator and source is important. The approaches used are reinforced, and necessary sincerity and conviction must be conveyed to the source. (*USArmyIIH 2005*: 94–5)

The MI understanding of interpreting is controversial. On the one hand, it should be practiced as if it were transparent. This is how translation in any of its allomodes viewed by many clients everywhere and this is not a surprise for the interpreter/translator or the scholar of translation/interpreting. But this view is found in the same documents, such as the cited *USArmyIIH 2005* instructions, together with a detailed and frank discussion of interpreting as a factor that must be taken into consideration by the interrogator, that is, as a tangible and important agency to which entire sections are denoted. In some respects interpreting is seen as complicating the interrogation process, but in the other respects it is appreciated as facilitating the work of the interrogator. Moreover, *USArmyIIH 2005* advises to use reports that interrogators submit about their interpreters to the senior interrogator not only to update information about individual interpreters. “This evaluation may also be used to develop training programs for interpreters” (*USArmyIIH 2005*: 95). This is an extremely important point for the present social-systemic discussion of the MI interpreting. While the MI endohomorous agents wish the translation/interpreting ectohomorous agency to be invisible, they contribute to its institutionalisation: they theorise it, albeit in the prescriptional and therefore somewhat idealistic fashion; they also champion a better interaction between the endo- and ectohomorous agents; and finally, they advise collecting information for MI interpreting training.

10. Conclusion

Interrogation is normally described as an interaction between two parties: "An interrogation involves the interaction of two personalities—the source and the interrogator" (*USArmyIIH 2005*: 8). Interrogators are specially trained officers. Interrogatees are primarily enemy prisoners of war.

When it is necessary and possible, interpreters may constitute a third party. Obviously the interaction of three, instead of two, personalities is more complex as it takes yet another set of psychological characteristics as well as capabilities, but the focus of the present discussion is not on the psychological interactions of the parties in the interrogation process. The focus is on the socio-systemic structure of interrogation.

Whether there are the two or three parties involved, the MI interrogation is inevitably an interaction of the endo- and ectohomorous agencies. This means that there is a dialogue between the source and the interrogator across the socio-systemic boundary. Crossing the boundary requires a great deal of knowledge on the part of the interrogator. A part of the knowledge is military but another part is the nonmilitary linguo-socio-culture. While in the former, the interrogator claims undivided expertise, the latter is best provided by the ectohomorous agent – the interpreter/translator (often referred to as linguist in the MI literature).

Even when there is no third party (the interpreter) in an interrogation session, the socio-systemic structure of interrogation is the same as with an interpreter/translator/linguist present. There is the internal boundary, or endohomorous, agency – the interrogator or interrogatee, that crosses the socio-systemic (linguo-socio-cultural) boundary with the help of the ectohomorous agency – translation, whether exercised infrapersonally or in the personified mode. If the interrogator or the interrogatee speak the other side's language, they translate intrapersonally. If there is an interpreter involved, translation, in its interpreting allomode, is personified.

Thus, the MI interrogation is more accurately defined as an interaction between the interrogators and interrogatees made possible by translation. Translation may be exercised by the interpreter/translator who can be a professional translator/interpreter ("linguist") or a "trustworthy" local (Newbery 2015: 39). Sometimes interrogators themselves can act as interpreters for their colleagues. Ideally, the endo- and ectohomorous agencies should be in as close a contact as possible – they may occasionally be even combined in one person. However, nowadays, this option is viewed as exceptional: "The challenge is for interrogators to be proficient linguists and skilled members of a highly organised collection activity.

This ensures the acquisition of the maximum amount of pertinent information regardless of time available" (*USArmyIIH 2005*: 8). So, the interrogator's language proficiency allows them to act directly on the interrogatee and save time. But in real life, the two agencies are kept apart and for good reasons (Russano et al. 2014b: 842).

Overall, the dynamic of the relationship in the interrogation team (including the interrogatee) is complex. From the socio-systemic point of view, it is an interaction of the two boundary phenomena – MI and translation. There are various scenarios of their interaction but both boundary phenomena are always at work in the MI interrogation.

References

Baigorri-Jalón, Jesús. 2021/2019. *Languages in the Crossfire Interpreters in the Spanish Civil War (1936–1939)*. Translated by Holly Mikkelson. London and New York: Routledge.

Bowen, David & Bowen, Margareta. 1985. "The Nuremberg Trials. Communication through Translation," *Meta* 30 (1): 74–77.

Deacon, Richard. 1978. *The Silent War: A History of Western Naval Intelligence.* London: Grafton Books.

Fry, Helen. 2017. *The London Cage: The Secret History of Britain's World War II Interrogation Centre.* New Haven and London: Yale University Press.

Gaiba, Francesca. 1998. *The Origins of Simultaneous Interpretation. The Nuremberg Trial.* Ottawa: University of Ottawa Press.

HICO. 2006. *Human Intelligence Collector Operations.* Washington, DC: Headquarters. Department of the Army.

Inghilleri, Moira. 2012. *Interpreting Justice: Language, Ethics and Politics.* London & New York: Routledge.

Luhmann, Niklas. 1995. *Social System.* Translated by John Bednarz, Jr. with Dirk Baecker. Stanford, California: Stanford University Press.

Morris, Ruth. 1998. "Justice in Jerusalem – Interpreting in Israeli Legal Proceedings," *Meta* 43 (1): 110–8.

Newbery, Samantha. 2015. *Interrogation, Intelligence and Security: Controversial British Techniques.* Manchester: Manchester University Press.

Pöllabauer, Sonja. 2005. "Interpreting in Asylum Hearings," *Interpreting* 6:2: 143–80.

Russano, Melissa B., Fadia M. Narchet & Steven M. Kleinman. 2014a. "Structured Interviews of Experienced HUMINT Interrogators," *Applied Cognitive Psychology* 28: 847–59.

Russano, Melissa B., Fadia M. Narchet & Steven M. Kleinman. 2014b. "Analysts, Interpreters, and Intelligence Interrogations: Perceptions and Insights," *Applied Cognitive Psychology* 28: 829–46.

Schumann, Carsten. 2020. "Interrogation-Related Challenges of Using Interpreters. Analysis and Description of Problem Patterns for the Optimisation of Interrogation of Foreign-Language Suspects," *SIAK-Journal – Journal for Police Science and Practice (International Edition Vol. 10)*, 65–73.

Scott, Len. 2015. "Human Intelligence," in Robert Dover, Michael S. Goodman & Claudia Hillebrand (eds.), *Routledge Companion to Intelligence Studies*, 96 – 104. London and New York: Routledge.

Snellman, Pekka. 2016. "Constraints on and dimensions of military interpreter neutrality," *Linguistica Antverpiensia, New Series – Themes in Translation Studies*, 15: 260–81.

Tryuk, Małgorzata. 2016. "Ethical Issues of Community Interpreting and Mediation: The Case of the Lagerdolmetscher," in Lieven D'hulst, Carol O'Sullivan & Michael Schreiber (eds.), *Politics, Policy and Power in Translation History*. Berlin: Frank & Timmer, 53–68.

Tyulenev, Sergey. 2012. *Applying Luhmann to Translation Studies*. New York & London: Routledge.

Tyulenev, Sergey. 2018. *Translation in the Public Sphere*. Basingstoke: Palgrave Macmillan.

Tyulenev, Sergey. 2021. "Translation and (Counter-)Intelligence: The Interpenetration of Social-Systemic Boundary Phenomena," *Perspectives* 29 (3): 339–53.

Tyulenev, Sergey. 2022. "Translation and Diplomacy: The Ins and Outs of Social-Systemic Boundaries," in *Diplomacy & Statecraft* (in print).

USArmyIIH 2005: *U.S. Army Intelligence and Interrogation Handbook*. 2005. Guilford, Connecticut: The Lyons Press.

U 76 1941: "U 76" Interrogation of Survivors. 1941 (May). A file. London: Naval Intelligence Division. N.I.D. 08409/43. Available at https://www.uboatarchive.net/U-76A/U-76INT.htm (Last accessed 4 July, 2022).

Wolf, Michaela (ed.). 2016. *Interpreting in Nazi Concentration Camps*. London: Bloomsbury.

Elisabet Tiselius

Chapter 4 Ethics of interpreting professions: One size fits all?

Abstract: As pointed out by Horváth and Tryuk (2022: 291), the codes of ethics of different interpreting professions share certain characteristics such as commitment to accuracy, competence, confidentiality, impartiality, integrity, invisibility, neutrality, transparency and working conditions. Although, these can be seen as a least common denominator for ethics in interpreting, it can also be argued that depending on the profession or specialisation, the ethics differ, just as the expectations on the interpreter differ.

Skaaden (2019) has introduced the concept of discretionary power to interpreting and argues that just as public servants have a certain margin of manoeuver when making rule-based decision, so has the interpreter when making language-based decisions. One could argue in this context as well that different interpreter professions may have different margins of manoeuver when it comes to the discretionary power.

This article will discuss the ethics and loyalties of different interpreter professions (see also Tryuk 2015), how they may differ and in what way they are similar.

Keywords: ethics, interpreting profession, codes, guidelines, deontology

1. Introduction

Interpreting, at least in the western world, is normally divided into professions – sign language interpreters, public service interpreters, conference interpreters, military interpreters and so forth. The professions are sometimes divided even further following their setting, court interpreters, medical interpreters, educational interpreters, UN-interpreters are cases in point. I have argued elsewhere (Tiselius 2022, see also Downie 2020) that all interpreters, regardless of specialisation or profession most likely share the basic cognitive processes (bi- or multilingual decoding, encoding and producing a series of language units), as well as the basic skills and competences (e.g. language, active listening, mnemonic, reformulation, anticipation, problem solving, monitoring and attentional capacity management). Naturally, depending on experience, training and specialisation some skills may become more developed than others.

Similarly, as pointed out by Horváth and Tryuk (2022: 291), the codes of ethics of the interpreting professions share certain common characteristics such as commitment to accuracy, competence, confidentiality, impartiality, integrity, invisibility, neutrality, transparency and working conditions. Although these can be seen as a least common denominator for ethics in interpreting, it can be argued that depending on the profession or specialisation, the ethics differ, just as the expectations on the interpreter differ (see Tryuk 2015).

In this chapter, I will discuss the moral philosophy underlying codes of professional ethics of interpreting professions, how they may differ and in what ways they are similar. This chapter is not based on a study of codes of professional ethics, but rather a discussion based on how previous publications on professional ethics have presented such codes.

2. Moral philosophy, ethics and professional ethical guidelines

Before going further into the professional ethics of interpreting professions, I will shortyly outline different types of ethics, for a fuller description of ethics and moral philosophy see for instance Wolff (2020) or Rudvin (2020). Ethics, or moral philosophy, revolves around eternal questions of human morality such as good and evil or right and wrong. As the human understanding of these issues vary over time and between cultures, so does the theories on ethics. Moral philosophers aim to answer questions such as what can be defined as good (*meta-ethics*), or how an action or a deed can be qualified as good (*normative ethics*) or, what is the right way to act in a particular situation (*applied ethics*). Normative ethics can further be divided into two opposing theories: *consequentialism* or *teleology*, where the consequences of a person's action is in focus; *deontology*, which concentrates on the action itself, and whether that action is right or wrong according to certain rules and human duties. The third theory of normative ethics, *virtue ethics*, implies that a person will know what is the right thing to do based on theoretical or practical wisdom or the knowledge of what other virtuous individuals do.

In fact, as pointed out by Kermit (2020), the professional ethics of different professions, such as interpreters, and what we link to them may be very far from theories of ethics, understood as reflections and theorisation about moral issues. Kermit (2020: 3) uses the confidentiality principle as a case in point. The confidentiality principle is part of most code of ethics for interpreters, while confidentiality as such is not seen by the general public as a moral principle. However, some may argue that the praise of confidentiality could be found in proverbs like – speech is silver, but silence is golden. Furthermore, Tryuk (2015: 50), by using a grim example of interpreters in concentration camps, points to the fact that an interpreter may be well aware of the fact that their action is not one of doing good, or that the consequences of the action will not be good (i.e. does not follow the basic moral principles). Yet, for lack of other choices and immediate fatal consequences if they do not interpret, they may choose to interpret as well.

Rudvin (2020: 30) argues that the three main principles underlying interpreting ethics identified by Hale (2007), accuracy, impartiality and confidentiality can be traced back to the macro areas of normative ethics, i.e. consequentialism/teleology, deontology and virtue ethics. To these three areas Rudvin adds the concepts of justice and equality, concepts perhaps more connected to political or legal philosophy than to moral philosophy. Rudvin (2020: 33) further argues that the central virtue of interpreting is accuracy. Accuracy as a central virtue should not be understood as the absolute agreement between an utterance and its rendition, but rather the *telos* (the ultimate goal, the final cause) of an interpreter action. Accuracy as the *telos* is a theoretical understanding of an interpreter's purpose, not a measure for the correctness in an interpreting. If the interpreter's *telos* or central virtue is accuracy in their practice, one could argue that we are no longer dealing with interpreting. From a teleological or consequentialist perspective, one would argue that accuracy in interpreting is always better than any of the other alternatives, and therefore the interpreter has to strive towards that. From a deontological perspective one would argue that accuracy in itself is good. From this perspective, we cannot automatically know that the interpreter always strives for the best outcome in any given situation but, given that since accuracy is good in itself, it is imperative. Finally, from a virtue ethics perspective, one would argue that accuracy is a virtue and therefore the interpreter must be accurate.

These rather theoretical and abstract ideas develop into ethical guidelines of interpreting through norms, described by Schäffner (1999) as codified, collective, intersubjective standards of practice. The norms become the ethics of a profession when they function prescriptively and impact the professional's decisions. For interpreting, Rudvin (2020: 69) links accuracy in terms of relationship between utterance and rendition as related to the virtue ethics; and accuracy in terms of the duty and relationship to clients as related to the deontology; and finally, respecting what is ultimately beneficial for clients to consequentialism. Thus, according to Rudvin, accuracy could be construed following the three approaches to moral philosophy, depending on the context of accuracy. Rudvin links impartiality and confidentiality to the concepts of justice and equality. Justice and equality can be said to be parts of Kant's (1785) deontological moral philosophy. In the writings of Kant, a categorial imperative is a type of moral law that must be upheld, because some actions cannot be defended by being the better alternative. Kant argued this as people not always act in ways that are only good; they are also driven by fear, greed, or even desire to harm. Therefore, he argued, some absolute rules or categorical imperatives are needed.

As said above, ethical guidelines of interpreting can be distilled into certain basic principles, and looking at authors who have mapped the principles, such as Bancroft (2005), Hale (2007), Setton and Prunč (2015), Rudvin (2020) and Horváth and Tryuk (2022), accuracy, impartiality and confidentiality come up as the distillate. As pointed out above, the underlying ethics of these actions can be traced down to virtue ethics, deontology and consequentialism/teleology. Despite the fact that a distillate can be found, in a similar vein as the basic cognitive skills, or the basic skills and competences, there is not one universal code for all interpreters in all settings (Setton & Prunč 2015). This is most certainly due to the fact pointed out by Horváth and Tryuk(2022: 293) "that no code of ethics can anticipate all the professional situations interpreters may encounter". One can imagine that settings, modes or modalities (Tiselius 2022) would impact the type of ethical guideline in use, and that certain aspects of normative ethics could be more highlighted than others depending on the setting, mode or modality. In the next sections, I will look further into settings (conference, court, medical and military) and modalities (spoken or signed) with the aim to chisel out what types of norms the ethical guidelines reflect, and possibly the underlying moral philosophy guiding them.

3. Moral philosophy in conference interpreting code of ethics

The professional code of ethics of AIIC[1], the international association of conference interpreters, can be said to strive to be universal document of professional ethics for conference interpreters. As an international organisation, AIIC strives for the code to cover their members, conference interpreters throughout the globe. Furthermore, it is a living document, updated after deliberations and voting by its members. An example of this is that older versions (e.g. from 1994) do not explicitly mention "independence, impartiality and responsibility" (§ 2 art. 8, AIIC 2022), nor does the 1994 version mention the "fidelity of the interpretation" (§ 2 art. 10, AIIC 2022), or "errors in interpretation" (§ 2 art. 11, AIIC 2022). The version of 1994 focuses on "integrity, professionalism and professional secrecy". Thus, one could argue that the version from 1994 does not handle the issue of accuracy as described above (Rudvin 2020), and that the underlying ethical

1 https://aiic.org/document/10277/CODE_2022_E&F_final.pdf (accessed March 20, 2023)

principles are more related to deontology (the right or the wrong of an action in relation to rules and duties) and the concepts of justice and equality, rather than consequentialism/teleology or virtue ethics. In the version of 2022, the concept of accuracy is introduced into the code, and thereby also the link to consequentialism (based on the idea that the accuracy of the interpreting will always be the better alternative), and to virtue ethics (accuracy if a virtue and good interpreters are accurate). This is of course not to argue that accuracy as the telos, or ultimate goal, of the interpreter was not part of the AIIC members' habitus (c.f. Bourdieu 1977) prior to 2022, only that it was not spelled out in the professional code of ethics.

However, it may be argued that the telos of interpreters is not accuracy, as the consequences for accuracy may not be the best possible alternative in a given context. Alternatively, it could be said that the understanding of accuracy differs depending on setting. As pointed out by Slaughter Olsen et al. (2022), the border between conference interpreting and diplomatic interpreting is sometimes very blurred. They define diplomatic interpreting as "a special type of conference interpreting provided to sovereign governments and intergovernmental organizations […]" (2022: 67). Thiéry (2015: 107) points to the fact that the term is often taken to refer to settings involving heads of states and dignitaries. By this definition, both UN and EU interpreters can be seen as diplomatic interpreters, since they are (at least for some meetings) providing conference interpreting for heads of states and dignitaries in intergovernmental organizations. AIIC is organising interpreters at these institutions and negotiate on behalf of the freelance interpreters. Interpreters working for these institutions abide by AIIC's code of professional ethics, and also in-house rules (Horváth and Tryuk 2022: 295). However, one could argue that part of the AIIC code may not be as obviously applicable to the interpreters at these institutions, nor to certain types of diplomatic interpreting. I will not argue that the institutional interpreters or diplomatic interpreters do not strive to be independent, impartial and responsible as stated in article 8 of the professional ethics. Yet, there may be a certain clash between the underlying ethics of consequentialism/teleology and deontology here. In a diplomatic context, the loyalty of the interpreter may clearly lie with one of the parties. This is touched upon by Slaughter Olsen et al. (2022: 70) who describe the use of diplomatic interpreters as a soft power tool to "help negotiate alliances, deescalate tensions, and defend national interest". The interpreting task thus seems to have a very different approach to whether the outcome of providing accurate interpreting is the best possible one, and therefore whether the action of providing accurate interpreting is right or wrong. The key issue here is instead the loyalty to the party, and what is the best possible outcome for that party (Slaughter Olsen et al. 2022: 73). The diplomatic interpreter, in many cases, constitutes a guaranteed loyalty to one party, rather than what Skaaden (2013) labelled bi-partial interpreter (i.e. loyal to both parties in the encounter). Slaughter Olsen et al. (2022: 73) also points to the fact that both the US and China describe their interpreters as "represent[ing] the US government interests" (the US) and "resolutely safeguard[ing] China's national interests" (China). Regarding the fact that many AIIC members work as institutional or diplomatic interpreters, it is perhaps not surprising that earlier versions of the code of professional ethics did not mention impartiality, as also pointed out by Liu (2018). Without the mention of impartiality, the code of professional ethics does indeed encompass this extreme of conference interpreting in all its expressions and contexts.

AIIC's code of professional ethics is, as said in the introductory paragraph to this section, aiming to encompass all the situations of their members. Yet, as also argued in this section and by many other authors, depending on setting and context, principles of deontology and consequentialism/teleology may clash, showcasing the challenge to honour the code. In this respect, the older version of the code could be argued to leave issues possibly related to teleological or deontological interpretations outside the code, concentrating solely on the justice and equality side, i.e. confidentiality. The following section will deal with professional ethics in the public sector, e.g. in court or medical settings.

4. Moral philosophy in public services interpreting codes of ethics

The public services are closely intertwined with local structures, traditions and cultures. As a consequence, for interpreters working in the public sector, there is no universal professional codes of ethics, but many regional ones. For countries with a more organised and thus codified interpreting profession, some even have specific codes of professional ethics for the courts and for the medical sector (Phelan 2020). This section will not go through different versions of codes of ethics, but rather try to approach some general tendencies reported by other authors.

Ozolins (2015: 322–323) points out that in codes for the courts there is a stronger stress on how interpreters shall only translate, and that an interpreter's rendition shall deviate as little as possible from the original utterance. He contrasts this with medical interpreters who in many codes are allowed to intervene in an advocating way by providing additional information or pointing out lack of understanding (Ozolins 2015: 323). The differences in these codes relate to the interpreter's role in the encounters as discussed by Setton and Prunč (2015). However, one may argue that the moral philosophy behind the codes (rules), and the practitioner's role (duties) in relation to the code, is based on a deontological approach, and that specific codes trigger different roles. I argue that this focus on the interpreter's role, and the discussions around it, links back to virtue ethics.

I argue for the differences between codes for court interpreters and codes for medical interpreters to be traced to virtue ethics, since the codes can be said to have been created with regards to what a *good* person, a *good* interpreter, would do. The codes use many words to describe what the interpreter shall or shall not do, possibly stemming from the perception of a *good* interpreter, and then attempt to describe the characteristics of *good* interpreting in these contexts.

The codes in the public services include accuracy, confidentiality and impartiality. As described in the introductory section, accuracy can be seen as a manifestation of certain approaches to moral philosophy depending on how we choose to frame it. On the other hand, confidentiality and impartiality relate to equality and justice, and therefore to a deontological approach.

5. Moral philosophy in ethical codes for interpreters in conflict zones

Interpreters in conflict zones can be humanitarian interpreters or military interpreters. I argue that there is a major difference between these two, as well as a major difference between interpreters in the military setting and perhaps all other interpreter settings. If aware of them, humanitarian interpreters follow codes of ethics with traditional ethical commitments for interpreters, e.g. the safety guide lines by Red-T (2012) or the UNHCR guidelines (2017). I will not handle them in detail here as I argue that these codes of ethics share the same underlying ethical theories as those of public service interpreting discussed above.

5.1. Moral philosophy in military interpreter's code of professional ethics

Military interpreting is a very particular setting, where loyalty and trust are perhaps the most important underlying philosophical concepts. Military interpreters are partial with one side in an encounter, perhaps more clearly than other interpreting professions (e.g. Snellman 2016; Baker 2010). One type of military interpreters (type 1), described by Dahnberg (2022) and

Snellman (2016), are trained and employed by a nation's armed forces, sharing the nationality with that armed forces and go on missions to conflict zones in or outside their own nation. An example of this can be a Swedish military interpreter learning Dari in Sweden as part of military training, employed as a Swedish specialist officer and following a Swedish army unit on a mission to Afghanistan. The other type of military interpreters (type 2) are locally recruited interpreters, who share the language and nationality or ethnical background with one of the nations or ethnical groups of the conflict zone, and who have a knowledge of a foreign language, often English. Many military interpreters, both type 1 and type 2, wear the uniform of the army they serve, and live and travel with their units, thus, they are seen as representatives of that army. And as pointed out by Tryuk (2015), shown by the organization the Red-T[2], and also covered by many news outlets, this system puts especially type 2 interpreters at a significant risk, since they are seen as loyal to the armed forces they work for, rather than being impartial, or loyal to their country or ethnic. Admittedly, type 1 interpreters may also be suspected of not being loyal or being too involved in "the other party" with whom they do not share nationality or ethnicity, but since they learn the language and culture, or spend time in their country, naturally gain great understanding of that other. Whichever type of interpreter, interpreting in a conflict zone is a high-stake task, and in the words of Tryuk (2015: 150) "interpreters are among the first to die".

The Red-T has developed safety guidelines for interpreters in conflict zone which state, on the issue of impartiality, that "[r]egardless of who engages you, serve all parties equally without expressing your opinions or sympathies. You cannot be an advocate for any cause and must declare any conflict of interest" (Red-T 2012). Admittedly, this is a guideline for *civilian* interpreters in conflict zone, but how does one discern a civilian and a military interpreter in a conflict zone when both are employed by an armed force and deployed with them? The guidelines also state that the interpreters should be given "protective clothing and equipment, but not arms", and that as "a civilian, you are not required to wear a uniform unless you consent to do so". However, as pointed out by Dahnberg (2022), "[t]he notion of identity concerns not only how interpreters think of themselves. It can sometimes be of even greater importance how an interpreter is perceived by the parties in an armed conflict: if the interpreter is a friend or a foe, one of 'us' or one of 'them'." The fate of many type 2 military interpreters

2 https://red-t.org/ (accessed March 20, 2023)

when armed forces have left the territory, described by for instance Red-T, shows that these interpreters are perceived neither as impartial nor as "one of us".

Dahnberg (2022) describes type 1 military interpreters in Sweden, a context similar to other countries and points out that the interpreters share the code of ethics with all Armed Forces personnel, which includes anti-discrimination, respect for equal rights and loyalty. However, such codes of ethics do not include topics typical for interpreters' codes of ethics, such as confidentiality and impartiality. In fact, as underlined by Dahnberg (2022), and also Snellman (2016) and Baker (2010), the military code of conduct does not require military interpreters to see themselves as neutral[3].

The format of this chapter does not allow for a longer discussion of the moral philosophy of war, which is the underlying moral philosophy of the ethics of armed forces. Suffice to say that these theories comprise issues such as the right to go to war, and the code of conduct in war. The latter aspect contains issues such as distinction between combatants and non-combatants, proportionality of an action, the necessity of an action as well as the fair treatment of prisoners of war. Furthermore, as has been shown above the professional ethics of these interpreters are inconsistent. Type 1 interpreters follow the code of ethics of their armed forces while type 2, if they are aware of it, will follow the code of ethics of Red-T (2012) or perhaps the one of the UNHCR (2017) – although the latter concentrates on asylum hearings rather than military interpreting.

I will therefore shortly discuss the general ethical theories underlying the expected conduct of the military interpreters. Regardless of being type 1 or type 2 interpreter, I argue that they are expected, by all parties in a conflict, to be loyal to the army they serve. Furthermore, they are expected to be trustworthy in their task. Loyalty and trust will link us back to virtue ethics. However, both of these are tricky, loyalty is considered a virtue (Kleinig 2022) but is complicated as it comprises a potentially costly commitment. For military interpreters, a possible cost is their lives, thus indeed constituting a costly commitment. Therefore, one could imagine that military interpreters not only base their action on the virtue of loyalty, but also with an aspect of the *good* on an individual level of possible outcomes of certain actions (c.f., the discussion of Kant above and individuals acting out of fear, personal winning etc.). The same thing goes for trust, perhaps

---

3 It is beyond the limits of this chapter to discuss the difference between neutrality and impartiality, but *neutral* is the term used by these authors, and for the purpose of the understanding of whether military interpreters align with one side or not, I believe neutral is sufficient here.

an even more deceitful virtue (McLeod 2021). Trust allows us to depend on other people, but involves the risk of others deceiving that trust and possibly putting us in difficulty or danger. Trust, in terms of truthful interpreting, is therefore an absolute cornerstone for the military interpreter, in addition to a trust to not disseminate sensitive information. Although accuracy and confidentiality are not necessarily spelled out in the military codes of ethics, their essence may be there anyway. For the type 2 military interpreter trust goes the other way too, of course.

6. Moral philosophy in sign language interpreters' codes of ethics

Sign language interpreters have perhaps had (at least in the Western industrialised world) a very distinct movement from helpers to professionals, more so than any of the other interpreting professions. Wilcox and Shaffer (2005) argue, for instance, that the reason for the conduit model (i.e. the interpreter being a vessel void of agency and previous experiences) becoming popular in interpreting practice was part of this movement away from the helper discourse. However, Tate and Turner already pointed out in 2000, that in ethically complex contexts either the code itself or interpreters' readings of it often were at odds with actual practice. Leneham and Napier (2003) concluded that codes are needed, but that they needed to adapt to modern understandings of the interpreters' role. These discussions have led to new models of the sign language interpreter's role being put forward such as the role-space (Llewellyn-Jones & Lee 2014) and the demand-control schema (Dean & Pollard 2001). The foundations of these models being that the role of or the demands on the interpreter differ, and as a consequence, the interpreter's approach to the encounter must differ.

The issue does not lie in whether codes of ethics are appropriate or not, but one can observe that more recent codes of ethics in sign language interpreting, such as the Swedish code of professional ethics (2004), the American NAD-RID code of professional conduct (2005), or the British NRCPD guidelines for professional practice (2009), and the Australian ASLIA code of ethics (2009), all contain formulation about respect and non-discrimination. It should be stressed that these also contain the distillate discussed above and identified by Hale (2007); accuracy, impartiality and confidentiality.

Authors like Dean and Pollard (2011) have argued, in support of their demand-control schema, that traditional codes of ethics have a deontological approach, and that this make them restrictive in a possibly harmful way. The demand-control schema instead allows for a teleological or consequentialist approach, where the possibly good outcome of the action would dictate whether the action is right or wrong. Contrary to this, one could of course argue, along the lines of Kant, that we may not know whether the individual interpreter acts only with the idea of the ultimately best outcome. In fact, the interpreter may not be aware of all the factors and consequences following their action, or they may simply act for their own good (such as wanting to get home earlier today, or to survive).

As discussed above, respect and non-discrimination, just as confidentiality and impartiality are part of a deontological approach to moral philosophy, whereas accuracy can be seen as both teleological, deontological and as a virtue. All these approaches of moral philosophy can thus be seen to underpin professional codes of ethics for sign language interpreters, and also for the codes of the other interpreting professions discussed in this text.

7. The rule-following paradox and professional codes of ethics in interpreting

Wittgenstein stated in his Philosophical Investigations (§201a. 1953) that "no course of action can be determined by a rule, because any course of action can be made out to accord with the rule". He meant that one understands a rule and applies it, but this does not mean that the rule is actually being followed. According to Wittgenstein we follow rules based on education, practice and experience. Now, Wittgenstein talked about rules governing language or mathematics, and admittedly this stance has been contested. I chose to use the example of Wittgenstein, as a starting point for arguing that the fact that someone is deviating from a rule must not be a reason for concluding that the rule is obsolete or wrong.

Rule-following is linked to the concept of moral blindness, which, although discussed already in antiquity, gained interest through Arendt's (1963) observation and recount of Eichmann during his trial in Jerusalem. Arendt pointed to the fact that Eichmann underlined his commitment to following Kant's categorical imperative, following absolute rules for the greater good. During this period two experiments about rule-following got a lot of attention: the Stanford prison experiment (Haney et al. 1973), and Milgram's (1963) rule-obedience experiment. Both of these concluded that participants were inclined to morally questionable things when they believed they were following the rules as if being (temporarily) morally blind.

Seen from this perspective, normative rules, or professional codes of ethics may be a necessary evil. As is perhaps the discussion about them. The way forward is then reflective practitioners aware of the accountability of the interpreter (Baker & Maier 2011). Practitioners now have understood that the interpreter has agency in the interpreted encounter (Downie 2017), as well as responsibilities for that encounter. In this context, Skaaden (2019) argues that the interpreter has discretionary power in their language-based decisions in interpreting, similar to public servants who have a certain margin of manoeuver when making rule-based decision. No course of action can perhaps be determined by a rule, in the words of Wittgenstein, but with discretionary power the rule can be followed through the course of action. As pointed out by Horváth and Tryuk (2022: 293) "codes are useful tools for defining professional behaviour or the *modus operandi* or interpreters", but the authors go onto underline the competence, experience and wisdom of the interpreter in order to handle ethical dilemmas on the ground based on the codes.

8. Conclusion

This chapter set out to explore the moral philosophy underlying codes of professional ethics for interpreting professions, how they may differ and in what ways they are similar. As has been shown, the underlying moral philosophy of the professional codes are similar on many levels. Depending on how one chooses to describe or construe the concepts put forward in the codes, they can be argued to represent different and possibly contradicting approaches of moral philosophy. This means that depending on the understanding of the concepts in the professional codes of ethics competing and opposing approaches of moral philosophy will form the base of the understanding of the codes. Hence, perhaps, the reason for the sometimes very animated debates around the professional codes of ethics.

Despite their similarities, I would argue that one size of professional ethics does not fit all. As pointed out by Tryuk (2015: 163), as well as others, an interpreter's work is carried out "in concrete conditions and with concrete aims". It is a situated activity, of which neither the interpreter not the other participants may have the full understanding. And just as one size does not fit all in terms of the interpreting professions, one size may not fit all in terms of every specific encounter either. As said previously by, Tate and Turner (2000), a code of professional ethics will not have an answer to every situation.

Certain contexts, as the ones described by Tryuk (2015) for instance, may perhaps never, nor should ever, be covered by codes of professional ethics. And as Tryuk argues (2015: 173) one must understand that the ideal situation for which these codes were written will perhaps never exist. Yet, that should not lead to the conclusion that we are in no need of professional ethics, but rather that we, like Kant argued, cannot expect everyone to act for the highest good in any situation, and therefore we need professional codes of ethics, and, not the least, we need to discuss and dispute them.

References

AIIC. 2022. Code of Professional Ethics. https://aiic.org/document/10277/CODE_2022_E&F_final.pdf

Arendt, Hannah. 1963/1968/2006. *Eichmann in Jerusalem: A Report on the Banality of Evil.* London: Penguin.

Baker, Mona. 2010. Interpreters and translators in the war zone: Narrated and narrators. *The Translator, 16*(2), 197–222.

Baker, Mona & Carol Maier. 2011. Ethics in interpreter & translator training. *The Interpreter and Translator Trainer, 5*(1), 1–14. https://doi.org/10.1080/13556509.2011.10798809

Bancroft, Marjory. 2005. *The Interpreters World Tour: An Environmental Scan of Standards of Practice for Interpreters.* The California Endowment. https://www.ncihc.org/assets/documents/publications/NCIHC%20Environmental%20Scan.pdf

Bourdieu, Pierre. 1977. *Outline of a Theory of Practice.* Cambridge: Cambridge University Press.

Dahnberg, Magnus. 2022. Military interpreter training for context specific situations. In Ruiz Rosendo, Lucía & Marija Todorova (eds.), *Interpreter Training in Conflict and Post-conflict Situations.* London: Routledge, 35–36.

Dean, Robyn K. & Robert Q Pollard Jr. 2011. Context-based Ethical Reasoning in Interpreting, *The Interpreter and Translator Trainer, 5*(1), 155–182. https://doi.org/10.1080/13556509.2011.10798816

Dean, Robyn K. & Robert Q Pollard Jr. 2001. Demand-control schema. *Journal of Deaf Studies and Deaf Education, 6*(1), 1–14.

Downie, Jonathan. 2017. Finding and critiquing the invisible interpreter – A response to Uldis Ozolins. *Interpreting, 19*(2), 260–270. https://doi.org/10.1075/intp.19.2.05dow

Downie, Jonathan. 2020. "Interpreting is interpreting: Why we need to leave behind interpreting settings to discover Comparative Interpreting Studies." *Translation and Interpreting Studies, 16*(3), 325–346. https://doi.org/10.1075/tis.20006.dow

Hale, Sandra. 2007. *Community Interpreting.* New York: Springer.

Haney, Craig, Curtis Banks & Philip Zimbardo. 1973. Interpersonal Dynamics in a simulated prison. *International Journal of Criminology and Penology, 1*(1): 69–77. https://doi.org/10.21236/AD0751041

Horváth, Ildiko & Małgorzata Tryuk. 2022. Ethics and Codes of Ethics in Conference Interpreting. In Michaela Albl-Mikasa & Elisabet Tiselius (eds.). *Routledge Handbook of Conference Interpreting*. London: Routledge, 290–304. https://doi.org/10.4324/9780429297878-27

Kant, Immanuel. 1785. *Fundamental Principles of the Metaphysic of Morals*. Project Gutenberg.

Kermit, Patrick Stefan. 2020. Introduction. In Mary Phelan, Mette Rudvin, Hanne Skaaden, & Patrick Stefan Kermit (eds.), *Ethics in Public Service Interpreting*. London: Routledge, 1–23

Kleinig, John. 2022. Loyalty. In Edward N. Zalta (ed.), *The Stanford Encyclopedia of Philosophy*. https://plato.stanford.edu/archives/sum2022/entries/loyalty/

Leneham, Marcel & Napier, Jemina. 2003. Sign language interpreters' codes of ethics: Should we maintain the status quo? *Deaf Worlds: International Journal of Deaf Studies, 19*(2), 78–98.

Liu, Henry. 2018. Help or hinder? The impact of technology on the role of interpreters. *FITISPos International Journal, 5*(1), 13–32. https://doi.org/10.37536/FITISPos-IJ.2018.5.1.162

Llewellyn-Jones, Peter & Lee, Robert G. 2014. *Redefining the Role of the Community Interpreter: The Concept of Role-space*. Carlton-le-Moorland: SLI Press.

McLeod, Carolyn. 2021. Trust. In Edward N. Zalta (ed.), *The Stanford Encyclopedia of Philosophy*. https://plato.stanford.edu/archives/fall2021/entries/trust/.

Milgram, Stanley. 1963. Behavioral study of obedience. *Journal of Abnormal and Social Psychology, 67*(4): 371–378. https://doi.org/10.1037/h0040525

Ozolins, Uldis. 2015. Ethics and the role of the interpreter. In Holly Mikkelson & Renée Jourdenais (eds.), *The Routledge Handbook of Interpreting*. London: Routledge, 319–336.

Phelan, Mary. 2020. Codes of ethics. In Mary Phelan, Mette Rudvin, Hanne Skaaden, & Patrick Stefan Kermit (eds.), *Ethics in Public Service Interpreting*. London: Routledge, 85–146.

Red-T. (2012). *Conflict Zone Field Guide for Civilian Translators/Interpreters and Users of Their Services*. https://library.fit-ift.org/public/Resources/Documents/CZG_201203_EN.pdf

Rudvin, Mette. 2020. Situating interpreting ethics in moral philosophy. In Mary Phelan, Mette Rudvin, Hanne Skaaden, & Patrick Stefan Kermit (eds.), *Ethics in Public Service Interpreting*. London: Routledge, 24–84.

Schaffner, Christina. 1999. *Translation and norms*. London: Multilingual matters.

Setton, Robin & Prunč, Erich. 2015. Ethics. In Franz Pöchhacker (ed.), *Routledge Encyclopedia of Interpreting Studies*. London and New York: Routledge, 144–148.

Skaaden, Hanne. 2019. Invisible or invincible? Professional integrity, ethics, and voice in public service interpreting, *Perspectives, 27*(5), 704–717. https://doi.org/10.1080/0907676X.2018.1536725

Skaaden, Hanne. 2013. *Den topartiske tolken* [The bipartial interpreter]. Oslo: Universitetsforlaget.

Slaughter Olsen, Barry, Henry Liu, & Sergio Viaggio. 2022. Diplomatic conference interpreting. In Michaela Albl-Mikasa & Elisabet Tiselius (eds.), *Routledge Handbook of Conference Interpreting*. London: Routledge, 67–79. https://doi.org/10.4324/9780429297878-8

Snellman, Pekka. 2016. Constraints on and dimensions of military interpreter neutrality. *Linguistica Antverpiensia, New Series: Themes in Translation Studies, 15,* 260–281.

Tate, Granville & Graham Turner. 2000. The code and the culture: Sign language interpreting–in search of a new breed's ethics. In Frank J. Harrington & Graham Turner. *Interpreting Interpreting – Studies & Reflections on Sign Language Interpreting.* Coleford: Douglas McLean, 53–66.

Thiéry, Christophe. 2015. Diplomatic interpreting. In Franz Pöchhacker (ed.), *Routledge Encyclopedia of Interpreting Studies*. London: Routledge, 107–108.

Tiselius, Elisabet. 2022. Conference and community interpreting – Commonalities and differences. In Michaela Albl-Mikasa & Elisabet Tiselius (eds.), *Routledge Handbook of Conference Interpreting*. London: Routledge, 49–64. https://doi.org/10.4324/9780429297878-6

Tryuk, Małgorzata. 2015. *On Ethics and Interpreters*. Frankfurt: Peter Lang.

UNHCR. 2017. *Handbook for Interpreters in Asylum Procedures*. Vienna: UNHCR Austria. https://www.unhcr.org/dach/wp-content/uploads/sites/27/2017/09/AUT_Handbook-Asylum-Interpreting_en.pdf

Wilcox, Sherman & Shaffer, Barbara. 2005. Towards a cognitive model of interpreting. In Terry Janzen (ed.), *Topics in Signed Language Interpreting: Theory and Practice.* Amsterdam and Philadelphia: John Benjamins Publishing Company, 27–50.

Wittgenstein, Ludvig. 1953. *Philosophical Investigations*, ed. G. E. M. Anscombe & R. Rhees, trans. G. E. M. Anscombe. Oxford: Blackwell.

Wolff, Jonathan. 2020. *An Introduction to Moral Philosophy*. New York: W. W. Norton & Company.

Agnieszka Biernacka

Chapter 5 Still *the Cinderella of interpretation*[1]? Court interpreting in Poland revisited

Abstract: A volume in honour of Professor Małgorzata Tryuk is undoubtedly an excellent opportunity to refer to the findings of her milestone publication devoted to community interpreting (2006). Without leaving the methodological frames that enabled her to show similarities and differences between then still almost undiscovered community interpreting and well-rooted conference interpreting, this chapter aims at revisiting court interpreting as juxtaposed to community interpreting. The veiled purpose is also to elaborate on the question in the title whether court interpreting as oral communication contextualised within legal interpreting is an underestimated setting? This chapter focuses on revisiting such aspects of court interpreting as: status of interpreters, scope of their competences vs. skills, professional organisations, interpreter training, bidirectional nature of interpreted encounters, participant status, interpreting modes, interpreted communicative acts as trilogues, personal context, note-taking, ethics, as well as recent challenges resulting from COVID-19-related changes in the interpreter's work environment. What is excluded from this review is the historical aspect that has already been profoundly elsewhere analysed.

Keywords: court interpreting, community interpreting, competences, skills, confidentiality, interpreter, institutional setting

1. Introduction

Community interpreting is carried out in "a specific institutional context, i.e. in a legal, judicial, medical, public, humanitarian milieu, e.g. in an office, lawyer's office, court, doctor's office, also during a psychotherapy session or negotiation"[2] (Tryuk 2006: 32–33), thus, it is pictured as a kaleidoscopic grid of settings. Nonetheless, from among all these varieties, court interpreting is

1 The title refers to a widely known metaphorical description of court interpreting coined by Repa (1991: 595): "**The Cinderella of interpretation: an unglamorous girl who is only of late developing a degree of appeal**".

2 „w środowisku prawno-sądowym, medycznym, publicznym, humanitarnym, np. w urzędzie, kancelarii adwokackiej, sądzie, gabinecie lekarskim, również podczas sesji psychoterapeutycznej lub negocjacji" (unless otherwise stated, all translations in this chapter are mine).

considered a specific type of community interpreting (Roberts 1997: 9; Wadensjö 1998: 51; Pym 1999: 265; Dąmbska-Prokop 2000; Garber 2000: 14; Apfelbaum 2004: 32; Tryuk 2006: 25; Biernacka 2010, 2014; Kościałkowska-Okońska 2010). As Bancroft (2015: 221) puts it, "there is no clear consensus on whether the court interpreter is a community interpreter or not". As far as International Standards are concerned, there are two different documents dedicated to either community or court interpreting, i.e. *ISO 13611:2014 Interpreting — Guidelines for community interpreting* and *ISO 20228:2019 Interpreting services — Legal interpreting — Requirements*. In the former it is indicated that a possible distinction between community and legal (i.e. police, court, etc.) interpreting is up to national standards and legislation.

A diversity of settings is reflected in a multiplicity of denominations of community interpreting. The catalogue includes *community-based interpreting* (Roberts 2002: 161), *public service interpreting, liaison interpreting, bilateral interpreting, bidirectional interpreting; dialogue interpreting, triangle interpreting, cultural interpreting, consecutive interpreting, contact interpreting, face-to-face interpreting, triad interpreting, discourse interpreting, social interpreting, intra-social interpreting* (Bancroft 2015: 218), *ad hoc interpreting* and *escort interpreting* (Roberts 2002), as well as *three-cornered interpreting* (Hsieh 2015: 1). The terms *community interpreting* and *public service interpreting* are commonly used, nonetheless, as Bancroft explains, "the term 'community interpreter' has come into use to describe less qualified interpreters who perform the same work as public service interpreters" (2015: 218). Moreover, *cultural* (*intercultural*) *mediation* and *language mediation* are added to that list (Bancroft 2015: 218), however, some researchers believe that mediation and interpreting are two different activities (Vargas-Urpi and Arumí Ribas 2014: 1–2).

Court interpreting is a reserved name for interpretation services rendered in the courtroom (Edwards 1995; Hale 2004; Gamal 2009: 63; Biernacka 2019) thus it is also referred to as *courtroom interpreting* (Morris 2015). Tryuk, clearly elaborating on a similar nature of community and court interpreting, applies an expression "an interpreter in a court setting" (2006: 101; transl. by the author)[3]. Yet another term, *tribunal interpreting*, although associated with the court, is limited to interpreting done for the needs of ad hoc international courts to judge war criminals (Takeda 2015: 424). A widely used term *legal interpreting* is a broad concept covering not only court interpreting but also interpretation services in other law-related settings, such as "police stations, courts, prisons, etc."[4], while

3 "tłumacz w środowisku sądowym".

4 ISO 13611:2014 *Interpreting – Guidelines for community interpreting.*

Hertog (2016) points out that legal interpreting is carried out through the entire legal procedure.

2. Status of interpreters

As Biernacka (2019: 45–46) writes about court interpreters in Poland, "(c) ourt interpreting has obtained the status of a separate variety of community interpreting which is due to legal developments relating to the need to make interpreting services available in all public settings, and to the necessity for professionalization of interpreting". As elsewhere indicated, not only the EU legislation in force, but also the Polish national legislation provides for the criteria to be fulfilled by court interpreters, who are required to possess specific competences and obliged to satisfy the principles of professional ethics (Biernacka 2019: 36–38, 41–44). Grbič (2015: 322) refers to a list proposed by Wilensky (1964) that includes five stages of professionalisation: "(1) making the occupation full-time; (2) establishing formal training; (3) developing a professional association; (4) pushing for legalized protection; and (5) adopting a code of ethics". In the light of the aforesaid catalogue, what Polish court interpreters lack on their way to professionalisation is the provision of services on commission, and not as a full-time job. Other stages of professionalisation give court interpreting in Poland the status of a prestigious profession.

As far as professional organisations are concerned, court interpreters in Poland have their dedicated associations. Nonetheless, there are two professional associations of sworn translators. These organisations attract also those professionals who render their services as either community or court interpreters, or both. One of them is the Polish Society of Sworn and Specialised Translators established in 1990 to consolidate and represent the profession[5], and the other is, since 2017, the Trade Union of Sworn Translators in Poland[6], advocating for working conditions of the profession. Both organisations are very active in the field of offering training for candidates for the profession and as part of life-long learning for both their members and non-members, filling in a gap existing in court and community interpreter training.

In Poland, training courses for court interpreters are available at the level of postgraduate studies. The Interdisciplinary Postgraduate Studies in Translation

5 Polskie Towarzystwo Tłumaczy Przysięgłych i Specjalistycznych TEPIS. http://tepis.org.pl (March 4, 2023).

6 Związek Zawodowy Tłumaczy Przysięgłych w Polsce. http://www.zztp.pl/ (March 4, 2023).

and Interpreting at the Institute of Applied Linguistics, University of Warsaw is the first program of this type established in 1998.[7] Apart from formal training, Polish court interpreters indicate other sources of their knowledge and informal ways of gaining skills: specialised literature, dictionaries, experience gained 'on the spot', parallel texts, Internet, training courses, and help provided by lawyers; interpreters also point out that they expect an open attitude on the part of their more experienced colleagues who could share their experience, but at the same time declare that "interpreters are a hermetic clan, nobody has ever given me advice, I don't know why [...]" (Biernacka 2014: 41)[8]. Also Skorek claims the need for training prospective court interpreters by their experienced colleagues, indicating however, that this issue has been broadly discussed and afterwards rejected "by the experts" (2014: 263).

Court interpreters are obliged to observe principles of ethics which is a consequence of the nature of the legal process, and which distinguishes court interpreting from other varieties of interpreting (Gamal 2009: 63). Such a viewpoint is in complete agreement with the comprehensive approach to professionalism; even though there are countries in which the code of ethics does not exist, "the welfare of the client demands ethical practices" (Gentile et al. 1996: 57). Moreover, it proves, that in those countries in which there is no requirement of training before becoming a professional interpreter, ethics provides guidelines for practicing court interpreting (Hale 2007: 103). Codes of ethics are a source of knowledge of the principles that should govern court interpreters' approach to their activities, i.e. accuracy, impartiality, and confidentiality. As investigated by Hale (2007) who compared 16 codes of ethics binding in 9 countries, these principles most frequently appear in the analysed codes[9]. As elsewhere stated, "(t)wo of the aforementioned principles—accuracy and impartiality—are of particular importance as they directly refer to the interpretation in the courtroom, and what is more, the (non-)compliance with them can directly and (adversely) affect the proceedings and judgments" (Biernacka 2019: 30). Moreover, the codes help identify a profession in order to

---

7 For a detailed presentation of the program see Jopek-Bosiacka 2014.

8 "tłumacze to taki zamknięty w sobie klan, nikt nigdy nie udzielił mi żadnej porady, nie wiem tylko, dlaczego".

9 Hale (2007: 108) puts these three principles under the heading of the "interpreters' responsibility to the authors of the utterances", and distinguishes two other groups of principles: those which include "interpreters' responsibility to the profession" (solidarity), and those covering "interpreters' responsibility to self as a professional" (professional development, working conditions and role definition).

enable to share knowledge and experience (Corsellis and Fernández 2001: 77), from which it can be inferred that codes of ethics not only assume a function of guidelines for court interpreters, but play a vital role in consolidating the profession as well.

According to the Polish *Sworn Translator and Interpreter's Professional Code*[10] accuracy means not only preserving exactly the form of original statements, i.e. rendering the whole content, without omitting, adding or modifying anything, but also commenting on what has been said if such a procedure contributes to a better understanding of the original statement. Impartiality imposes on an interpreter a prohibition to express personal opinions or views of the clients or other persons involved. These ethical recommendations are a direct consequence of the wording of an oath taken by the sworn translator and interpreter pursuant to the Act on the Profession of Sworn Translator of November 25, 2004[11].

3. Scope of competences

An important aspect of court interpreting is the required scope of competences. Zimman (1994), who refers to community interpreting, proposes the following catalog of competences: language, culture, common knowledge, knowledge of social systems, knowledge of a topic of the encounter, as well as an ability to make interpreting decisions that are the fundamental skills. Kaczmarek (2008) proposes a descriptive model of community interpreter competence recognising its three-fold nature structured by: the individual system (knowledge, skills and motivation), episodic system (variables considered during a particular episode of interaction), and relational system (based on the protracted observations of interpreter-mediated encounters with participation of the same interlocutors). As regards the competences of court interpreters, Bednarek emphasises textual and discourse competences, claiming that they are subject to dynamic modifications due to implementing new EU legislation binding for court interpreters (2014a,

---

10 The recommendations of *the Sworn Translator and Interpreter's Professional Code* (2019) are reproduced after previous versions of the Polish code of ethics, i.e. *The Court Translator and Interpreter's Code* [*Kodeks tłumacza sądowego*] (1991), *The Sworn Translator and Interpreter's Code with a Commentary* [*Kodeks tłumacza przysięgłego z komentarzem*] (2005) and the Sworn Translator and Interpreter's Code [*Kodeks tłumacza przysięgłego*] (2011).

11 Ustawa o zawodzie tłumacza przysięgłego z dnia 25 listopada 2004 r. (Dz.U. 2004 Nr 273 poz. 2702). https://isap.sejm.gov.pl/isap.nsf/DocDetails.xsp?id=wdu20042732702 (March 12, 2023).

2014b). A list of competences relating to court interpreters suggested by Hertog is detailed and distinguishes pre-requisite and specific competences. The former include: general language competence; listening, speaking, reading and writing skills; interpersonal skills and attitudes; and knowledge of relevant countries and their cultures, while the latter cover: knowledge of legal systems and legal language; knowledge of resources and information retrieval; interpreting and oral sight translation skills; as well as knowledge of the professional code of conduct and guidelines to good practice (2016).

Notwithstanding the fact that the above researchers use the term "competence" to describe the abilities that court interpreters should demonstrate, international standards and frameworks expressly distinguish between skills and competences. Skills are defined as "the ability to apply knowledge and use know-how to complete tasks and solve problems", while competence as "the proven ability to use knowledge, skills and personal, social and/or methodological abilities, in work or study situations and in professional and personal development"[12]. In the same vein, ISO 20228:2019 follows the above frame definitions and mentions: "skills critical to effective linguistic decision-making" (2019: 7), speaking, listening, reading and writing skills within linguistic competences (2019: 8) and "memory skills, note-taking, and stress management" within interpreting competences (2019: 8), as well as "communication and interpersonal skills" within interpersonal competences (2019: 8), and furthermore specifies also technical and intercultural competences.

As far as the specific competences of Polish sworn translators[13] are concerned, it is *Ordinance of Minister of Justice of January 24, 2005 on Particulars of Performing the Examination for Sworn Translators and Interpreters*[14] which provides for a catalog of categories on the basis of which both a written and an oral part of the examination for sworn translators is assessed. These categories cover: accurate

---

12 COUNCIL RECOMMENDATION of 22 May 2017 on the European Qualifications Framework for life-long learning and repealing the recommendation of the European Parliament and of the Council of 23 April 2008 on the establishment of the European Qualifications Framework for lifelong learning (2017/C 189/03).

13 "In the Polish legislative tradition relating to court interpreters, they have been referred to as sworn translators (*tłumacze przysięgli*), which is an umbrella term for officially appointed professionals who render both translation and interpreting services" (Biernacka 2019: 38).

14 Rozporządzenie Ministra Sprawiedliwości z dnia 24 stycznia 2005 r. w sprawie szczegółowego sposobu przeprowadzenia egzaminu na tłumacza przysięgłego https://isap.sejm.gov.pl/isap.nsf/DocDetails.xsp?id=wdu20050150129 (March 12, 2023).

rendition of the original message, use of terminology and idiomatic expressions, correct grammar and vocabulary, appropriate register and correct intonation, pleasant pace and diction. Hence, it is the content and form of the renditions that is assessed, while such criteria as an ability to speak in public, to talk with people and to manage stress are not taken into consideration.

Both legal and ethical requirements of a quality interpretation in the courtroom are in the case of Polish court interpreters heavily embedded. It seems, however, that one of the consequences of a large number of former regulations relating to admitting candidates for the profession, and, in particular, these concerning (not) examining candidates for sworn translators, is that not only court interpreters whose competences were verified in the course of harsh examinations, but also those who obtained permission to interpret in the courtroom on the basis of completion of higher education philological or foreign language studies and had never been trained to render court interpreting services, are entered onto the list of sworn translators and can exercise their profession. Therefore, it can be stated that not all court interpreters in Poland are highlyqualified specialists.

4. Bi-directionality and languages

According to Tryuk, "[community] [i]nterpreting takes place in the context of a meeting, a dialogue, a conversation; it is also a two-way interpreting, i.e. from language B to language A and vice versa"[15] (2006: 33). This bi-directionality forced by a dialogue nature of an interpreted encounter is also noticeable in court interpreting. In the case of Poland it also means that the languages that a language combination of a court interpreter is limited to A and B languages and excludes C languages.

What is equally important, "(c)ommunity interpreting concerns countless languages and even dialects, registers or jargons, rare or little-known languages"[16] (Tryuk 2006: 34). Maliszewski (2001: 35), when concluding on the interpreter's competences in police settings, states that "(t)he interpreter must patiently enrich professional vocabulary from various fields in order to be able to cope with the duties imposed on him. Among the most common are medical and technical

15 „Tłumaczenie odbywa się w kontekście spotkania, dialogu, rozmowy; jest to również tłumaczenie dwustronne, tj. z języka B na A i odwrotnie".

16 „Tłumaczenie środowiskowe dotyczy niezliczonej liczby języków, a nawet dialektów, rejestrów lub żargonów, języków rzadkich lub mało znanych".

vocabulary as well as all kinds of specialist and social jargons"[17]. According to ISO 13611:2014, "the community interpreter should be able to understand and produce technical and non-technical language for a variety of speakers and listeners who vary in age, gender, race, ethnicity, and socio-economic status"[18]. The linguistic requirements for court interpreters are even more strict; ISO 20228:2019 determines that court interpreters need "to be able to comprehend various regional accents and/or dialectal differences, recognize various language registers, including formal and informal, be familiar with subject-specific vocabulary, idiomatic expressions, colloquialisms, and slang"[19].

5. Participant status

In community interpreting "(p)articipants in the interpreted encounter have different status, competencies, knowledge, capabilities, rights; relations of superiority/subordination between them are evident; in this type of interpreting, one of the participants in the encounter is the person who asks, demands the right, seeks justice from the other participant who holds the right; relations of equality/inequality between the participants may affect the way the interpreter does his job[20] (Tryuk 2006: 33). It is also true as regards a court setting where all parties involved in the proceedings, in case they do not understand the language of the courtroom, require interpretation services to be delivered. These parties include "(…) persons deprived of liberty, suspects, accused, defendants, plaintiffs, claimants, complainants, witnesses, victims, (…)", that is, the interpreter's non-institutional clients, and "(…) judges, lawyers, prosecutors, (…)" who are the interpreter's institutional clients"[21]. As Biernacka (2019: 24) concludes, "(t)he lack of balance between the participants (with the judge being the most powerful

---

17 „Tłumacz musi cierpliwie wzbogacać słownictwo fachowe z różnych dziedzin, aby móc podołać nałożonym na niego obowiązkom. Pośród najczęściej spotykanych wymienić należy słownictwo medyczne i techniczne oraz wszelkiego rodzaju żargony specjalistyczne i społeczne".

18 ISO 13611:2014 *Interpreting – Guidelines for community interpreting.*

19 ISO 20228:2019 *Interpreting services – Legal interpreting – Requirements.*

20 „Uczestnicy tłumaczonego spotkania mają inny status, kompetencje, wiedzę, możliwości, prawa; relacje nadrzędności/podrzędności między nimi są widoczne; w tego typu przekładzie ustnym jeden z uczestników spotkania jest osobą, która prosi, domaga się prawa, szuka sprawiedliwości u drugiego uczestnika, który dysponuje tym prawem; stosunki równości/nierówności między uczestnikami mogą wpływać na sposób wykonywania pracy przez tłumacza".

21 ISO 20228:2019 *Interpreting services – Legal interpreting – Requirements.*

figure (Morris 2015)) in the interaction results not only from the fact that they represent different backgrounds (Shackman 1984), do not speak the language or do not know the culture of the other party, but is also related to the power and the shifts of control over the interpreted event". What distinguishes dialogues in community interpreting where "a spontaneous exchange of sentences is interpreted" (Tryuk 2006: 34) from courtroom interactions is that they are, or at least are supposed to be, monitored by the judges. As Biernacka (2019: 23) concludes, "[a]part from being the "oral interpretation of speech from one language to another" (Edwards 1995: xv), [...], court interpreting (Hale 2004; Gamal 2009: 63) or courtroom interpreting is characterised by "complex ritualized interaction and power hierarchies" (Morris: 2015: 91)". It is especially the case of those instances where a judge, as a "master of ceremony" (Biernacka 2019: 61) is a party to a dialogue, e. g. when they are hearing a witness. They are able to control both verbal and non-verbal attitude of the heard party: by asking for short or long answers, for providing more or less details, to stand up or sit down. In the same vein Toledano Buendía and Aguilera Ávila (2017: 52) characterise courts as "very hierarchical organizations in which the interpersonal relations are very protocolarized".

6. Interpreting mode

According to Tryuk (2006: 33), who refers to community interpreting, "[i]t is consecutive, sentence-by-sentence interpreting, sometimes fragments of sentences". It is also true in the case of court interpreting, where question-and-answer dialogues are interpreted consecutively. Moreover, court interpreters consecutively render fragments of (e.g. witness') declarations, which may have various length. Also, whispered interpreting is provided to a foreign language-speaking party who is listening to the interactions between a judge, a lawyer or a prosecutor hearing a witness. Yet another mode is sight translation of written documents, such as expert reports, indictments, and judgements.

7. Trilogue

In community interpreting "(c)ommunication with participation of the interpreter takes the form of a trilogue in which all participants have a role to play; the interpreter can thus influence the other participants, but the other participants can also influence him; often the interpreter resolves conflict situations or is emotionally involved in the conversation"[22] (Tryuk 2006: 34). As Valero-Garcés (2017: 33) points out, "[…] the interpreter does not merely carry out linguistic conveyance but also coordinates, mediates, and negotiates cultural and social meaning. The problem lies in setting the exact boundaries of this intervention".

In court interpreting "the interpreter is situated in-between an institutional client (the court) and a private client (a suspect, an accused, etc.)" (Biernacka 2019). As elsewhere shown (Biernacka 2014, 2016) court interpreters assume different roles. Nonetheless, they are forbidden to influence other participants as this would be considered a violation of impartiality, which is one of the ethical principles governing court interpreting. Unbiased interpreters who refrain from expressing their own opinions or judgements (Edwards 1995: 64–65; Ostarhild 2001: 28) and comply with the "prohibition against giving advice, legal or otherwise, and the inappropriateness of ever advocating for one side or the other" (Framer 2005: 4) are "essential to the integrity of the judicial system" (Najarro Smith 2005: 163). González et al. (1991: 314) indicate that impartiality is prohibition to make assumptions as to the intentions of original speakers, while Cal-Meyer (2013: 1) understands impartiality as "equilibrium" between information in the source language and the information in the target language.

8. Personal context

According to Tryuk, in the community interpreting "the milieu is individualised, personal, sometimes of a confidential nature"(2006: 33). Court interpreting, as well, requires satisfying a principle of confidentiality, which is defined in the Act on the Profession of Sworn Translator of November 25, 2004 as an obligation to keep in secret any sensitive (i.e. personal or other related to the proceedings) information obtained by the interpreter in relation to their assignment. The Polish *The Sworn Translator and Interpreter's Professional Code* [*Kodeks zawodowy tłumacza przysięgłego*] (2019: 27), recommending the principle of confidentiality, provides for destroying any notes taken during the court proceedings immediately after providing the interpretation[23]. This is due to

22 „Komunikacja z udziałem tłumacza ma postać trialogu, w którym wszyscy uczestnicy mają do odegrania jakąś rolę; tłumacz może więc wpływać na pozostałych uczestników, ale inni uczestnicy mogą też wpływać na niego; często tłumacz rozwiązuje sytuacje konfliktowe lub jest zaangażowany emocjonalnie w rozmowę".

23 "After the interpretation, in accordance with the principle of confidentiality, the interpreter is obliged to destroy the notes in a way that prevents third parties from recreating them" [„Po wykonaniu tłumaczenia, zgodnie z zasadą zachowania poufności,

frequently appearing personal context of court interpreting. As Nagao (2005: 3) and Gentile et al. (1996: 30–31) point out, court interpreting is one of these types of community interpreting that is done for the clients whose life depends on the interpreter. Furthermore Nagao (2005) and Katschinka (2000) claim that court interpreting needs to be viewed within the context of personal tragedies where it is much more important for a foreign language speaking party to be understood by other parties to the proceedings through the professional interpretation than it is in the case of conference settings. As Biernacka (2019: 25) concludes, "[…] the personal context of the interaction means a great (both professional and personal) liability of an interpreter; channels an interpreter who is to deal with emotionally charged communicative acts individually (there is no teamwork in the courtroom) […]".

9. Note-taking

Contrary to the opinions expressed by Dąmbska-Prokop (2000) and Tryuk (2006: 34), according to whom "[c]ommunity interpreting is done without notes" because note-taking could "adversely affect the participants (e.g. cause a lack of faith in the discretion of the interpreter) or distract the participants of the exchange", other researchers consider it a value added in the interpreter-mediated encounters. Heimerl-Moggan and John (2007) observe that note-taking is a memory aid for public service interpreters by helping them in precise and correct rendering of long, emotionally loaded, and redundant original utterances, in particular when primary speakers change pace and use specific terminology. Notwithstanding its undoubtful values, note-taking is underappreciated and considered useless in the settings where interpreters transmit dialogues (Allen 2014). *The Sworn Translator and Interpreter's Professional Code* expressly allows note-taking, which can be however done only on condition that "after the interpretation, in accordance with the principle of confidentiality, the interpreter is obliged to destroy the notes in a way that prevents third parties from recreating them"[24] (2019: 27).

tłumacz ma obowiązek zniszczyć notatki w sposób uniemożliwiający osobom trzecim ich odtworzenie"] (2019: 27).

24 „Po wykonaniu tłumaczenia, zgodnie z zasadą zachowania poufności, tłumacz ma obowiązek zniszczyć notatki w sposób uniemożliwiający osobom trzecim ich odtworzenie".

10. Physical distance

Among the skills a community interpreter should display ISO 13611 indicates "the ability to use the equipment (such as tele- and videoconferencing technology) that can be necessary for on-site or remote interpreting, including microphone etiquette (e.g. pressing the mute button when coughing)"[25]. This means that a physical distance between the interpreter and their clients might be huge. In the light of the quoted requirement and considering the recent pandemic developments that forced the humanity to communicate by videoconferencing, a physical distance in community interpreting touched upon by Tryuk (2006: 33) takes on a metaphorical meaning:

> This is a face-to-face interpreting; in this communication, the two parties want to understand each other; the third participant is the interpreter, who must find the most appropriate place for himself in this contact so that eye contact is possible between the participants of the conversation; this gives participants equality in the act of communication; it is best to arrange a meeting in a triangle configuration[26].

In the same vein, and indeed, being unable to foresee a COVID-19 explosion of interest in remote court interpreting, Biernacka (2019: 25) concludes, "[…] the personal context of the interaction […] may make an interpreter feel involved in the interaction due to a short physical distance between the interpreter and main speakers". Similar to community interpreters, court interpreters should be able "to use interpreting equipment (such as microphone, audio- and video-conferencing technology) that can be required for interpreting in a given legal setting (e.g. volume control, microphone etiquette)"[27].

The academic research in videoconference interpreting and remote interpreting shows that they are deployed in all institutional settings, including legal (Braun 2013; Napier 2012; Locatis et al. 2010, 2011). Furthermore it has been proven that although remote interpreting facilitates the organisation of events (Mouzourakis 2006), certain constraints imposed on communication (Mouzourakis 2006; Braun 2015) may include: unstable sound quality, background noise, and scarce eye contact as well as social interaction problems in consecutive interpreting via

---

25 ISO 13611:2014 *Interpreting – Guidelines for community interpreting.*

26 „Jest to tłumaczenie twarzą w twarz; w tej komunikacji dwie strony pragną się porozumieć; trzecim uczestnikiem jest tłumacz, który w tym kontakcie musi dla siebie znaleźć najodpowiedniejsze miejsce tak, aby między uczestnikami rozmowy był możliwy kontakt wzrokowy; zapewnia to uczestnikom równorzędność w akcie komunikacji; najlepiej zaaranżować spotkanie w konfiguracji trójkąta".

27 ISO 20228:2019 *Interpreting services – Legal interpreting – Requirements.*

videoconferencing (Braun 2007); remoteness ("loss of co-presence", Setton and Dawrant 2016: 36), affecting a feeling of alienation and decreased motivation of the parties to the remote communicative act (Mouzourakis 1996; Braun 2007); the parties being "left out" (Moser-Mercer 2005; Mouzourakis 2006; Roziner and Shlesinger 2010); possible poor visibility (Mouzourakis 2006); decreased concentration, lack of handouts (Seleskovitch and Lederer 2002); and a need to adapt to new communication situations (Braun 2007).

As regards court proceedings, in many countries, "[v]ideo-hearings did not start with the pandemic" (Sanders 2021: 3). In the EU Member States, the "use (of) communications technology at the performance of the taking of evidence, in particular by using videoconference and teleconference" is governed by Article 10 and Article 17 of the Council Regulation (EC) No 1206/2001 of 28 May 2001 on cooperation between the courts of the Member States in the taking of evidence in civil or commercial matters. In Poland, distant taking of evidence via videoconferencing is provided for in Article 177 1a of the Code of Criminal Procedure, Article 235(2) and (3) of the Code of Civil Procedure, and the Regulation of the Minister of Justice of 24 February 2010 on the technical equipment and resources that enable evidence to be taken remotely in civil proceedings. In line with these regulations more than 1,500 courtrooms have been equipped with video conferencing facilities in 2011–2017.[28] Thus, even before the COVID-19 outbreak, videoconferencing was possible as far as taking evidence of witnesses staying abroad, children and disabled persons was concerned.

In the pandemic, it was the *Act of 2 March 2020 on special solutions related to preventing, counteracting and combating COVID-19, other infectious diseases and crisis situations arising therefrom* (Journal of Laws of 2020, item 374)[29], *which enabled remote working, while the Act of 14 May 2020 on amendment on certain acts concerning protective measures in connection with the spreading of the SARS-CoV-2 virus* (Journal of Laws of 2020, item 875)[30] *admitted videoconferencing as a way for all parties to participate in court proceedings.*

28 For more statistical details of the implementation of the regulations on court technical equipment see Ministerstwo Sprawiedliwości.2015. Opis wdrożenia at https://www.arch.ms.gov.pl/pl/sady-w-internecie/e-protokol/opis-wdrozenia/ (March 14, 2023).

29 Ustawa z dnia 2 marca 2020 r. o szczególnych rozwiązaniach związanych z zapobieganiem, przeciwdziałaniem i zwalczaniem COVID-19, innych chorób zakaźnych oraz wywołanych nimi sytuacji kryzysowych (Dz.U. 2020 poz. 374).

30 Ustawa z dnia 14 maja 2020 r. o zmianie niektórych ustaw w zakresie działań osłonowych w związku z rozprzestrzenianiem się wirusa SARS-C0V-2 (Dz.U. 2020 poz. 875)

While in December 2020 it was reported that, as a result of implementing the above-mentioned legal regulations, statistically every 36th court hearing was held via videoconference, however, in some courts even every 4th hearing was held online (Słowik 2020), the statistics provided by the Polish Ministry of Justice show an even greater increase in the number of online hearings:

> In total, from July 3 to October 22, 2020, a total of 1,080,854 cases were held at hearings and public hearings, of which 24,726 (2.29%) were held by videoconference. From October 23 to December 31, 2020 – 671,693 of which 19,393 online – 2.89 percent. From January 1 to December 31, 2021, there were 3,418,356 such hearings and sessions in total, of which 250,076 were videoconferences – 7.32 percent. In turn, from January 1 to January 27, 2022, a total of 233,090, including 31,007 online – 13.3 percent[31].

A remote court hearing via videoconferencing is a decision of the judge and does not require the consent of those attending the hearing nor can they object to it. Also, *an application, which is used for conducting a remote hearing* (e.g. MS TEAMS, Avaya SCOPIA, or JITSI), *and which "guarantee confidentiality and integrity of audio and video data between participants in the proceedings"*[32] *is chosen by a judge*[33]. *Technically speaking, t*he court sends a summons, or notice of hearing, or just an email, to all parties, their lawyers, and the interpreter which, among other data, includes a set of such information as: a link to a virtual video conference room enabling participation in the hearing; recommended equipment (a computer equipped with a camera, microphone and loudspeaker, or alternatively a smartphone); a need to verify the proper functioning of the camera, microphone and speakers; a reminder that the Internet is indispensable; instructions that it is the duty of the party to participate in a remote hearing

---

31 „W sumie od 3 lipca do 22 października 2020 r. odbyło się łącznie 1 080 854 spraw na rozprawach i posiedzeniach jawnych, z tego 24 726 (2,29 proc.) w trybie wideokonferencji. Od 23 października do 31 grudnia 2020 r. – 671 693 z czego 19 393 w trybie online – 2,89 proc. Od 1 stycznia do 31 grudnia 2021 r. łącznie takich rozpraw i posiedzeń był 3 418 356 z czego 250 076 wideokonferencji – 7,32 proc. Z kolei od od 1 do 27 stycznia 2022 r. łącznie 233 090 w tym 31 007 w trybie online – 13,3 proc." (Aleksandra Partyk and Patrycja Rojek-Socha, „W sądach coraz więcej e-rozpraw. I wciąż pytania o prawa stron", 18.02.2022, available at https://www.prawo.pl/prawnicy-sady/rozprawy-zdalne-statystyki-za-2020-2021-i-styczen-2022-r,513546.html (March 12, 2023)).

32 *Rozprawy zdalne*, available at https://suwalki.so.gov.pl/rozprawy-zdalne,m,m2,320 (March 30, 2022).

33 *Rozprawy zdalne – co warto wiedzieć?*, available at https://bip.warszawa.so.gov.pl/artykuly/1921/rozprawy-zdalne (March 30, 2022).

in a place and under circumstances that will not violate the solemnity, peace and order of court activities; advice to provide a telephone number in advance to the e-mail address of the court division so that the party can be contacted in case of problems related to the organisation of the videoconference or its course (delay, technical problems); as well as instructions that if the party does not have technical facilities or internet, while other parties agree to a remote hearing, it is theoretically (as the decision is up to the presiding judge) possible for that particular person to appear in court on the day of the hearing and use the equipment provided to them by the court, e.g. in a different room than the one used by the judge and reporter.[34] During the online session it is again the judge who "[…] plays a central role in administrating the interpretation and in giving instructions to the witness or the interpreter during the hearing, in particular as regards the order in which the parties involved speak"[35] . In order to overcome these challenges, Valero-Garcés and Cayron emphasise a need to re-discuss "the ethical considerations, [and] best practices" (2022: 26) for remote interpreting.

11. Final remarks what's the future of court interpreting?

It seems that court interpreting in Poland is a fully-fledged type of interpretation performed mostly by competent professionals. Unlike interpreters rendering their services in settings other than legal, court interpreters are required to certify skills during the exam for a sworn translator, observe the oath and the rules of professional ethics as well as improve skills in the process of life-long learning. Among the required competencies, technical competencies in particular, resulting from the transition from face-to-face to online mode, came to the fore as the fastest evolving and most needed. As far as the future of court interpreting is concerned, re-discussing of the issues of professional ethics and standards is necessary.

References

Allen, Katharine. 2014. "Note-taking for public service interpreters: towards a sector-specific teaching model." In *(Re)Considerando ética e ideología en situaciones de conflicto. (Re)Visiting Ethics and Ideology in Situations of Conflict*,

34 *Rozprawy zdalne – co warto wiedzieć?*, available at https://bip.warszawa.so.gov.pl/artykuly/1921/rozprawy-zdalne (May 30, 2022).

35 *Guide on videoconferencing in cross-border proceedings*, General Secretariat of the Council of Europe, 2013: 11.

edited by Carmen Valero Garcés, 232–239. Alcalá de Henares: Servicios de Publicaciones Universidad de Alcalá.

Apfelbaum, Birgit. 2004. *Medical Interpreting and Cross-cultural Communication*. Cambridge: Cambridge University Press.

Bancroft, Marjory A. 2015. "Community interpreting. A profession rooted in social justice". In *The Routledge Handbook of Interpreting*, edited by Holly Mikkelson and Renée Jourdenais. Routledge. https://www.routledgehandbooks.com/doi/10.4324/9781315745381.ch14 (March 11, 2023).

Bednarek, Grażyna Anna. 2014a. *Polish vs. American Courtroom Discourse: Inquisitorial and Adversarial Procedures of Witness Examination in Criminal Trials*. New York/Basingstoke: Palgrave Macmillan.

Bednarek, Grażyna Anna. 2014b. "Polish vs. American courtroom discourse: inquisitorial and adversarial procedures of witness examination in penal trails. What court interpreters need to know about witness examination in criminal trails under disparate legal systems to provide high level interpreting services in the light of the Directive 2010/64/EU of the European Parliament and of the Council of 20 October 2010?" *Comparative Legilinguistics. International Journal for Legal Communication* 19: 77–115.

Biernacka, Agnieszka. 2010. Funkcje tłumacza w rozprawie sądowej. Ph.D. Thesis. Warsaw: University of Warsaw.

Biernacka, Agnieszka. 2014. Tłumacz w rozprawie sądowej. Warszawa: Studi@ Naukowe. https://portal.uw.edu.pl/documents/7732735/0/SN+16+Agnieszka+Biernacka+T%C5%82umacz+s%C4%85dowy.pdf (April 23, 2023).

Biernacka, Agnieszka. 2016. "Quality in Court Interpreting vs. (?) Role(s) of Court Interpreters." In *Interchange between Languages and Cultures: The Quest for Quality*, edited by Jitka Zehnalová, Ondřej Molnár, and Michal Kubánek, 89–102. Olomouc: Palacký University.

Biernacka, Agnieszka. 2019. *Interpreter-Mediated Interactions of the Courtroom. A Naturally Occurring Data Based Study*. Berlin: Peter Lang.

Braun Sabine. 2007. "Interpreting in small-group bilingual videoconferences: Challenges and adaptation". *Interpreting*, 9(1), 21–46. https://doi.org/10.1075/intp.9.1.03bra

Braun Sabine. 2013. "Keep your distance? Remote interpreting in legal proceedings: A critical assessment of a growing practice". *Interpreting*, 15(2), 200–228. https://doi.org/10.1075/intp.15.2.03bra

Braun Sabine. 2015. "Videoconference interpreting". [in:] F. Pöchhacker (ed.), *Routledge Encyclopedia of Interpreting*. Routledge: London/New York, 437–439.

Cal-Meyer, Pilar. 2013. "Clarifying pragma-linguistic incongruences when conveying meaning between sociocultural words/worlds." *Proteus,* 22(1). www.najit.org/proteus (May 21, 2014).

Corsellis, Ann, and Leandro F. Fernández. 2001. "Code of ethics and conduct and guidelines to good practice." In *Aequitas. Access to Justice across Language and Culture in the EU*, edited by Erik Hertog, 77–87. Antwerp: Departement Vertaler-Tolk, Lessius Hogeschool.

Council Recommendation of 22 May 2017 on the European Qualifications Framework for lifelong learning and repealing the recommendation of the European Parliament and of the Council of 23 April 2008 on the establishment of the European Qualifications Framework for lifelong learning (2017/C 189/ 03).

Council Regulation (EC) No 1206/2001 of 28 May 2001 on cooperation between the courts of the Member States in the taking of evidence in civil or commercial matters.

Dąmbska-Prokop, Urszula. 2000. *Mała Encyklopedia Przekładoznawstwa.* Kielce: Wyd. WSU im. Stanisława Staszica.

Edwards, Alicia B. 1995. *The Practice of Court Interpreting.* Amsterdam and Philadelphia: J. Benjamins.

Framer, Isabel. 2005. "*Interpreters as officers of the Court: Scope and limitations of practice.*" *Proteus*, 14(2), 3–5.

Gamal, Muhammad Y. 2009. "Court interpreting." In *Routledge Encyclopedia of Translation Studies*, edited by Mona Baker and Gabriela Saldanha, 63–67. London and New York: Routledge.

Garber, Nathan. 2000. "Community interpreting: A personal view." In *The Critical Link 2: Interpreters in the Community. Papers from the Second International Conference on Interpreting in Legal, Health, and Social Service Settings, Vancouver, Canada, 19–23 May 1998*, edited by Roda P. Roberts, Silvana E. Carr, Diana Abraham, and Aideen Dufour, 9–20. Amsterdam/ Philadelphia: J. Benjamins.

Gentile, Adolfo, Uldis Ozolins, and Mary Vasilakakos. 1996. *Liaison Interpreting.* Melbourne: Melbourne University Press.

González, Roseann D., Victoria F. Vásquez, and Holy Mikkelson. 1991. *Fundamentals of Court Interpretation: Theory, Policy and Practice.* Durham, NC: Carolina Academic Press.

Grbič, Nadja. 2015. "Profession." In *Routledge Encyclopedia of Interpreting Studies*, edited by Franz Pöchhacker, 321–326. London and New York: Routledge.

Guide on videoconferencing in cross-border proceedings. 2013. General Secretariat of the Council of Europe.

Hale, Sandra. 2004. *The Discourse of Court Interpreting. Discourse Practices of the Law, the Witness and the Interpreter.* Amsterdam/Philadelphia: J. Benjamins.

Hale, Sandra. 2007. *Community Interpreting.* Houndmills, Basingstoke, Hampshire: Palgrave Macmillan.

Heimerl-Moggan, Kirsty, and Vanessa Ifeoma John. 2007. *Note-taking for Public Service Interpreters.* Altrincham: Interp-Right Training Consultancy Ltd.

Hertog, Erik. 2016. "Legal interpreting competences in civil justice and mediation." In *Understanding Justice. An enquiry into interpreting in civil justice and mediation*, edited by Brooke Townsley, 51–89. London: Middlesex University.

Hsieh, Elaine. 2015. "Interpreting for Institutions." In *The International Encyclopedia of Language and Social Interaction*, edited by Karen Tracy, Cornelia Ilie, and Todd Sandel. John Wiley & Sons, Inc. doi: 10.1002/9781118611463/wbielsi004

ISO 13611:2014 Interpreting — Guidelines for community interpreting. 2014. Geneva: International Organization for Standardization.

ISO 20228:2019 Interpreting services — Legal interpreting — Requirements. 2019. Geneva: International Organization for Standardization.

Jopek-Bosiacka, Anna. 2014. "Poland: Court Interpreters' and Legal Translators' training at the Institute of Applied Linguistics of the University of Warsaw." In *New Tasks for Legal Interpreters and Translators in the Enlarged Europe*, edited by Danuta Kierzkowska, 199–208. Warszawa: TEPIS.

Kaczmarek, Łukasz. 2008. "Proposing a model of community interpreting competence." In *Investigación y práctica en traducción e interpretación en los servicios públicos. Desafíos y alianzas. Research and Practice in Public Service Interpreting and Translation. Challenges and Alliances*, edited by Carmen Valero Garcés, 240–254. Alcalá de Henares: Servicios de Publicaciones Universidad de Alcalá.

Katschinka, Liese. 2000. *What is Court Interpreting?* Last modified 2015. https://aiic.net/page/239/what-is-court-interpreting/lang/1 (February 17, 2017).

Kodeks tłumacza przysięgłego. 2011. Warszawa: Wyd. Tepis.

Kodeks tłumacza przysięgłego z komentarzem. 2005. Warszawa: Wyd. Tepis.

Kodeks tłumacza sądowego. 1991. Warszawa: Wyd. TEPIS.

Kodeks zawodowy tłumacza przysięgłego. 2019. Warszawa: Wyd. Tepis.

Kościałkowska-Okońska, Ewa. 2010. "Interpreters in the courtroom: The importance of competence and quality." *Comparative Legilinguistics. International Journal for Legal Communication,* 2, 39–47.

Locatis, Craig et al. 2010. "Comparing in-person, video, and telephonic medical interpretation." *Journal of General Internal Medicine*, 25(4), 345–350.

Locatis, Craig et al. 2011. "Video medical interpretation over 3G cellular networks. A feasibility study." *Telemedicine and-e-Health*, 17(10), 809–813. doi: 10.1089/tmj.2011.0084

Maliszewski, Julian. 2001. "Pragmatyka przekładu policyjnego. Warsztatowe zagadnienia pracy tłumacza w warunkach ekstremalnych." *Lingua Legis*, 9: 27–36.

Ministerstwo Sprawiedliwości. 2015. Opis wdrożenia. https://www.arch.ms.gov.pl/pl/sady-w-internecie/e-protokol/opis-wdrozenia/ (March 14, 2023).

Morris, Ruth. 2015. "Courtroom interpreting." In *Routledge Encyclopedia of Interpreting Studies*, edited by Franz Pöchhacker, 91–93. London and New York: Routledge.

Moser-Mercer, Barbara. 2005. "Remote interpreting: Issues of multi-sensory integration in a multilingual task." *Meta*, 50(2), 727–738. https://doi.org/10.7202/011014ar

Mouzourakis, Panagiotis. 1996. "Videoconferencing: Techniques and challenges." *Interpreting*, 1(1), 21–38.

Mouzourakis, Panagiotis. 2006. "Remote interpreting: A technical perspective on recent experiments." *Interpreting*, 8(1), 45–66. https://doi.org/10.1075/intp.8.1.04mou

Nagao, Hiromi. 2005. "Sprawa z Melbourne: niewłaściwe tłumaczenie przyczyną oskarżenia o niepopełnione przestępstwa." *Lingua Legis*, 13: 3–7.

Najarro Smith, Nadia. 2005. "Resolving ethical dilemmas for court interpreters." In *Traducción como mediación entre lenguas y culturas. Translation as Mediation or how to Bridge Linguistic and Cultural Gaps*, edited by Carmen Valero Garcés, 161–167. Alcalá de Henares: Servicios de Publicaciones Universidad de Alcalá.

Napier, Jemina. 2012. "Here or there? An assessment of video remote signed language interpreter-mediated interaction in court." In *Videoconference and Remote Interpreting in Criminal Proceedings*, edited by S. Braun and I. J. Taylor, 167–214. Intersentia: Cambridge.

Ostarhild, Edda. 2001. "*Linguistic standards for legal interpreters and translators at Diploma or Fist Degree Level and at MA level.*" In *Aequitas. Access to Justice across Language and Culture in the EU*, edited by Erik Hertog, 21–72. Antwerp: Departement Vertaler-Tolk, Lessius Hogeschool.

Partyk, Aleksandra and Patrycja Rojek-Socha. 18.02.2022. W sądach coraz więcej e-rozpraw. I wciąż pytania o prawa stron. https://www.prawo.pl/prawnicy-sady/rozprawy-zdalne-statystyki-za-2020-2021-i-styczen-2022-r,513546.html (March 12, 2023).

Polskie Towarzystwo Tłumaczy Przysięgłych i Specjalistycznych TEPIS. http://tepis.org.pl (March 4, 2023)

Pym, Anthony. 1999. "'Nicole Slapped Michelle'. Interpreters and theories of interpreting at the O.J. Simpson Trial." In *Dialogue Interpreting. Special Issue of The Translator: Studies in Intercultural Communication*, edited by Ian Mason, 265–283. Manchester: St Jerome Publishing.

Repa, Jindra. 1991. "Training and certification of court interpreters in a multicultural society." *Meta*, 36(4), 595–605.

Roberts, Roda P. 1997. "Community interpreting today and tomorrow." In *The Critical Link 1: Interpreters in the Community. Papers from the First International Conference on Interpreting in Legal, Health, and Social Service Settings, Canada, June 1–4, 1995*, edited by Silvana E. Carr, Roda P. Roberts, Aideen Dufour, and Dini Steyn, 7–26. Amsterdam and Philadelphia: J. Benjamins.

Roberts, Roda P. 2002. "Community interpreting: A profession in search of its identity." In *Teaching Translation and Interpreting 4*, edited by Eva Hung, 157–175. Amsterdam: J. Benjamins. doi:10.1075/btl.42.20rob

Roziner Ilan and Shlesinger Miriam. 2010. "Much ado about something remote: Stress and performance in remote interpreting." *Interpreting*, 12(2), 214–247. https://doi.org/10.1075/intp.12.2.05roz

Rozporządzenie Ministra Sprawiedliwości z dnia 24 stycznia 2005 r. w sprawie szczegółowego sposobu przeprowadzenia egzaminu na tłumacza przysięgłego https://isap.sejm.gov.pl/isap.nsf/DocDetails.xsp?id=wdu20050150129 (March 12, 2023).

Rozporządzenie Ministra Sprawiedliwości z dnia 24 lutego 2010 r. w sprawie urządzeń i środków umożliwiających przeprowadzenie dowodu na odległość w postępowaniu cywilnym (Dz.U. 2010 nr 34 poz. 185).

Rozprawy zdalne. 2022. Sąd Okręgowy w Suwałkach. https://suwalki.so.gov.pl/rozprawy-zdalne,m,m2,320 (March 30, 2022).

Rozprawy zdalne – co warto wiedzieć? 2022. Sąd Okręgowy w Warszawie. https://bip.warszawa.so.gov.pl/artykuly/1921/rozprawy-zdalne (March 30, 2022).

Sanders Anne. 2021. "Video-Hearings in Europe before, during and after the COVID-19 pandemic." *International Journal for Court Administration*, 12(2), 1–21. http://doi.org/10.36745/ijca.379

Seleskovitch Danica and Lederer Marianne. 2002. *Pédagogie Raisonée de l'Interprétation*. OPOCE/Didier Érudition: Luxembourg/Paris.

Setton, Robin and Dawrant Andrew. 2016. *Conference Interpreting. A Complete Course*. Amsterdam/Philadelphia: J. Benjamins.

Shackman, Jane. 1984. *The Right to be Understood: A Handbook on Working With, Employing and Training Community Interpreters*. Cambridge: National Extension College.

Skorek, Marta. 2014. "Apprenticeship: The value of hands-on experience in court interpreter training." In *New Tasks for Legal Interpreters and Translators in the Enlarged Europe*, edited by Danuta Kierzkowska, 258–266. Warszawa: Wyd. TEPIS.

Słowik Patryk. 2020. "Sąd nie(przeniesiony) do sieci." *Dziennik Gazeta Prawna*. https://prawo.gazetaprawna.pl/artykuly/1498315,posiedzenia-sadow-online-statystyki.html (November 12, 2021).

Takeda, Kayoko. 2015. "Tribunal interpreting." In *Routledge Encyclopedia of Interpreting Studies*, edited by Franz Pöchhacker, 424–425. London and New York: Routledge.

Toledano Buendía, Carmen and Aguilera Ávila, Laura. 2017. "Stress, interpersonal communication and assertiveness training in public service interpreting." In *Interdisciplinary encounters: Dimensions of interpreting studies*, edited by Andrzej Łyda and Katarzyna Holewik. Katowice: Wyd. Uniwersytetu Śląskiego.

Tryuk, Małgorzata. 2006. *Przekład ustny środowiskowy*. Warszawa: Wyd. Naukowe PWN.

Ustawa o zawodzie tłumacza przysięgłego z dnia 25 listopada 2004 r. (Dz.U. 2004 Nr 273 poz. 2702) https://isap.sejm.gov.pl/isap.nsf/DocDetails.xsp?id=wdu20042732702 (March 12, 2023).

Ustawa z dnia 2 marca 2020 r. o szczególnych rozwiązaniach związanych z zapobieganiem, przeciwdziałaniem i zwalczaniem COVID-19, innych chorób zakaźnych oraz wywołanych nimi sytuacji kryzysowych (Dz.U. z 2020 r. poz. 374).

Ustawa z dnia 14 maja 2020 r. o zmianie niektórych ustaw w zakresie działań osłonowych w związku z rozprzestrzenianiem się wirusa SARS-COV-2 (Dz.U. 2020 poz. 875).

Valero-Garcés, Carmen. 2017. "Evolution, trends and gaps in public service interpreting training in the 21st century." In *Interdisciplinary Encounters: Dimensions of Interpreting Studies*, edited by Andrzej Łyda and Katarzyna Holewik. Katowice: Wyd. Uniwersytetu Śląskiego.

Valero-Garcés Carmen and Cayron Samantha. 2022. "The impact of the COVID-19 pandemic on Public Service Interpreting and Translation (PSIT) and its future developments." *FITISPos International Journal*, 9(1), 24–39. https://doi.org/10.37536/FITISPos-IJ.2023.1.9.336

Vargas-Urpi, Mireia and Marta Arumí Ribas. 2014. "Estrategias de interpretación en los servicios públicos en el ámbito educativo: estudio de caso en la combinación chino-catalán." *inTRAlinea*, 16, 1–2. http://www.intralinea.org/archive/article/2040 (March 11, 2023).

Wadensjö, Cecilia. 1998. *Interpreting as Interaction*. London and New York: Longman.

Wilensky Harold L. 1964. "The professionalization of everyone?" *The American Journal of Sociology*, 70(2), 137–158.

Zimman, Leonor. 1994. "Intervention as a pedagogical problem in community interpreting." In Teaching Translation and Interpreting 2: Insights, Aims and Visions, edited by Cay Dollerup and Annette Lindegaard, 217–224. Amsterdam and Philadelphia: J. Benjamins.

Związek Zawodowy Tłumaczy Przysięgłych w Polsce. http://www.zztp.pl/ (March 4, 2023).

Aleksandra Kalata-Zawłocka

Chapter 6 Preparation for interpreting in TV settings: Strategies employed by signed language interpreters across Europe

Abstract: Preparation is a vital tenet of a majority of interpreters' codes of ethics and professional standards, a fundamental principle advocated by educators and endorsed by interpreters' professional organisations. Its significant role is emphasised in relation to any settings where the interpreter has to deal with texts that may be challenging with respect to terminology, density or potential consequences. One of such demanding settings is television. The primary aim of the study, conducted by means of an online survey, was to identify and document the preparation strategies employed by signed language interpreters working in television settings across Europe. It examined, among others, the participants' approaches to the concept of preparation, the amount of time spent on it, specific activities undertaken to secure the efficacy of the interpreted output, and the reasons behind preparation. The results revealed many similarities among the preparation strategies employed by the surveyed interpreters. The activities they engaged in could be tentatively classified as (1) pre-assignment, (2) on-assignment, and (3) post-assignment strategies. The study fills the gap in research on preparation, especially in the context of television interpreting. It shows the potential to support the interpreting community in providing deaf viewers with high-quality services.

Keywords: preparation, television interpreting, signed language interpreting, strategy, deaf

A successful interpreting situation is only the tip of the iceberg; before that there are many hours of unseen and unheard work in preparing for assignments.[1]

1 https://www.facebook.com/AICIInterpreters/photos/a.216574362342386/29295230 4704591/?type=3 (Accessed 4 February 2023).

1. Signed language interpreting on TV – Background

Television interpreting, otherwise referred to as TV interpreting or broadcast interpreting (Dal Fovo, 2016; Gile, 2011; Tsuruta, 2011), is a category of media interpreting which, alongside dubbing, subtitling and audio description, is sometimes included in a broader field of audio-visual translation. As reported by Ladd (2007), the first records of signed language interpreting on TV can be traced back to around the 1950s. However, in many countries, it is still a "relatively recent development" (Roberson & Shaw, 2018 after de Wit, 2020: 1) that competes for recognition and validity with other traditional accessibility services for the deaf[2] and hard of hearing audiences, such as closed-captioning and live subtitling. As opposed to spoken language-based alternatives that serve mainly bilingual, hard of hearing or late-deafened viewers, signed language interpreting aims to make television content accessible primarily to those deaf viewers whose first, preferred or the only language is visual-spatial.

The presence of signed language interpreting on TV has been frequently called for by Deaf communities, signed language interpreters, and scholars. It has long been recognised that television interpreting not only constitutes "a major source of information and entertainment" (Xiao & Li, 2013: 1), providing deaf people with access to information of general interest (Mäkipää & Hämesalo, 1993; Neves, 2007), but gets them out of informational and social isolation (Kurz & Mikulasek, 2004). Sometimes it may even save lives, as in the case of natural disasters or emergency situations that are frequently announced to the public on television (McKee, 2014). Most importantly, it allows Deaf community members to exercise their rights as responsible and autonomous citizens (Seleskovitch, 1997).

At the international level, the provision of deaf-accessible broadcasts became better-recognised with the advent of such legislative initiatives as the United

2 According to a previous convention commonly used in the field of deaf studies, sign linguistics and sign language translation/interpreting studies, people with hearing loss who do not use a signed language and do not identify with the community of signed language users should be referred to as "deaf", whereas deaf people who use a signed language and identify with the signing community should be referred to as "Deaf". Yet, some researchers (Kusters at al., 2017; Napier, 2021), having observed changes to the patterns of deaf community membership, suggest using a generic "deaf", in order to avoid making "judgement about the hearing and linguistic identity or status of people who use a signed language" (Napier, 2021: 33). The author subscribes to this convention, albeit partly, by using a small "d" with reference to deaf individuals and a capital "D" when referring to the Deaf community as a linguistic-cultural minority.

Nations Convention on the Rights of Persons with Disabilities (UNCRPD)[3] or the European Audio-visual Media Services Directive[4]. The implementation of the new laws and policies, however, has been taking place at a different pace in various countries. Where available, the provision of signed language interpreting services may vary in terms of the percentage of TV content that is being interpreted, the types of programmes available via signed language interpreting, and the forms of signed language rendition (interpretation/translation). What contributed to both public and state-level acknowledgment of the need for formal regulations was also the rapidly increasing visibility of signed language interpreting in the media (McKee, 2014). Furthermore, there have been such misfortunate situations as the one with the non-professional interpreter during Nelson Mandela's funeral or the outbreak of the COVID-19 pandemic that suddenly left millions of deaf people cut off from vital information disseminated mainly through press conferences or announcements available on television (de Wit et al., 2020).

2. Signed language interpreting in television settings

At first sight, television interpreting shares many characteristics with conference interpreting (Pinhas, 1972; Strolz, 1992 after Kurz, 2002). Both are mainly performed by qualified professionals, in a simultaneous mode, under severe time pressure, on high-density texts (often prepared or scripted), and to large audiences. Both may be delivered on-site or remotely. However, considering new insights from the growing body of research on TV interpreting, many scholars seem to agree that television interpreting is a specific type of language transfer (Mack, 2002; Kurz, 2002; Pöchhacker, 2011). It is one that "requires an entirely new 'mind-set' compared to everyday practice of conference interpretation" (Bros-Brann, 1993: 1). One of the first distinctions to be made pertains to the form of interpretation delivery – television interpreting may be performed live, synchronously with the broadcast, for example in the case of news programmes and other live broadcasts, public announcements, press conferences, etc. It can also be performed asynchronously with the broadcast, that is pre-recorded, for example for the sake of TV films, series, educational or entertaining programmes, etc. While the former is performed by an interpreter in real time, either by listening to the incoming text (hearing interpreters) or reading the written text

3 https://www.un.org/disabilities/documents/convention/convoptprot-e.pdf (Accessed 3 February 2023).

4 https://eur-lex.europa.eu/legal-content/EN/TXT/HTML/?uri=CELEX:32018L1808&from=EN (Accessed 3 February 2023).

displayed on the autocue (deaf interpreters), the latter can be watched/listened to by the interpreter repeatedly in preparation for the recording of their rendition, which is why it is referred to as translation (Leneham, 2007; Wurm, 2010 after Napier & Leeson, 2015).

Another issue is the unidirectional character of televised communication – interpreters work by transferring information presented on TV to viewers with rare, or no opportunity for retour. The only exceptions are live debates, interviews, talk shows or press conferences including a Q&A part.

Finally, within the existing body of literature on interpreting, television and media settings are often referred to as among the most difficult and stressful to work in (Strolz, 1997; Kurz, 2002; Mack, 2002; Serrano, 2011). Simultaneous interpreting being a highly demanding cognitive activity in itself (Herbert, 1952; Gile, 1995; Moser-Mercer, 2003; Leeson, 2005), when combined with the specificity and a multitude of requirements and challenges posed by television settings that constantly put the interpreter's physical and physiological abilities to the test (Dal Fovo, 2016), proves more stressful than ordinary conference interpreting (Kurz, 1997, 2002). The stress factors responsible for the extra strain experienced by interpreters working in television as opposed to other settings can be divided into three categories:

(1) Physical environment
(2) Work-related issues
(3) Psycho-emotional issues (Kurz, 2002).

The stress-inducing factors related to the television environment are of two main kinds. First, it is the very place in which the interpreter provides her/his renditions – s/he may be doing it either from the TV studio or from a distance. In the case of the former, especially if the interpreting is delivered from a newsroom shared with other TV professionals, the interpreter may be exposed to various "distractions and disturbances" (Kurz, 2002: 195), such as noise from other people's conversations, equipment being shifted, and other TV crew members crossing in between her/him and the camera or appearing unexpectedly in the scope of her/his vision. Even if the interpreter can work from a separate studio, abrupt opening of the door or noises coming in from the outside may affect her/his concentration on the task. Apart from focusing on her/his job, the interpreter needs to exert a certain degree of control over the equipment s/he is surrounded with (headphones, autocue, camera) and bear in mind the limitations on the use of signing space imposed on her/him by the camera scope. On top of that is the special lighting that is necessary to make the interpreter visible and well lit, but which may add to the temperature and sometimes may be hurtful to the eyes.

The second type of factors affecting the interpreter's performance and wellbeing is connected with the very essence of the television medium. First, there is a lack of direct contact with the recipients of one's interpreting. Televised communication being unidirectional in nature, the interpreter is deprived of the immediate reactions to her/his renditions. Unlike in other settings, s/he cannot rely on positive or negative feedback from the audience. This is something many interpreters may find disheartening and difficult to cope with.

Additionally, in the majority of cases, there is no opportunity to pause during interpreting, ask for clarification, etc. For one thing, the very fast rate of the texts that are interpreted (pre-prepared and read out) means that any pause or longer hesitation threatens the interpreter with losing track of the incoming text, for another, the interpreter cannot afford to interrupt a news presenter or debating politicians to ask for repetition or clarification (Pöchhacker, 2011; Pignataro, 2011).

Finally, unlike in any other interpreting setting, television interpreters have to work with a great variety of speakers: from different backgrounds, of different status, with different accents or speaking styles, with a different degree of competence in public speaking. On the other side of TV sets there are deaf audiences that are even more diverse (Pöchhacker, 2011). They differ in terms of their signed language variety (national/regional) and competencies, as well as interpreting preferences (form-based/meaning-based). Interpreters thus face a serious challenge in adjusting their language transfer so that it is understandable and suitable to as many viewers as possible.

Last but not least, work-related issues may also pertain to working times. Sometimes there are very early/late hours, other times there is very short notice (emergency situations, there are impromptu press conferences). What adds to the irregularity, which may be disturbing in itself, is the frequent lack of opportunity to prepare for the task ahead. On many occasions preparatory materials, such as the script of the programme, are obtainable only minutes before the programme goes on air, or state officials do not want to share the text of their speeches prior to the press conference, etc. (Issa, 2016).

One of the issues that may distinguish interpreting in television from interpreting in other settings is the frequent or total, as in Poland, lack of a team partner. In spite of the fact that a particular assignment may not last long, due to the fast rate, informational density, or weight of the interpreted content, signed language interpreters may wish for language, technical, or emotional support from another professional (this may not be the case with pre-recorded interpreting, where the decision to consult fellow interpreters/deaf signers or to cooperate on the interpretation prior to its recording belongs to the interpreter).

Among the psycho-emotional factors that, according to scholars and practitioners, most noticeably contribute to the stressfulness of television interpreting are the exposure to a mass audience and the fear of failure in front of it (Pöchhacker, 2011; Kurz, 2002). Moreover, the fact that TV interpreters are perceived by many as "the face of the Deaf community, role models for those acquiring signed language" (Neves, 2007) and an image of the profession (Viaggio, 2001), adds to a further sense of responsibility.

Apart from the great diversity of speakers and audiences of television interpreting, interpreters have to deal with a wide array of topics and speech genres. It is particularly visible in the case of the news programmes, but also debates or talk shows. It requires exceptional flexibility, broad world knowledge, and quick reactions. Interpreters need to switch from topic to topic sometimes within an instance and they must orientate themselves nearly expertly. The particularly high expectations of the viewers (Moreau, 1998; Kurz, 2002) do not make the interpreters' work any easier.

Bearing in mind all of the above and considering the scarcity or even the lack of specialised education or training for interpreters working on TV (de Wit et al., 2020), it comes as no surprise that signed language interpreting in television settings calls for only the most fluent and experienced interpreters (Pöchhacker, 2011) – those who are very special amongst those who are already special (Bros-Brann, 1994). High language fluency and extensive interpreting experience are undeniably the two features that contribute to the interpreter's success in TV interpreting. They are discussed as such in the literature and among practitioners (see the results section below). However, the participants of the present study point out that the third factor that ensures successful interpreting performance is preparation.

3. "By failing to prepare, you are preparing to fail"[5]

Quotations such as the one above emphasise the need for preparation prior to all sorts of ventures. Interpreting scholars and practitioners subscribe to this notion no less fervently than Benjamin Franklin, indicating that the time when many would agree that "interpreters are born not made" (Herbert, 1978 after Stern & Liu, 2019) is long gone in the area of Interpreting Studies.

5 A quote attributed to Benjamin Franklin by *The Minneapolis Tribune* (Page 10, Column 2, Minneapolis, Minnesota) https://quoteinvestigator.com/2018/07/08/plan/ (Accessed 3 February 2023).

Preparation is a vital tenet of a majority of interpreters' codes of ethics and professional standards (Nicodemus et al., 2014), a fundamental principle advocated by educators and endorsed by interpreters' professional organisations:

> If ensuring proper working conditions is the first pillar of quality in conference interpreting, diligent preparation is the second. (…) A conference interpreter needs to have as good a knowledge of the terrain as any trekker heading into the Himalayas. (AIIC, 2016: 6)

The ever growing awareness of the complexity of interpreting nurtures the belief that preparation is an indispensable part of interpreter's work. The necessity to prepare before an assignment stems from the need to ensure the highest possible quality of interpretation (Mathers, 1999). The significant role of preparation in achieving it is emphasised particularly in relation to conference or platform interpreting, but also in any settings where the interpreter has to deal with texts that may be challenging with respect to terminology (medical encounters), density (academic lectures), or potential consequences (court trials). Television is definitely one such demanding setting.

As some of the more recent studies reveal, preparation increases accuracy of interpreting (Díaz-Galaz et al., 2015) and helps reduce stress related to exposure to a mass audience (Pöchhacker, 2011). These theoretical findings are reflected in what practitioners reveal about the role of preparation in their interpreting routines:

> Going into a job without receiving any preparation or having any idea of the content puts me on the back foot. I feel worried that something will come up which will be beyond my comprehension or life-experience, and this psychological stress adds to the physical burden of the job. I might also feel tense about possible humiliation of being unable to function in front of an audience. (Knox, 2006: 184) [6]

Calls for and guidance on interpreter preparation come in a wide range of forms and levels, from professional and occupational standards[7], documents regulating interpreting services[8], educational materials[9], to professional

6 In spite of the fact that the author of the quotation is an academic interpreter, her attitude overlaps with what participants of the survey report when enumerating reasons for undertaking preparation for their interpreting assignments in TV settings.

7 NOS (2017), "National Occupational Standards for interpreting", Section 1 – Access your ability to undertake an interpreting assignment. Available at: https://www.ukstandards.org.uk/PublishedNos-old/CFAINT01.pdf (Accessed 4 February 2023).

8 *ISO 18841:2018 Interpreting services – General requirements and recommendations*, https://www.iso.org/obp/ui/#iso:std:iso:18841:ed-1:v1:en (Accessed 4 February 2023).

9 A presentation delivered by Barbara Dumara in a series of lectures for the European Masters of Conference Interpreting programme held at the Institute of Applied

blogs[10]. However, academic publications on preparation, especially in the field of signed language interpreting, are not that numerous.

Witter-Merithew (2001) and Winston and Monikowski (2005) wrote about discourse mapping – a form of text analysis that can be considered a useful preparation strategy. It consists of visualising the text the interpreter is about to interpret in the form of a map of relations between its context, content and language, thereby helping achieve equivalence between the source and target languages in those three areas.

Stone (2009) discussed the preparation by deaf and hearing British Sign Language interpreters/translators working in television settings in the broader context of what he called a "Deaf community translation model" (ibid.: 172). Amidst similar and differing patterns of preparation in the two groups of interpreters/translators with respect to different types of texts – spontaneous and scripted – he indicated rehearsing as an especially effective form of preparation.

Dean and Pollard (2013) refer to preparation as a powerful control that can be used to deal with the demands of TV interpreting. According to their theory, while at work interpreters face various demands (environmental, interpersonal, paralinguistic, and intrapersonal) that may affect the outcome of their interpreting. In order to perform their work successfully, they need to control these demands, for example by taking specific actions before, during and after an assignment. Predicting the potential demands of a particular assignment is a form of preparation that may help them through difficult situations.

The most comprehensive study on preparation strategies the author has encountered was the one conducted by Nicodemus et al. (2014). The researchers analysed strategies employed by American Sign Language interpreters in preparation for rendering President Obama's inaugural address. The authors identified the most common strategies and evaluated the effect they had on the interpreting output. Although they discovered many similarities among the strategies employed by the participants of their study, they did not observe a standard approach or good practice.

As presented above, there is a growing body of literature available in relation to both signed language interpreting in television settings and the preparation

---

Linguistics, University of Warsaw, https://www.emcinterpreting.org/emci/resources/theory-interpreting/preparation-interpreting-assignment (Accessed: 3 February 2023).

10 An interpreting blog by Jonathan Downie https://www.integritylanguages.co.uk/2017/08/29/another-look-behind-the-scenes-of-conference-interpreting/ (Accessed 4 February 2023).

towards it. To the author's knowledge, however, apart from the abovementioned study by Stone (2009), hardly any research has been conducted on the combination of the two issues.

4. Study

The aim of the present study was to explore preparation strategies employed by signed language interpreters working in television settings in different European countries. The survey questionnaire designed for the purpose of this study was to explore the approaches of signed language interpreters to the notion of preparation and its place in their daily interpreting practice. Furthermore, it was to help identify similarities and differences in interpreters' preparations with respect to the amount of time available prior to an interpreting assignment, specific activities they engage in prior to their assignments, and motivation, among others.

The study was exploratory in nature, hence designed with no prior hypotheses in mind. One of the rationales underpinning the research was to provide a source of good practices as well as pedagogically-relevant information for signed language interpreters and educators.

4.1. Research method and procedure

For the purpose of this study, an online questionnaire was designed using the LimeSurvey website. It was piloted by 3 English-speaking signed language interpreters (2 from Poland and 1 from a different country). Following their feedback, some minor changes regarding the order of the questions or their wording were introduced. Next, using network and snowball sampling techniques (Hale & Napier, 2013) an invitation with the link to the questionnaire was distributed among professional interpreter organisations and via personal contacts all over Europe. The questionnaire was available online from April to June and in November of 2019. Interestingly, although the study targeted European signed language interpreters, the invitation with the link reached beyond Europe and the questionnaire was completed by an American citizen. As it was a single case, it was included in the total number of returns.

The language of the questionnaire was written English. The questionnaire consisted of a total of 24 questions covering three main areas: (1) demographic and professional information, (2) participants' understanding of and attitude towards preparation, and (3) methods and strategies used for preparation. The questions were both close- and open-ended, with some allowing for additional comments in an "other" option, others could be bypassed, one question required respondents to rank the options listed in the question, and in the final question of the survey participants were also invited to share their general comments regarding preparation.

The collected survey data were exported from LimeSurvey to MS Excel. The total number of returned questionnaires was 113, out of which 83 were complete. The incomplete ones were discarded. Each respondent was then given a unique identifying number, e.g., I01, I02, I03… I83. The data collected, being both numerical and descriptive in nature, were subjected to quantitative as well as qualitative analysis conducted by means of the MS Excel spreadsheet and a word processor. Qualitative data were subjected to thematic analysis and coding for quantification.

4.2. Limitations

The method of self-administered questionnaires while having many obvious advantages, such as widespread distribution or quick and easy completion, is also known for its limitations (Hale & Napier, 2013). First of all, as the respondents complete the questionnaires on their own, they may find some questions vague or confusing, and the researcher will not be there to provide explanations to dispel their doubts. As a result, participants may sometimes provide responses that do not fit the purpose of the study or become discouraged and abandon the questionnaire. In a similar vein, because the questionnaire requires some time to process, especially its open-ended questions, respondents may not have enough time or will to engage in the process. That may negatively affect the return rate. In the present study, the return rate was not high, which is also one of the reasons why its results cannot be generalised: a small sample of a population cannot be considered representative. It must also be borne in mind that when completing questionnaires respondents *report* what they do/did, and not necessarily what they actually do/did.

Evident limitation of the study is the lack of a clear distinction between preparation for live programmes and pre-recorded ones that could help identify some standard approaches among interpreters when preparing for interpreting these two types of programmes. Finally, a higher number of deaf respondents could also help explore similarities and differences among strategies undertaken by hearing and deaf interpreters to inform educational practices and facilitate collaboration between these two groups.

4.3. Findings

4.3.1. Participants

The survey was addressed to signed language interpreters working in television settings. As presented in Figure 1, it was completed by 83 individuals from 30 countries.

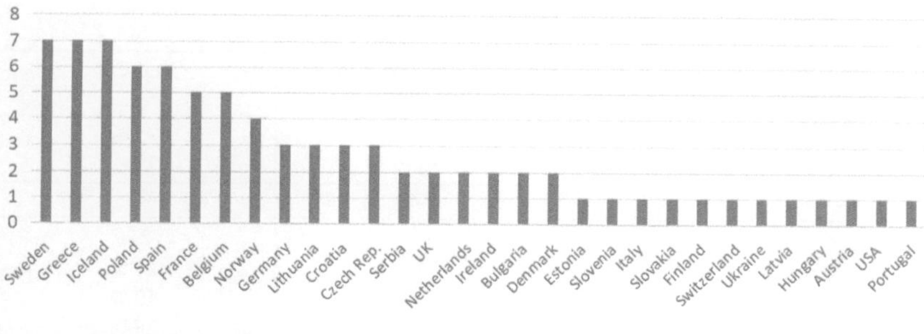

Figure 1. Number of responses by country

Their demographic and professional data are presented in Tables 1 and 2 respectively. As expected, given other studies and reports on signed language interpreter communities (Cokely, 1984; Bontempo et al., 2006; Kalata-Zawłocka, 2017), the majority of participants were female (76 %). Similarly, nearly all interpreters were hearing (94 %). The explanation of this tendency may be at least twofold: in many countries where deaf interpreters do not have access to education and professionalisation on par with their hearing colleagues, they have not been recognised as a professional group (Boudreault, 2005). Consequently, as in Poland, there may be very few deaf professionals working as signed language interpreters. Another reason for deaf interpreters being so poorly represented in this study may be the specific nature of the television setting. The population of deaf individuals working as interpreters is generally smaller than that of hearing individuals; therefore, those who manage to pursue careers in television are even fewer. Again, in some countries, the UK and its BBC station being an example, deaf interpreters are as valued as their hearing colleagues (Stone, 2009). In countries such as Poland, however, where only a small fraction of all interpreting assignments in different settings are completed by deaf professionals, and where signed language interpreting on television performed by hearing professionals is a newly-established practice, TV stations are not open-minded about employing deaf individuals.

The participants were aged 23–64 (M = 42, SD = 8.69). Their education was predominantly university-level with occasional cases of vocational training, secondary, or even primary education. 9 (11 %) participants did not specify their level of education. 23 (28 %) interpreters declared having acquired their signed language at home, 17 (20 %) as heritage signers,[11] and 6 (7 %) having learnt it from other family members (grandparents, siblings, children).

Table 1. Participants' demographic data

Gender	**Number of participants (N = 83)**	**Percent**
Female	63	76 %
Male	20	24 %
Age		
18–25	2	2 %
26–35	20	24 %
36–45	33	40 %
46–55	23	28 %
56–65	5	6 %
Audiological status		
Hearing	78	94 %
Deaf	5	6 %
Education		
PhD	2	2 %
MA or BA degree	65	78 %
Vocational training	1	1 %
Secondary education	5	6 %
Primary education	1	1 %
Unspecified	9	11 %
Signed language background		
Deaf family members	23	28 %
- parents	17	20 %
- other	6	7 %
Education and Deaf community	60	72 %

With few exceptions, participants in the study were mostly experienced interpreters, actively practising from 1 to 38 years (M = 16, SD = 7.88). This

11 A term introduced by Napier (2021) in place of the formerly used term CODA (Children of Deaf Adults) to refer to hearing people having deaf parents.

appears to confirm a view expressed by many respondents that television interpreting requires extensive prior experience in a multitude of settings. Participants' experience in television interpreting ranged from less than 1 year to 33 years (M = 8.15, SD = 6.74). The majority of them (N = 67, 81 %) worked more or less on a regular basis – from every day (N = 25, 30 %), through a few times a week (N = 19, 23 %) or once a week (N = 10, 12 %), to a few times a month (N = 9, 11 %), or once a month (N = 4, 5 %). 16 (19 %) interpreters reported performing television interpreting occasionally. Slightly more than a half (N = 44, 53 %) respondents declared a certain degree of regularity as to the time of day at which they worked.

Television interpreting is a very broad term that encompasses different types of aired programmes. The three programmes most commonly interpreted by the participants in this study were TV news (83 %), public/political debates (66 %), and interviews (53 %). Other types of broadcasts they had interpreted are summarised in Table 2. Naturally, in each country, different types of programmes may be available for interpreting, depending on the existing laws that regulate the provision of television content. In other words, types of interpreted programmes may be country-specific.

Table 2. Types of programmes interpreted by the participants

Types of interpreted programmes[12]	Number of interpreters (N = 83)	Percent
News	69	83 %
Public/political debates	55	66 %
Interviews	44	53 %
Political announcements/speeches	42	50 %
Cultural programmes	34	41 %
Sports programmes	28	34 %
Talk shows	25	30 %
Programmes for children	23	28 %
Social campaigns	21	25 %
Knowledge-based contests	17	20 %
TV series	15	18 %
Films	13	16 %

(*Continued*)

12 A multiple-choice question.

Table 2. Continued

Types of interpreted programmes[12]	Number of interpreters (N = 83)	Percent
Commercials	12	14 %
Programmes about wildlife	11	13 %
Emergency announcements	10	12 %
Talent shows	7	8 %
Religious programmes	3	4 %

4.3.2. Preparation – General data

Following the part of the questionnaire devoted to demographic and professional information, there were questions aimed at establishing the participants' general understanding of the concept of preparation, its place in their interpreting practice, and their attitudes towards it. To begin with, the respondents were asked how they had learnt about the need to prepare, and different preparation methods. Most frequently (N = 21, 25 %), interpreters declared that they had learnt about preparation on their own, or through professional development (courses, workshops, etc.) (N = 14, 17 %). A group of 13 (16 %) participants became familiar with preparation through a combination of university education, professional development, and their own work. For 12 (14 %) individuals, professional development was the only source of knowledge about preparation. In the "other" option, 9 (11 %) respondents admitted that they had learnt about preparation from their colleagues. University education combined with professional development equipped 6 (7 %) interpreters with knowledge about preparation, and 5 (6 %) more learnt about it at university alone. The remaining 3 (4 %) individuals mentioned different combinations of options.

As regards the frequency with which respondents declared preparation for their interpreting assignments in television settings, 52 (63 %) interpreters selected the option "always". 24 (29 %) respondents admitted they "usually" prepare before TV interpreting. According to 4 interpreters (5 %), their preparation takes place "from time to time", in 2 (2 %) cases it occurs "rarely", and in 1 case (1 %), "whenever time and materials are available".

Out of 74 (89 %) participants who were able to estimate the average amount of time spent on preparation before interpreting on TV, 16 (22 %) participants reported that it was around 1 hour, for the same number of respondents it took around 30 minutes. A group of 15 (20 %) interpreters claimed that their preparation took on average 2 hours, and 12 (19 %) individuals spent around 2.5 hours to prepare. 7 (9 %) people prepared for around 15 minutes on average, and

5 (7 %) for around 1.5 hours. For 3 interpreters (4%), the average preparation time was as much as 3 hours. For 8 (10 %) participants, the preparation time varied so greatly that they found it impossible to provide any estimates and wrote "it depends". 1 (1 %) person did not provide any answer. To sum up, the mean reported preparation time was 83 minutes (SD =21.5).

4.3.3. Preparation strategies

The main aim of the study was to learn what preparation strategies interpreters use prior to their interpreting assignments in TV settings. Respondents were asked about it in an open-ended question in which they were required to write what they actually do when preparing for their television assignments. The surveyed interpreters reported engaging in three types of activities that could be identified as (1) *pre-assignment strategies*, (2) *on-assignment strategies*, and (3) *post-assignment strategies*. The distinction is not always clear-cut, as some of the strategies may fall into more than one category. Hence, the proposed taxonomy below should be considered tentative.

Pre-assignment strategies

This group encompasses activities in which the respondents engaged usually much ahead of the assignment, often prior to the arrival at the TV studio. These could be divided into four categories:

(1) *Keeping abreast with the general news* (reading newspapers, listening to the radio, watching TV news, etc.) – this means both staying up-to-date with current international, national, and local events on a daily basis, as well as on the very day of the assignment (e.g., a press review), in some cases even minutes before it. Engagement in such activities was declared by 21 (25 %) respondents.
(2) *Selecting appropriate attire and makeup/hairdo* was reported by 7 (8 %) interpreters. As regards the choice of clothing, it nearly always took place at home, but makeup or hairdo were often, although not always, reported as being taken care of on-site, by television specialists.
(3) *Sleep and diet* – activities not necessarily connected with interpreting, at least at first sight, but by 4 (5 %) interpreters considered important aspects of their preparation that contribute to sustaining their mental condition and stamina. They usually take place outside the TV studio, but some interpreters mentioned strengthening themselves with snacks or drinks while on the job (obviously, not in front of the camera).
(4) *Keeping fit* – 2 (2 %) respondents declared taking care of their physical condition to help them endure work-related stress and work long/late hours.

1 (1 %) person reported performing some light physical exercise (stretching, warming up hands and fingers) just before beginning interpreting.

On-assignment strategies

Classified in this group are activities that pertain more directly to the assignment *per se*, which is often, though not always, undertaken inside a television studio. They can be further divided into several narrower sub-categories of (1) *content-related strategies*, (2) *context-related strategies*, (3) *language-related strategies*, (4) *interpreting-related strategies*, (5) *venue-related strategies*, and (6) *self-centred strategies*. Again, some of the sub-categories may overlap, thus the division is tentative and may be a subject of further discussion.

(1) *Content-related strategies* include activities undertaken by interpreters to familiarise themselves with the content of the programme they are about to interpret: its formula and character, dynamics, purpose, etc. 57 (69 %) respondents reported *reading the text/script of the programme* and 38 (46 %) *watched/listened to the pre-recorded programme* when available. Some (N = 5, 6 %) would also try to *find out what additional materials will be shown or discussed* during the programme (visual presentations, videos, audio-recordings, etc.).

(2) *Context-related strategies* involve *research for background or further knowledge* on the issues covered in the programme, for example to learn about the speakers, make connections between people and events, arrange events in chronological order, explore unknown concepts and topics, learn/check/recall names, dates, etc. 29 (35 %) respondents declared engaging themselves in similar activities. 2 (2 %) interpreters made an effort to *watch previous programme releases* or similar programmes, to better understand/remember arguments, comments, or events.

(3) *Language-related strategies* imply activities such as *terminological preparation* in one or both languages: consulting dictionaries, preparing glossaries, finding definitions, etc. 33 (40 %) participants declared doing that before their assignments. More than one-third (N = 29, 35 %) of the surveyed interpreters mentioned *consulting their deaf and hearing colleagues* for advice regarding lexical and grammatical issues. To cope with the amount of new information to learn, process, and remember in the course of preparation, some interpreters (N = 4, 5 %) resorted to *mnemonic techniques* in relation to dates and names. 1 person (1 %) *practised fingers*pelling some of them.

(4) *Interpreting-related strategies* encompass three types of activities related to the interpreting process. Some interpreters (N = 15, 18 %) *practised or*

rehearsed their interpreting before the actual assignment, for example by having a script of the programme in front of them. They would think about different strategies or techniques they could employ to render a particular phrase, collocation, metaphor, joke, etc. They would try using their signing space by placing different referents in it or coming up with alternate versions of signed utterances to select the best one. Some pondered about how they could incorporate background or multimodal presentations into their interpreting. A few of the respondents (N = 8, 10 %) declared doing similar activities mentally, *visualising the interpreting* process. 5 (6 %) individuals *watched interpretations of similar programmes* done by their colleagues for inspiration.

(5) *Self-centred strategies* are activities aimed at *focusing on one's own wellbeing and state of mind*, such as positive self-talk, concentration, mindfulness, relaxation (meditation, breathing exercises), or silence. These types of activities were mentioned by 7 (8 %) surveyed interpreters. Naturally, mental preparation can be practised long in advance of the assignment (at home, on the journey to the TV studio, during make-up) as well as just before facing the camera. 3 (4 %) people admitted that they like to *keep good atmosphere* in the workplace, as this reduces stress and helps them focus on the task ahead.

(6) *Venue-related strategies* include different types of *technical arrangements* that interpreters made to get ready in terms of the space and conditions (including their technical aspects) in which they were about to interpret, such as positioning themselves in front of the camera (framing, focus), adjusting earphones, checking for sound and lighting, etc. 6 (7 %) respondents reported engaging in these activities.

Post-assignment strategies

As the name suggests, post-assignment strategies are employed once the interpreting has finished. They were not very common among the participants of this study, still they seem worth mentioning.

(1) *Asking for feedback*, that is requesting evaluation of the performed interpreting, either from other interpreters on the team or those not involved in the assignment, or from deaf viewers. This activity was mentioned by 17 (20 %) participants of the study. For 2 (12 %) of this group, it meant cooperation with a deaf consultant/advisor that took place on a regular basis.

(2) *Reflection* – recalling those aspects of the assignment that either appeared problematic and unsatisfactory or turned out successful (e.g., decisions,

reactions, solutions). 10 (12 %) participants of the study reported *watching their recorded interpretations* with the aim of analysing the outcome, 2 (2 %) individuals would *write down the troublesome fragments* for further analysis and consultations with colleagues, 1 (1 %) person admitted to writing down everything they were happy about in their interpreting, as examples of good practice for future assignments.

(3) *Self-critique* – an activity reported by 3 (4 %) interpreters that means critical evaluation of their work both in terms of the overall effect as well as particular decisions made during interpreting. Sometimes it involved chastising oneself for a mistake or failure.

Importantly, out of the 83 surveyed interpreters, the majority (N = 75, 90 %) declared engaging themselves in more than one of the abovementioned activities from different categories, which sometimes resulted in very elaborate strategies. As few as 8 (10 %) individuals mentioned only one of the activities as their preparation.

Apart from the activities that were categorised above as preparation strategies, respondents mentioned at least four others that they believed were important in terms of their interpreting performances in television settings. They were not counted as part of preparation by the respondents, and the author is not convinced that they belong to any of the abovementioned categories, however, they may be considered preparatory in nature, especially in a broader perspective. Moreover, interpreters underlined the beneficial effects of these on the overall quality of their interpreting performance on TV, their self-assurance, and on their stress levels. Additional activities undertaken by the respondents encompassed the following:

(1) *engaging themselves in continuous professional development* in the area of language skills, interpreting skills, and other subjects (N = 17, 20 %),
(2) *exchanging and sharing interpreting experiences with other interpreters* (N = 9, 11 %),
(3) *watching and analysing other interpreters' work*, for example to expand their array of strategies, visualisation techniques, signing styles (N = 7, 8 %),
(4) *staying in touch with the Deaf community* in order to be up to date with the latest developments and issues important for the community as well as sign vocabulary currently in use – an activity that helps interpreters provide more culturally-adequate renditions (N = 5, 6 %).

Participants of the survey revealed that their preparation strategies may vary, depending on many factors, most of all related to the programme to be interpreted: its linguistic complexity (N = 67, 81 %), type (N = 59, 71 %), subject matter (N = 55, 66 %), and the level of specialisation of its content (N = 55, 66 %). Over half of the respondents (N = 47, 57 %) pointed out that their preparation depends on the amount of time available before the interpreted programme - as many of them have busy schedules and other assignments, sometimes they are informed about the interpreting on very short notice. The surveyed interpreters admitted that their preparation is further conditioned by their interpreting experience (N = 39, 47 %), and sometimes also by their own physical condition and mood (N = 17, 20 %) (it may take more time when they are tired, did not have enough sleep the night before, etc.). Finally, for 3 (4 %), individuals it was the time during which preparatory materials were available that influenced their preparation.

Interestingly, as many as 69 (83 %) of the surveyed interpreters claimed that their preparation strategies had evolved with time. According to 10 (11 %) individuals, their preparation strategies had remained the same despite time passing by. 3 (4 %) respondents noticed both some stable elements in their preparation, activities in which they engaged in regardless of the assignment, as well as differences, especially due to changes that had occurred over the time of their interpreting practice (technological, educational, social, etc.), but also due to acquired routine, or flexibility gained with experience.

5. Final thoughts on preparation

In one of the final questions of the survey, respondents were asked to evaluate the significance of preparation when compared to other factors affecting the quality of interpreting. To be precise, the question included a catalogue of suggested factors, including preparation, that the interpreters were to arrange in order of importance. Out of 8 factors (see Table 3 below) the three most important ones turned out to be: signed language fluency (N = 65, 78 %), interpreting experience (N = 62, 75 %), and preparation (N = 49, 59 %).

Table 3. Significance of preparation in relation to other factors affecting the quality of interpreting

Factors affecting quality of interpretation	Number of responses (N = 83)	Percent
Signed language fluency	65	78 %
Interpreting experience	62	75 %
Preparation	49	59 %
World knowledge	26	31 %
Familiarity with the subject matter	18	22 %
Immunity to stress	11	13 %
Speed of interpreting	10	12 %
Quick reactions	8	10 %

When asked why they prepare for their interpreting assignments in television settings, 33 (40 %) surveyed interpreters replied that they do it in order *to provide interpreting services of high quality*. Many of them emphasised that it was their responsibility to provide deaf viewers with full access to information. Sometimes, based on the interpretation, deaf people may want to make some political decisions (e.g., during elections) or other life choices, sometimes their safety depends on it. In general, it is their right to receive high quality renditions. In the same vein, 15 (18 %) respondents believed that due to preparation, they are able *to ensure renditions that are more linguistically precise, clear, and culturally appropriate*. According to this group of participants, deaf viewers deserve to fully understand the interpreted information and enjoy receiving it without struggle.

Other responses reflected a more interpreter-centred approach. According to some interpreters (N = 12, 14 %), preparation provided them with the *sense of security, readiness, calm, made them feel easy and in control of the situation*. It helped them cope better with the high speed of information delivery (N = 12, 14 %), as well as other *challenges typical of television interpreting*, such as the diversity of subjects, speakers, texts, linguistic complexity and density of texts, lack of sign vocabulary, proper names, numbers, dates, etc. (N = 12, 14 %). For 11 (13 %) respondents preparation *facilitated understanding of the general situation* in which they found themselves, *provided context knowledge* that increased their orientation in the issues discussed, procedures, protocols, and rules.

9 (11 %) individuals reported the *sense of pressure and responsibility* resulting from exposure to a very large and very diverse audience. They perceived preparation as a means to cope with it. Likewise, 6 (7 %) participants of the study declared that preparation was very helpful in *lowering their stress level* and coping with persistent thoughts of being evaluated (N = 4, 5 %).

Finally, for 11 (13 %) respondents, preparation was *an integral part and the expression of their professionalism*. 7 (8 %) more individuals confirmed that by stating, "I prepare for any interpreting assignment and TV interpreting is not different", (I18) and according *to* 3 (4 %) others, by preparing for an assignment they set good examples for other interpreters.

6. Conclusions

The survey findings have shown that signed language interpreters are generally well aware of the challenges of interpreting in television settings. Their responses indicate a strong sense of responsibility towards their profession and wish to provide deaf viewers with full access to the information they convey as interpreters. With this in mind, they treat preparation as a fundamental part of their interpreting practice, third, after language fluency and experience, as among the most significant factors that affect the quality of their interpreting.

Interpreters learn about the need to prepare via different routes, sometimes in the course of formal education, or on the job. Their preparation strategies usually evolve with them – through experience and continuous development, for many (nearly two-thirds of the respondents), preparation is an indispensable element of their interpreting assignments (with the average preparation time exceeding an hour).

The responses collected by means of the survey provide an overview of the preparation strategies employed by signed language interpreters working in television settings. They demonstrate that interpreters diversify their preparation strategies with regard to the anticipated level of linguistic complexity of the programme, its type and subject matter, as well as their own skills, knowledge, and wellbeing. Many of them develop preparation strategies that include different types of activities, that may be roughly classified as (1) *pre-assignment*, (2) *on-assignment*, and (3) *post-assignment strategies*. The division cannot be considered definitive, as some of the activities may be undertaken long before, during, as well as after the assignment. Some of the identified strategies, such as eating and sleeping well before the assignment, practising positive self-talk, rehearsing interpreting, or visualising it, are consistent with those mentioned in the literature on preparation.

Despite differences in languages and cultures represented by the participants of the survey, its findings have revealed that there are many similarities among the identified preparation strategies. Furthermore, it was observed that the majority of the surveyed interpreters used a combination of strategies, even though no common approach or pattern was identified.

To the author's knowledge, this is the first study aimed at exploring and documenting preparation strategies employed by signed language interpreters working in television settings in different European countries. Further in-depth research is needed on this topic in order to support interpreters in their goals to provide high quality interpreting services to deaf viewers.

References

AIIC. (2016). "Practical guide for professional conference interpreters", https://aiic.org/document/547/AIICWebzine_Apr2004_2_Practical_guide_for_professional_conference_interpreters_EN.pdf (Accessed 2 February 2023).

Bontempo, K., Napier, J., & Lenaham, M. (2006). Sign language interpreting in Australia: An overview. *VIEWS: Magazine of the Registry of Interpreters for the Deaf*, Vol. 2006, April edition: 1, 7, 8, 45. Alexandria: RID.

Boudreault, P. (2005). Deaf interpreters. In Janzen, T. (Ed.), *Topics in Signed Language Interpreting*. Amsterdam: John Benjamins, 323–356.

Bros-Brann, E. (1993). Simultaneous interpretation and the media: Interpreting live for television. In Picked, C. (Ed.), *Translation – The Vital Link*. London, Institute of Translation and Interpreting 11, 267–271.

Bros-Brann E. (1994). Interpreting live on television: Some examples taken from French television. Unpublished report at UIMP course The Interpreter as a Communicator, La Coruna, 26–29/7/1994.

Cokely, D. (1984). *Towards a Sociolinguistic Model of the Interpreting Process: Focus on ASL and English*. Washington, DC: Georgetown University.

Dal Fovo, E. (2016). The interpreter's role in dialogue interpreting on television: A training method. In Bianchi, F. & Gesuato, S. (Eds.), *Pragmatic Issues in Specialised Communicative Contexts*. Leiden and Boston: Brill/Rodopi.

de Wit, M., Peréz, S. M., & Peterson, P. R. (2020). Sign language interpreting on TV and media: Sharing best practices. A report of the first European seminar, https://www.mayadewit.nl/publications (Accessed 3 February 2023)

Dean, R. K. & Pollard, R. Q. (2013). *The Demand Control Schema: Interpreting as a Practice Profession*. North Charleston, SC: Create Space Independent Publishing Platform.

Díaz-Galaz, S., Padilla, P., & Bajo, M. T. (2015). The role of advance preparation in simultaneous interpreting. *Interpreting. International Journal of Research and Practice in Interpreting*, 17(1), 1–25.

Gile, D. (1995). *Basic Concepts and Models for Interpreter and Translator Training*. Amsterdam: John Benjamins.

Gile, D. (2011). Errors, omissions and infelicities in broadcast interpreting: Preliminary findings from a case study. In Alvstad, C., Hild, A., & Tiselius, E. (Eds.), *Methods and Strategies of Process Research: Integrative Approaches in Translation Studies*. Amsterdam: John Benjamins, 201–218.

Hale, S. &,Napier, J. (2013). *Research Methods in Interpreting. A Practical Resource*. London–New York–New Delhi–Sydney: Bloomsbury Academic.

Herbert, J. (1952). *Manuel de l'interprète*. Genève: Georg.

Herbert, J. (1978). How conference interpretation grew, In Gerver, D. & Sinaiko, W. H. (Eds.), *Language interpretation and communication, Proceedings of the NATO Symposium on language interpretation and communication*, New York, Plenum, 5–10.

Issa, S. (2016). Challenges Facing Conference and Television Interpreters. A Thesis submitted to the Auckland University of Technology.

Kalata-Zawłocka, A. (2017). *Społeczne i językowe konteksty tłumaczenia języka migowego w Polsce*. Warszawa: Wydział Polonistyki Uniwersytetu Warszawskiego.

Knox, S. (2006). Sign Language interpreting in an academic setting: Preparation strategies and consideration, *SITES: New Series*, 3(1), 183–204.

Kurz, I. (1997). Getting the message across. Simultaneous interpreting for the media, In Snell-Hornby, M., Jettmarova, K., & Kaindl, K. (Eds.), *Translation as Intercultural Communication*. Amsterdam and Philadelphia: John Benjamins, 195–205.

Kurz I. (2002). Physiological stress responses during media and conference interpreting. In Garzone, G. & Viezzi, M. (Eds.), *Interpreting in the 21st Century. Challenges and Opportunities*. Amsterdam and Philadelphia: John Benjamins, 195–202.

Kurz, I. & Mikulasek, B. (2004). Television as a source of information for the deaf and hearing impaired. Captions and Sign Language on Austrian TV. *Meta* 49(1), 81–88.

Kusters, A., O'Brien, D., & De Meulder, M. (2017). Innovations in Deaf Studies: Critically mapping the field. In A. Kusters, M. De Meulder, & D. O'Brien (Eds.), *Innovations in Deaf Studies: The role of deaf scholars* (pp. 1–53). Palgrave: Basingstoke.

Ladd, P. (2007). Signs of change: Sign language and televisual media in the UK. In Cormack, M. & Hourigan, N. (Eds.) *Minority Language Media: Concepts, Critiques and Case Studies*. Bristol, Blue Ridge Summit: Multilingual Matters, 229–247.

Leeson, L. (2005). Making the effort in simultaneous interpreting: Some considerations for signed language interpreters. In Janzen, T. (Ed.), *Topics in Signed Language Interpreting: Theory and Practice.* Amsterdam and Philadelphia: John Benjamins, 5–68.

Leneham, M. (2007). Exploring power and ethnocentrism in sign language translation. *Babel: Journal of the AFMLTA*, 41(3), 4–12.

Mack, G. (2002). "Conference interpreters on the air: Live simultaneous interpreting on Italian television." In Gambier, Y. & Gotlieb, H. (Eds.),

(Multi)Media Translation. Concepts, Practices and Research. Amsterdam and Philadelphia: John Benjamins, 125–132.

Mäkipää, A. & Hämesalo, A. (1993). *Towards Full Participation and Equal Rights*. Helsinki: World Federation of the Deaf.

Mathers, C. (1999). Preparation: More than Just a Good Idea. *RID Views*, Vol. 16, Issue 8, Aug./Sept.

McKee, R. L. (2014). Breaking news: Sign language interpreters on television during natural disasters. *Intepreting*, 16(1), 107–130.

Moreau, H. (1998). L'interprétation sur la chaîne ARTE, In Gambier, Y. (Ed.), *Translating for the Media*. Turku: Painosalama OY, 225–229.

Moser-Mercer, B. (2003). Remote interpreting: Assessment of human factors and performance parameters. https://aiic.org/document/516/AIICWebzine_Summer2003_3_MOSER-MERCER_Remote_interpreting_Assessment_of_human_factors_and_performance_parameters_Original.pdf (Accessed 3 February 2023).

Napier, J. (2021). *Sign Language Brokering in Deaf-Hearing Families*. London: Palgrave MacMillan.

Napier, J. & Leeson, L. (2015). Sign/ed language interpreting. In Pöchhacker, F. (Ed.), *Routledge Encyclopedia of Interpreting Studies*. New York: Routledge, 376–381.

Neves, J. (2007). Of pride and prejudice. The divide between subtitling and sign language interpreting on television. *The Sign Language Translator and Interpreter*, 1(2), 1–24.

Nicodemus, B., Swabey, L., & Taylor, M. M. (2014). Preparation strategies used by American Sign Language-English interpreters to render President Barack Obama's inaugural address. *The Interpreters' Newsletter*, 19, 27–44.

NOS (2017). "National Occupational Standards for interpreting", Section 1 – Access your ability to undertake an interpreting assignment. Available at: https://www.ukstandards.org.uk/PublishedNos-old/CFAINT01.pdf (Accessed 4 February 2023).

Pignataro, C. (2011). Skilled-based and knowledge-based strategies in Television Interpreting. *The Interpreters' Newsletter*, 16, 81–98.

Pinhas, R. (1972). Les retombeés scientifiques des opérations 'Apollo' sur l'interprétation simultanée. *La linguistique* 8(1), 143–147.

Pöchhacker, F. (2011). Researching TV interpreting: Selected studies of US Presidential Material. *The Interpreters' Newsletter*, 16, 21–36.

Roberson, L. & Shaw, S. (Eds.). (2018). *Signed language interpreting in the 21st century: An overview of the profession*. Washington, DC: Gallaudet University Press.

Seleskovitch, D. (1997). Interview de Mme Arlette Morel, présidente de la Féderationnationale des sourds de France. *Meta*, 42(3), 560–63.

Serrano, O. J. (2011). Backstage conditions and interpreter's performance in live television interpreting: Quality, visibility and exposure. *The Interpreters' Newsletter*, 16,115–136.

Stern, L. & Liu, X. (2019). Interpreting studies. In Laviosa, S. & González-Davies, M. (Eds.), *The Routledge Handbook of Translation and Education*. London: Routledge.

Stone, C. (2009). *Toward a Deaf Translation Norm*. Washington, DC: Gallaudet University Press.

Strolz, B. (1992). *Theorie und Praxis des Simultandolmetschens. Argumente für einen kontextuellen Top-down-Ansatz der Verarbeitung und Produktion von Sprache*. Unpublished Dissertation, Universität Wien.

Strolz, B. (1997). Quality of media interpreting. A case study. In Gambier, Y., Gile, D., & Taylor, C. (Eds.), *Conference Interpreting: Current Trends in Research*. Amsterdam and Philadelphia: John Benjamins, 194–197.

Tsuruta, C. (2011). Broadcast interpreters in Japan: Bringing news to and from the world. *The Interpreter's Newsletter*, 16, 157–173.

Viaggio, S. (2001). Simultaneous interpreting for television and other media: Translation doubly constrained. In Y. Gambier & H. Gottlieb (Eds.), *(Multi)Media Translation. Concepts, Practices and Research*. Amsterdam and Philadelphia: John Benjamins, 23–3.

Winston, E. & Monikowski, C. (2005). Discourse mapping: The GPS of translation. In Roy, C. B. (Ed.), *Advances in Teaching Signed Language Interpreters*. Washington, DC: Gallaudet University Press, 49–77.

Witter-Merithew, A. (2001). Understanding the meaning of texts and reinforcing foundation skills through discourse analysis. In Nettles, C. (Ed.), *Tapestry of Our Worlds: Proceedings of the 17th National Conference of Registry of Interpreters for the Deaf*. RID, 177–192.

Wurm, S. (2010). *Translation across Modalities: The Practice of Translating Written Text into Recorded Signed Language – An Ethnographic Case Study*. PhD dissertation, Heriot-Watt University.

Xiao, X. & Li, F. (2013). Sign language interpreting on Chinese TV: A survey on user perspectives. *Perspectives*, 21(1), 100–116.

Heidi Salaets / Katalin Balogh

Chapter 7 Access to justice for vulnerable groups in society: Minors in Belgium as a case

Abstract: At the start of the DG Justice research projects on interpreter-mediated questioning of minors in 2012, we could not have foreseen that, ten years later, this would be so topical. Unfortunately, it is mainly wars but also ethnical, racial, religious and environmental challenges that make people flee, and amongst them many children. In this contribution, we will describe how we started our research by mapping out the field of interpreter-mediated questioning of minors (Co-Minor-IN/QUEST I); then how, in the second project (Co-Minor-IN/QUEST II), using an experimental approach, we asked minors and stakeholders about their experiences. We will also present the voices of vulnerable minors on communication issues they experienced (ChiLLS, Children in Legal Language Settings), as well as the website that was built and concluded in 2021. Finally, we will report on Interprofessional Education (IPE) a programme we organised for stakeholders involved in interpreter-mediated questioning of minors. In illustrating how we managed to have impact on the way stakeholders work with minors during an ImQM (interpreter-mediated questioning of minors)– including non-accompanied minors, like Ukrainian children recently – we wish to pay tribute to Małgorzata Tryuk as a highly dedicated researcher with a strong commitment.

Keywords: minors, interpreter-mediated questioning of minors (ImQM), vulnerability, foreign language vulnerability (FLV)

1. Introduction

As an interpreting and translation scholar, Małgorzata Tryuk has always paid close attention to vulnerable people in society and has shown abundantly how language barriers can add an extra layer of vulnerability, which we will define in this contribution as Foreign Language Vulnerability (FLV; see Salaets et al., 2023:125). The community interpreter is an actor who can empower people in precarious situations where FLV represents an extra barrier. Research and practice has shown, however, that an interpreter is not such a "miraculous" solution, because of a lack of professionalisation (Hale, 2015, 2007), hence a lack of trained interpreters in all kind of language combinations, the languages of lesser diffusion (LLDs) being the most scant as far as availability and training is concerned (Hlavac, 2013).

In her publications, Małgorzata Tryuk has largely focussed on community interpreting and the difficult road to professionalisation (Tryuk, 2007), more specifically to the delicate and heavily discussed topic in the literature of ethics for interpreters (Tryuk, 2015) and the interpreter's roles as perceived by users, be they medical doctors, magistrates or immigration officers (Tryuk, 2012, 2017) who all come in contact with potentially vulnerable people. In particular, she has united the topics mentioned in crisis and war situations (Tryuk, 2020), more specifically on interpreting and translation during Fascism and in Nazi concentration camps during World War II (Tryuk, 2021, 2016a, 2016b, 2010) where extreme vulnerability, unfortunately, was a daily reality in one of the most brutal periods in human history.

This is why, to pay tribute to such a respected scholar as Małgorzata Tryuk, we decided to highlight the concept of vulnerability in **foreign language (FL)-speaking minors**, presenting the concept of potential vulnerability in every individual as a metaphor:

> If an object is easily broken or damaged, we deal with it cautiously and treat it in a certain careful way. We even place a warning label on the box it is packed in or on the wrapping, reminding everyone who comes into contact with it, that it is fragile. We, human beings, 'subjects', although we have no warning label attached, are all fragile; […] some of us are even more fragile, or, to use another term, more vulnerable than others due to certain personal or external characteristics and features. (Virág, 2015, pp. 77–78)

This notion applies particularly to children. As Virág notes, "[…] a child is regarded as different from an adult not only in quantity, but also in quality, characterized by the lack of social, biological, sexual (and legal) maturity. This immaturity is, in general, what makes minors vulnerable in most social contexts including, in particular, legal procedures" (Virág, 2015: 78). Of course, childhood is not a homogeneous period and is characterised by several developmental stages (Virág, 2015: 78), which for lack of space we will not go into here.

In what follows, we will briefly present the results of our research by referring to former publications which contain more details, while focussing on interprofessional education (IPE) as a way to impact society and strengthen outreach in research, a good example of which we have found in Małgorzata Tryuk. We will show that solutions to overcoming language barriers when working with minors are within arm's reach through collaboration with professionals, which should always be a solution in the best interest of the child to enhance their resilience in stressful, frightening, awkward, lonely and other situations.

2. Co-Minor I

In the first research project (JUST/2011/JPEN/AG/2961, with financial support from the Criminal Justice Programme of the European Commission DG Justice), which dates back to 2012–2014, we firstly wished to map out the "landscape" of interpreter-mediated questioning of minors in Europe, including collaboration patterns among the stakeholders, firstly police officers, youth judges and lawyers, prosecutors, psychologists, child-support workers amongst each other, but then mostly with interpreters. This gave birth to the acronym of the project(s): *Cooperation in interpreter-mediated questioning of minors* (Co-Minor-IN/QUEST) and the first mapping of interpreter-mediated questioning of minors (ImQM) in several EU member states (at that time still involving the UK (Scotland), next to Belgium, France, Hungary and Italy). We wanted to verify if the common belief made sense, namely that minors do not have a language problem since they learn languages quickly. A lot of research existed already on questioning minors (Lamb et al., 2000, 2007, 2008, 2011; Lamb & Fauchier, 2001[1]), but little had been published at that time on situations where minors do not speak the official language of the authorities and, by extension, the person they sometimes need to talk to (a social worker, (forensic) psychologist, etc.) (Matthias & Zaal, 2002; Fontes, 2009, 2010; Keselman et al., 2010a, 2010b).

More specifically, we wanted to present a needs analysis of the parties involved in the questioning of children by sending questionnaires to police officers, legal actors (magistrates, lawyers, prosecutors etc.), child-support workers, psychologists, interpreters and any other possible stakeholder (e.g. paediatricians). For details about methodology and extensive findings we refer to Salaets and Balogh (2015a) freely available on our website, like other materials (e.g. the used questionnaire)[2].

According to our analysis of the respondents' answers, the "common belief" was not validated, since we have to keep in mind that minor victims especially

---

1 Just to name a few: Lamb & colleagues have developed the *National Institute of Child Health and Human Development (NICHD)* Protocol on International Evidence-Based Investigative Interviewing of Children. This research-based technique is used in many countries, amongst which Belgium. Information on the NICHD protocol is available at https://nichdprotocol.com/ where also translations of the questioning techniques and tactics are available (https://nichdprotocol.com/the-nichd-protocol/). Unfortunately, there is no Polish version yet.

2 https://www.arts.kuleuven.be/english/rg_interpreting_studies/research-projects/co_minor_in_quest

have difficulty expressing what their experiences are in whatever language, even in their mother tongue or preferred language[3]. If the newly acquired language can be used as a "shield" to lessen the emotional intensity, then an interpreter is not the answer. However, the challenge is for the interviewer to discover this, which is not an easy task that maybe cannot be solved even after only one encounter. Anyway, if a child has not had the chance to learn another language than the home language (because of recent arrival, a lack of education, impairments or for many other reasons), a professional interpreter can be a solution. The problem at that time (2012–2014) was that no legal interpreter was trained to do so – at least not in Belgium.

The findings of the first project can be summarised in four eye-catching keywords that drew our attention: the need for more **time**, **trust** building, **briefing/teamwork** and **training** which can be both specialised training for a professional group or joint training for all professional groups together. This is not surprising, because these are key elements that are unmistakably interdependent: more time before the interview ensures a better briefing and clear agreements accordingly on the teamwork that all professionals in an ImQM will fulfil during the interview; more time and good teamwork, where professionals trust in each other's competences and professionalism will assure that this trust is displayed to the minor. But before knowing and understanding the relevant (re) actions and competences of all the professionals present in "the room" (be they the social worker, the psychologist, the legal actor and/or the interpreter) and before being confident about their own performance, it could be good to undergo some additional training.

But before organising that, we decided to at least share the findings concerning the experiences of several actors and stakeholders in an ImQM in the freely available volume *Children and Justice: overcoming language barriers*[4] (Balogh & Salaets, 2015), where signed and spoken languages interpreters, interpreting scholars, a psychotherapist, a chief inspector of the Federal Police, a child

3 "a language learned after the early childhood years can serve as a protective psychic defence (de Zulueta, 1995). It can help clients to talk about traumatic events. If, for example, the trauma happened in one language, an individual may find that they are able to talk about it in one of their other languages with a lessening of the emotional intensity, which, in turn, makes it bearable" (Costa, 2010: 16).

4 https://www.arts.kuleuven.be/tolkwetenschap/projecten/co_minor_in_quest/children-and-justice

rights expert, a family mediator, (forensic) psychologists, an expert on learning difficulties and intellectual disabilities and a youth lawyer took part[5].

To meet basic and first needs of all parties involved, we made leaflets with recommendations in five languages (Dutch, English, French, Italian and Hungarian) on what to do before, during and after an encounter with a minor during an ImQM[6]. These three parts are then further subdivided in two sub-headings namely *for interpreters* and for *other professionals* (i.e. the primary participants who are in the room with the child, and the other primary non-professional participant). Briefing from "both sides" before the encounter is indicated as an essential part before starting the actual interview; then recommendations on ethical behaviour for both parties "during the interview" are formulated, and finally debriefing is also mentioned as an enriching, instructive part after the ImQM.

3. Co-Minor II

The outcomes of the first project made us decide to write a proposal to continue the work that clearly was not finished. Only after a second call, European DG Justice fundings for Co-Minor-IN/QUEST II (JUST/2015/JTRA/AG/EJTR/8678) were obtained in 2016. The aim of the second project was to have the findings of Co-Minor I confirmed in focus group discussions with the stakeholders of ImQM, given the fact that the first project results were exclusively built on survey results.

These discussions confirmed the findings of the survey as summarised in the 4 keywords, however participants stressed two types of **trust**: trust of the minor for the interviewer, which emerged from the survey, but also trust amongst the stakeholders themselves in the ImQM, to make the minor feel at ease. If minors feel tension amongst the people in the room, they will not trust them and will have difficulty sharing unpleasant and uncomfortable content.

To obtain enhanced trust amongst the people in the room (be they police officers, psychologists, magistrates, etc.) and, in the case of an ImQM, the interpreter, we have organised IPE or interprofessional education, a need that was also thrown up by our previous research.

5 An extensive version of the results of the project consortium can be found in Salaets & Balogh (2015a) while a summarised version of the results of Belgium can be found in Salaets & Balogh (2015b). Finally, findings of Italy and Belgium were compared in Salaets & Balogh (2017). Salaets & Balogh (2015a) is freely available.

6 https://www.arts.kuleuven.be/english/rg_interpreting_studies/research-projects/co_minor_in_quest/recommendations

What was also innovative in this project, was the experiment with minors on their perception of the interpreter and the whole multilingual situation: as primary participants in an ImQM, minors themselves had not been heard yet. As stated before, only the professional stakeholders in the encounter had been heard.

3.1. IPE: Interprofessional education

With the results of the Co-Minor I – the importance of briefing and teamwork which, in turn, create trust and the demand for additional training – we decided to write a manual to organise such trainings with all stakeholders in an ImQM. The content of the manual was based on actual training sessions held in 2017 (pilot) and 2018 (final workshop).

The manual (Balogh et al., 2018) itself is freely available[7] in five languages (Dutch, English, French, Italian and Hungarian) and enables the facilitator to organise an IPE-event with the different stakeholders in an ImQM. In the first part, the background of and the need for the training manual is explained, in the second part actual ready-made materials are presented: an icebreaker to start with, brainstorming exercises, mini case studies (short stories) as well as controversial issues to debate and role-plays. The animation movie (one of the deliverables of the project) can also be used for discussion: it shows stakeholders how misunderstandings can originate from language issues and leave the minor isolated[8].

To better prepare the training, two toolkits are also available in the manual for the facilitator/organiser of the training. The first helps to identify the participant's professional background and experience by seeking answers to the following questions: job description, training and education and experience in working with minors (e.g. which age groups, how often, in which contexts) as well as experience in working with an interpreter.

The second toolkit helps to look at participants' attitudes towards training-related issues. For instance, they are asked to give their opinion on some controversial issues or to reflect on a concrete ImQM situation.

The toolkits mainly help the facilitator to tailor the training according to the most relevant needs of the potential participants who by definition are diverse and come from different backgrounds.

---

7 https://www.arts.kuleuven.be/english/rg_interpreting_studies/research-projects/co-minor-in-quest-ii/manual-interpreter-mediated-child-interviews

8 https://videolab.avnet.kuleuven.be/video/?id=08f1246ce5f9efca72a977d8b4ae792b&height=390&width=640&autoplay=false

3.2. The voice of the children: An experiment

In Co-Minor II, the voices of the children were heard for the first time in an experimental approach that was undertaken in Belgium, France, Italy and Hungary.

It was experimental in the sense that a bilingual interview situation was set-up with "normal" children[9], who first looked at a short video of a pick-pocket stealing a wallet and then were asked to comment on it. This was done as prescribed in child questioning: by letting the children speak, by asking open questions that generate narratives, introduced by "Tell me about the movie" instead of closed and even suggestive questions like "Do you want to share with me what the thief in the movie looked like?". The interviewers (FL speaker, namely Hungarian or Italian) were trained to do so and invited the children to speak with a minimum of questions asked. The children were between 5 and 17 years old, the interpreters were professional interpreters who alternated between two interpreting modes, namely consecutive and simultaneous interpreting. After a break, the researchers came in and asked questions about the experience as such. Detailed information on methodology and findings can be found in Salaets and Balogh (2019) where we also describe the results of the Belgian case regarding rapport between the minor and the interviewer, or in Salaets and Balogh (2017) were we compare the Italian and Belgian case when talking about the role of the interpreter.

In a nutshell, what can be concluded from the experiment is that the children preferred the consecutive mode, which gives them the time to reflect and the possibility to hear the interviewer (although they don't understand him/her), whereas the simultaneous mode distracts them and makes them wonder if it is polite to speak at the same time (interpreter and child) or whether they must then raise their voice during the simultaneous whispering. This is important information for the interviewer.

Important findings from the study need to be highlighted. Firstly, despite the fact that the interviewer wants to build trust with the minor, it is the interpreter who actually receives that trust from the child. This is understandable, since they are the only ones present in the room who speak the same language. The data

9 In the sense that they were not in an (at least visibly) vulnerable situation, for instance, as non-accompanied minor, as asylum-seeker, as child placed in foster care etc. They were all members of 'ordinary' families and had at least one characteristic in common: they had no experience with interpreters, except the deaf child (who by default is used to working with interpreters) and did not understand a word of the languages used (Hungarian and Italian).

show that when children answer the questions, they do so mostly when looking at the interpreter – although the answers are meant for the interviewer.

This leads us to the next important finding and condition for trust building, namely: positioning. The classic triangular setting often makes it impossible for the interviewer to have eye contact with the minor. Moreover, everything and everybody must be audio recorded through a sensitive microphone, so the interpreter should not position him/herself too far from the microphone either. Having tested different positionings during an ImQM, we have found that the ideal setup of an interview is when the interpreter takes a seat next to the interviewers so that the latter at least get the impression that the minor is looking at them. The direction of gaze is then determined in this way. Eye contact between interviewer and minor contributes significantly to trust building between them. This however is not feasible for a deaf child, since the only way to give or receive information is through sign language which must be seen, and which is provided only by the interpreter.

When the children are asked about trust – to whom would you give your chocolate (young children) or with whom would you share a secret (older children) – almost all the children choose the interpreter as their trusted person.

This is important for all stakeholders to know, which allows us to conclude the following: "that rapport building with the interviewer must be encouraged, but also that we must take into account the children's reality and their perceptions. This should be discussed in a briefing before starting the actual interview, so that everybody's role is clear to all the professionals involved in the ImQM." (Salaets & Balogh, 2019: 39)

Like those for the stakeholders, animation movies are available for younger (3–6) and older minors (6–18) to explain – without using language – what the interpreter's job is, how they bring understanding to people who have different language uses[10].

4. Children in Legal language settings (ChiLLS)

After having finished the two Co-Minor projects, there were two major elements that had to be consolidated. So we decided to seek funding for the ChiLLS-project (Children in Legal Language Settings), which was obtained through a DG Justice

---

10 https://videolab.avnet.kuleuven.be/video/?id=5af49e61d19c500705d82bdef891056e&height=390&width=640&autoplay=false (3–6 years)
https://videolab.avnet.kuleuven.be/video/?id=033e00870b742c03fa15aad54cb07907&height=390&width=640&autoplay=false (6–18 years)

project of the European Commission (JUST-JACC-AG-2017). Next to KU Leuven, the partners were, the University of Bologna, the Hintalovon Foundation in Hungary (a children's rights centre) and the following experts: Dimitri Elman and Richard Redwood (both from the International Criminal Court, The Hague, The Netherlands); György Virag (Forensic Psychologist, Institute for Criminology, Hungary) and Eric Van der Mussele (Youth Counsellor, Belgium). Firstly, there was the need to bring together all the materials available, not only on the university websites (because of limited access and publicity for non-academic parties), but on a website created for ImQM stakeholders and for minors themselves[11]. Secondly, we wanted to broaden and consolidate the participation of the minors themselves. When talking about child-friendly justice, we asked some minors – ambassadors for the project – their opinion on the matter and received some valuable insights from them. They reported on their experience as participants, also during the final online conference on October 19 & 20 in 2020 (since the COVID pandemic didn't allow us to have a physical conference)[12]. But most of all, we were able to interview minors who really found themselves in a vulnerable situation, being either non-accompanied minors and/or involved in a criminal procedure. Due to the pandemic (with the lockdown starting March 13, 2020), we managed to speak only with 8 minors. Still, their experiences are important to share: contrary to the former projects, this is the first publication on the findings of qualitative research involving vulnerable minors. In what follows, we will briefly outline participants' demographics, the methodology used in the study and results, which are limited here to the Belgian case.

4.1. Demographics of the respondents

The children we interviewed were all males ranging in age from 12 to just under 18. Seven of them were involved in an asylum procedure as non-accompanied minors, of which one was involved in both asylum and criminal procedure. One boy was involved in a criminal proceeding. Their mother tongues were English/Crio, Pashto, Dari, Somali and Romanes/Slovak. Only the boy with English was interviewed without an interpreter; the others were interviewed with the assistance of a professional interpreter. Three of them were interviewed at the asylum centre in the presence of their guardian, one at home with his mother present, the others were interviewed in a room at KU Leuven University: one face

11 Website: chills.expedite.dev – Just another WordPress site (chills-research.eu)

12 Reference to online conference of October 19–20 2020: Online conference – 19 & 20 October 2020 – chills.expedite.dev (chills-research.eu)

to face without audio recording, only field notes (since it was his right to refuse recording); the other three were interviewed through remote interpreting[13] of which only the audio was recorded. Ethical clearance was obtained by SMEC (*Sociaal-maatschappelijke ethische commissie* – Social and societal ethical committee) of KU Leuven, informed consents were signed by either a parent or in the case of non-accompanied minors, by their guardian.

4.2. Methodology

With the experts and members of the consortium, we prepared a semi-structured interview that gauges the minors' ideas and experiences concerning communication: we asked about the communication needs they felt, the emotions they experienced during communication issues (support or hostility) and their idea about relationships in the encounter (trust and safety). The intention was to determine their vulnerability, especially there foreign language vulnerability, although this is not a quantifiable given.

The interviews were transcribed, translated, read through several times for annotation, after which categories were created through colour coding by two independent coders, to assure triangulation. The categories and the key words were discussed amongst the coders to reach a consensus. Next the analysis (codes, keywords) was put together in an excel sheet and striking quotes from the interviews were inserted to illustrate the findings from the analysis.

4.3. Results

When asked about their journey towards Belgium, the respondents (see 4.1) reported that they did not have many resources. For instance, nobody – except the oldest respondent – mastered English, which indicates that English as so called "lingua franca" is far from being mastered by everybody on the globe. This, in turn, confirms what Blommaert (2010) stresses: "sociolinguistically, the world has not become a village. That well-matured metaphor of globalization does not work"(Blommaert, 2010: 1). It means also that the refugee minors testified they had to search for people who were in Belgium for a longer period and to ask them to interpret into Dutch. Ultimately, if there were no solutions, they had to express themselves through gestures.

---

13 The interpreter was located remotely; the interviewers and the minor were at the same location.

When asked about their **needs** as far as communication is concerned, what came out as categories in the coding were the need to **give** and of course, **receive** information. The minors had a very clear idea about these communication needs and especially about the interpreter's tasks and roles.

First of all, it was minor 7 who gave an excellent definition of what he expects from the interpreter

> The interpreter has an important task. Actually a crucial task. The interpreter has to transfer what the person is saying in the best way possible in the other language. (M7)

If we break down this broader theme, according to the minors, the interpreters need good language skills, as well as good comprehension and listening skills. Moreover, they must be accurate and preferably speak the same language variant as the minor. That was signalled by minor 1 with Creole and English, who referred to an interpreter who was trying to do their best, while another really spoke Creole in minor 1's case:

> And then, yea, the person have [sic] to know that we don't speak the same thing. Because yes, she can understand some, a bit of what I was saying. But if I start talking really deeply, she cannot understand because she is not from my country. […] But this one I did in Brussels, the person was from my country she can understand what I was saying. (M1)

Accuracy was also explained by minor 5 as transferring messages without omissions:

> Yes, that interpreter for example, I said some things to him, and he didn't understand some terms or words, then skipped […] he omitted them. (M5)

The need for accuracy was also intertwined with deontological behaviour according to the minors: the interpreters should not express their opinion (M7), should not interrupt and step out of their role (M5), should not have their own "interpretation" of what they think they have understood, but should ask for confirmation (M7). Some remarkable quotes illustrate these communication needs expressed by the minors:

> The interpreter is not allowed to form or express an opinion. (M7)
> He [the interpreter] has to understand me well, he should know Dutch well, that he doesn't communicate everything immediately, but lets me finish, and if he didn't understand me, then he has to ask me and only interpret afterwards. (M7)
> In the middle of my interview, suddenly he [the interpreter] became angry with me, because I understand English and I understood he was talking in English and at a certain moment in time he said to me 'you talk a lot, you ought to wait for a moment.' (M5)

Regarding **emotions,** positive feelings of self-confidence were indicated by only one minor, the one who mastered English; the others experienced feelings of frustration or were confronted with the anger of one of the other speakers in the encounter (e.g. the interpreter who became angry was already mentioned above).

Both minor 5 and 7 expressed their frustration about the choice of the interpreter: minor 7 indicates that there is not much chance to choose an interpreter, and minor 5 refers to the absurdity of the question they asked him before the interview and in the end about the quality of the interpreter. The minor refers to politeness and the fact that, especially as a minor, you cannot tell an adult to his face that he did not do a good job:

> They ask in the beginning of the interview and at the end whether you understood the interpreter well, but yeah, you can't say it at that moment, because he is looking you in the eye. You can't say anything in his presence.

When asked about relationships and trust, all minors had complete trust in their guardian because "he knows everything about my story" (M1). Both trust and distrust in the interpreter were expressed: again minor 7 seemed to understand very well what the tasks of the interpreter are and even mentions the note-taking technique spontaneously:

> The first interpreter that was very pleasant [...] I could understand the interpreter well, his Somali was good, so I had trust in him, that he was able to interpret to Dutch as well. [...] Some interpreters took notes, and I found that better, because it is also better for the memory of the interpreter. Some of them only listened. (M7)

However minors 5 and 6 express distrust (M5) or what we would call "forced trust" in the interpreter (M6):

> But my interpreter was of Afghan origin, and I am not completely sure, but he saw himself ... he thought, he was different than us. He saw himself as a better person than us. He behaved in a distinct manner. (M5)
> Now well; your asylum story, these are ... this is a private matter, you don't tell this to everyone. [...] R[esearcher]1: But you do to the interpreter? M: Yes, definitely. [...] But no, I don't trust it, but I have no other choice, I have to tell it there. (M6)

4.4. Conclusion

We can conclude at a meta-analytical level that minors know very well what privacy is and don't want to tell their story to just anyone. They would prefer to tell their story without interpreter and would feel more "free" to do so, but since there is no other solution than talking through the interpreter, they feel they should trust them. In other words, they are looking for a safe space which we as adults, practitioners and professionals should try to give them as much as possible.

However, a kind of forced trust in the interpreter emerges in this study, which renders it different from the experiment where the trust in the interpreter was almost unconditional. This can probably be explained through the fact that the children in the experiment were not experiencing a really difficult or dangerous situation or had not been previously confronted with a difficult journey fleeing from war, oppressive regimes, famine or natural disasters.

However, children feel that they can trust the interpreters if they have good language, listening and comprehension skills; if they are accurate; if they can be neutral and impartial without expressing – even subtly – an opinion or cultural and societal differences in power and social class (see the Afghan origin of the interpreter in the quote of M5).

Basically, the minors provide a clear definition of a professional interpreter without having any notion of the concept itself. It shows that we, as adult researchers, can learn a lot from the participation of minors in our research. Namely, it shows that minors don't need to be paternalized; they need protection but it is not always easy to draw the line (Pleysier et al., 2019). We have also learned in person that linked to the concept of vulnerability there is the concept of resilience (Fineman, 2010): the minors we met were extremely mature and strong, but like the concept of vulnerability, this varies from minor to minor. Finally, it must be stressed that of course, one meeting doesn't tell anything about their general state of mind.

5. Impact and outreach

Both academic (see references) and societal outreach have been realised through this line of research, not only in Belgium but also elsewhere, namely in Italy (Amato & Mack, 2022) and Hungary[14]. The authors of this contribution gave workshops on ImQM for Associations of professional interpreters in the UK (the APCI, Association of Police and Court Interpreters) on June 28, 2021 and in Spain for APTIJ (Asociación Profesional de Traductores e Intérpretes Judiciales y Jurados) on December 19 and 20, 2022.

14 https://hintalovon.hu/en/2020/10/22/chills-child-participation/

In what follows, we will concentrate on Belgium where the projects have had structural impact and led to collaboration with the Belgian Federal Police[15].

First of all, the authors of this chapter have given training to all T.A.M[16]. police officers (N = 500) in Belgium (which meant that we had to have one day in French, one in Dutch) about the role and tasks of the interpreting, about their deontological code, about how to work with an interpreter (where we systematically distribute the flyers with recommendations, see § 2).

Secondly, this has resulted in two workshops for the trainers of new T.A.M. police officers, where the number of participants was significantly lower to enable interaction, namely about 15 trainers for the French- and 15 for the Dutch-speaking parts of Belgium. This allowed us not only to discuss with the police trainers about the aforementioned topics that regard the interpreter, but also to exchange information about the specific questioning technique they apply. The theory was then practised in three role plays: one in French, one in Hungarian, one in Flemish sign language using scenarios from the database of the Federal police. All participants were professionals (T.A.M. police officers and interpreters), only the "child" was an adult actor since one cannot use children as actors in such destressing scenarios.

Thirdly, these workshops and training sessions have resulted in a very special initiative: in 2016, the Federal Police has nominated our research group as candidates for the Society award in the KU Leuven Humanities. Ultimately, we received a special mention,[17] not the actual prize, because KU Leuven had never been confronted with an academic nomination (which is supposed to be given by other academics) being proposed by non-academics, in this case the Federal Police. Nevertheless, it has given a lot of visibility to the research in the academic world, which has generated a short video as a show-case of an actual

15 Moreover, a (retired) member of the Belgian Federal Police and expert in T.A.M. (Danny Sluyts) has been training police officers in Hungary since 2018 about the questioning technique for minors, always taking into consideration the interpreter, if necessary, for FL speaking minors. In 2023, he will train the trainers (the first group that will pass on the questioning technique to further generations) so that they can continue working autonomously in the future. Moreover since 2021, one of the authors (Dr. K. Balogh) has been training Hungarian judges in working with an interpreter, also in cases involving minors.

16 T.A.M. is the French-Dutch acronym for *Audiovisual Techniques for questioning of minors*.

17 https://ghum.kuleuven.be/NL/prijzen2016

interpreter-mediated questioning of a minor. It comprises a summary of a role play we did with the Federal Police during the training of trainers[18].

In the years 2020–2021 and 2022, together with the Federal police, the authors of this contribution "moved" (the focus of) the workshop from adults to children during the Children's University. The goal of this exercise was to let minors witness an interpreter-mediated questioning of a minor and to make them participate in assisting the police officer (also present) who has to communicate through the interpreter. The minor indeed did not speak Dutch and had been a victim of bullying at school, which is very recognisable for minors under 13. Minors had to reflect on how to solve the situation with somebody the police officer does not understand. Every year, the workshop has been a big success and we managed to work with about 60 children in total.

When the war in Ukraine started, we tried to make a small contribution by offering free interpreting training for bilingual citizens (Ukrainian/Russian-Dutch) to work as "interpreters". Of course, it is not possible to become an interpreter in a 30 hours course, but the main guidelines and instructions were given about the code of ethics (including such forms of behaviour as impartiality), terminology, note-taking and role plays, which were done with doctors and social workers. Part of the 30 hours was a 6-hour specialisation class with a T.A.M. police officer in working with Ukrainian minors, per definition a vulnerable group in war time who needs special attention. Foreign Language Vulnerability makes them even more vulnerable, of which smugglers and people with bad intentions, unfortunately took advantage, as we could read in the press.

Last but not least, the most fundamental and structural outreach and impact has been obtained from that year on (2016): since then, the authors of this contribution have been training all new candidates for a T.A.M. specialisation training at the National Police Academy twice a year. The fixed module in the two week training of is entitled "T.(E).A.M-work: how to work with an interpreter when questioning minors." This means that since then, we have trained about 250 new T.A.M. officers (about 30 candidates per year). Vice versa, T.A.M. police officers train future legal interpreters who want to specialise in questioning minors on how to behave during questioning of minors, and how to respect the specific questioning technique for minors. The general comment the T.A.M. office receives from the shopfloor is that practitioners clearly see the difference between an interpreter and/or officer who has received the IPE, in

18 https://www.arts.kuleuven.be/english/rg_interpreting_studies/research-projects/co_minor_in_quest/trainingfgp

contrast to those who have not. Briefing, teamwork during the questioning and debriefing run much more smoothly and efficiently[19].

We hope that this contribution shows that research takes time; needs teambuilding and a lot of effort; that it requires networking during which awareness raising about FLV for minors and the need for professional interpreters is stressed… but also that continuous efforts can cause the stone in the river to change the course of the water.

References

Amato, Amalia & Mack, Gabriele (Eds.) (2022). *La comunicazione multilingue con mindorenni nei contesti legali*. LED. Edizioni Univeristarie di Lettere Economia Diritto. Freely available at: https://www.ledonline.it/public/files/journals/9/998-1/Comunicazione-multilingue-minorenni.pdf

Balogh, Katalin, Salaets, Heidi, & Van Schoor, Dominique (2018). *Interpreter-mediated Child Interviews. Tools for Interprofessional Training*. Lannoo.

Balogh, Katalin & Salaets, Heidi (Eds.) (2015). *Children and Justice: Overcoming Language Barriers. Cooperation in Interpreter-Mediated Questioning of Minors*. Intersentia. Freely available at: https://www.arts.kuleuven.be/tolkwetenschap/projecten/co_minor_in_quest/children-and-justice

Blommaert, Jan (2010). *The Sociolinguistics of Globalization (Cambridge Approaches to Language Contact)*. Cambridge University Press. https://doi:10.1017/CBO9780511845307

Costa, Beverley (2010). Mother tongue or non-native language? Learning from conversations with bilingual/multilingual therapists about working with clients who do not share their native language. *Ethnicity and Inequalities in Health and Social Care, 3*(1), 15–24. https://DOI:10.5042/eihsc.2010.0144

Fineman, Martha Albertson (2010). The vulnerable subject and the responsive state. *Emory Law Journal, 60*, 251–275.

Fontes, Lisa Aronson (2010). Interviewing immigrant children for suspected child maltreatment. *Journal of Psychiatry and Law, 38*(3), 283–304.

Fontes, Lisa Aronson (2009). Interviewing immigrant children and families for suspected child maltreatment. *APSAC Advisor*, 7–11.

Hale, Sandra Beatriz (2015). Community interpreting. In Franz Pöchhacker (Ed.), *Routledge Encyclopedia of Interpreting Studies* (pp. 65–69). Routledge.

19 Unfortunately, we have no statistics or numbers about the impact: the source are informal conversations.

Hale, Sandra Beatriz (2007). *Community Interpreting*. Palgrave Macmillan.

Hlavac, Jim (2013). A cross-national overview of translator and interpreter certification procedures. *Translation & Interpreting, 5*(1), 32–65.

Keselman, Olga, Cederborg, Ann-Christin & Linell, Per (2010a). 'That is not necessary for you to know!' Negotiation of participation status of unaccompanied children in interpreter-mediated asylum hearings. *Interpreting, 12*(1), 83–104.

Keselman, Olga, Cederborg, Ann-Christin, Lamb, Michael E., & Dahlström, Örjan (2010b). Asylum-seeking minors in interpreter-mediated interviews: What do they say and what happens to their responses? *Child & Family Social Work, 15*(3), 325–334.

Lamb, Michael E., La Rooy, David J., Malloy, Lindsay C., & Katz, Carmitz (Eds.) (2011). *Children's Testimony: A Handbook of Psychological Research and Forensic Practice*. Wiley-Blackwell.

Lamb, Michael E., Hershkowitz, Irit, Orbach, Yael, & Esplin, Phillip W. (2008). *Tell Me What Happened: Structured Investigative Interviews of Child Victims and Witnesses*. Wiley.

Lamb, Michael E., Orbach, Yael, Hershkowitz, Irit, Esplin, Phillip W., & Horowitz, Dvora (2007). "Structured forensic interview protocols improve the quality and informativeness of investigative interviews with children: A review of research using the NICHD Investigative Interview Protocol". *Child Abuse & Neglect, 31*(11–12), 1201–1231. https://doi:10.1016/j.chiabu.2007.03.021

Lamb, Michael E. & Fauchier, Angèle (2001). The effects of question type on self-contradictions by children in the course of forensic interviews. *Applied Cognitive Psychology, 15*(5), 483–491. https://doi.org/10.1002/acp.726

Lamb, Michael E., Sternberg, Kathleen J., & Esplin, Philip W. (2000). Effects of age and delay on the amount of information provided by alleged sex abuse victims in investigative interviews. *Child Development, 71*(6), 1586–1596. https://doi.org/10.1111/1467-8624.00250

Matthias, Carmel & Zaal, Noel (2002). Hearing only a faint echo? Interpreters and children in court. *South African Journal on Human Rights, 18*(3), 350–371.

Pleysier, Stefaan, Herbots, Katrien, & Molenberghs, Sanne (2019). Het recht op participatie vs. bescherming: Ethische kwesties in onderzoek bij kinderen en jongeren. *Tijdschrift voor Jeugd en Kinderrechten, 4*, 321–333.

Salaets, Heidi, Balogh, Katalin, & Aelbrecht, Stefan (2023). The right to an interpreter: Taking stock, looking forward. In Roxanna Dehaghani, Samantha Fairclough, & Lord Mergaerts (Eds.), V*ulnerability, the Accused, and the Criminal Justice System*. Multijurisdictional Perspectives, (pp 125–144). Routledge.

Salaets, Heidi & Balogh, Katalin (2019). Interpreter-mediated questioning of minors (ImQM): The voice of children and their rapport with interpreters. *Revista de Llengua I Dret, Journal of Language and Law, 71*, 27–44. http://dx.doi.org/10.2436/rld.i71.2019.3257

Salaets, Heidi & Balogh, Katalin (2017). Participants' and Interpreters' perception of the Interpreter's role in interpreter-mediated investigative interviews of minors: Belgium and Italy as a case. In Carmen Valero-Garcés & Rebecca Tipton (Eds.), *Ideology, Ethics and Policy Development in Public Service Interpreting and Translation* (pp. 151–178). Multilingual Matters.

Salaets, Heidi & Balogh, Katalin (2015a). Chapter 4. Co-Minor-IN/QUEST Research findings. In K. Balogh & H. Salaets (Eds.), *Children and Justice: Overcoming Language Barriers. Cooperation in Interpreter-Mediated Questioning of Minors* (pp. 175–227). Intersentia.

Salaets, Heidi & Balogh, Katalin (2015b). Co-Minor-IN/QUEST. Improving interpreter-mediated pre-trial interviews with minors. *Trans. Revista de traductologia, 191*, 57–76.

Tryuk, Małgorzata (2021). Translation under Fascism and Nazism. In Christopher Rundel (Ed.), *The Routledge Handbook of Translation History* (pp. 469–484). Routledge.

Tryuk, Małgorzata (2020). Translating and interpreting in conflict and crisis. In Kaisa Koskinen & Nike K. Pokorn (Eds.), *The Routledge Handbook of Translation and Ethics* (pp. 398–414). Routledge.

Tryuk, Małgorzata (2017). Conflict. Tension. Aggression. Ethical issues in interpreted asylum hearings at the Office for Foreigners in Warsaw. In Carmen Valero-Garcés & RebeccaTipton (Eds.), *Ideology, Ethics and Policy Development in Public Service Interpreting and Translation* (pp. 179–194). Multilingual Matters.

Tryuk, Małgorzata (2016a). Interpreting and translating in Nazi concentration camps during World War II. *Linguistica Antverpiensia, New Series – Themes in Translation Studies, 15*, 121–141.https://doi.org/10.52034/lanstts.v15i.386

Tryuk, Małgorzata (2016b). Interpreters in the concentration camp of Majdanek (1941–1944). In Michaela Wolf (Ed.), *Interpreting in Nazi Concentration Camps* (pp. 115–133). Bloomsbury.

Tryuk, Małgorzata (2015). *On ethics and Interpreters*. Peter Lang.

Tryuk, Małgorzata (2012). The judge, the doctor, the immigration officer and the interpreter. Community interpreters' role perception-a Polish perspective. *The Interpreters' Newsletter*, 17, 117–138. https://www.openstarts.units.it/bitstream/10077/8621/1/Tryuk_IN17.pdf

Tryuk, Małgorzata (2010). Interpreting in Nazi concentration camps during World War II. *Interpreting*, 12(2), 125–145. https://doi 10.1075/intp.12.2.01try

Tryuk, Małgorzata (2007). Community interpreting in Poland. In Cecilia Wadensjö, Birgitta Englund Dimitorva, & Anna-Lena Nilsson (Eds.), *The Critical Link 4. Professionalisation of Interpreting in the Community* (pp. 95–105). John Benjamins.

Virág, György (2015). "Interpreted interview with highly vulnerable children". In Heidi Salaets & Katalin Balogh (Eds.), *Children and Justice: Overcoming Language Barriers: Cooperation in Interpreter-Mediated Questioning of Minors* (pp. 77–93). Intersentia. https://doi.org/10.1017/9781780685144

Websites

APCI Association of Police and Court Interpreters https://apciinterpreters.org.uk/

APTIJ Asociación Profesional de Traductores e Intérpretes Judiciales y Jurados https://www.aptij.es/

ChiLLS (Children in Legal Language Settings) chills.expedite.dev – Just another WordPress site (chills-research.eu)

Hintalovon Hungary https://hintalovon.hu/en/2020/10/22/chills-child-participation/

NICHD protocol: International Evidence-Based Investigative Interviewing of Children https://nichdprotocol.com/

Research Group Interpreting Studies, KU Leuven https://www.arts.kuleuven.be/english/rg_interpreting_studies

Carmen Valero Garcés

Chapter 8 Exodus, refugees, and inclusion of the Afghan population in Spain. The project *Get To Know To Keep In Mind*

Abstract: Since the end of the twentieth century and in this twenty-first century, migration and humanitarian crises have taken on gigantic quantitative proportions and have become a challenge of the first magnitude to which no existing organisation has provided a solution or response in accordance with the dignity that human beings deserve. The Afghanistan crisis is a good example of this. In a context of pandemics and globalisation, the lack of communication and understanding due to linguistic and/or cultural issues makes the situation even worse outside the *lingua franca* zone, where languages of lesser diffusion (LLD) are the most frequently used by humanitarian aid workers or professionals who help refugees or asylum seekers. This chapter focuses on the presentation and development of the project *Get to Know to Keep in Mind. Conversations with mediators, translators, interpreters and refugees,* an action carried out between March 2022 and March 2023 to contribute[1], first, to the integration of Afghan refugees in Spain following the invasion by the Taliban and the exodus of thousands of Afghans, and secondly, to recognise the value and need of effective communication in LLD.

Keywords: Humanitarian action, multilingual communication, asylum seekers and refugees, Afghan crisis, languages of lesser diffusion, LLD

1. Introduction. Humanitarian action and communication in multilingual settings

Humanitarian action is often a multilingual effort in which translation and interpreting between different languages and cultures can have life-saving consequences. Displacement has become a global challenge to which no existing international body (UN, EU) has provided a solution or answer beyond politically or economically interested proposals.

1 The project *Conocer para no Olvidar. Conversaciones con mediadores, traductores e intépretes* (*Get to Know to Keep in Mind. Conversations with mediators, translators, interpreters and refugees)* was funded by CASA ASIA, Beca Ruy de Clavijo 2022–2023.

Protagonists of the global order are not only states and the different forms of political organisation (international, national, regional or local), but also the emerging civil society committed to the task of defending universal interests.

In this global context of pandemics and globalisation, the lack of communication and understanding due to linguistic and/or cultural issues makes the situation even worse when the cushion of *lingua franca* or most widely used languages do not exist and humanitarian actors have to confront the languages of lesser diffusion (LLD) or migration languages, which are the ones most frequently encountered by humanitarian aid workers or professionals who help refugees or asylum seekers (Valero-Garcés, 2022).

The significant differences in the responses to the challenges of multilingualism in humanitarian crises by institutions and NGOs indicate that declarations and legislation are necessary and urgent, but this alone does not guarantee that change will happen. The current war in Ukraine is a case in point. The EU is providing an unprecedented response to the Ukrainian exodus following the outbreak of war in February 2022. The European Directive on Temporary Protection[2], activated on 4 March 2022 for the first time since it was drafted 20 years ago, determines and makes unique the solidarity response of its EU partners. After the outbreak of war, many EU governments reacted swiftly with the deployment of reception resources, express procedures, reception centres, information telephones and daily announcements committed to the welfare of those fleeing war at the gates of the EU, including a call for professional Tr&In and/or ad-hoc volunteers and bilinguals to help with communication (EU Migration and Home Affairs 2022)[3].

In the case of Spain, this is not the first migration challenge faced by the government and society. Since the beginning of the socialist government mandate in June 2018, the country has faced an ongoing refugee situation. To contextualise the study, references to of some of these episodes follows.

One of such challenges was the rescue of the "Aquarius" in June 2018 when 629 people were rescued in the Central Mediterranean. Another case is the Canary Islands crisis, a e escape route from the Sahel desert, in 2020 in the midst of the pandemic. In May 2021 Spain experienced a massive influx of more than 10,000 people into Ceuta with the largest humanitarian crisis in the world, according

2 The European Directive on Temporary Protection at https://www.consilium.europa.eu/en/infographics/temporary-protection-displaced-persons/ (accessed 3 April 2023).

3 EU Migration and Home Affairs 2022. https://commission.europa.eu/about-european-commission/departments-and-executive-agencies/migration-and-home-affairs_en (accessed 3 April 2023).

to UNHCR. A year later- in March 2022-, a historic jump at the Melilla fence took place at the same time that the intensification of the Russian offensive in Ukraine.

Two months later, in August 2021, the Afghan crisis broke out and Spain, like other EU Member states, was involved in the evacuation and reception of refugees. In February 2022 the Ukraine was started- and still continues one year later- and different European countries, including Spain, simplified their procedures for receiving Ukrainian refugees in response to the EU's decision to activate a Directive for unlimited reception and the granting of temporary residence permits and provision of adequate accommodation.

While I was writing this chapter, another unprecedented humanitarian crisis, the consequences of which are yet to be seen, has struck the world: the earthquake in Turkey and Syria on February 6th, 2023. The effects of the emergency situation have not yet ceased with deadly new tremors that have trapped more people under rubble on February 20, 2023 (BBC news, 21/2/2023).[4]

This chapter focuses on the Afghan crisis after the invasion by the Taliban and the exodus of thousands of Afghans. The main aim is the description of an initiative carried out to contribute to the integration of Afghan refugees in Spain. First, I will contextualise the arrival and situation of Afghans to Spain after Taliban invasion and exodus. Secondly, the project objectives, methodology, development and results carried out so far will be explained, and finally, I will conclude with some lessons learned and tips to continuing contributing to the integration of Afghan refugees in Spain.

2. Contextualization. Afghanistan and Afghan refugees in Spain

Spain was among the countries to evacuate Afghans who had helped their troops and diplomats. During the withdrawal by Western forces, Spain airlifted more than 2,000 people out of the country, most of them Afghans at risk of reprisals from the new Taliban rulers. The first group to arrive following the takeover by the Taliban landed at Torrejón de Ardoz air base (Madrid) on August 19, 2021. The Spanish Prime Minister said at the time that Madrid would not lose interest in the Afghans who had remained in their country but wanted to leave. Since

4 BBC News. 2023. Turkey earthquake: Deadly new tremor traps people under rubble. 21 2 2023. https://www.bbc.com/news/world-europe-64711228 (accessed 3 April 2023).

then, planes have brought to Spain hundreds more Afghan citizens who had managed to cross into other nations such as Pakistan, Turkey and Iran.

Afghan evacuees were arriving in Spain in a state of "extreme exhaustion," and carrying just the few belongings that they could carry with them amid the chaos of Kabul. They were (and still are) also worried about the families that they were leaving behind, according to the organizations that were assisting with their arrival. Despite having escaped their home country, ahead of them awaited a challenging process, which would involve further travel and a wait that would last months until their requests for protection were resolved. These processes often take longer than the legal limits, but the Spanish government announced that the asylum requests would be dealt with as "special" and would be processed "urgently." Figures from the OAR (*Oficina de Asilo y Refugio*, in English Asylum and Refugee Office), which belongs to the Interior Ministry showed that the rate of acceptance for Afghan asylum seekers in Spain was 74 %, a percentage that is in stark contrast to the 5 % average for all requests filed. Finally, once their documents were processed, they were given a special residency permit for a 15-day period. According to normal procedures, after a month they must be informed as to whether their request has been accepted for processing. If it has, the authorities have six months to decide whether to grant them refugee status or subsidiary protection, or reject the request. If their application is accepted, and more than six months have passed without a response, the applicants are allowed to work in Spain.

While the asylum process is managed by the Interior Ministry, their shelter in Spain is organized by the Ministry of Inclusion, Social Security and Migration, which distribute them to state centres all around the country. Those seeking international protection are managed by organizations such as the Spanish Commission for Refugee Assistance (CEAR) and the Red Cross, among others. CEAR, in their annual report 2021 pointed out that in August 2021, following the evacuation of people from Afghanistan, it was necessary to urgently respond to the communication needs of the people being transferred to Spain, most of whom could only communicate in LLD Dari and Pashto. CEAR had to managed to immediately reinforce the number of interpreters. They also pointed out to the main difficulties faced: locating interpreters for such minority languages in Spain, coordinating the presence of interpreters upon arrival at the airport, as well as facilitating their presence during transfers and access to military installations. (CEAR, 2021).

A year after the Taliban's return to power in Kabul, Afghans still keep arriving to Spain, thus, around 300 Afghans who worked for Spain, and their families, arrived in Madrid from Pakistan on August 2022 (Info Migrants, 2022). While moving to Spain, they have saved their lives, one year later, some of them are still struggling to build a life and find employment (Lopez & Rodrigo, 2022).

At institutional level, however, cultural and linguistic issues are often not a priority or are hardly mentioned at all. This is the eternal paradox of multilingual communication: on the one hand, mediators, translators, or interpreters (Tr&In) or bilinguals who share language and culture in some ways are a fundamental link to inclusion. On the other hand, institutions do not always recognise them as professionals, and they are practically invisible to society. There are many people who serve as liaisons without being professionals and many contexts in which they must act, with generally poorly paid recognition, endless working hours or lack of (supply of) training and failures in communication. This is the context of the project I am presenting.

3. The project

The project *Get to Know to Keep in Mind. Conversations with mediators, translators, interpreters and refugees* was developed thanks to the funding by Casa Asia, Beca Rui de Clavijo (2022–2023). It started in March 2022 and ended in March 2023.

3.1. Objectives

The project is based on two hypothesis. First, a mutual knowledge of the traditions, cultures and languages of the two countries (Spain and Afghanistan) will lead to an advance in the integration of the Afghans welcomed in Spain, and second, this mutual knowledge will also help as a stimulus for greater international cooperation and greater work and training opportunities from and to both sides.

In this context, the general objectives of the project are:

1. To encourage the level of interdependence between the different active agents,
2. To share cooperation practices,

3. To contribute to the integration of people hosted in Spain in line with the 2030 UN Sustainable Development Goals (DGS), and
4. To contribute to the government's efforts in Afghans inclusion itineraries.

This leads to a series of more specific objectives, which are:

1. To promote joint actions and interventions by social agents, mediators, psychologists, educators who are collaborating with the migrant population,
2. To get to know the necessary work of experts in communication with the foreign population (interpreters, mediators, and translators), and their situation in conflicts such as the one in Afghanistan, and
3. To disseminate strategies or guidelines to facilitate linguistic and cultural communication aimed at untrained bilingual people who wish to go further and to be trained as a professional translator and interpreter.

3.2. Methodology

The methodology followed is both qualitative and quantitative. The first is based in conversations and interviews to the different agents involved in the project, as well as a compilation and analysis of materials (videos, texts, drawings, etc.) that help know each other. As for the quantitative method, data come from two surveys, one to Afghans and the other one to nationals. More information follows in the next sections.

3.3. Resources

The project was developed in collaboration with members of the FITISPos Research groups (Training and Research in Translation and Interpreting in Public Services) at the University of Alcalá, Madrid, Spain[5], the non-profit organization AFIPTIPS[6], and some NGOs as well as the collaboration of professional mediators, interpreters and translators.

3.4. Development

The project was developed in two phases, 1. March – October 2022 and 2. November 2022 – March 2023.

5 FITISPos Research Group: https://fitisposgrupo.web.uah.es/ (accessed 3 April 2023).
6 AFIPTIPS: https://www.afiptisp.org (accessed 3 April 2023).

3.4.1. *First phase. March – October 2022*

Two actions were taken: 1. Creation of a multilingual, multidisciplinary and multifunctional working group, and 2. Compilation of materials to create a repository.

1. Creation of a multilingual, multidisciplinary, and multifunctional working group (WG):

The main objective was to create a tool to critically analyse the differences and similarities between the two counties (Spain & Afghanistan). Five specific areas were considered: education, family life and customs, health care, working life, women and education. Once the topics were decided, a call for help to NGOs assisting migrants and refugees and government representatives from the Asylum and Refugees Office was sent. The NGOS contacted were CEAR (the Spanish Commission for Refugee Assistance (CEAR), ACCEM (Spanish Catholic Association of Immigrants) (ACCEM) Red Acoge-Guadalajara), and Red Cross. They provided contacts with professionals who had been in touch with Afghans. Finally, after some conversations and interviews with these contacts the WG was initially composed of 6 people: two professional interpreters and translators who were present at the arrival of the first Afghan refugees at the Torrejón de Ardoz airport in 2021, and who have continued to collaborate with NGOs and the Government to date; a psychologist specialising in mental health and with experience in working with host families, refugees and collaborating with NGOs in the inclusion of some Afghan families in the central area of Spain called Corredor del Henares; and two Afghan women who arrived a year ago as refugees at the Torrejón de Ardoz base. One of them is a lawyer, an activist of human rights in her country as an advisor in an NGO, and the other is a student with a degree in computer science from the Polytechnic University of Kabul, and currently studying a master's degree in computer science at the University of Valencia, where she has been admitted through a programme to help Afghan refugees. Later on (in the second phase) members of the AriA-E Association (Association for Afghan-Spanish Friendship and Intercultural Reinforcement), interpreters who collaborate with UNHCR (United Nations High Commissioner for Refugees) and other NGOs have joined throughout the development of the project. The group remains still open for the incorporation of new people interested in the subject.

Once the WG was consolidated, on the 30th of September 2022, this initial team participated in a round table organized at the University of Alcalá to celebrate the Translator's Day. The topics and subjects discussed and their protagonists were: family life and customs by a professional mediator and interpreter; health care by a psychologist helping Afghans in different NGOs; women by a woman professional interpreter and mediator who has been helping Afghans since their first arrival; education, by an Afghan refugee, lawyer and activist on the defense of human rights in her country; and work and technologies in our lives by an Afghan refugee student having being recently admitted to a MA in technology in a Spanish university, as already mentioned. The speakers tried to compare the issues in both countries so as to increase knowledge from both sides.[7]

2. Compilation of materials to create a repository.

The compilation of materials about Afghanistan and Afghans in Spain was initiated using google drive. So, a link was created and circulated to upload all type of the materials (e.g. institutional reports, news on national TV or the social media, NGOs memorandum, and news from international channels about Afghanistan) in the repository in order to get first-hand knowledge of the communicative needs of the Afghan population in Spain.

3.4.2. Second phase: November 2022 – March 2023

In November 2022, as a step further, a new initiative called Vocinares+2[8] was developed. The main motivations for developing this action were:

1. To increase visibility to the fundamental role of communication as a tool for social insertion, and
2. To advance in mutual knowledge and collaboration between the people in the area of Alcalá de Henares (Northeast Madrid, called Corredor del Henares) and the Afghan Community.

The objectives established for this action were:

1. To get closer to the Afghan population of the surrounding area,
2. To try to establish contacts with people who are acting as a linguistic and cultural bridge,
3. To get to know, through them, the main difficulties that this population have to integrate,

---

7 The recording is available on you tube at: https://youtu.be/CmQKujm-818 (accessed 3 April 2023).

8 More information about Vocinares +2 at: https://biblioteca.uah.es/export/sites/biblioteca/.galleries/Galeria-Documentos-Biblioteca/VOCINARES-2_Resultados.pdf (accessed 3 April 2023).

4. To exchange information on strategies or guidelines to facilitate linguistic and cultural communication, and
5. To describe or elaborate guidelines to facilitate communication

In this phase, a qualitative and quantitative methodology was followed. Three activities were carried out: 1. WG sessions to exchange and increase knowledge, 2. To develop one survey to get quantitative data, and 3. To collect first- hand information about specific topics to help integration.

Action 1. WG sessions were held to exchange and increase knowledge. 4 sessions took place both face-to-face and online-synchronous via Blackboard Collaborative platform with the coordinator of the project, the initial WG, and new members who joined the group to discuss materials on the repository, and to develop the two surveys, as well as collect and discuss the data.

Action 2. One survey addressed to Afghans was designed with the tool provided by UAH, Microsoft Forms, completely anonymous and voluntary. It was distributed by email and social channels (WhatsApp, social networks, etc.) to all those people and/or associations that could be interested in this project and in contract with Afghans in Spain. Only 14 answers were obtained and results indicate the following: 10 women and 4 men. In terms of age, the highest percentage was for people between 26 and 35 (6); followed by people between 36–45 (3) and 45–55 (3). 2 people indicated they were between 16 and 25. When asked about the languages they spoke: 54 % said they spoke English; 70 % knew 3 languages; and most Afghans (78 %) have been in Spain for less than 2 years.

We wanted to know among those who had worked or assisted as interpreters or mediators, if they observed the code of ethics for interpreters. Confidentiality was ranked first, followed by neutrality and fidelity – but only 1 person valued linguistic and cultural competence. This leads us to consider the differences between bilingual and translators and interpreters in the training materials.

Despite the short number of answers, a close look at the data from the Afghans indicated that most of them spoke 3 or more languages or dialects demonstrating the large number of dialects that could be found in this country, and that the most frequently spoken languages are: Dari, Pashtun, English and Spanish. In the case of Spanish, most of the participants had learned Spanish in Spain through language courses.

Action 3. The next activity developed to increase awareness and knowledge through first-hand information to know each other was to ask both groups, Spanish and Afghans, to write or record an audio for the four specific situations shown in the tables below:

In the case of Afghans, they were asked to write or record an audio (in Spanish or in their native language) for the following:

Afghans	Some cultural differences between Spain and your country of origin (clothing, food, services offered, etc.)
	Some topics that most caught your attention when you first arrived in Spain (gestures, posters, clothing, etc.).
	The main difficulties you encountered when you arrived in Spain (communication, culture, customs, etc.).
	Some suggestions or advice to people (from the same country of origin as you) who have just arrived in Spain on how to integrate more quickly

In the case of Spanish, they were asked the following:

Write or record an audio	
Nationals	First impressions when you met foreigners who did not know the Spanish language and/or culture.
	Some cultural differences that you have observed in Afghans who have just arrived in Spain.
	Some suggestions or advice for people who have just arrived in Spain about culture, communication, customs, etc.
	Some tips on how to integrate better in Spain if you are a foreigner.

The next tables indicate the answers to questions by Afghans.

Question 1. Some cultural differences between Spain and your country of origin (clothing, food, services offered, etc.)
➢ Sometimes they (Spanish people) speak too loudly. ➢ They gesticulate a lot when they speak. ➢ There is a lack of interaction/knowledge of each other each or with other countries and nations which has decreased drastically in the last 40 years in our country. ➢ As for clothes, in Spain it is like in the Kurdish region, very beautiful and colourful, especially for women, but this goes against the Islamic culture which suggests dark colours. ➢ The Afghan cuisine is very diverse, we have a variety of delicious and different kebabs and stews served with rice. We use lot of rice and carbohydrates as well as special spices which are used less here in Spain.

Question 2. Some topics that most caught your attention when you first arrived in Spain
➤ Very friendly and smiling. ➤ They always try to help (positive). ➤ The first thing that struck me about Spain is the architecture and ancient buildings that have been common in this country for decades and even centuries. ➤ The language of the people of this country has its own rhythm and beauty. ➤ The climate.

Question 3. Main difficulties you encountered when you arrived in Spain (communication, culture, customs, etc.)
➤ Communication (both verbal and non-verbal). ➤ Space (invasion of personal space). ➤ The language. This is the most important problem for a foreigner. People who are not from Latin America do not know Spanish, and Spaniards are not familiar with English, especially in small towns. ➤ An important difference in Spanish culture is the excessive relaxation of its people. It is good in some respects, but it really requires patience when it comes to administrative work.

Question 4. Some suggestions or advice to people from your country who have just arrived in Spain on how to integrate more quickly
➤ Ask your neighbours and the people to trust on you more. ➤ Accept that Spanish bureaucracy is slow. ➤ If you don't know the language, ask for an interpreter service. ➤ Try to find out everything you need to know before you do anything. ➤ Take part in the various workshops organised by the associations. ➤ Use public transport is cheaper and everything is very well connected.

The next tables indicate the answers by Spanish people

Question 1. Some recommendations you would make to newcomers to Spain (refugees, immigrants, foreigners, etc.)
➤ Participate in neighbourhood activities, cultural centres. ➤ If you do not understand the language well, ask to communicate through interpreters. ➤ Explain their rights and obligations as well as the administrative procedures to regularise their situation. ➤ Try to do a professional course in order to have more job opportunities. ➤ Don't refuse to do the customs of the country, and invite your neighbours to participate in your customs (e.g. New Year's celebration/your New Year…).

Question 2. Some cultural differences that you have observed in foreigners who have just arrived in Spain
➢ Language ➢ Food and drink ➢ People skills ➢ Clothing, customs ➢ Timetable
Question 3. Some tips on how to integrate better in Spain if you are a foreigner
➢ Seek support from public bodies and establish relationships with neighbours. ➢ Live with the citizens by participating in everything they can: cultural activities, activities in libraries… ➢ Adapt to the neighbourhood where they want to live, be good people, go to an association that can help them. ➢ Practice Spanish and get to know Spanish traditions and culture better.

Question 4. Tell us about your first impressions of a foreigner or refugee living in Spain
➢ Accept that Spanish bureaucracy is slow. ➢ If you don't know the language, ask for an interpreter service. ➢ Try to find out everything you need to know before you do anything. ➢ Take part in the various workshops organised by the associations. ➢ Use public transport is cheaper and everything is very well connected.

4. Main conclusions

Migration and humanitarian crises are becoming one of the most significant challenges in our globalised society. The Afghans crisis is a good example. Starting in August 2021, Spain like other EU Member states, contributed to the evacuation and protection of refuges, prioritising their reception and speeding up their request for asylum and work permits. However, their adaptation to the Spanish reception system as well as their inclusion in the society and daily life routine has not been easy. Among other factors, problems of communication due to sociocultural and linguistic differences were- and still are insurmountable – barrier in some cases. Assuming that a mutual knowledge of the traditions, cultures and languages of the two countries could be a step forward the integration of the Afghans welcomed in Spain, the project *Get To Know To Keep In Mind* was developed by a multilingual, multidisciplinary and multifunctional team (psychologists, social workers, interpreters, translators, refugees, academics). Differences and similarities between the two countries in four main areas – education with a focus in women, family life and customs, health care, working life- were discussed a repository – still open- of different materials based on the experience, contacts and results of the different actions carried out was created. It is our intention to continue reaching out to Afghans and national populations in search of better communication, either by presenting the results in congresses or in publications.

As a final point, the conclusions we have reached can be summarised as follows: The project has allowed us to get closer to the Afghan and foreign population and to contact with people who are acting as linguistic and cultural bridges, helping in communication – some as professionals and others as simple bilingual friends or relatives or volunteers who know the languages to a certain level. Through all these collaborators and the multidisciplinary group, both groups – the Afghan participants and the research team – have gathered information based on experience and day-to-day life, have learned relevant information about each other, and have exchanged information on strategies or guidelines to facilitate integration.Finally, it is worth mentioning that the repository has been and continues to be disseminated by NGOs – such as CEAR, ACCEM, GUADACOGE, CARITAS, etc. – and by the contacts of the participants in the project, as well as in conferences and seminars organised by the FITISPos research group.

We also continue working on the three main lines of action opened:

1. Development of joint actions by social agents, mediators, psychologists and educators who are collaborating with the migrant population.
2. Dissemination of the necessary work of experts in communication with the foreign population (interpreters, mediators, and translators), and their situation in conflicts such as the one in Afghanistan.
3. Promotion of training proposals addressed to untrained bilingual people and as a prior step to promote and recognise the work of translators and interpreters in LLD.

We are convinced that multilingual staff from international, EU or local organisations as well as professional mediators, translators and interpreters play a critical role in ensuring effective communication in humanitarian emergency situations. We hope that our efforts help contribute to the achievement of the UN 2030 Agenda for Sustainable Development, and the efforts of the Spanish government in its inclusion itineraries.

References

ACCEM. https://www.accem.es/.

BBC News. 2023. Turkey earthquake: Deadly new tremor traps people under rubble. 21 February 2023. https://www.bbc.com/news/world-europe-64711228. (Accessed 4 April 2023).

CEAR. 2021. Memoria 2021. https://www.cear.es/wp-content/uploads/2022/07/Memoria-2021.pdf. (Accessed 4 April 2023).

EU Migration and Home Affairs. 2022. https://commission.europa.eu/about-european-commission/departments-and-executive-agencies/migration-and-home-affairs_en. (Accessed 3 April 2023).

Info Migrants. 2022. Afghan refugee flight arrives in Spain. Published on 11 August 2022. https://www.infomigrants.net/en/post/42545/afghan-refugee-flight-arrives-in-spain. (Accessed 4 April 2023).

López, Javier and Rodrigo, Ana. 2022. Afghan refugees in Spain struggle to rebuild their lives. Published on 18 August 2022. https://www.laprensalatina.com/afghan-refugees-in-spain-struggle-to-rebuild-their-lives/. (Accessed 4 April 2023).

Red Acoge-Guadalajara. http://www.guada-acoge.org/.

The European Directive on Temporary Protection. https://www.consilium.europa.eu/en/infographics/temporary-protection-displaced-persons/. (Accessed 3 April 2023).

Valero-Garcés, Carmen. 2022. "Ética, instituciones y sociedad civil. Hacia una ética cosmopolita en TISP". In Bourne, Julian, Fernández Sánchez, M. Manuela, Gutiérrez Artacho, Juncal, Portnova, Tatjana, Pradas Macías, E. Macarena y Quero Gervilla Enrique F. (eds.), *Reflexiones sobre ética profesional de traductores e intérpretes y buenas prácticas*. Granada: Comares.

Alessandra Riccardi

Chapter 9 Interpreter training: A never-ending process

Abstract: *Historia magistra vitae est*: interpreting history is no exception, in addition to being a fascinating subject, and can offer the opportunity to reflect on the interpreter's role and how it developed through centuries, in particular during turning points in civilisation. The result can be a more objective and critical stance towards present events and changes.

Similarities may be detected between interpreters' experiences in wartime, for example during Nazi-occupation or in concentration camps and in present-day conflict-zones. Simultaneous interpreting introduced during the 1920s at international conferences and especially its use during the Nuremberg trial required considerable adaptation to the new mode of interpreting comparable to the revolution brought about by the massive use of remote simultaneous interpreting during the Covid-pandemic. Interpreting history and the memoirs of interpreters themselves provide examples to enable students to overcome difficulties during their conference interpreting studies.

Keywords: simultaneous interpreting, *Lagerdolmetscher*, Nuremberg Trial, interpreter training, skills, RSI

1. Introduction

First of all, I would like to say how grateful I am to the colleague whose birthday is being celebrated with this volume, prof. Małgorzata Tryuk, because she was the researcher who first drew my attention to and interest in the *Lagerdolmetscher*, the interpreters in the Nazi concentration camps. I remember her telling me about her studies and investigations and how impressed I was by the research she was conducting at the time. I remember her asking me about an Italian quote of Primo Levi and informing me about her intention of writing an article on the concentration camp interpreter Marta Weiss featured in the film *The Last Stage* by Wanda Jakubowska (Tryuk 2019). Recent interpreting history is one of the subjects of my Interpreting Studies course and is often a starting point for students to debate present developments comparing them to the past.

In the present contribution I will first introduce the *Risiera di San Sabba* – the *San Sabba* Ricemill situated in Trieste, a city in the north-eastern part of Italy, very near to the border with Slovenia. The *Risiera* buildings, in the *San Sabba* suburb, became a police detention camp (*Polizeihaftlager*) after the armistice of

September 8 1943,[1] and, later, the only Nazi concentration camp[2] in Italy with a crematory furnace. Here, from 1944 until the end of the war, prisoners were tortured, selected and deported to Auschwitz or other concentration camps. At the *Risiera*, interpreting with the prisoners was carried out by civilians, Italian or Volksdeutsche[3], they were not prisoners as they mostly were in Nazi concentration camps elsewhere. Their treatment and duties will be compared and contrasted with those of the *Lagerdolmetscher* as reported by Tryuk (2010, 2016, 2019) and Wolf (2016).

The second historical event examined in this contribution is the Main Nuremberg Trial. Interpreters' recruitment and preparation for the hearings will be examined and compared to the present situation. Last year, 2022, it was possible[4] in Trieste to organise AIIC's travelling exhibition *One process – Four languages*[5] dedicated to the fascinating and often dramatic lives of the pioneers of simultaneous interpreting: the interpreters who in 1945–1946 worked for the International Military Tribunal in the first of the Nuremberg Trials during which the leaders of the Nazi regime were tried. Modern simultaneous interpretation as we know it today was used there for the very first time. Without simultaneous interpretation, a trial of this magnitude and duration in the four languages spoken by the judges, witnesses, defendants, members of the prosecution and of the defense (English, French, Russian and German) would have been unthinkable[6].

---

1 After the armistice of September 8 1943 between Italy and the Allies during World War II, the region Venezia Giulia became a territory under the direct administration of the Third Reich, *Operationszone Adriatisches Küstenland*.

2 Between 1933 and 1945, Nazi Germany and its allies established more than 44,000 camps and other incarceration sites (including ghettos). The perpetrators used these sites for a range of purposes, including forced labour, detention of people thought to be enemies of the state, and mass murder; see https://encyclopedia.ushmm.org/content/en/article/concentration-camp-system-in-depth, 28.1.2023.

3 Volksdeutsche: people whose language and culture had German origins but who did not hold German citizenship.

4 The exhibition in Trieste had to be postponed for some years because of the Covid-19 pandemic.

5 The exhibition was organized as one of the series coordinated by Elke Limberger-Katsumi under the patronage of AIIC. The first exhibition *One Process – Four Languages* was held 2013 in Nuremberg. In the following years, the travelling exhibition was held in many European and non-European cities. https://www.profession-of-interpreting.org/en/one-trial-four-languages/, 14.1.2023.

6 The hearings in the main trial alone, with the depositions of 360 witnesses, lasted 218 days.

Following the publication in 1998 of Francesca Gaiba's book *The origins of Simultaneous Interpretation – The Nuremberg Trial*, research into interpreting history, which was still scarce at the time, experienced a boost (see Kurz/Bowen 1999; Baigorri-Jalón 2002, 2017; Behr/Corpataux 2006; Kalverkämper/Schippel 2008; Andres/Behr 2014). Probably the latest publication on the subject is the 2022 Special Issue of *The Interpreters' Newsletter*, *Looking back at Interpreting in Nuremberg*, with three contributions from a panel organised during the Trieste exhibition.[7] Much has been written on simultaneous interpreting at Nuremberg, also by the three contributors to this issue[8]. In their contributions, the authors were able to draw on sources hitherto unused before, thereby adding new features to their reflections and analyses. The exhibition aroused my interest in learning more about the circumstances under which interpreters had to work and how they could manage to prepare for their assignments.

2. The *Risiera di San Sabba*

The *Risiera* buildings date back to 1898. With the September 8 armistice in 1943 and the establishment of the fascist Republic of Salò, they became a centre for the confinement and transit of the prisoners later deported to Germany and Nazi-occupied Poland. In the camp, the prisoners were Italians, Slovenes, Croats, Jews, partisans and political opponents.

Studies on *Lagerdolmetscher* have shown that the role of the interpreter in concentration camps would change according circumstances, there is no rigid and fixed model. His/her role can be identified as one of the points of a continuum, with different gradations and facets, where on one pole there is unconditioned compliance, servility and collaboration with superiors and on the other empathy, solidarity and altruism (Wolf 2016: 76). Through their actions, individual interpreters can be found on the side of the victims, the executioners or on one of the possible points in between.

7 The title of the panel was *Simultaneous Interpreting at Nuremberg: a groundbreaking event* and offered an in-depth examination of the role of interpreters during the trials.

8 The contributions selected for the special issue of *The Interpreters' Newsletter* are: "The Nuremberg Trial as a turning point in the history of interpreting: Notes on historical transitions" by Jesús Baigorri-Jalón; Francesca Gaiba's "'*I have done some digging in my memory files and some old folders*': An intimate look through my correspondence with Nuremberg interpreters from 1995 to 1998 Interpreting for the Nuremberg Trials"; and "Four Eyewitness Accounts" by Ingrid Kurz .

The *San Sabba Risiera* was different. In addition to the Nazi personnel, the *Risiera* camp was able to function thanks to a network of officers and civil servants recruited directly in the region. They were employed in several sectors, from the administrative, to the economic, propaganda, police, racial sector as well as in relations with Italian civilians and military authorities. Trieste, the capital city, had many Nazi headquarters and, here, civilians were employed with various duties: interpreter, administrators, secretary, simple employer and maintenance personnel (Scalpelli 1995: I 31).

Information on the period can be found in the two volumes *San Sabba: istruttoria e processo per il Lager della Risiera* by ANED[9], on the preliminary hearings and the trial[10] for the *Risiera* lager, it is the reference work for the historical reconstruction of what happened and includes documents and testimonies. Here can be found the depositions of prisoners and officers working at the Risiera, interpreters included. Thirty years passed before the sentence was delivered. Among the collaborators, 74 were defined as interpreters. Compared to the *Lagerdolmetscher*, they were in a totally different position. They were civilians regularly recruited by the Reich administration, their workplace was at the Risiera as well as in offices outside the lager. Their duties included translating correspondence, assisting during questionings and interrogations, searches and also during executions (Santarelli 2019). These employees with interpreting duties are an example of how interpreters may operate inside a particular ideological and cultural system and consequently be loyal to the forces employing them. War time interpreters, as stated by Tryuk (2015), are almost always in the position of representing the interrogator and in the worst cases, as in the Gestapo offices, "interpreters not only interrogated them like other investigators, but even took part in the beatings and torture of those detained" (Tryuk 2015: 156). The persons who were interpreting the prisoners in the *Risiera* had no training or preparation, they were bilinguals, and interpreting was only one of their mansions. During the process they admitted that they had

9 ANED (*Associazione Nazionale ex deportati nei campi nazisti*) is the National Association of Italian political deportees from Nazi concentration camps. It is made up of survivors of Nazi extermination, and families of victims of the camps. ANED is a non-profit organization.

10 The trial against the *Risiera* crimes began on the 16th February 1976, more than 30 years after the end of WW II and 30 years of preliminary hearings. It ended on the 29th April 1976 and those in charge of the camp were sentenced, most of them had already died, the only survivor was the head of the *Risiera*, Joseph Oberhauser who was convicted in absentia.

collaborated with the Nazis, but they all denied any knowledge of the atrocities committed by the regime they served (Scalpelli 1995: I 35).

3. Interpreter training at the Nuremberg trial

A completely different interpreting situation emerges at the end of WW II during the Main Nuremberg Trial. For the first time in history, the leaders of a nation, the Nazi leaders, were put on trial. To ensure a fair criminal trial within a reasonable timeframe the decision was taken to use simultaneous interpretation in four languages for the proceedings (Gaiba 1998; Baigorri-Jalòn 2002, 2014). Consecutive interpreting was the preferred mode at most international conferences at the time, although simultaneous interpretation had been already tested during the 1920s and 1930s. Technical problems and the difficulty in monitoring its quality had until then impeded its diffusion.

The decision to use simultaneous interpreting was accepted by the International Military Tribunal because it would guarantee an orderly and fair trial within an acceptable time even with four languages being used. Consecutive interpretation would have lengthened the proceedings enormously, three or four times, which would have meant between three and four years' time if compared to the eleven months duration of the Nuremberg main trial. The idea of using the telephonic interpretation that had been used in Geneva at the ILO headquarters during their conferences in the 1920s (see Baigorri-Jalón 2021) was indeed a revolutionary idea at the time, given the scant experience with the Filene-Finlay Speech Translator system (Baigorri-Jalón 2014: 7).

One of the problems linked to the decision of adopting the simultaneous mode of interpreting was the scarcity of interpreters who had had already worked with it. Actually, according to Baigorri-Jalón only two of those hired in Nuremberg "had had prior experience with simultaneous at the ILO Conference in Philadelphia" in April 1944 (2014: 221). Given the scarce request, interpreter training programmes concentrated thus far only on consecutive interpreting. Recruitment of interpreters was therefore no easy task; neither was ensuring training to prepare interpreters for the new modality. The recruitment consisted of two stages: first on location, in Paris, London, Washington, Geneva to test their language command and general knowledge; successful candidates would be tested again in Nuremberg to verify whether they could cope with listening and speaking at the same time in two languages.

All delegations were aware of the fact that the language system at Nuremberg would be effective only if three requirements were met: an efficient mechanical system; the court had to be disciplined in speaking, this meant that people had to speak slowly and one at a time; the third condition was that the system would only work "if delegations recruited top-notch interpreters" (Gaiba 1998: 45). As interpreting scholar and trainer, I was very curious to learn more on the intellectual background of the selected interpreters. For example, what was their preparation, their age, their professional training, because there was no school at the time to learn simultaneous interpreting. The AIIC exhibition has filled to a certain extent this gap with the biographies of many of the interpreters. Other studies have also contributed to learn more about these pioneers of simultaneous interpreting (Gaiba1998; Baigorri-Jalón 2002, 2017, 2022; Andres/ Behr 2014). Many of them were very young, in their twenties, some had just finished their interpreting training in consecutive, other were in their forties or older, sometimes with a very adventurous life as emigrants or with a military background (Ramler 1988; Kurz 2017; Baigorri-Jalón 2014). Only two, as mentioned above, had already had experience with simultaneous interpreting. They had usually grown up as bilingual or trilingual, possibly adding other languages during their career as journalists, writers, linguists or serving in the army; some were Jews who had emigrated or had been detained in concentration camps or witnessed terrible family experiences.

Recruiters would test or look for persons who in addition to an excellent language command would also possess a vast background knowledge, good knowledge of legal and military terminology together with a high level of resilience to stress (Matasov 2017; Baigorri-Jalón 2014). The younger interpreters would probably have weaker terminology and background knowledge compared to their more mature colleagues with their work experience in different fields possibly compensated by more rapid reactions. Some would experience an intolerable psychological stress when confronted with the Nazi criminals or testimonies.

4. Stefan Priacel

To indicate how interpreters went about their preparation and to obtain some first-hand answers, I would like to quote reflections by Stefan Priacel, interpreter at the Nuremberg Trial, from his posthumously published book (1974/2016). His reflections on simultaneous interpretation and the examples given of how he acquired the necessary skills can help interpreting students to recognise the importance of self-study and self-reflection when, during simultaneous interpreting classes, they are confronted with certain stumbling blocks they find difficult to overcome.

Stefan Priacel was born in 1904 in Breslau of Jewish origin and grew up with Polish, German, French, Italian and English. He was a journalist, translator, writer, theatre and film critic and later an anti-fascist political journalist.[11] He was arrested in 1941 and interned in the Camp du Vernet in Ariège, subsequently in the prisons of Figueras de Jaraba in Spain. He was freed eleven months later and in 1944 he joined the Free French Forces in Algiers. He obtained French nationality in 1945. In February 1946, having just returned to Paris, he was offered the job of interpreter at the Nuremberg trials. After his first simultaneous interpreting experience in Nuremberg, Priacel continued to work as an interpreter in international institutions, for the UN, for the Council of Europe and for the European Community. He also taught for several years at ESIT in Paris.

The test Priacel had to go through in Nuremberg consisted in a text read out by an American second lieutenant of German origin. It was a passage, rich in figures, from a statement made that day by the former finance minister of the Third Reich. Priacel had already interpreted in the past, but only in consecutive. He did not even know of the existence of simultaneous and his first reaction after having understood what was expected of him as an interpreter, was to decline the offer and go back to Paris on the first plane, because he was not sure about being able to sustain for long the effort of concentration required (Priacel 1974/2016: 22). Major Jean Mayer and Colonel Léon Dostert, who were there listening to him, insisted and, finally, he accepted spending two weeks in Nuremberg to practice simultaneous interpretation.

Priacel had vast background knowledge and knew how to prepare for assignments. Every evening, as soon as the hearing was over, he would return to his room carrying the minutes of the proceedings and as many documents as possible relating to the trial to help him to understand the words and the arguments of the speakers and grasp the nuances, the allusions of those men the French version of whose voice and words he was to become (Priacel 1974/2016: 25).

Priacel was familiar with radio resources having worked in military listening centres[12] as listener/translator as well as head of the control of radio programmes in Paris. He had learned the skill of reproducing the main ideas and realised that his recipients were interested in the rigor of thought not in the reproduction of the terms used. He had soon recognised the utmost importance, for simultaneous

11 See https://maitron.fr/spip.php?article142706, 26.01.2023.

12 Listening centres were a monitoring service that informed military, political authorities and the press about the reactions of foreign broadcasts – allied or enemy – to the events of the war.

interpreting too, of the skills acquired earlier as listener/translator – rapid analysis, synthesis and working memory. Therefore, he began practicing them with the help of radio broadcasts and news bulletins (Priacel 1974/2016: 26).

Above all, what helped him immensely for a smooth interpretation from German was a thorough understanding of the context, the subject, the speaker's point of view and the thesis he wanted to defend. Acquiring insight into the question at hand, he knew he would be able to anticipate the speaker's thoughts including the verb, as a logical conclusion of the speaker's ideas.

> L'essentiel, pour l'interprète, serait de bien saisir l'enjeu de la discussion et de s'interdire toute forme d'automatisme afin de réussir, par une sorte de sens de la divination, à précéder l'orateur dans sa propre pensée et à découvrir ainsi, presque toujours à coup sûr, le verbe, voire la négation ou l'affirmation qui, en toute logique, devait conclure son propos (Priacel 1974/2016: 27)[13]

The recruiters had rightly seen in Stefan Priacel an ideal candidate to become a simultaneous interpreter at the Nuremberg Trial. Not only did he have the required command of languages, a vast encyclopaedic knowledge and specific knowledge of legal terminology[14], but was able to devise a system of self-study to cope with the various requirements of the Nuremberg trial. Under the pressure of the working conditions of the Nuremberg trial and the responsibility he faced as interpreter he exploited as rapidly as possible all his knowledge sources to be able to stand the challenge of simultaneous interpretation he and all his colleagues were confronted with.

5. Simultaneous interpreting skills

In Nuremberg there was a high turnover of interpreters for a variety of reasons. Some were on loan from other organisation, some could not keep up with the fatigue deriving from the interpreting situation and had to be replaced. Many interpreters were very young (Matasov 2017) only few of whom had attended

---

13 The essential thing for the interpreter is to understand what is at stake in the discussion and refrain from any form of automatism to succeed, through a kind of sense of divination, in anticipating the speaker's own thoughts thereby discovering, almost always with certainty, the verb, or even the negation or the assertion, which, logically, would be the conclusion of his or her remarks (translation by the author).

14 Between 1934 and 1936, he had followed and attended as a journalist the trials of communists in Berlin and Romanian antifascists in Romania with reports published in several journals and on these political trials he published three books, see https://maitron.fr/spip.php?article142706, 25.02.2023.

interpreting classes in Geneva, and then only in consecutive. Various forms of training were devised for those who were considered apt for the job to fill their terminological and cultural gaps. There was sometimes too little time to make up for their shortcomings. In extreme cases there was almost none, perhaps a couple of days or weeks or, in certain cases, up to two months. To learn and practice terminology, candidate interpreters would first work in the Translation Department for a while, they would follow the hearings as often as possible, in the courtroom or in the public gallery, participate in simultaneous exercises outside the proceedings, in mock trials or with colleagues reading speeches before beginning the real job, interpreting in the booth (Baigorri-Jalón 2014: 221–223).

Most experience would be gained in the field, as on-the-job training. There were three interpreter teams, comprising all together thirty-six interpreters. While one team was on duty interpreting in the courtroom, a reserve team would be in a room next door, connected to the sound system, following the proceedings, ready to intervene in the event of difficulties. The third team, not on duty, could follow proceedings from the above-mentioned spectator's gallery. This teams' shift arrangements gave interpreters who were not in the booths the opportunity to prepare and exercise for what they could expect next during their turn, in addition, they could hear their colleagues working and learn new vocabulary, new techniques or tactics (Baigorri-Jalón 2014: 224–225). Interpreters' duties included checking the stenographers' transcriptions with the recordings, another kind of exercise to contribute to refining their interpreting skills. The revision was necessary to avoid errors in translation. Further help for the interpreters came over time from the monitors and coordinators who would also learn to recognise defects or infelicities and sometimes even from the listeners. The teamwork implied discussions and exchanges among interpreters and from the users, the judges, for example, but also from the defendants (Baigorri-Jalón 2014: 226–227). The feedback received from colleagues and also the public at large would help interpreters understand better what was more suitable in terms of terminology, accents and pitch under varying circumstances.

In Nuremberg, interpreters, monitors and coordinators developed the basics of simultaneous interpreting training that would be further improved and elaborated in the following decades. Given the exceptional circumstances under which they had to work and considering the extreme time pressure they were exposed to, it is no wonder that they would exploit every possibility to improve their interpreting skills together with the cultural, legal and technical notions required during the trial. Their capacity to overcome different kinds of difficulties was the result of joint cooperation inspired by the willingness and determination to fulfil a common duty and reach a common goal. Self-study, group-exercise as well as feedback from different sources were the means to improve the interpreting skills needed during the Nuremberg trial to guarantee communication among the parties for a fair trial.

6. Interpreters conditioning and transition processes

Studies on wartime interpreters have examined the question of applicable interpretation norms and Tryuk's (2015) conclusion on interpreting norms is that in crisis or wartime situations the concept of the objective and neutral interpreter is just a myth, because in these instances the interpreter there is at the heart of the conflict where there is no neutral ground. Therefore, she suggests to discarding "the notion that an interpreter is always a neutral and impartial intermediary. Recognition of the reality in which interpreters work would allow for the preparation of a new code of behaviour which would more adequately suit the various conditions under which contemporary interpreters work" (Tryuk 2015: 162).

The many difficulties encountered by interpreters when on duty in wartime and conflict situations, together with the knowledge of what interpreters had witnessed in the past, have contributed not only to define rights and duties in present times, but also raise awareness of the extreme risks they are exposed to.

A discussion on interpreting ethical norms and their applicability depends on the kind of assignment and interpreting required always linked to a concrete situation, a given time and place.

Raising the awareness of all stakeholders and actors of these factors – perhaps above all including interpreters themselves – will result in a more precise understanding of the work of interpreters as responsible and active participants in a process and event, and not only as supposedly neutral and impartial intermediaries or 'machines' who are always faithful to the original (Tryuk 2015: 163)

The perspective of a transition process in the history of interpreting put forward by Baigorri-Jalón (2022) is to the present writer's opinion extremely useful to gain an understanding of the evolution witnessed in the profession and in interpreting modes and training:

> That transition involved not only technological developments but also an evolution in the interpreters' training, selection and working environment, in the users' education on what to expect from interpreting services, and in the relationship between interpreters and the recipients of their services. (Baigorri-Jalón 2022: 2)

7. Final remarks

In the 1920s, telephone technology paved the way for the Filene-Finlay system of telephone interpretation, the ancestor of modern simultaneous interpreting systems. Several tests were conducted at the ILO in the second half of the 1920s and 1930s to assess the feasibility of the system. SI as it is now known, was called direct or instantaneous interpretation. It typically led to difficulties when the speaker's delivery was too fast or when figures were given. It was therefore only used occasionally. Telephone interpreting was also used in what was called simultaneous telephone interpretation – the simultaneous delivery of the interpreted speech in several languages after the source language speech had been made and while it was being interpreted from the platform into one of the official languages, enabling interpreting to be provided to delegates with limited knowledge of English or French, ILO's official languages (Baigorri-Jalón 2021). It was a great challenge at that time – a technical revolution partially overcoming the time-related limitations inherent in the consecutive mode. It took many years, though, before simultaneous interpreting began being used more systematically at international meetings and conferences.

An extraordinary event such as the main trial in Nuremberg, requiring real time interpretation into four languages, contributed to the awareness of simultaneous interpreting and led to its adoption at international level, despite initial reservations and resistance from delegates and interpreters.

A set of favourable circumstances combined to allow the successful launch of simultaneous interpretation – four languages to be interpreted back and forth, time issues, the need to have real time interpreting and the availability of new technology.

Between the late 1990s and 2005 several tests were conducted at the European Institutions and at the UN to investigate the viability of remote interpreting as a means to solve issues of interpreter availability and costs brought about by physical building constraints, a shortage of meeting rooms with the number of booths matching the increasing number of EU official languages or the impossibility to equip small or medium-sized meeting rooms with additional booths (Mouzourakis 2006; United Nations Report 1: 2001a; United Nations Report 1: 2001b).

Interpreters found remote interpreting characterised by technical audio and video conditions inferior to those commonly present in onsite interpreting, which caused greater fatigue and stress. They complained about sore eyes, back and neck pains, headaches as well as loss of concentration and motivation and a feeling of alienation due to the remote interpreting conditions.

During the last twenty years, new technologies have become an important feature of conference interpreting working conditions and interpreter training has gradually adapted to the new requirements of the profession introducing them into regular classes. New technologies may be used to complement traditional interpreting classes, for blended learning – combining face-to face instruction and computer-mediated instruction – and/or to support students' self-study. Online search engines, terminological databases such as IATE, interpreter-specific glossary management software, for example Interpreters' Help or InterpretBank have become part and parcel of conference interpreter training.

Looking back at interpreting history, while the Nuremberg trial marked the first revolution in conference interpreting with the massive adoption of simultaneous interpreting, the Covid pandemic marked the second, with the massive use of platforms for virtual conference interpreting and remote simultaneous interpreting (RSI). ICT tools such as platforms for RSI had been around for a while and technically viable, but had been much less used than onsite simultaneous interpreting until Covid-related lockdowns left no other option for continuing to interpret at the events that were still held.

Remote interpreting and remote simultaneous interpreting had to be introduced in conference interpreting training from one day to the next, when it became the only viable option for interpreting classes during lockdowns. In the meantime, RSI has become part of the profession of conference interpretation, it is one of the competences, skills, techniques of a modern conference interpreter. In the same way as other ICTs were integrated into interpreter training, RSI platforms are finding their place in conference interpreter programmes. The choice of the right moment is vital, probably, preference should be given in the last part of the programme, when simultaneous and consecutive techniques are already strong enough to include the new skill in a progressive manner.

Today, simultaneous interpreting is a well-established subject, but the difficulties remain. Students have to overcome them when they begin memorising, analysis and synthesis exercises or when they go into the booth for the first times. They have been told that their languages need to be fluent and rich in vocabulary if they wish to keep up with the speaker and reduce their reaction times. They know perfectly they need to distribute their mental resources between listening, comprehension and speaking and feel terribly frustrated when, notwithstanding their efforts, their output is wrong, they loose parts of the speech or cannot find the suitable vocabulary they have been studying so intensively. The training is effortful, results scarce and they become demotivated. Examples taken from the pioneers may help them understand that even great interpreters had to struggle to obtain a fluent delivery and the right pace that seem so natural and spontaneous encouraging them to continue their studies knowing that present circumstances are much easier compared to what pioneer interpreters had to go through in the past. Knowing how they mastered difficulties can assist them in devising new forms of self-study and persuading them not to give up.

References

Andres Dörte / Behr Martina (eds.) (2014) *Die Wahrheit, die reine Wahrheit und nicht als die Wahrheit,* Berlin, Frank & Timme.

Baigorri-Jalón Jesús (2002) *De Paris à Nuremberg: Naissance de l'interprétation de conférence,* Ottawa, University of Ottawa Press.

Baigorri-Jalón Jesús (2014) *From Paris to Nuremberg. The birth of conference interpreting,* translated by H. Mikkelson and B. S. Olsen, Amsterdam / Philadelphia, John Benjamins.

Baigorri-Jalón Jesús (2017) "*Interpreting at the main Nuremberg Trial (1945–1946) and its impact on conference interpreters' professionalization*", in Guillaume Mouralis / Marie-Bénédicte Vincent (eds.), *Comparativ, monograph issue The Nuremberg Trials. New Perspectives on the Professions, Band 2016,* 4, 28–42.

Baigorri-Jalón Jesús (2021) "Once upon a time at the ILO: The infancy of simultaneous interpreting", in Kilian Seeber (ed.), *100 Years of Conference Interpreting: A Legacy,* Cambridge, Cambridge Scholars Publishing, 1–25.

Baigorri-Jalón Jesús (2022) "The Nuremberg Trial as a turning point in the history of interpreting: Notes on historical transitions", *The Interpreters' Newsletter, 27* bis, 1–24

Behr Martina / Corpataux Maike (2006) *Die Nürnberger Prozesse. Zur Bedeutung der Dolmetscher für die Prozesse und der Prozesse für die Dolmetscher,* München, Martin Meidenbauer.

Gaiba Francesca (1998) *The Origins of Simultaneous Interpretation: The Nuremberg Trial,* Ottawa, Ottawa University Press.

Kalverkämper Hartwig / Schippel Larisa (eds.) (2008) *Simultandolmetschen in Erstbewährung: Der Nürnberger Prozess 1945,* Berlin, Frank & Timme.

Kurz Ingrid (2017) "Mit Anfang 20 als Dolmetscher dabei – Richard W. Sonnenfeldt und Siegfried Ramler im Justizpalast in Nürnberg 1945", in Dörte Andres, Klaus Kaindl, und Ingrid Kurz (eds.), *Dolmetscherinnen und Dolmetscher im Netz der Macht,* Berlin, Frank &Timme, 153–170.

Kurz Ingrid / Bowen Margaret (eds.) (1999) *The history of interpreting in the 20th century, Special Issue of Interpreting, 4*(1).

Matasov Roman A. (2017) "Nuremberg: The Trial of Six Million Words", AIIC, https://aiic.org/document/995/, 26.01.2023.

Mouzourakis Panayotis (2006) "Remote interpreting – A technical perspective on recent experiments", *Interpreting*, *8*(1), 45–66.

Priacel Stefan (1974/2016) *L'Interprète de Conférence: Cet Inconnu*, (Manuscrit repris et numérisé par Helga Priacel avec la collaboration de Anne et Matthieu Freund-Priacel, Janvier 2016), Internet Archive: https://archive.org/details/9500-priacel-fr-interprete-conference-ce-inconnu/mode/2up, 23.01.2023.

Ramler Siegfried (1988) "Origins and challenges of simultaneous interpretation: The Nuremberg trial experience", in D. Lindberg Hammond (ed.), *Languages at Crossroads*, Medford, Learned Information, 437–440.

Santarelli Mattia (2019) *Contro "l'eclissi della parola" – L'interpretazione nei campi di concentramento nazisti*, unpublished master thesis, University of Trieste.

Scalpelli, Adolfo (ed.) (1995) *San Sabba: istruttoria e processo per il Lager della Risiera*, ANED, Trieste, LINT.

Tryuk, Małgorzata (2010) "Interpreting in Nazi concentration camps during World War II", *Interpreting*, *12*(2), 125–145.

Tryuk, Małgorzata (2016) Interpreting and translating in Nazi concentration camps during World War II. *Linguistica Antverpiensia, New Series – Themes in Translation Studies*, *15*, 121–141.

Tryuk, Małgorzata (2015) *On Ethics and Interpreters*, Frankfurt am Main, Berlin, Bern, Bruxelles, New York, Oxford, Wien, Peter Lang.

Tryuk Małgorzata (2019) "The cinematic figure of an interpreter at a Nazi concentration camp: Marta Weiss in *The Last Stage* by Wanda Jakubowska", *Przekładaniec*, Special Issue 38/2019, *Translation and Memory*, 175–191, https://www.ejournals.eu/Przekladaniec/English-issues/Special-Issue-Translation-and-memory/art/15654/, 15.10.2023.

United Nations Report 1 (2001a) "Provision of interpretation services to other locations from permanent interpretation structures in New York, Geneva, Vienna and Nairobi", *The Interpreters' Newsletter*, 11, 153–162.

United Nations Report 2 (2001b) "Remote Interpretation", *The Interpreters' Newsletter*, 11, 163–180.

Wolf Michaela (ed.) (2016) *Interpreting in Nazi concentration camps*, New York, Bloomsbury.

Danielle D'Hayer

Chapter 10 When a CoP mindset combined with hybrid pedagogy breaks silos to enhance interprofessional multilingual experiential learning and an inclusive participation of multiple communities. The case study of mock conferences for conference interpreting education at London Metropolitan University

Abstract: The COVID 19 pandemic had a transformative impact on the interpreting profession. But what about interpreting education? This case study showcases the high potential of a community of practice that brings together students, educators and alumni as partners on repurposing mock conferences as a construct of three cycles of inclusive multilayered events. The innovative use of technologies enables the strategic participation of a multilingual audience that enhances the value of experiential learning for students and staff. It opens the doors to the interprofessional participation of students and staff who experience the value of their own multilingual identity in professional settings. The community of practice mindset empowers students to be agents of their own learning. Finally, the ambition of the chapter is to initiate inclusive pedagogical conversations to optimise the value of conference interpreting studies as a catalyst to enhance language and culture identity in Higher Education.

Keywords: Students as Partners (SaP), Experiential Learning, Simulated Based Learning (SBL), Community of Practice (CoP), mock conferences, Students as Co-creators, Student-staff Partnership

1. Introduction

This chapter provides an insight on the COVID-19 influenced pedagogical strategies that underpin the mock conferences in interpreting studies at London Metropolitan University. The objective of the chapter is twofold. First it aims at inviting conference interpreting educators to consider technology as an enabling factor to revisit the purpose, design and impact of mock conferences in interpreting pedagogy. It then introduces underexplored pedagogical concepts to interpreting studies, that will hopefully encourage interpreting educators to move beyond the individual performative approach and the apprenticeship model, and engage further with Experiential Learning (Morris, 2019), Simulated Based Learning (Frei-Landau et al., 2022; Hu, 2019), Students as Partners and Students as Co-Creators of the curriculum (Lubicz-Nawrocka, 2018; Nawrocka-Lubicz, 2022). These pedagogical developments that place mutual engagement and trust at the heart of the debate traditionally underpin social learning and the community of practice pedagogical approach. This case study will hopefully offer a narrative that illustrates how this approach can evolve into becoming a mindset that enhances the teaching and learning experience of interpreting students and educators. Only then can interpreting studies claim the recognition it deserves in Higher Education and play to its full potential in the wider debate on multilingual and cultural social educational inclusion.

2. Pedagogical approach for interpreting education: Too exclusive to be inclusive?

Conference interpreting programmes are often considered to be fairly exclusive in the wider context of Higher Education (D'Hayer, 2022). This reflects the conference interpreting professional landscape that is renowned to be competitive and selective. In the absence of protected title (Gentile, 2014; Setton & Dawrant, 2016a, p. 358; Rudvin, 2018), professional interpreters rely on their skills and reputation to access interpreting assignments abiding by the AIIC standards, working conditions and pay (D'Hayer, 2022).

Unsurprisingly, interpreting education map the professional landscape and aim at developing a high reputation with quality labels (Orlando, 2016, 2021) such as EMCI[1], AIIC listed courses[2], CIUTI[3], UN MoU network[4] and cooperation with European institutions[5].

So far, the pedagogy principles that underpin interpreting studies have been based on the apprenticeship model (Pöchhacker, 2004; Orlando, 2016; Setton & Dawrant, 2016a) adopting a transmissionist approach whereby tutors who are

1 European Masters in Conference Interpreting https://www.emcinterpreting.org/ (Accessed 16 January 2023)

2 AIIC Schools Directory: https://aiic.org/site/dir/schools (Accessed 16 January 2023)

3 CIUTI https://www.ciuti.org/about-us/our-profile/ (Accessed 16 January 2023)

4 MoU network: https://www.un.org/dgacm/en/content/mou-network (Accessed 16 January 2023)

5 Directorate General Interpretation: https://ec.europa.eu/education/knowledge-centre-interpretation/universities_en (Accessed 16 January 2023)

practising professional interpreters transmit their skills, knowledge and expertise to students, adopting the novice-expert paradigm (Moser-Mercer, 1997, 2000). Over the years, there has been an attempt to shift from a tutor-centred approach to a student-centred approach, adopting a pedagogical perspective inspired by Vygotsky' constructivist model (Defrancq et al., 2022).This model was then further enhanced by the adoption of the theory of situated learning (Lave & Wenger, 1991) that suggests that learning is collective and social within 'a community of practice'. According to Wenger et al. (2002, p. 4), 'Communities of Practice are groups of people who share a concern or a passion for something they do, and learn how to do it better as they interact regularly'.

However, even though the theories of community of practice and social learning have evolved over the years (Bandura & Walters 1963, 1977; Wenger 1998, 2008, 2010; Wenger et al., 2014; Wenger-Trayner & Wenger-Trayner, 2019, 2020), they have been surprisingly under-explored or even neglected in the world of interpreting studies (Sawyer, 2004, p. 77). Setton and Dawrant (2016b, p. 75) make an attempt at challenging the traditional apprenticeship model and state that 'apprenticeship should be more than teaching by mere inspiration' and that 'a more intrusive coaching approach wherever appropriate' (p. 75) would be welcome, adopting 'a more student focused learning' and that 'a first step (…) would be to recognise the individual variability of students' learning trajectories' (p. 75). Duflou's research (2016) seems to be the only extensive work that illustrates how a community of practice can facilitate the inclusion of newly accredited EU interpreters to the workplace and contribute to professional development and identity transformation. Finally, D'Hayer's doctoral thesis (2022) demonstrates that the apprenticeship model operating with a top-down tutor-student model is not conducive to a Community of Practice model. A CoP is a more egalitarian horizontal model that fosters pedagogical approaches and values that are underpinning the case study presented in her paper. The outcome of her three year longitudinal research demonstrated that:

> Commitment and belonging to the community [of practice] motivates members to take an active role and exercise agency to continuously negotiate meaning so as to define the purpose of the community, its practice and who they are becoming in the process. *Converging towards a common interest* contributes to developing *trust* and creating a safe space so that *learning within a community by caring, giving and sharing* takes place. The values of participation, such as *learning by caring, giving and sharing, trust, a collaborative mindset* and *a professional activity* based on *togetherness*, reside in participants even beyond the CoP experience, and contribute to transform their identity and approach to learning as *motivated social lifelong learners* and *professionals actively engaged in a landscape of practice.* (D'Hayer, 2022, p. 225)

The Covid19 pandemic was a reminder that in the face of crisis, solutions to move forward in the unknown, and the creation of new knowledge never are the result of one person's contribution, but the outcome of a reflexive process that brings people together in networks or communities. This shift from a competitive to a more collaborative approach was illustrated by the numerous online webinars and contributions on social media that were formally and informally organised by individuals (e.g. El Metwally, M. (2019)[6], Goldsmith, J. (2019)[7]), professional associations such as the Association Internationale des Interpretes de Conference[8] and international institutions (e.g. Mock conferences organised by DG SCIC[9]). Some of them were punctual, others were network based, whereas very few fostered a community-based approach. One of them was initiated by Sophie Llewellyn Smith who was able to bring together interpreting trainers to share their challenges and know-how on a very successful Facebook group, Interpreter trainers blundering through online teaching in a pandemic[10]. This group initiative has now evolved into the inspiring community-based annual event, The Terp Summit.

3. The Covid 19 pandemic: Catalyst for change for the interpreting profession, but what about interpreting education?

3.1. It is not all about the technology

The pandemic undeniably shook the interpreting profession and education globally. Actually, in the face of the crisis, the pandemic stimulated stakeholders to come together formally and informally to find immediate operational solutions, such as understanding how interpreting platforms worked, how to protect the hearing of interpreters and avoid acoustic shock, what equipment to get for excellent sound quality, or again what to do to preserve the interpreter's well-being or financial survival. For interpreting education, the focus mainly was practical; how to teach and assess simultaneous interpreting to a multilingual

6 https://www.youtube.com/@culturalbridgesbymahael-me2305/featured (Accessed 22 January 2023)

7 https://www.innovationininterpreting.com/insiders (Accessed 22 January, 2023)

8 https://aiic.asia/regional-webinars-supporting-members-during-the-covid-crisis/ (Accessed 18 January 2023)

9 https://ec.europa.eu/education/knowledge-centre-interpretation/en/news/new-training-support-videos-mock-conferences-0 (Accessed 20 January 2023)

10 https://www.facebook.com/groups/1452814461639873 (Accessed 20 January 2023)

group of students remotely (Chen-En & Zou, 2022), using more than one device; or again finding new opportunities for interpreting students to practise with peers in the absence of the traditional onsite dummy booth practice or interpreting assignments offered to interpreting students. On the one hand, conversations about technology had to take centre stage to continue teaching interpreting in the face of this unprecedented emergency. However, the pedagogical conversations about the impact of the Covid19 on interpreting education have not yet moved beyond that point. The pandemic has impacted how people feel, work and think. It is an opportunity to question, rethink and create a more adapted pedagogical approach that reflects what the 'new normal' means for educators, students and professionals.

3.2. The 'new normal': Pedagogical trends

As we move away from emergency remote teaching[11], the 'new normal' educational context is emerging. Even though technology is fully integrated into the conversation, it is mainly as a tool that enables change.

Post Covid19 Higher Education literature in the UK, the USA and Australia such as Lubicz- Nawrocka & Owen (2022) contribute to defining new trends and report how students and educators have engaged as equal partners to navigate new learning spaces, in a synchronous or/and asynchronous mode, either online or in hybrid contexts. Healey et al. (2014, cited in Mercer-Mapstone et al., 2017) describe SaP as 'a relationship in which all involved—students, academics, professional services staff, senior managers, students' unions, and so on—are actively engaged in and stand to gain from the process of learning and working together' (p. 12).

Together as partners (Healy, 2017), students and educators have fostered trust and engaged collaboratively to co-create learning and teaching (Metthews et al., 2019); they have negotiated a mutually beneficial decision making process and a more egalitarian and inclusive approach to teaching whereby the student voice is highly represented. The role of educators has shifted from the expert to the designer and facilitator of safe learning spaces where actors come together across traditional boundaries to experience new teaching and learning partnerships[12]

---

11 https://www.uopeople.edu/blog/emergency-remote-teaching-vs-online-learning/ (Accessed 17 January 2023)

12 According to Cook-Sather et al. (2014, pp. 6–7, cited in Mercer-Mapstone et al., 2017) 'Partnership is a "reciprocal process through which all participants have the opportunity to contribute equally, although not necessarily in the same ways, to curricular or

(Mercer-Mapstone et al., 2017). The relationship between students and educators is a form of engagement, a partnership where together students and educators co-design, co-create and co-evaluate learning. This is illustrated in the Student Futures Manifesto from the UPP Foundation Student Futures Commission (2022, p. 4) that introduces a comprehensive shift in framing learning in a post covid era (Table 1).

Table 1: A Student Futures Manifesto, UPP Foundation. Student Futures Commission (2022, p. 4)[13]

The future is not what it used to be	→	**subtle shifts in framing**
Physical places	→	Physical and/or digital places
Teaching	→	Learning
Blended/Hybrid	→	Multi-modal
Consultation	→	Co-creation
Academic outcomes	→	Graduate outcomes
Volunteering	→	Service learning
Extra-curricular	→	Co-curricular
Student Engagement	→	Belonging
Student Journey	→	Learning Journey
Team	→	Community

These themes have been explored for a number of years (Bergmark & Westman, 2016, 2018; Healy & Healy, 2014; Harrington et al., 2016; Mercer-Mapstone et al., 2017; Cook-Sather & Felten, 2017). But rather than the norm, they were the exception. The experience of the pandemic in education currently is a catalyst to question the role of universities, how students want to learn, and what learning spaces should be like (The Times Higher Education, 2023[14]). This transition period is an invitation to open up an inclusive debate on optimising the potential of interpreting studies to not only benefit the interpreting community but also the wider community of educators and learners.

pedagogical conceptualisation, decision-making, implementation, investigation, or analysis"'.

13 https://upp-foundation.org/wp-content/uploads/2022/02/A-Student-Futures-Manifesto-Final-Report-of-the-Student-Futures-Commission.pdf (Accessed 19 October 2023)

14 Up to date articles in: https://www.timeshighereducation.com/campus/spotlight/higher-educations-lessons-crisis (Accessed 18 January 2023)

4. From traditional mock conferences to an inclusive interprofessional simulated model: The London Metropolitan University MACI case study

Mock conferences are increasingly popular in interpreting education, especially since the introduction of situated learning in interpreting studies (Li, 2015). According to Albl-Mikasa (2013) and Li (2015, p. 6, figure 1) mock conferences come as a transitional stage between the 'skills development stage' and the 'professional interpreting situations'. They may not be fully considered as bridging the gap between interpreting education and the workplace (Duflou, 2016), but they remain a relevant form of experiential learning (McLellan, 1994) that offers an opportunity for students to engage in a rich authentic context where they have to perform as interpreters (Defrancq et al., 2022). During the Covid 19 pandemic, in the absence of in situ dummy booth practice and pedagogical assistance, the interpreting services of the European Commission (DG-SCIC) chose the mock conference format[15] to continue their support to interpreting students and educators. This initiative enhanced the relevance of sharing mock conferences as a valid pedagogical approach (Duong & Nguyen, 2021; Pan, 2016; Risku, 2016) that benefits a network of universities, in a synchronous and asynchronous mode of participation. This inclusive approach offers an example of a community mindset that has the potential to transform networks where 'members pass on a multitude of information on many topics' into communities of practice where 'members share a common interest in developing practices in a specific field and aim at improving members' know-how on a specific domain' (Probst & Borzillo, 2008, p. 336). However, for a lack of a better word, the term CoP may also 'refer to a certain mode of learning interaction in which people engage with each other as learning partners' (Wenger-Trayner & Wenger-Trayner, 2020, p. 31). Wenger-Trayner and Wenger-Trayner (2020, p. 32) interestingly draw a list of key characteristics that they define as characterising communities of practice in opposition to other forms of social learning spaces. They are:

- *'Identification with a shared domain*
- *Commitment to applying, developing and improving a shared practice*
- *Longevity and continuity as a social structure*
- *Definition of a regime of competence over time*

15 New training support videos: mock conferences https://ec.europa.eu/education/knowledge-centre-interpretation/en/news/new-training-support-videos-mock-conferences-0 (Accessed 18 January 2023)

- *Recognition of membership and construction of identity based on the regime of competence*'. (Wenger-Trayner. B.E, 2020, p. 32)

4.1. Turning challenges into opportunities

At London Met the postgraduate interpreting programmes started in 2004, which is fairly recent compared to conference interpreting programmes in France, Switzerland, Poland or the Czech Republic. Mock conferences were included from the onset; they have always been very popular with students, perhaps too popular at times for staff as they tend to generate a workload that is not fully accounted for by the university-wide workload model.

From the very beginning, experiential learning (Kolb, 1984) has underpinned the mock conference pedagogical design, that aims at offering students an opportunity to experience their role as interpreters in a safe simulated multilingual and multicultural professional environment[16] with confidence (D'Hayer, 2006). Experiential learning fosters a continuous process approach that is initiated with a 'concrete experience'; it is followed by a 'reflective observation' approach that leads to forming 'abstract conceptualisation', that can then be tested in 'active experimentations' (Kolb, 1984). Even though experiential learning remains one of the leading learning frameworks that underpins the mock conferences, it encapsulates pedagogical values that have been generated by a community of practice approach, such as *learning by teaching, caring and sharing* (D'Hayer, 2022).

Mock conferences have evolved a great deal over the years. Some of the changes have resulted in the need to adapt to university policies, such as access to resources and budgets. Others have been motivated by a strong desire to continuously align the pedagogical approach with the currency and relevance of professional developments both in interpreting and teaching practices (Zeff, 2003; Chouc & Conde, 2016). Optimising learning experience and enhancing the students' confidence to become agents of their own lifelong professional development have unceasingly led the desire for change. This process was enabled by the continuous conversations and open exchange within the community of students, alumni, staff, and professionals in the field of interpreting, IT and education. It defines a community of practice mindset that fosters trust, encourages the students as partners approach, and leads to developing a students-staff partnership. This form of leadership across boundaries highlights how to create relevant inclusive

---

16 The course includes between 6 and 11 languages paired up with English.

change grounded in the community experience, to transform challenges into opportunities.

4.1.1. *Strategic timetabling to reduce stress and enhance professional development*

The dialogue between staff and students is formal and informal. Twice a year, the student representatives[17] elected by students meet the teaching team during the course committee[18]. This is a university-wide formal initiative that aims at democratising education, bringing the students' voice to the attention of staff so that together relevant changes can occur. Furthermore, the alumni who are members of the Ambassadors Scheme[19] (D'Hayer, 2014b, 2022) offer a more informal opportunity to bring in feedback from students who may feel more at ease to confine into peers rather than staff. Finally, the community approach to teaching and learning facilitates conversations for change.

As a result, collective feedback identified that even though mock conferences were highly valued for professional development, they occurred too often and generated stress and a challenging workload for both students and staff. As a result, over the years, changes were made. But the pandemic reinforced the potential for change; as a result a strategic approach to timetabling and workload was revisited.

This was an opportunity to reconsider the best ways to optimise the added value of mock conferences for students, staff, alumni and employers, and reduce challenges. The number of mock conferences was reduced (from 12 to 8) and reorganised over three semesters, rather than two. They were redesigned to fit into three evolutive cycles (see 4.2). The third semester, traditionally dedicated to the dissertation, was fully explored to integrate a third cycle of mock conferences to enhance practice and reinforce self confidence, especially as mock conferences integrated further challenges to reflect the reality of the professional landscape.

As a result, students had more time to deepen their knowledge, enhance their skills, and reflect on their practice during class, and their semi guided or

---

17 Students reps at London Met: https://www.londonmetsu.org.uk/studentreps/ (Accessed 17 January 2023)

18 Course committees bring together student representatives and staff together twice a year to review the course, the teaching and learning experience. It is an opportunity to hear the students voice and act upon it.

19 https://communityofpracticeforinterpreting.blogspot.com/2014/04/the-interpreting-ambassadors-scheme-at.htm

independent studies. This includes the integration of terminology management with software (e.g. InterpretBank, Google sheet, database, Quizlet), a collaborative paperless approach (e.g. Google drive, Google docs, uploading video recordings on their YouTube channels), and dedicated time to practise and reflect for their weekly Portfolio of Practice; for every module, students have access to a personal Portfolio of Practice (PoP) which is accessible by their peers and tutors. The PoP is an online space dedicated to semi guided and independent practice. The PoP is included in the final assessment with a pass/fail.

As a result, students felt better prepared and enjoyed the experience of the mock conferences. The stress they experienced was far more embedded in the experiential learning strategy rather than accidental and unplanned. Each mock conference has become a landmark in the professional development of students. It is constructed so as to offer a gradual approach in the professional challenges and learning outcomes.

4.1.2. Three cycles of mock conferences: A constructed approach

The mock conferences in Cycle 1 and Cycle 2 are mainly led by staff with the contribution of students who may contribute to find speakers, help with the set up or provide support in logistics. They represent the first two cycles of experiential learning that focuses on the students in their role of interpreters.

After the final practical exams at the end of Cycle 2 in May, Cycle 3 includes four student-led mock conferences that spread over June and July (simultaneous interpreting). They are student-led, with staff supporting in the background. At this stage, students have gradually gained confidence in their skills and role as interpreters. They have gained an understanding and an insight into what constitutes a multilingual and multicultural event with interpreting services. They have internalised the experience and adjusted their strategies to efficiently prepare for the assignment, interpret during the assignment and reflect on their performance. They are familiar with the tools and technology they use. They still need some practice to reach a professional level but they are on the right path. But most importantly, they have worked collectively, supported one another, and developed trust in each other and the community. Students have internalised that the development of their professional identity and achievements is closely connected to their engagement and collective work within a community. As a result, the last four mock conferences in Cycle 3 are much more than the traditional mock conferences, they have become student-led simulated multilingual events that are shared synchronously and asynchronously for the benefit of an inclusive audience that has gradually evolved from being safe and supportive for students to being open to all.

4.1.3. *Adapting to a more 'agile' workforce: Rethinking assessment strategies for mock conferences*

Over the last 15 years, access to human resources has changed a great deal. Following the widespread adoption of a more 'agile workforce'[20] approach by universities in the UK, there has been a shift to reduce the number of permanent staff and increase the use of hourly paid visiting lecturers. This has had an impact on the access to human resources available and the language combinations they represent to provide speeches and assess students. With the hourly payment policy, the objective has been keen to reduce expenses and spread cost and expenses equally across courses.

Unfortunately for interpreting studies, this approach highlights the high human cost to budget holders, especially when compared to other courses. As a result, the viability of interpreting courses could have been questioned and access to human resources had to be reduced. The decrease in the number of permanent members of staff was compensated by a rise in the number of hourly paid visiting lecturers. In this context, the rationale behind every contact hour with a language specific interpreting tutor is to optimise learning and impact.

This shift was an opportunity to rethink the role of tutors as contributors (delivering speeches in different languages) and assessors (providing feedback to students during the event). Following consultation with staff and students, it was agreed that teaching and learning with language specific interpreting tutors was optimised during small practice groups rather than during larger complex mock conferences. As a result, the number of teaching hours was kept to the same number, but the focus was on tutorials alone.

However, this raised the question of finding contributors and assessors. As a result, the purpose and participation (discussed in 4.2), and assessment of intended learning outcomes (discussed below) were revisited.

As recommended by Li (2015) mock conferences should be video recorded to provide an opportunity to assess students. This observation allowed students and staff to define that the tutors' main added value was to provide language specific feedback on the students' performance as no one else could do that.

---

20 The Benefits and Drawbacks of Implementing Agile Working in the Modern Workplace https://agile.org.uk/the-benefits-and-drawbacks-of-implementing-agile-working-in-the-modern-workplace/ (Accessed 19 January 2023)

During formal and informal conversations with students, alumni and tutors, it was also reported that students often felt they were interpreting for their tutors during the mock conference, rather than an audience of people that would need the interpretation to understand and contribute to the debate. Students and tutors felt this approach distorted the purpose of mock conferences that aimed at introducing students to an authentic professional context that would include some reasonable pressure. Instead the stress level of students was focused on what tutors would say. Students somehow felt paralysed, knowing that their tutor may critique every single word they utter. Furthermore, the feedback breaks during the mock conferences and after the mock conferences were never long enough for students and tutor to constructively engage in the assessment process. As the mock conferences offered multiple language options, tutors only listened to their students interpreting for a limited time. Students may have had to use the relay interpretation from their peers, understanding that the quality of the relay varied according to the skills of the interpreting students that provided the relay. As a result, the relay interpreters were often criticised by the students and tutors, which generated a demotivating context for all.

Instead, it was agreed that the small tutorial format would be ideal to listen to the recording of the students' interpretation to get feedback in a pedagogical context that would favour a conversational exchange based on the initial self and peer assessment reflections captured in the Portfolio of Practice. The PoP strategy for assessment was introduced in 2019, independently of the COVID 19 pandemic. Initially, it was introduced to one practical module but on students' demand[21], there is now a PoP for every single module of the course. This personal and collective space on Google Drive is the students' home of practice and reflection. Tutors can access the PoP, and so can other students. Every week, tutors set some tasks based on a three step approach: research, practice, reflect. This weekly experience then contributes to defining the following SMART[22] objectives. The PoP space is also a space of freedom where any other work can be inserted using any tool or mode of communication that suits the learning style of the students. As a result, reflections can be expressed in writing, audio or video recorded. The PoP is included in the final assessment of each module with a Pass or Fail based on the regular weekly engagement with the PoP and its strategic use to develop a reflexive approach to professional development.

---

21 Feedback officially captured in the course committees in 2019 and 2020.

22 SMART: Specific, Measurable, Achievable, Realistic, in a Timely fashion.

What could have been perceived as a challenge that would weaken the teaching and learning experience, was actually an opportunity to rethink strategically about the role of tutors as assessors during the mock conferences. It has not only opened the doors to innovative assessment tools such as the PoP, but it has also enhanced students' agency to adapt the mock conferences cycles to their needs and professional development. This form of student staff partnership contributes to a more horizontal exchange that promotes a constructive professional form of feedback that is initiated by the student and reinforced by peers and the tutor during tutorials. As the student verbalises reflection in the PoP, the student is more ready to listen and engage in the conversation with peers and tutor in a safe small format teaching space that is less threatening, and more conducive to change, especially when further exercises are integrated to apply changes to the interpreting practice. This approach reinforces the added value of the experiential learning framework. It is felt that the PoP have democratised feedback and contributed to enhance student agency and the student-tutor partnership. This was further illustrated during the COVID19 online summative assessment approach that was negotiated and defined by students and staff working together as partners (D'Hayer, 2020a, 2020b).[23]

4.2. A community of practice approach: Optimising participation and purposes

Most papers that explore mock conferences offer insights on the role they have in the learning process, their purpose, their design and the impact on the students' learning experience. However, little has been said on the relevance of having an audience. Students are so often reminded that the purpose of interpreting is to bridge a linguistic and cultural divide and promotes multicultural and multilingual communication. However, literature on mock conferences focuses on the interpretation itself, often using assessment criteria that are used in standard interpreting classes or for final assessments. It has been acknowledged that the real value of mock conferences is to move away from the interpreting class and embrace the challenges of a simulated authentic environment. And for an interpreter, the real assessor would not then be the tutor that continuously monitors the performance of the interpreter, but the audience, also referred to as

23 'Our online interpreting exam experience: students as partners' (D'Hayer, 2020b) https://communityofpracticeforinterpreting.blogspot.com/2020/06/our-online-interpreting-exam-experience.html

'the pure customer'[24] who is actually always present during the EU accreditation test for interpreters.

However, in the context of interpreting studies, the audience is often under-explored. It may be due to a number of potential factors; the increased pressure on students who do not yet perform well enough because they have not yet finished their training; or it could also be because it is difficult to organise and would require quite a lot of resources and logistics. It has already been established in 4.1.3 that language specific human resources are increasingly getting scarce.

When reflecting on the purpose of mock conferences over the past years with staff and students, it has been established that an audience was highly relevant to add value and authenticity to the simulated experience. Initially, twenty years ago, the only audience that may attend was face to face in situ. However, as technology has developed, it has allowed the inclusion of an audience that has been strategically designed to bring authenticity to the simulated event, add pedagogical value, and support to students. The evolution of technology has enabled staff and students to think further about the boundaries of participation of different communities that could join the mock conference as an audience for the benefits of the interpreters and their own too. With the Covid19 pandemic acting as a technical catalyst for the development and use of new technologies to connect and participate beyond boundaries, the strategies to develop an audience have evolved at great speed.

Operating as a community of practice, the concept of participation, engagement and inclusion are recurrent. Using the concept of trajectories in the CoP, the audience has been conceptualised to gradually include different layers of participation, adapted to the level of exposure interpreting students can benefit from. What follows is the outcome of a continuous reflexive process that mapped the students' needs, the motivation to enhance authenticity in simulated events with an authentic audience, and the technology available. It is not so much a focus on what technology can do, but rather how technology is fully included in the conversation to inspire change and optimise learning impact at multiple levels.

24 The freelance accreditation test: part 4 – jury deliberation: https://www.youtube.com/watch?v=U_q0L-zb3MU&ab_channel=EUInterpreters (Accessed 19 January 2023)

4.2.1. *Cycle 1: Mock conferences for consecutive interpreting (semester 1): a supportive audience of friends and family*

In the first semester, students' interpreting skills are still young. As they focus on consecutive skills, it is important to experience the purpose of consecutive skills in an authentic environment so that students can project themselves as professionals, and feel how they perform as an interpreter. The purpose of this first exposure is to offer students an opportunity to contextualise interpreting, experience the demands of a formal event that generates stress, and the internalisation of coping strategies. At this stage, as students develop their skills and confidence, they need support and guidance. This reality guided the strategies to invite a non-threatening audience to contribute to the development of confidence. This is an opportunity to open up the traditionally secluded educational boundaries and include a community that is usually left out, but plays an incredibly supportive role: friends and family. As mock conferences take place in a hybrid synchronous mode on Zoom and in the interpreting suite in situ, supportive friends and family selected by the students are given the link to join the event. They are invited to leave their camera on so that interpreters can feel the audience in the room.

What has been noticed is that the audience not only brings a sense of immediate authenticity, but also excitement and pride to the interpreters. Interpreters feel they want to perform at their very best to impress their audience. The sense of motivation, determination and resilience goes beyond what has been experienced in any class before. Furthermore, as the audience keeps their cameras on, it provides an inclusive opportunity to talk about the support they get from their audience, for example a parent, a sibling, a friend or even a former teacher. It has been observed that during the classes that followed this experience, students still referred to members of the audience as a way to engage or motivate each other. This is an inclusive invitation to enhance the authenticity of the simulated event, but it also brings into the world of education the students identity and their supporting communities.

4.2.2 *Cycle 2: Mock conference for simultaneous interpreting (semester 2): A multilayered interprofessional approach to enhance experiential learning*

In the second semester, students have experienced the two mock conferences for consecutive interpreting. They now understand the purpose, set up and formality of a simulated event. They understand how much progress they can make between mock conferences. They are able to situate their performance in a professional context. They have taken their consecutive interpreting exams.

As they now embark on the simultaneous interpreting adventure, they are ready to engage in two more mock conferences. They are now experienced in interpreting for an audience in a protected environment. As a result, students are now ready to engage with further challenges and add layers of participation to enhance the authenticity of the simulated event.

In addition to their friends and family, students with languages are encouraged to take part. The obvious choice is to first invite linguists from the BA and MA Translation programmes[25] who enjoy participating as speakers or listeners to expand their professional horizons. For some, this experience will act as a catalyst to join the MACI and add interpreting skills to their professional profile.

However, linguists are not the only students with languages at university. Even though the popularity of language learning has decreased in the UK,[26] it does not mean that languages are no longer visible in universities or the workplace. The UK has always been a pole of attraction for migration over centuries[27] and remains so even in a post Brexit era. Furthermore, British universities have always attracted a high number of international students[28]. Even though home and international students speak English, it is often their second or even third language. London Met is no exception. Whilst the Covid pandemic and the Black Lives Matter[29] movement have reinforced the education trends to evolve towards a more inclusive approach to social justice[30], the correlation between multilingualism and social justice has been overlooked. In contrast in

25 There is an interpreting module in the third year of the BA Translation. BA Translation at London Met: https://www.londonmet.ac.uk/courses/undergraduate/translation---ba-hons/ (Accessed 16 January 2023) and MA Translation: https://www.londonmet.ac.uk/courses/postgraduate/translation---ma/ (Accessed 16 January 2023)

26 https://epi.org.uk/publications-and-research/15043/ (Accessed 16 January 2023). This led to the closure of a number of language, translation and interpreting programmes in the UK.

27 https://migrationobservatory.ox.ac.uk/resources/briefings/migrants-in-the-uk-an-overview/ (Accessed 17 January 2023)

28 https://www.studying-in-uk.org/international-student-statistics-in-uk/ (Accessed 17 January 2023)

29 https://blacklivesmatter.com/ (Accessed 17 January 2023)

30 Education for Social Justice Framework at London Met: https://www.londonmet.ac.uk/about/equity/centre-for-equity-and-inclusion/a-fair-outcomes-approach-to-teaching-and-learning/the-degree-awarding-gap/education-for-social-justice-framework/ (Accessed 17 January 2023)

professional settings, languages are highly valued and considered to be an asset[31] to access employability in a competitive market.

This gap motivated the desire to open mock conferences to students and staff from other professional courses. As a community of practice, students and staff are used to negotiating boundaries to open meaningful safe learning spaces to others. As a result, students and staff managed to convince their multilingual peers from other professional courses to participate as speakers, listeners, journalists or even organisers.

In Cycle 2, the professional courses that have been involved in the mock conferences are:

- The International Business Management BSc students[32]
- The Diploma in Law (Mooting competition[33])
- BA Journalism[34]

Negotiations have now been extended to:

- the law students for our mock conference on immigration;
- the BA Fashion Marketing and Business Management students[35] to take part in the mock conference on recycling in the world of fashion;
- the BA Events Management[36] students to help organise the conferences.

Interprofessional experiential learning events such as mock conferences are highly beneficial to interpreting students. This was recently demonstrated by Defrancq et al. (2022, p. 54) who reported that in their case study, their mock conference had been 'seen as an opportunity to learn *with* the other professional group'. The paper also highlights that there could have been further engagement between the two groups of students. This could be due to the lack of trust between

---

31 https://eures.ec.europa.eu/five-reasons-why-learning-language-can-boost-your-employability-2021-06-22_e(Accessed 17 January 2023)

32 'Experiential learning for interpreting and international business students'https://www.londonmet.ac.uk/news/articles/experiential-learning-for-interpreting-and-international-business-students/ (Accessed 17 January 2023)

33 https://www.londonmet.ac.uk/news/articles/law-students-reach-quarter-final-of-major-mooting-competition/ (Accessed 17 January 2023)

34 https://www.londonmet.ac.uk/courses/undergraduate/journalism---ba-hons/ (Accessed 17 January 2023)

35 https://www.londonmet.ac.uk/courses/undergraduate/fashion-marketing-and-business-management---ba-hons/ (17 January 2023)

36 https://www.londonmet.ac.uk/courses/undergraduate/events-management---ba-hons/ (Accessed 17 January 2023)

the two groups who do not yet know each other. It showcases how instilling a community of practice mindset at an early stage is essential. Negotiating boundaries to invite others in existing learning spaces takes a long time as trust has to be nurtured gradually. Opening up mock conferences to other students/staff with languages and professions not only brings together language specific communities across courses, but it also represents a new inclusive trend in the evolution of the curriculum.

The first interprofessional mock conference with the International Business Management BsC students and staff was a great success and can still be watched on our YouTube Channel[37]. However, it was hard work for all as it was a new concept. It took a lot of effort to bring all parties to understand the multilayered multilingual participative vision. Communication strategies adopted on the interpreting course had to be extended further to include a much larger group of business students. The event was streamed and the business students really enjoyed this aspect of learning they had not experienced before. They too invited friends and family to watch their performance. Speaking their mother tongue as speakers was a revelation as they were not used to bringing this linguistic dimension of their identity at university with their peers. This simulation-based learning activity (Chernikova et al., 2020), required preparation and a level of professionalism that business students had not experienced before. It was such a steep learning curve that often interpreting students doubted the conference would ever materialise. At this stage, the role of the tutor changes. It is the bridge that brings the two communities together. The tutor facilitates communication and leads in a supportive manner to also enable collaborative solutions. This first attempt was not perfect but it stimulated the imagination of staff and students as one community.

This powerful vision was enabled by a community of practice mindset, a constructed approach to simulation-based learning, and a strong desire to use technology as a tool to include a multilayered level of participation that was highly beneficial to interpreting students and students from other professional courses.

Beyond the immediate result of one event, inclusive interprofessional mock conferences have been motivated by the following:

- Optimising the visibility of mock conferences across the university to promote multilingualism;

37 https://www.youtube.com/watch?v=DWOHkGYD2Rg&t=54s&ab_channel=InterpretingatLondonMet (Accessed 17 January 2023)

- Promoting the relationship between identity and languages in students and staff;
- Situating multilingualism in professional studies other than translation and interpreting;
- Raising awareness that languages in a professional context are an asset that needs to be explored and integrated in university studies;
- Promoting the role interpreters play in professional settings;
- Gaining experience in how to work in a multicultural and multilingual professional setting;
- Offering students from other professional courses the opportunity to apply their languages to the skills and purposes of their studies, as highly valued speakers in the mock conference;
- Increasing the impact of mock conferences to other courses;
- Enhancing the value of experiential learning and simulation-based learning
- Forming a community of staff that work across course specific boundaries to pool resources and ambition to create multilayered experiential learning opportunities, such as simulation-based learning for the benefit of all students.

This powerful experience has enabled interpreting students and staff to work as partners. Together, students and staff had to negotiate learning, to build confidence and trust with one another and become agents of their own learning; they had to overcome barriers and go beyond their remit to make the mock conference work for everyone. This transformative experience for both staff and students brought them closer to adapting to the current professional market in their respective field. Students are now ready to engage further into the third cycle of mock conferences.

4.2.3 Cycle 3: Student-led mock conferences for simultaneous interpreting (semester 3). Engaging applicants who passed the aptitude test to join the MACI

During the third semester, students traditionally conduct their research to write their dissertation. Even though there is a placement element included in the course, this period often is a form of disconnect with the intensive practice of the first two semesters. This is why students and staff have gradually come to define the third cycle for mock conferences to not only increase the practice but also gain professional independence as learners, interpreters and conference managers. This cycle is made of a total of four mock conferences (two in June, and two in July).

At this stage, students have gained experience in simultaneous interpreting practice and they have taken their exams in both consecutive and simultaneous interpreting. Their level of skills is growing but practice remains essential to consolidate their professional development. The level of relevance of the mock conferences is increasing as their focus is on the professional transition to enter the interpreting market. Their stress level for the exams is behind them. The authenticity of the simulated event is now getting extremely close to what they will encounter on the market as professional interpreters.

From the previous mock experiences, they now feel confident in using the equipment and the technology. They understand how mock conferences are organised. They know how to write speeches. From their module on ethics and the code of conduct for the interpreting profession, they have engaged in the reflexive process of their professional identity, building in continuous professional development, marketing strategies and business communication.

They are now ready to apply their newly acquired leadership skills to run the mock conferences as a community and set up a team of interpreters, understand the language regime and put together a team sheet. Students have to find speakers, brief them, guide them, define a collaborative space for a paperless approach, collect notes and presentations, understand the hybrid technology as well as how to share the event with the streaming on social media. To cover all these tasks, a set of roles has been designed:

- Head of the event
- Head of the agenda
- Head of speakers
- Head of interpreters (Chef d'equipe)
- Head of technology

These roles were defined and allocated to the team of students at the beginning of Cycle 2. As a result, they are ready to embrace this additional layer of commitment and their additional new roles. As students now feel more confident as interpreters, they can now embrace the conference management challenges. This not only offers an additional layer of authenticity to the simulated event and experiential learning; it also offers a wider spectrum of employment opportunities that may motivate students to initially work in the field of conference management as employees whilst consolidating their professional networks to launch their interpreting careers as freelancers. Students are now the full agents of their learning. They have full ownership of the events that increasingly improve in quality and complexity as time goes by. However, it is important to note that there is an element of flexibility so that students only take onboard the workload they feel they can manage. Students may be in charge of the organisation in the morning and interpret in the afternoon and vice versa[38].

In cycle 3, the increased level of complexity in terms of participation, interpretation and exposure to a multilayered audience, offers a third opportunity for students to operate in a safe guided collaborative space as one community, to deliver an event that is real, authentic, professional, and even motivating for a brand new group of participants, i.e. the applicants to the MACI that have passed the MACI aptitude test for the next academic year. At this stage, applicants often feel anxious but also motivated. They have a long wait ahead of them before the course starts. Their participation in the mock conferences is an opportunity to join a community of like minded students who were in their shoes a year ago. As a result, applicants have an opportunity to project themselves and imagine what they will be able to do by the end of the academic year. This experience initiates a process of learning before the course even starts. They understand how they can use their time before the course starts to improve their skills. Their motivation is captured to encourage them to not only learn from observation, but also participate. For example, they are encouraged to formally take part in the debates with the speakers. Furthermore, they are encouraged to informally engage during the debriefing of the event, by sharing their feelings and impressions on the experience.

The connection between the applicants and the students continues beyond the event. After the mock conferences, applicants will continue to ask students for advice, meet to share experience and even ask for practical help to get accommodation for example. Meanwhile, students will continue their journey and graduate, and often engage in the Ambassadors Scheme for the following academic year.

The mock conferences in cycle 3 are an opportunity to break silos and fluidify boundaries between applicants, students and graduates. The multilayered participation in the mock conferences offers a momentum that keeps the community of practice alive over the rigidity of the academic cycles. It is crucial to assure the continuity of the community of practice for the course from one academic year to the next. Otherwise, the momentum slows down and the community may disintegrate, especially as the community is of a fairly small size.

38 We are currently designing a new module that will be dedicated to conference management only so that students can exclusively focus on new skills and roles should they wish to.

Table 2 summarises how a community of practice mindset supported by technology enables a complex multilayered approach to participation in mock conferences over an academic year:

Table 2: Overview of the three cycles of inclusive mock conferences, with the multilayered levels of participation enabled by the technology and a community of practice mindset

Temporal cycles -------------------- **Specificities**	**Cycle 1**	**Cycle 2**	**Cycle 3**
Main learning outcome	Ability to perform short and long contributions in the context of a professional multilingual event to a supportive audience	Ability to prepare and interpret an interprofessional multilingual event collaboratively with a team of interpreters and speakers and staff, for a controlled audience	Ability to collaboratively organise, lead and interpret a multilingual event for an open audience
Interpreting mode	Consecutive	Simultaneous	Simultaneous
Leadership	The tutor	The tutor in partnership with students	Students with the tutor's support in the background
Technology for participation for interpreters	Hybrid: interpreters can be on site or online.Synchronously	Hybrid: interpreters can be on site or online. Synchronously	Hybrid: interpreters can be on site or online. Synchronously
Audience: a strategic inclusive approach:	Audience cycle 1: Friends and family	Audience cycle 2: Audience cycle 1 + Students with languages from other courses (BA Translation, MA Translation, other professional courses) Wider community streaming on Zoom Webstreaming with #InterpretWithUs	Audience cycle 1, 2 and Candidates who have passed the aptitude test for the following academic year. Participants to the introduction to conference interpreting short course.

Table 2: Continued

Temporal cycles ------------------- **Specificities**	**Cycle 1**	**Cycle 2**	**Cycle 3**
Who are the speakers?	– Tutors, – Friends and family, – Graduates (the Ambassadors) – Students from the BA and MA translation – Guest from our networks	– Tutors, – Friends and family, – Graduates (the Ambassadors) – Students from the BA and MA translation – Guest from our networks – **Students from other professional courses**	– Tutors, – Friends and family, – Graduates (the Ambassadors) – Students from the BA and MA translation – Guest from our networks – **Candidates to the MACI who have passed the aptitude test and will join the course in the next academic year**
The audience: Who can hear the main event with interpretation?	– The onsite community (interpreting suite) – The online community with access via a Zoom link.	– The onsite community (interpreting suite) – The online community with access to a Zoom webinar with interpretation	– The onsite community (interpreting suite) – The online community with access to a Zoom webinar with interpretation

(*Continued*)

Table 1: Continued

Temporal cycles -------------------- **Specificities**	**Cycle 1**	**Cycle 2**	**Cycle 3**
The audience: Who can hear the main event without the interpretation? Opportunity for the wider community to practise interpreting Invitation is launched on social media using #InterpretWithUs	No one	Anyone who is connected to our live event on our YouTube channel: Interpreting at LondonMet The mock conference recordings remain available on our channel for anyone to practise, but also for students and tutors to access. This has been used by students and tutors in other universities.	Anyone who is connected to our live event on our YouTube channel: Interpreting at LondonMet The mock conference recordings remain available on our channel for anyone to practise, but also for students and tutors to access. This has been used by students and tutors in other universities.
Enabling technology	Traditional equipment for interpreting purposes (Brahler). Zoom meeting accessible via a link for the online community. Please note that the onsite community is also connected to the same online meeting. Streaming to a private link on YouTube channel (only available to students and staff). Integration of the interpreting system to the AV system. Integration of the Zoom platform on the AV system. Recording of AV output as one event.	Traditional equipment for interpreting purposes (Brahler). Zoom webinar accessible via a link for the online community. Interpretation add-on is available on Zoom for the online interpreters. Please note that the onsite community is also connected to the same online webinar. Streaming of the webinar without interpretation mto a public link on YouTube channel. Integration of the interpreting system to the AV system. Integration of the Zoom platform on the AV system. Recording of AV output as one event.	Traditional equipment for interpreting purposes (Brahler). Zoom webinar accessible via a link for the online community. Interpretation add-on is available on Zoom for the online interpreters. Please note that the onsite community is also connected to the same online webinar. Streaming of the webinar without interpretation mto a public link on YouTube channel. Integration of the interpreting system to the AV system. Integration of the Zoom platform on the AV system. Recording of AV output as one event.

5. Conclusive remarks

This chapter offers an insight into the experience of students, alumni and educators working in partnership within a community of practice. The aim of the chapter was not to provide a traditional piece of evidence based research with conclusions. On the contrary, the ambition of this chapter is to tell and share a story in the hope to start conversations, however uncomfortable they may feel so that interpreting studies evolve beyond the apprenticeship model and embrace new pedagogical ambitions that are less exclusive and more inclusive.

On the one hand, this chapter tells the story of a pedagogical construct (Vygotsky, 1978) for mock conferences as a form of simulated based learning (Madsgaard et al., 2022) within an experiential learning framework (Kolb, 1984). This experience may feel overwhelming and challenging to 'reproduce'. But the purpose of this chapter is not to provide a model to follow to the letter. The story that was presented in this chapter responds to the needs of the London Met interpreting community. Each community has its own identity and the identity evolves every year as new students come in and others leave (Wenger-Trayner & Wenger-Trayner, 2020). In this community, the approach reflects the ambition of the community that strongly feels that inviting others in, to create additional layers of participation to mock conferences, enhances the learning experience for all.

From the outside, the story may feel complex. But from within, the complexity is deconstructed into simple and accessible steps that were democratically negotiated by students, alumni and educators working together as partners and co-creators of the curriculum (Bergmark & Westman, 2016, 2018). The objective has been to:

- revisit the aims and objectives of mock conferences as simulation based learning activities
- build trust and empower students to have their voices heard and acted upon
- promote student agency
- align interpreting education with the authentic development of the interpreting profession
- creatively transform challenges into reflective opportunities (see 4.1.3)
- demonstrate the role of technology as opportunities to enhance an inclusive participation
- enhance motivation and shape ambitions to embrace new roles (4.2.3)
- use mock conferences as an inclusive opportunity to validate the linguistic identity of participating interprofessional students,
- promote multilingualism to maximise interprofessional experiential learning.

The Covid pandemic was the catalyst to speed up change in the interpreting profession and education. Even though the temptation to go 'back to normal' is always there, it is the 'moving forward' that offers the exciting opportunity to bring together an inclusive community of partners made of students, educators, alumni, technicians, professionals, employers and service users, to question what stands as 'normal', and create new opportunities for interpreting education to fulfil its potential for interpreters in the making, but also for multilingual students and staff across universities. Beyond the resistance and fear that such a change of perspective may instil, there is an opportunity to build a trusting, resilient and inclusive community of practice that would not only consolidate interpreting studies in Higher Education but also offer an opportunity to place interpreting studies at the forefront of innovative experiential learning.

6. Further research

This chapter tells the story of a community on the theme of mock conferences. Before publication it was read, discussed and edited by two alumni involved in the Ambassadors Scheme.[39] This process was the most enjoyable part of the experience of writing this chapter. Even though this is quite a cutting edge approach (Mercer-Mapstone et al., 2017), co-researching and co-writing with students, alumni and educators would offer a full perspective on the added value of the teaching and learning experiences gained in stories that shape interpreting education. This exciting approach would contribute to the 'moving forward' into a new era of interpreting education and research.

References

Albl-Mikasa, M. (2013). 'Developing and cultivating expert interpreter competence'. *Interpreters' Newsletter,* 18, pp. 17–34.

Bandura, A. and Walters, R. (1963). *Social Learning and Personality Development.* New York: Holt, Rinehart and Winston, 1st edition (1 Jan. 1963).

Bandura, A. (1977). *Social Learning Theory*. Englewood Cliffs, NJ: Prentice-Hall.

Bergmark, U. and Westman, S. (2016). 'Co-creating curriculum in higher education: Promoting democratic values and a multidimensional view on

39 The author would like to thank Elsa Haughton and Yanitsa Dimitrova, two MACI alumni for offering their feedback on the chapter. Their contribution was an eye opening experience on the powerful experience of co-editing together.

learning'. *International Journal for Academic Development*, 21(1), pp. 28–40. https://doi.org/10.1080/1360144X.2015.1120734.

Bergmark, U. and Westman, S. (2018). 'Student participation within teacher education: Emphasising democratic values, engagement and learning for a future profession'. *Higher Education Research & Development*, 37(7), pp. 1352–1365. doi: 10.1080/07294360.2018.1484708.

Chen-En, H. and Zou, Y. (2022). 'Teaching interpreting in the time of COVID: Exploring the feasibility of using Gather'. In K. Liu and A. K. F. Cheung (Eds.), *Translation and Interpreting in the Age of COVID-19* (pp. 311–330). Singapore: Springer.

Chernikova, O., Heitzmann, N., Stadler, M., Holzberger, D., Seidel, T., and Fischer, F. (2020). 'Simulation-based learning in higher education: A meta-analysis'. *Review of Educational Research*, 90(4), pp. 499–541. https://doi.org/10.3102/0034654320933544.

Chouc, F. and Conde, J. M. (2016). 'Enhancing the learning experience of interpreting students outside the classroom: A study of the benefits of situated learning at the Scottish Parliament'. *Interpreter and Translator Trainer*, 10(1), pp. 92–106. https://doi.org/10.1080/1750399X.2016.1154345.

Cook-Sather, A., Bovill C., and Felten, P. (2014). '*Engaging Students as Partners in Learning and Teaching: A Guide for Faculty*'. San Francisco: Jossey-Bass.

Cook-Sather, A. and Felten, P. (2017). 'Where student engagement meets faculty development: How student-faculty pedagogical partnership fosters a sense of belonging'. *Student Engagement in Higher Education Journal*, 1(2), 3. Available at: https://sehej.raise-network.com/raise/article/view/cook (Accessed 12 April 2023).

Defrancq, B., Delputte, S., and Baudewijn, T. (2022). 'Interprofessional training for student conference interpreters and students of political science through joint mock conferences: An assessment'. *The Interpreter and Translator Trainer*, 16(1), pp. 39–57, doi: 10.1080/1750399X.2021.1919975.

D'Hayer, D. (2006). 'Training conference interpreters: An experiential approach to teaching and learning'. *Investigations in University Teaching and Learning*, 3(2), pp. 67–72. ISSN: 1740–5106.

D'Hayer, D. (2014b). 'The Interpreting Ambassadors' Scheme at London Metropolitan University moving towards a Community of Practice'. *Community of Practice: The Missing Link*. 24 April. Available at: http://communityofpracticeforinterpreting.blogspot.com/2014/04/the-interpreting-ambassadors-scheme-at.html (Accessed 27 March 2021).

D'Hayer, D. (2020a). 'Rising to the challenge with pride: A community of practice at work'. *Community of Practice: The Missing Link*. 23 March. Available at: http://communityofpracticeforinterpreting.blogspot.com/2020/03/rising-to-challenge-with-pride.html (Accessed 27 March 2021).

D'Hayer, D. (2020b). 'Our online interpreting exam experience: Students as partners'. *Community of Practice: The Missing Link*. 3 June. Available at: http://communityofpracticeforinterpreting.blogspot.com/2020/06/our-online-interpreting-exam-experience.html (Accessed 27 March 2021).

D'Hayer, D.(2022). 'To what extent and in what ways do communities of practice facilitate learning in the context of professional development for interpreting students and practitioners?' PhD thesis (awaiting publication on https://repository.londonmet.ac.uk/)

Duflou, V. (2016). *Be(com)ing a conference interpreter. An ethnography of EU interpreters as a professional community*. Benjamin's Translation Library. Volume 124. Amsterdam. Philadelphia.

Duong, D. A. and Nguyen, P. L. (2021). 'Using mock conference to teach consecutive interpreting – A case study at Vinh University'. *International Journal of Education and Social Science Research (IJESSR)*, 4(6), pp. 361–384. http://dx.doi.org/10.37500/IJESSR.2021.4627.

El Metwally, M. (2019) Cultural Bridges. Available at: https://www.youtube.com/@culturalbridgesbymahael-me2305 (Accessed 19 October 2023).

Frei-Landau, R., Orland-Barak, L., and Muchnick-Rozonov, Y. (2022). 'What's in it for the observer? Mimetic aspects of learning through observation in simulation-based learning in teacher education'. *Teaching and Teacher Education*, 113. https://doi.org/10.1016/j.tate.2022.103682.

Gentile, P. (2014). 'The status of conference interpreters: A global questionnaire into the profession'. *Rivista internazionale di tecnica della traduzione – International Journal of Translation*, 15, pp. 63–82.

Goldsmith, J. (2019) Innovation in Interpreting Summit. Available at: https://www.innovationininterpreting.com/insiders. (Accessed 19 October 2023).

Harrington, K., Sinfield, S., and Burns, T. (2016). 'Students engagement'. In H. Pokorny and D. Warren (Eds.), *Enhancing Teaching Practice in Higher Education* (pp. 106–124). London: Sage.

Healey, M. and Healey, R. (2014). *Student Engagement through Partnership: A Guide and Update to the Advance HE Framework*. York: Higher Education Academy.

Hu, W. (2019). 'Examining the effectiveness of the simulated interpreting projects: Students' Perspectives'. *Review of European Studies*, 11(2), pp. 118–129. doi:10.5539/res.v11n2p118.

Kolb, D. A. (1984). The process of experiential learning, Chapter 2. In *The Experiential Learning: Experience as the Source of Learning and Development*. Englewood Cliffs, NJ: Prentice-Hall.

Lave, J. and Wenger, E. (1991). *Situated Learning: Legitimate peripheral participation*. New York: Cambridge University Press.

Li, X. (2015). 'Mock conference as a situated learning activity in interpreter training: A case study of its design and effect as perceived by trainee interpreters'. *The Interpreter and Translator Trainer*, 9(3), pp. 323–342. doi: 10.1080/1750399X.2015.1100399.

Lubicz- Nawrocka, T. M. (2018). 'From partnership to self authorship: The benefits of cocreation ofthe curriculum'. *InternationalJournal for Students as Partners*, 2(1), pp. 47–63. https://doi.org/10.15173/ijsap.v2i1.3207.

Lubicz-Nawrocka, T. M. and Owen, J. (2022). 'Curriculum co-creation in a postdigital world: Advancing networked learning and engagement'. *Postdigital Science and Education*, 4(2), pp. 793–813. doi: 10.1007/s42438-022-00304-5.

MacPherson Institute. (2017). *Mick Healey – Students as Partners*. Available at: https://www.youtube.com/watch?v=TNKhQghFV1Y (Accessed: 25 January 2023).

Madsgaard, A., Røykenes, K., Smith-Strøm, H., and Kvernenes, M. (2022). 'The affective component of learning in simulation-based education – Facilitators' strategies to establish psychological safety and accommodate nursing students' emotions'. *BMC Nursing*, 21(91). https://doi.org/10.1186/s12 912-022-00869-3.

McLellan, H. (1994). 'Situated learning: Continuing the conversation'. *Educational Technology*, 34(10), pp. 7–8.

Mercer-Mapstone, L., Dvorakova, S. L., Matthews, K. E., Abbot, S., Cheng, B., Felten, P., Knorr, K., Marquis, E., Shammas, R., and Swaim, K. (2017). 'A systematic literature review of students as partners in higher education'. *International Journal for Students as Partners*, 1(1). doi: 10.15173/ijsap. v1i1.3119.

Metthews, K., Cook-Sather, A., Acai, A., Dvorakova, S. L., and Felten, P. (2019). 'Toward theories of partnership praxis: An analysis of interpretive framing in literature on students as partners in teaching and learning'. *Higher Education Research & Development*, 38(2), pp. 280–293.

Morris, T. H. (2019). 'Experiential learning – A systematic review and revision of Kolb's model'. *Interactive Learning Environments*, 28(8), pp. 1064–1077. doi: 10.1080/10494820.2019.1570279.

Moser-Mercer, B. (1997). 'The expert-novice paradigm in interpreting research'. In E. Fleischmann, W. Kutz, and P.A. Schmitt (Eds.),

Translationsdidaktik: Grundfragen der Übersetzungswissenschaft (pp. 255–261). Tubingen: Gunter Narr.

Moser-Mercer, B. (2000). The rocky road to expertise in interpreting: Eliciting knowledge from learners. In K. Kaindl Kadric and F. Pocchacker (Eds.), *Translationswissenschaft. Festschrift für Mary Snell-Hornby zum 60. Geburtstag* (pp. 239–352). Tubingen: Stauffenburg.

Nawrocka-Lubicz, T. (2022). 'Conceptualisations of curriculum co-creation: It's not them and us, it's just us'. *Curriculum Perspectives*. https://doi.org/10.1007/s41297-022-00180-w.

Orlando, M. (2016). *'Training 21st Century Translators and Interpreters: At the Crossroads of Practice, Research and Pedagogy'*. Berlin: Frank & Timme.

Orlando, M. (2021). 'The interpreter as partner in a multidimensional act of communication'. In K. Seeber (Ed.), *100 Years of Conference Interpreting. A Legacy* (pp. 202–204). Newcastle upon Tyne: Cambridge Scholars Publishing.

Pan, J. (2016). 'Linking classroom exercises to real-life practice: A case of situated simultaneous interpreting learning'. *The Interpreter & Translator Trainer*, 10(1), pp. 107–132. http://dx.doi.org/10.1080/1750399X.2016.1154346.

Pöchhacker, F. (2004). *Interpreting: First Studies*. Oxon: Routledge.

Probst, G. and Borzillo, S. (2008). 'Why communities of practice succeed and why they fail'. *European Management Journal*, 26, pp. 335–347.

Risku, H. (2016). 'Situated learning in translation research training: Academic research as a reflection of practice'. *The Interpreter and Translator Trainer*, 10(1), pp. 12–28. http://dx.doi.org/10.1080/1750399X.2016.1154340.

Rudvin, M. (2018). *Interpreting and Professional Identity*. The Routledge Handbook of Interpreting (pp. 432–446). Oxon: New York

Sawyer, D. (2004). *Fundamental Aspects of Interpreter Education: Curriculum and Assessment*. Amsterdam: John Benjamins.

Setton, R. and Dawrant, A. (2016a). Conference interpreting. A complete course. Benjamin's Translation Library. Volume 120. Philadelphia: John Benjamins Publishing Company.

Setton, R. and Dawrant, A. (2016b). Conference interpreting. A trainer's guide. Benjamin's Translation Library. Volume 121. Philadelphia: John Benjamins Publishing Company.

The Times Higher Education (2023) Higher education's lessons from the crisis. Available at: https://www.timeshighereducation.com/campus/spotlight/higher-educations-lessons-crisis. (Accessed 19 October 2023).

UPP Foundation. (2022). 'Student Futures Manifesto'. Student Futures Commission. Available at: https://upp-foundation.org/student-futures-commission/ (Accessed 17 January 2023).

Vygotsky, L. S. (1978). *Mind in Society: The Development of Higher Psychological Processes*. Cambridge, MA: Harvard University Press.

Wenger, E. (1998). *Communities of Practice. Learning, Meaning and Identity.* Cambridge: Cambridge University Press.

Wenger, E., McDermott R., and Snyder W. (2002). *Cultivating Communities of Practice. A Guide to Managing Knowledge*. Boston: Harvard Business School Press.

Wenger, E. (2008). *Communities of Practice, Learning, Meaning and Identity.* Cambridge: Cambridge University Press.

Wenger, E. (2010). 'Communities of practice and social learning systems: The career of a concept'. In C. Blackmore (Ed.), *Social Learning Systems and Communities of Practice* (pp. 179–198). London: Springer.

Wenger, E. et al. (2014). *Learning in Landscapes of Practice: Boundaries, Identity, and Knowledgeability in Practice-Based Learning.* New York: Routledge

Wenger-Trayner, E. and Wenger-Trayner, B. (2019). Designing for change: Using social learning to understand organizational transformation. Learning 4 a Small Planet.

Wenger-Trayner, E. and Wenger-Trayner, B. (2020). '*Learning to Make a Difference – Value Creation in Social Learning Spaces*'. Cambridge: Cambridge University Press.

Zeff, E. (2003). 'Negotiating in the European Council: A Model European Union Format for Individual Classes'. *International Studies Perspectives*, 4(3), pp. 265–274. https://doi.org/10.1111/1528-3577.403003.

Ivana Čeňková

Chapter 11 Artificial intelligence from the perspective of students and interpreters

Abstract: Artificial intelligence is discussed everywhere today and is a topic that hits the headlines. International research and projects include it in their terms of reference in the hunt for subsidies. It is well established in numerous industrial sectors and is considered an integral part of new technologies. In short, artificial intelligence enters into all areas of human activity and is becoming an unavoidable and omnipresent subject in twenty-first century society, and in the everyday lives of all of us. But do we really know what it means – or will mean – for us, and notably for interpreters? Will it influence or change interpreter training and the whole profession? If so, how? The author will be taking a layman's view of this subject and put these questions (among many others) to students and interpreter trainers at the Institute of Translation Studies, Faculty of Arts, Charles University and also to Czech interpreters on the domestic and European market to see what they think, what they know, and how they view the future. She also compares some of the answers with the results of the questionnaire that she and her colleagues distributed later in the European Masters in Conference Interpreting Consortium (EMCI) and briefly comments on them. After going through and analysing all of the 77 answers from the first sample, the author presents the results of this survey and attempts to draw short conclusions which will be preliminary, as this area is developing at breakneck speed.

Keywords: artificial intelligence, conference interpreter training, the "augmented interpreter", toolbox, simultaneous translation of speech, community interpreting, speech-to-text, automatic speech recognition

1. Genesis and wider context

In April 2019, the Directorate General for Interpreting (DG SCIC) of the European Commission held its 23rd regular conference in Brussels for coordinators of interpreting masters or postgraduate programmes in conference interpreting from European and selected non-European universities. The conference is also attended by leaders of interpreting services and directorates from other European institutions, international organisations, as well as representatives of the main professional interpreting organisations (AIIC, CIUTI, FIT). The conferences have been held annually since 1996. A representative of the Institute of Translation Studies of the Faculty of Arts of Charles University is always present and has been invited several times to speak as one of the participants in a planned thematic panel discussion or to be an invited speaker on a specific conference topic. The 2019 conference was the last one to be held in person pre-covid. The next one, in 2020 was held online with simultaneous interpretation into the main EU working languages and also into International Sign (IS), which itself was a complete novelty. It was only in November 2022 that we were invited to Brussels for the first "post-covid conference", which was hybrid, a new format that will certainly be used in future as it allows participants who cannot attend in person to join the conference online and to participate actively. The 2019 conference chose a very topical issue[1] that has provoked and continues to provoke reactions of the whole interpreting community, namely how to prepare for the arrival of completely new information and communication technologies in the field of conference interpreting and how to use them in particular for the benefit of interpreters. The title of the conference itself sounded very "technological" and at the same time somewhat mysterious: *Preparing for Interpreting 3.0. Towards the augmented interpreter*[2]. The programme included presentations on the development, preparation and use of new IT support tools for conference interpreters in the booth (e.g. the DG SCIC project[3]) and on the possibilities of incorporating Artificial Intelligence[4] (AI) into the whole interpreting process, automatic subtitling, machine interpreting or machine translation of spoken language, etc. Ondřej Bojar from the Faculty of Mathematics and Physics of Charles University presented the international ELITR project,[5] part of the European Union's Horizon 2020 research programme. The Institute of Translation Studies has subsequently cooperated with Bojar, particularly in the recording of simultaneous interpreting of our MA students in the Interpreting

1 SCIC – Universities Conference (4. – 5.4.2019): *Preparing for Interpreting 3.0. Towards the augmented interpreter.* https://webcast.ec.europa.eu/scic-universities-conference-2019-04-05 (accessed 29.12.2022).

2 T*he Augmented interpreter* and other new technologies – see the website of DG SCIC / Knowledge Centre on Interpretation: The Digital Booth | Knowledge Centre on Interpretation (europa.eu) (accessed 29.12.2022).

3 https://www.youtube.com/watch?v=_Il53xdfNhQ: AI for Interpreter Support. Marc van Dommelen on DG SCIC's 'Interpreter's Digital Toolbox project' – 11.12.2020 (accessed 29.12.2022).

4 https://ec.europa.eu/education/knowledge-centre-interpretation/news/eu-host-paper-new-technologies-and-artificial-intelligence-field-language-and-conference_en: European Commission (2019). New Technologies and Artificial Intelligence in the field of language and conference services (accessed 29.12.2022).

5 www.elitr.eu: ELITR – European Live Translator – Many Languages, One Voice (accessed 29.12.2022).

study programme, and in the preparation of other European projects. The topic of the conference was a real challenge for us, as teachers of interpreting, and provoked much controversial discussion, conflicting opinions and diametrically opposed positions.

This led me to become more interested in the use of new technologies related to the involvement of artificial intelligence in interpreting. A further impulse was Julia Skadchenko's master's thesis *Machine Translation and Automatic Interpreting*, successfully defended at the Institute of Translation Studies in May 2019. I have progressively concentrated more systematically on publications on the involvement of artificial intelligence in the field of interpreting, which, especially after 2018, have become more and more numerous, and are also much more specialised and more focussed on specific tools, testing the use of the possibilities of artificial intelligence in interpreter training, but also directly in various specific interpreting situations. The last impetus to mention was the topic announced by CIUTI, the international organisation of universities offering translation and interpreting education (*Conférence Internationale Permanente d'Instituts Universitaires de Traducteurs et Interprètes*) at the end of 2019, for its regular international scientific conference, which is always held in parallel with the annual general assembly of its member universities. The conference, scheduled in Paris for June 2020, chose as its theme artificial intelligence and intercultural intelligence, their impact and interaction in translation, interpreting and in relation to the target language. The abstract I submitted to this conference in early 2020 was accepted by the scientific committee and included in one of the sections[6]. I wanted to find out through a small questionnaire survey among students of interpreting at our Institute of Translation Studies, graduates and professional Czech interpreters on the domestic and European interpreting market, what they know about the use of AI in interpreting and what their ideas about AI in this field are for the future. Again due to the coronavirus pandemic, the conference was postponed until December 2020, when it was held online and I had the opportunity to present the results of my survey in French (!), which is not so common nowadays. Since CIUTI does not usually publish such presentations or make them available in the long term, I decided that it might

6 CIUTI Conference 2020 (9. – 11.12.2020) online – *Artificial Intelligence & Intercultural Intelligence: Actions and Interactions in Translation, Interpreting and Target Contexts*, ISIT, Paris, France. Presentation in the section: Transitioning to interaction: training and professional perspectives – *Intelligence artificielle qui soulève beaucoup de questions parmi les étudiants et les interprètes*: https://ec.europa.eu/education/knowledge-centre-interpretation/de/node/17226#event-description (accessed 29.12.2022).

be interesting for Czech respondents and readers to become acquainted with the results of the questionnaire survey (which was of course conducted in Czech) and to add additional links and information about artificial intelligence and AI tools existing or being developed for interpreter training or for interpreting itself[7]. It should be mentioned here that the period at the end of 2020 and the beginning of 2021 was very rich in AI-related events in interpreting in general. This trend naturally continued in 2022. We could mention a series of webinars[8] organised by the International Association of Conference Interpreters AIIC (*Association internationale des interprètes de conférence*) on artificial intelligence in interpreting and translation, and other interpreting webinars organised by colleagues abroad, open to the public and lasting a number of days, thematically broader in focus, and which were dedicated to various interpreter training technologies, and/or other modern technologies and their possible applications in interpreting[9].

2. Working definition of artificial intelligence in interpreting

For the purposes of our survey, in the introduction to the online questionnaire we provided respondents with a brief definition of AI for translation and interpreting. Definitions of artificial intelligence, which is nowadays encountered in almost all fields of human activity, are available in many sources: in the literature, on the websites of various international organizations, European bodies[10] and academic institutions; in project documentation (Horváth: 15 March 2019); in electronic encyclopaedias[11] or other online and printed sources; in discussions, webinars (AIIC: 11 December 2020) and innumerable articles. On this basis,

---

7 A first version was published in Czech in *Acta Universitatis Carolina (AUC) Philologica* 2/2021: Čeňková Ivana, Umělá inteligence a tlumočníci – víme, co nás čeká? (Artificial Intelligence and Interpreters – Do we know what awaits us?), 105–118.

8 https://aiic.co.uk/site/uk-ie/AI-interpreting: *Artificial Intelligence and the Interpreter – AIIC UK & Ireland's webinar series on AI and Interpreting*: November 2020 – January 2021 (accessed 29.12.2022).

9 https://www.innovationininterpreting.com/: 23. – 25.2.2021: Innovation in Interpreting Summit (accessed 5.3.2021) or: https://terpsummit.com: 13. – 15.1.2021: Your comprehensive toolkit for a successful, lasting interpreting career – organiser Sophie Liewellyn Smith (accessed 15.1.2021).

10 https://commission.europa.eu/publications/white-paper-artificial-intelligence-europ ean-approach-excellence-and-trust_en (accessed 15.01.2023).

11 https://en.wikipedia.org/wiki/Artificial_intelligence (accessed 22.12.2022).

we prepared the following brief definition, which we felt was specific and clear enough to introduce the topic of the questionnaire. Artificial intelligence in our questionnaire is understood as:

> *The ability of machines and systems to imitate human intelligence while using deep neural networks. Machines are then able to think and work independently, to make decisions, to solve the most varied types of complex tasks, to learn, to be creative, to adapt and change their behaviour based on the evaluation of the consequences of their previous actions, constantly to absorb and subsequently use new data (at present, for translation and interpreting: text and speech corpora, as well as speech recordings of various speakers etc.). Like humans they have the capacity to improve and increase the efficiency of their behaviour*[12].

We will be interested here only in the field of interpreting. We distinguish between purely automatic interpreting and AI-assisted interpreting.

We did not want to underestimate or overestimate the respondents. We based ourselves on our own, still rather limited knowledge, information about and awareness of the possibilities and future use of artificial intelligence in the field of interpreting and translation, at the same time using our many years of experience as an active conference interpreter, as well as a teacher of theoretical and practical interpreting courses at the Institute of Translation Studies of Charles University.

3. Research methodology

The questionnaire on *"Artificial Intelligence and Interpreters – what lies ahead?"* was prepared and published online in October 2020, where it was available for thirty days. We decided to address both undergraduate and graduate students of the Institute of Translation Studies of the Faculty of Arts, graduates of the EMCI course (European Masters in Conference Interpreting), internal and external interpreter trainers and active or former professional Czech interpreters. Therefore, the link to the online questionnaire was posted not only on the website of the Institute, on the Facebook group dedicated to interpreters, but was also sent to students and graduates of our Institute, to JTP (Union of Interpreters and Translators), ASKOT (Association of Conference Interpreters) and to Czech interpreters in the European institutions. The questionnaire contained a total of 18 questions, only one of which was open-ended, the others closed, multiple

12 This definition originally in Czech was translated into English for the purposes of the questionnaire used in further research by the EMCI Consortium: https://www.emcinterpreting.org/emci/application/files/5216/2627/7927/AI_questionnaire_13-7-21_final.pdf (accessed 22.12.2022).

choice or enumerative, so that the whole questionnaire did not take more than 15 minutes of the respondents' time. For several questions, a comment option was included if anyone wanted to comment in more detail. At the end of the questionnaire there was an additional space for comments. The questions were worded quite explicitly to make them clear to as wide a group of respondents as possible. We received a total of 77 completed questionnaires (any incomplete answers!) with a large number of interesting and thought-provoking comments.

3.1. Analysis of the responses and comments received

In the first question (Study/professional career), we asked who our respondents were, whether they were studying or had studied interpreting, and whether they were working or had worked as interpreters. As there was more than one option to tick, the number of responses is higher than the total number of completed questionnaires. In total, 34 current students, 6 teachers, 20 alumni and 43 active interpreters responded. The vast majority of this last group are, of course, our alumni.

In the second question we asked about the age of respondents. The most represented age group was 21–25 years old (40 %), i.e. our students, followed by active interpreters aged 40–49 (21 %). In third place were also interpreters, this time aged 50–59 (16 %). Fourth and fifth place were shared by respondents aged 31–39 and in the 60+ category (9 % each).

In the third question we asked about respondents' experiences with so-called classic "automatic interpreters" or voice translators such as *Google assistant/ interpreter* or *Skype translator, MS Translator Live feature* or other "pocket interpreters" in a smartphone, and with so-called voice phrase translators (Skadchenko 2019, 17–19). The responses were surprising at first glance, as 83 % of respondents answered that they had never used these apps. It is possible that interpreters are somehow able to communicate without these technical conveniences, even if they are in a situation where they do not know the language of their communication partners. Those who had used them (only 16 %) answered in the next question whether they were satisfied with the automatic interpreting and whether it met their expectations. It turned out that they did, as expectations were not high and the quality was sufficient in the situation to obtain the information or service required. Despite this limited experience, in the next question we asked in which situations the respondents thought this "pocket interpreter" could be used *without any worries* and offered multiple choices (communication in a hotel, transport – how do I get to…?, restaurant, emergency doctor's visit, basic communication with locals, following a guide in a castle or museum, theatre/film performance in a foreign language). As expected, transport (75 %), basic communication with locals (58 %), hotel (54 %) and restaurant (44 %) received the most responses. At the very end were an emergency visit to a doctor (13 %) and watching a theatre or film performance (4 %).

These initial questions were intended as a sort of "warm-up round" before the next group of questions, which then looked more specifically at the use of AI in interpreting.

They were followed by a single open-ended question (No. 6), "What do you think of AI in interpreting?", which was intended to probe the respondents' knowledge of AI and its potential use in the interpreting process. All 77 respondents gave their views and we tried to trace whether the answers depended on the age or the education and experience of the respondents.

It turned out that this was not the case, that students are very much aware of new technologies[13] and know how to use them (Riccardi et al. 2020, 7–42). Seven respondents of different ages and interpreting experience stated that they did not have a specific idea and did not elaborate further on their answers. The other 70 responses can be divided into two quite clearly defined groups, with various intermediate positions relating to the development of technology over time. In the first group we include the responses that speak of AI as an assistant to the interpreter, making his or her work easier and more convenient, whether they call AI *a device, a tool, software, a utility, a system, a database, an interpreting programme, a virtual assistant, or automated technical and terminological support for the human interpreter, or a kind of safety net*. Respondents state that "if AI is to assist 'human' interpreters, it could, for example, search for relevant passages in available documents and display them visibly on the screen (like a colleague in the booth and finding the relevant document and pointing a finger at a term/number/definition…)". Others specifically mention automatic writing of numbers, names, preparation of documents for a meeting, creation of glossaries.[14] The second group includes answers that give more power to AI, but again they name it differently – *as a system, computer, intelligent device, programme*, etc. These respondents refer to AI as "an artificial interpreter that mediates interpersonal communication without human intervention" or as "a technology that, based on speech recognition, converts speech into a written

13 https://www.youtube.com/watch?v=lQO5VSWZInY&feature=youtu.be: Artificial Intelligence and Interpreter Training. Ildikó Horváth – 11.12.2020 (accessed 30.10.2022).

14 Wang and Wang (2019), Prandi (2018).

version, which it contextually analyses and translates into a second language and then converts back into speech". In between these two basic classifications of AI, we can identify in a number of responses the intermediate positions mentioned above, where respondents talk about incremental stages of development: "soon it will be a Google Translate/Trados/CAI[15] in the booth which will monitor the speeches and write the terminology from the glossaries on the screen. Later I expect fully-fledged interpreting robots as in Star Wars…" or "the ability of the machine to interpret instead of the interpreter, much like machine-translation translates instead of the translator. It will certainly be much more difficult to minimise errors when interpreting than when translating, because in addition to language, pronunciation, distracting sounds, etc. enter into it." (see e.g. also Zhang 2017; Massion 2017; Fink-Hooijer 2017; Skadchenko 2019).

This question no. 6 was positioned in the questionnaire in such a way that respondents did not see the follow-up questions, which anticipated the expected answers in the completed questionnaires.

Namely, question 7 asks "can AI serve as an assistant interpreter (augmented interpreter, more powerful interpreter)?[16]"

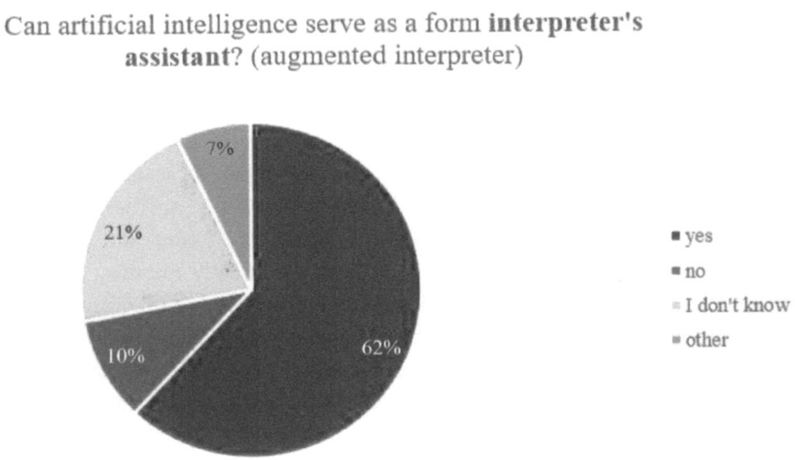

15 Computer-assisted interpreting.

16 See e.g. https://techforword.com/ Empowering language professionals through technology (accessed 29.12.2022).

We see that 62 % of respondents say yes, 21 % do not know, 10 % do not think so and the remaining 7 % also say yes but specify their opinion in further comments.

The eighth question then asks "for which type of interpretation would/could *AI assistance* be particularly useful?" There are several options to choose from: community interpreting, bilateral consecutive interpreting, high consecutive interpreting, simultaneous conference interpreting, court interpreting, accompanying interpreting, and possibly others (indicate in the comments).

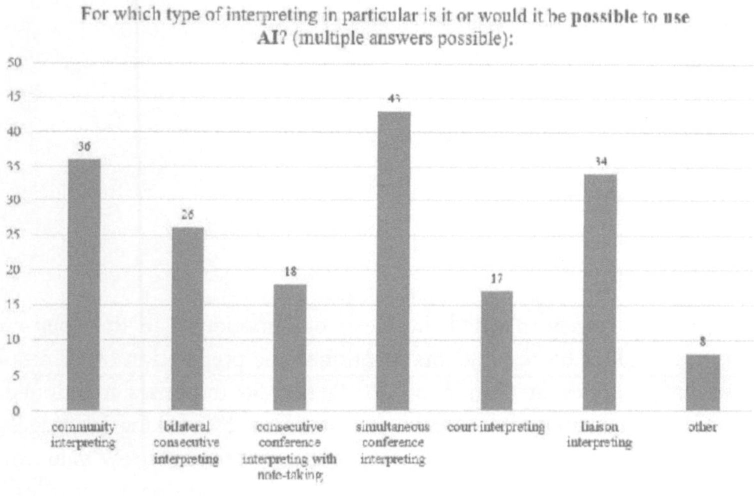

The majority of respondents (43) agreed that such assistance would be possible in the future for simultaneous conference interpreting, followed by 36 respondents who mentioned community interpreting and 34 who mentioned accompanying interpreting, which can overlap with community interpreting in many situations. The other types are less frequently mentioned, with AI assistance perceived to be least likely for court interpreting – cf. the table.

Question 9 asks even more specifically, "what could the use of AI consist of in conference setting especially?" Again, multiple choices were possible. The question took into account different types of support from AI[17] both before an event, during interpretation and possibly after an event.

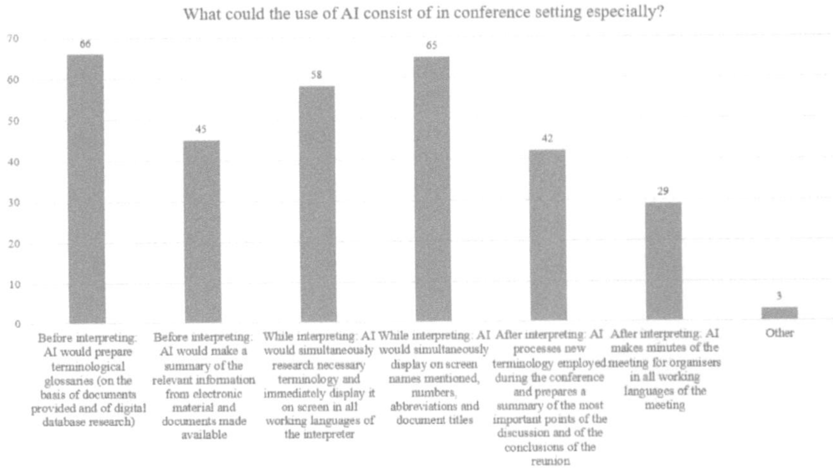

The responses largely matched the views of respondents in the open-ended question 6. A total of 66 respondents mentioned the preparation of terminology glossaries before an event (Fantinuoli 2017), and 58 responses mentioned the simultaneous search for terminology in the interpreter's working languages and instant display during interpretation. Even more respondents saw value in the simultaneous typing of numbers, names, abbreviations and document titles (65). As for AI assistance after the event, here the distribution is not so clear-cut, with 42 respondents choosing the processing of new terminology and outputs from the event content as appropriate assistance.

In the tenth question, we were interested to know whether respondents had also heard of ongoing projects such as *Speech Recognition*[18] or *Speech to text*

17 See e.g. Fantinuoli (2017, 2018) or Ortiz and Cavallo (2018) and others.

18 See e.g. https://ec.europa.eu/education/knowledge-centre-interpretation/news/european-commission-launches-speech-recognition-project (accessed 20.11.2022) or https://www.techforword.com/everything#innovation: Speech recognition for interpreters (accessed 26.01.2023), or Defrancq and Fantinuoli (2021).

or *ELITR*[19], mainly dedicated to the simultaneous conversion of speech in the source language into written text[20](subtitles) in the target language with the help of AI. Almost half of the respondents (49 %) said that they were familiar with these different projects or concepts, while 46 % wrote that they were not, and the remaining responded that they had only heard of some of them.

The eleventh question asked whether respondents thought that "AI is capable of subtitling a speech delivered in the source language instantaneously in the target language(s) on the displays of event attendees (*Simultaneous Subtitling* or *Simultaneous Translation*)"[21]. Only 30 % of the responses were positive, 20 % were negative, 14 % did not know what to answer, and as many as 36 % commented on their answers – a total of 25 comments that, while agreeing AI could perform simultaneous subtitling, put in a caveat with the word "but" ("the question is in what quality", "with many errors", "only partially", "depends on the sophistication of the technology", "to some extent", etc.).

The twelfth question then deals with this issue even more specifically and in more depth: "If AI is already partially capable of doing this (see question 11), what problems might it encounter and might its subtitling or simultaneous translation thus fail completely?" Again, multiple choices were offered – see Figure 12.

19 www.elitr.eu (accessed 10.12.2022).

20 https://www.youtube.com/watch?v=jiYQ0MeT-_U&t=1124s: AI: Speech Translation, interview Lourdes De Rioja / Ondřej Bojar – 8.1.2021 (accessed 20.01.2023).

21 Dávid Javorský, *Presentation of simultaneous speech translation* (Master thesis), Institute of Formal and Applied Linguistics, Faculty of Mathematics and Physics, Charles University, 2021.

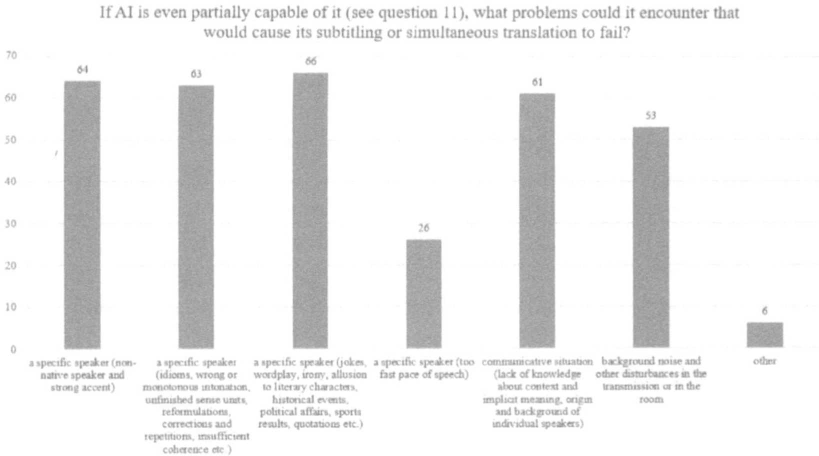

From the figure, we can clearly see that it is the speaker and various aspects associated with his/her speech (non-native speaker with heavy accent, idiomaticity, reformulations, corrections, lack of coherence, jokes, puns, references to literary characters and historical events, political causes, quotations, etc.), along with the specific communicative situation (66 and 61 responses respectively), that can negatively affect the AI's ability to provide simultaneous subtitling. Surprisingly, respondents often believe that the speed of the speaker does not have a significant impact on the quality of subtitling or simultaneous translation.

The thirteenth question partly returns to a topic that was already covered in question eight, where we only asked about possible help from AI. We used this inter alia to check for consistency in the answers of the respondents. We wanted to know "for which type of interpreting can we count on the gradual deployment of AI instead of a 'live' interpreter?". Here we go even further, no longer just mentioning AI support for the interpreter, but that AI would gradually replace the human interpreter completely. Again, respondents have more options, but they are more cautious. Community interpreting comes in first place with 40 responses (compared to 36 for question 8), and accompanying interpreting comes in second place with 36 votes (compared to 34 for question 8). We see a big drop especially for simultaneous conference interpreting, where we see only 16 positive responses (compared to question 8, where AI-assisted simultaneous interpreting took first place with 43 responses). However, this drop is quite logical and justified, also in the light of the previous questions and answers. We also checked this in the following, fourteenth, question.

The fourteenth question does not focus on particular types of interpreting, but on different interpreting situations and events in which we might expect the progressive use of AI instead of a live interpreter. Respondents were asked to mark their answers from most likely to least likely use of AI in a particular situation. They had a total of 13 situations to choose from (e.g. political and social science conferences, discussion fora, specialist technical and medical conferences, formalised parts of meetings – budget approval, annual reports, voting, ceremonial events, press conferences, plenary sessions of the European Parliament, or interpreting in courts of various instances, etc.). However, we must admit in self-criticism that this question was challenging both to fill in and to process. So, briefly and simply, we will state that the top places (for which the use of AI for interpretation can be considered) are formalised parts of meetings of various international organisations and institutions, technical conferences and expert working groups in EU institutions. Whereas the Court of Justice of the EU, the European Court of Human Rights, the International Court of Justice in The Hague or the plenary sessions of the European Parliament compete for the last places, clearly signalling that the use of AI here will only be hypothetical for a long time to come.

The fifteenth question asked respondents to estimate how long it is likely to take for AI to be deployed in multilingual meetings with simultaneous interpretation (presential or remote/online), noting that some scientific predictions already exist. Respondents were given a choice of five-year intervals, and the first possible time point was stated as 2030 at the earliest. A total of 34 % of respondents agreed that it would be in 2030, another 23 % that it would be in 2035 and 18 % in 2040. 9 % didn't know and another 9 % commented that they believed it will happen much earlier than 2030, that "pilot deployment will happen within two years for two languages" and that AI is being tested today, for example in China, although so far rather unsuccessfully, and it is very likely that certain types and segments of clients will adopt the use of AI perhaps even before 2025. Let us mention that experts' predictions speak more of 2050, when AI is expected to replace human interpreters completely.

The sixteenth question asked whether the use of artificial intelligence in interpreting will lead to an increase in multilingualism, i.e. will speakers speak more in their mother tongue? Respondents' views are divided: 29 % believe that it will, while as many as 36 % say it will not, and 27 % do not know. In addition, 8 % of respondents in their comments say yes, but that this will depend on the quality of machine interpretation. However, some of them also state very sceptically that everyone will prefer to speak bad English anyway.

The seventeenth question is more personal and asks whether respondents perceive AI involved in interpreting as a positive challenge and turning-point or as a threat? For 38 % it is a positive challenge, for 35 % a threat, 12 % don't know and 15 % comment on their answer to the effect that it is "probably neither", that they perceive AI neutrally and that it can make many things easier, or on the contrary they state that "it is both".

The final question was deliberately phrased somewhat speculatively: "Do you think that one day AI may turn against us, the interpreters and speakers, and rebel, like in Karel Čapek's drama *R.U.R.*?" Of course, we could cite other writers or scientists (Downie 2020) and personalities with similar thoughts (for example, Dan Brown and his 2017 novel *Origin*, or perhaps Bill Gates, Elon Musk, or Stephen Hawking).

The answers are as follows: 38 % of respondents say no, 23 % say yes, 20 % don't know, and a full 19 % answer evasively and comment on their answers (10 comments). Here are some of them: "I hope not, but it seems that we can destroy ourselves with our laziness and dependence on technology"; "yes, if the AI is so perfect that it starts correcting the interpreter's mistakes and proves to be more powerful and confident. The question is who will judge that performance and correctness. Personally, I think and hope that this is a utopia".

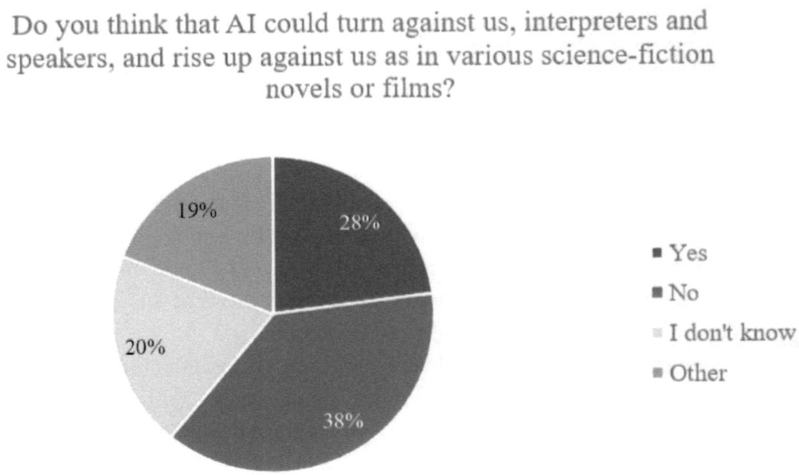

At the end of the questionnaire, respondents were still given space for further comments. A total of 20 of them took this opportunity to comment in more detail on other aspects related to the use of AI in the interpreting process. Again, there were views both for and against AI. We would like to mention explicitly those that cite specific cases where AI could (and should) be used – both for the benefit of the communicating parties and the interpreters themselves. These are in particular situations of community interpreting where interpreters are not available for some language combinations, although they are needed (e.g. hospitals in Africa). AI interpreting instead of a live interpreter could thus solve the difficulties caused by the language barrier in many situations where engaging interpreters would be difficult, economically prohibitive or ethically (e.g. war zones) unfeasible or difficult for various reasons.

3.2. New technologies in interpreting training

The use of these new technological tools in teaching was addressed in another questionnaire, which was sent out to all EMCI Consortium partner universities in spring 2021 and was completed by 111 respondents (55 students and 56 teachers). We were particularly interested in their ideas about the involvement of AI and new technologies in interpreter training itself. The detailed results and their analysis were published on the EMCI Consortium's website in the summer of 2021. We will take the liberty of presenting and partially quoting here just the answers to the questions that focussed on the pedagogical use of AI and all the supporting technological innovations mentioned above in our chapter (speech-to-text, automatic speech recognition, toolbox, intelligent terminology banks, etc.).

Two questions addressed interpreter training, specifically whether and how AI could or should be used in interpreter training, and whether the respondents think it is necessary for future generations of interpreters to be prepared for changes on the market, and whether universities are able, in terms of staffing, technically and financially, to achieve this.

The first question asked if the students and trainers have a clear idea of how AI could be introduced into interpreter training.

Almost 50 % of respondents answered "no" (of which 26 trainers and 34 students), the remaining answers being split almost equally between "yes" and "don't know", and that in both groups of respondents.

Some specified their replies in further comments. We can read for example: "By showing the tools available on the market, by raising awareness of students of the underlying issues such as AI ethics"(interpreter-trainer) or

"Students/Interpreters could learn to use and rely on AI for parts of the speech they miss (figures, names, etc.). It would just be another technique to include to interpreting learning" (student).

The second question asks very specifically what the use of AI in interpreter training could be, a selection of answers being proposed and multiple answers being possible. For the proposal: "AI could, during the source speech, search for terminology and show it on the student's display in the booth", there were 74 positive replies; for: "AI could, during the speech, display numbers and acronyms" – 82 positive replies; "AI could sub-title the source speech on the display, while the speaker can still be seen and heard" – 50 positive replies; "AI could simultaneously sub-title the speech in the target language, so that students can monitor their own output" – 22 positive replies. Further, there were three statements phrased as a negation: "No – it would be too expensive for universities" – 34 respondents agreed; "No – it would be technically too demanding for universities" – 25 agreed; and lastly "No – it would require further skills of the interpreter-trainers and supplementary expert technical and back-up staff" – 29 agreed. There were 15 comments to this question, some were very contradictory, some in favour, others very much against. It is interesting that these attitudes are distributed across both groups of respondents. Those who are rather against point out that students must first master basic interpreting skills and strategies, and only then could they, perhaps, use AI, for example for noting numbers, acronyms and names. The majority do not agree with simultaneous sub-titling in the target language, i. e. simultaneous translation or so-called speech to text[22].

3.3. Discussion

Any questionnaire is somewhat restrictive in its scope and type of questions and cannot capture all aspects and nuances of a given issue. However, we believe that the responses received indicate that our students, graduates and interpreters have, on the whole, a specific awareness and ideas about what AI (however we imagine it) might mean for the future of training and interpreting, how it might be helpful and how to use it to their advantage. A long road lies ahead for both artificial intelligence in interpreting and live interpreters because, as the researchers themselves state, "*machine interpreting does not really exist*

22 For the concrete quotations see the results of the questionnaire: https://www.emcinterpreting.org/emci/application/files/5216/2627/7927/AI_questionnaire_13-7-21_final.pdf (accessed 22.12.2022).

today. Only machine translation of spoken language is done. But first you have to recognise the spoken language accurately, which is a problem. […] For a neural network to interpret, we would need to give it the sound of the source speech as input and the sound of the target speech as output. If we could design such an architecture, and if we could understand how to run it so that there is a stable training process, in theory the system could machine-interpret. It would start doing all the things interpreters take for granted: adjusting speech rate, tone of voice, all the nonverbal aspects of the message."[23] But developments in the field of "understanding" language are extremely rapid, and the results are reflected in a whole range of AI applications (Horváth 2022, 1–13, or e.g. Open AI's Whisper engine for automatic speech recognition). We can therefore expect that AI will soon be able to assist interpreters and make their jobs easier, as we also tried to show in our questionnaire. The evidence is abundant, including in the field of training and education of future interpreters, where various supporting CAI tools and hybrid solutions are already being developed and tested. In the context of our discussion, let us mention at least one successful project, the already fully functional software tool *InterpretBank*[24] (Fantinuoli 2016), which is specifically designed to help future interpreters in an academic setting learn how better to search and prepare terminology and to automate the whole process of preparing for interpretation.

4. Conclusion

Artificial intelligence in interpreting will certainly attract more and more attention from professional interpreters, researchers and scholars, teachers and students, and will undoubtedly influence the content of curricula and technologies used in interpreter training. In interpreting theory, translation scholars talk about the different turns that occur in interpreting research (e.g. empirical, social or qualitative turns – Pöchhacker 2008), and now in the context of artificial intelligence we have made another major turn, namely the technological turn, as Fantinuoli (2019) has called it. The 2019 conference (see the introduction to our chapter) was titled *Interpreting 3.0.* This follows the practice of naming specific stages of development, particularly in various industrial, information and technological fields. Today, however, if we follow developments in the field

23 https://www.novinky.cz/kultura/salon/clanek/i-my-jsme-mozna-jen-stroje-rika-mate maticky-lingvista-ondrej-bojar-40308679: (accessed 10.12.2022).

24 http://interpretbank.com/: InterpretBank 8 | Software for interpreters – AI-based CAI tool (accessed 09.01.2023).

of interpreting closely[25] – also bearing in mind the huge leap forward made by online interpreting tools, applications and platforms in the wake of the covid-19 pandemic and the move to virtual reality – we are already talking about *Interpreting 4.0*. That, however, would already be a topic and subject for another article.

References

Čeňková, Ivana (2021) 'Umělá inteligence a tlumočníci – víme, co nás čeká?' (Artificial intelligence and interpreters – Do we know what awaits us?), *AUC Philologica*, 2/2021: 105–118.

Defrancq, Bart and Fantinuoli Claudio (2021) 'Automatic Speech Recognition in the booth: Assessment of system performance, interpreters' performances and interactions in the context of numbers', *Target*, 33(1): 73–102.

Downie, Johathan (2020) *Interpreters Vs Machines: Can Interpreters Survive in an AI-Dominated World?* New York: Routledge.

Fantinuoli, Claudio (2016) 'InterpretBank. Redefining computer-assisted interpreting tools', in *Proceedings of the Translating and the Computer 38*. Geneva: Editions Tradulex, 42–52.

Fantinuoli, Claudio (2017) 'Computer-assisted preparation in conference interpreting', *Translation & Interpreting*, 92: 24–37.

Fantinuoli, Claudio (2018) 'Interpreting and technology: The upcoming technological turn', in Claudio Fantinuoli (ed.), *Interpreting and Technology*. Berlin: Language Science Press, 1–12.

Fantinuoli, Claudio (2019) 'The technological turn in interpreting: The challenges that lie ahead', in Wolfram Baur, Felix Mayer (eds.), *Proceedings of the Conference Übersetzen und Dolmetschen 4.0. – Neue Wege im digitalen Zeitalter*, BDÜ, 334–354.

Fink-Hooijer, Florika (2017) 'Artificial Intelligence – The (un)desired revolution?', *Lebende Sprachen*, 62(2): 269–274.

Horváth, Ildikó (2019, March 15) 'Machine interpreting', lecture as visiting professor at the Institute of Translation Studies, Faculty of Arts, Charles University, within the *TO1 Internal competition projects* 2019–2020.

Horváth, Ildikó (2022) 'AI in interpreting: Ethical considerations'. *Across Languages and Cultures*, 23/1, 1–13.

25 https://smarter-interpreting.eu/theproject/: Remote Simultaneous Interpreting powered by Artificial Intelligence – A hybrid interpretation system that brings machines and humans together for a smarter interpreting (accessed 22.01.2023).

Javorský, Dávid (2021) *Presentation of simultaneous speech translation* (Master thesis), Institute of Formal and Applied Linguistics, Faculty of Mathematics and Physics, Charles University.

Massion, François (2017) 'Artificial intelligence, smart assistants and the role of language professionals', *Lebende Sprachen*, 62(2): 275–299.

Ortiz, Luis Eduardo Schild and Patrizia Cavallo, P. (2018) 'Computer-Assisted Interpreting Tools (CAI) and options for automation with Automatic Speech Recognition', *TradTerm*, 32, 9–31.

Pöchhacker, Franz (2008) 'The turns of Interpreting Studies', in Gyde Hansen, Andrew Chesterman and Heidrun Gerzymisch-Arbogast (eds.), *Efforts and Models in Interpreting and Translation Research: A Tribute to Daniel Gile.* Amsterdam: John Benjamins, 25–46.

Prandi, Bianca (2018) 'An exploratory study on CAI tools in Simultaneous Interpreting: theoretical framework and stimulus validation', in Claudio Fantinuoli (ed.), *Interpreting and Technology.* Berlin: Language Science Press, 29–59.

Riccardi, Alessandra, Čeňková, Ivana, Tryuk Malgorzata, Maček, Amalija and Pelea, Alina (2020) 'Survey of the use of new technologies in conference interpreting courses', in Dolores Rodríguez Melchor, Ildikó Horváth and Kate Ferguson (eds.), *The Role of Technology in Conference Interpreter Training.* Oxford, Bern, Berlin, Bruxelles, New York, Wien: Peter Lang.

Skadchenko, Julia (2019) *Strojový překlad a automatické tlumočení. (Machine translation and Machine Interpreting)* [MA thesis – in Czech], Institute of Translation Studies, Faculty of Arts, Charles University.

Wang, Xinyu and Wang, Caiwen (2019) 'Can computer-assisted interpreting tools assist interpreting?', *Transletters. International Journal of Translation and Interpreting*, 3: 109–139.

Zhang, Ailing (2017) 'Simultaneous Interpreting (SI): The Holy Grail of Artificial Intelligence – An SI practitioner's perspective', *Lebende Sprachen*, 62(2): 253–268.

Electronic resources

SCIC – Universities Conference (4. – 5.4.2019): *Preparing for Interpreting 3.0. Towards the augmented interpreter.* https://webcast.ec.europa.eu/scic-universities-conference-2019-04-05 (accessed 29.12.2022).

The Digital Booth | Knowledge Centre on Interpretation (europa.eu) (accessed 29.12.2022).

https://www.youtube.com/watch?v=_Il53xdfNhQ: AI for Interpreter Support. Marc van Dommelen on DG SCIC's 'Interpreter's Digital Toolbox project' – 11.12.2020 (accessed 29.12.2022).

https://ec.europa.eu/education/knowledge-centre-interpretation/news/eu-host-paper-new-technologies-and-artificial-intelligence-field-language-and-conference_en: European Commission (2019). New Technologies and Artificial Intelligence in the field of language and conference services (accessed 29.12.2022).

www.elitr.eu: ELITR – European Live Translator – Many Languages, One Voice (accessed 29.12.2022).

https://aiic.co.uk/site/uk-ie/AI-interpreting: *Artificial Intelligence and the Interpreter – AIIC UK & Ireland's webinar series on AI and Interpreting*: November 2020 – January 2021 (accessed 29.12.2022).

https://www.innovationininterpreting.com/: 23. – 25.2.2021: Innovation in Interpreting Summit (accessed 5.3.2021).

https://terpsummit.com: 13. – 15.1.2021: Your comprehensive toolkit for a successful, lasting interpreting career – organiser Sophie Liewellyn Smith (accessed 15.1.2021).

https://commission.europa.eu/publications/white-paper-artificial-intelligence-european-approach-excellence-and-trust_en (accessed 15.01.2023).

https://en.wikipedia.org/wiki/Artificial_intelligence (accessed 22.12.2022).

https://www.youtube.com/watch?v=lQO5VSWZInY&feature=youtu.be: Art ificial Intelligence and Interpreter Training. Ildikó Horváth – 11.12.2020 (accessed 30.10.2022).

https://techforword.com/ Empowering language professionals through technology (accessed 29.12.2022).

https://ec.europa.eu/education/knowledge-centre-interpretation/news/europ ean-commission-launches-speech-recognition-project (accessed 20.11.2022)

https://www.techforword.com/everything#innovation: Speech recognition for interpreters (accessed 26.01.2023).

www.elitr.eu (accessed 10.12.2022).

https://www.youtube.com/watch?v=jiYQ0MeT-_U&t=1124s: AI: Speech Translation, interview Lourdes De Rioja / Ondřej Bojar – 8.1.2021 (accessed 20.01.2023).

https://www.novinky.cz/kultura/salon/clanek/i-my-jsme-mozna-jen-stroje-rika-matematicky-lingvista-ondrej-bojar-40308679: (accessed 10.12.2022).

http://interpretbank.com/: InterpretBank 8 | Software for interpreters – AI-based CAI tool (accessed 09.01.2023).

https://smarter-interpreting.eu/theproject/: Remote Simultaneous Interpreting powered by Artificial Intelligence – A hybrid interpretation system that brings machines and humans together for a smarter interpreting (accessed 22.01.2023)

https://www.emcinterpreting.org/emci/application/files/5216/2627/7927/AI_questionnaire_13-7-21_final.pdf (accessed 22.12.2022).

Anna Jelec

Karol Bartkiewicz

Katarzyna Czarnocka

Joanna Ziobro-Strzępek

Chapter 12 Why not(es)? Automatic analysis of notes for consecutive interpreting training

Abstract: Conference interpreters have a very particular set of skills. Note-taking for consecutive interpreting is a system of conventions developed to aid memory and improve the faithfulness of interpretation. Traditionally, during a course on note-taking interpreting students learn to write down less, commit certain types of information to memory and structure text. In this study we show how instruction changes the way students take notes. We introduce two scales to measure the degree to which the interpreter writes information down (measured through their use of a blank page) and extent to which they structure notes (measured through text density). Using a computer algorithm, we analysed notes taken by 49 students of interpreting from three academic institutions, collecting 137 pages of notes in the "no training" condition and 179 pages of notes in the "after training" condition. Results show that following didactic intervention students' page use and text density have a tendency to decrease. We demonstrate the measurable effects of teaching note-taking on students' notes, which could help in the development of interpreter training curricula as well as assessment measures for teachers of consecutive interpreting, particularly in remote learning classrooms.

Keywords: interpreter training, consecutive interpreting, note-taking, remote learning, teaching consecutive

1. Introduction

Note-taking is a distinctive feature of consecutive interpreting (CI), particularly in the 'classic' consecutive where the interpreter relies on notes to reproduce longer fragments of speech[1]. This type of note-taking is practised by a vast majority of conference interpreters and traditionally taught during interpreter training. Although the terms 'notes' and 'note-taking' are relatively generic, in the context of conference interpreting, note-taking denotes a very particular skill. Different from any other type of writing, the interpreters' notes serve as memory activators, facilitating content memorisation and retrieval. Sustained scholarly interest in the subject has generated a considerable volume of literature on both notes, and teaching note-taking.

Chen[2] suggested that note-taking research is either prescriptive or descriptive. Indeed, much of the early work on the topic ought to be considered prescriptive, in that it focuses on developing note-taking systems and principles for interpreter training[3]. Prescriptivist approaches to interpretation (cf. the original didactic model by Gile[4]) divide consecutive interpretation into two phases: listening & analysis, and target text production. The two phases are accompanied by note-taking and note-reading, respectively. From a cognitive perspective, the operations involved in interpreting are seldom discreet, nor can they be neatly assigned to a single phase. Rather, they take place throughout the interpreting process. A similar view is embraced by Janikowski[5], who proposes CI is best described as a complex multimodal process where different modalities are involved at once. In the prescriptivist model, note-taking is associated with the early phase of listening and analysis. In practice, interpreters refer to their notes throughout both phases, introducing corrections, ticking off facts or even doodling on the margins. More recently, note-taking has been investigated from a descriptive perspective, including studies on the choice of form[6], preferred language[7], preferred directionality and target text fluency[8] or the relationship between note-taking and interpreting performance[9]. The latter, in particular, has

1 Pöchhacker, 2006
2 Chen, 2016
3 e.g. Matyssek, 1989; Rozan, 2002
4 Gile, 2009, p. 175
5 Janikowski, 2015, p. 142
6 words vs. symbols, e.g. Chen, 2017; Chmiel, 2010
7 target vs. source, e.g. Szabo, 2006; Dam, 2004
8 Mead 2011
9 e.g. Chen, 2020

shown that the relationship between note-taking and quality of target speech is perhaps more complex than originally thought. Precisely because interpreting is a complex process, isolating note-taking as a variable impacting the quality, accuracy or fluency of target speech is difficult. Researchers[10] have attempted to link certain qualities of notes (e.g. use of symbols, lists; writing in target or source language; quantity of notes) to the quality of interpreting output but their results were inconclusive.

Chen[11] observed that the quantity of notes did not affect the quality of output, in that there was no clear relationship between how much the interpreter wrote and how accurately they rendered the speech. Nai[12] concluded the relationship between the amount of notes taken by student interpreters and the quality of their interpretation is "not very close". Chmiel (2010) asked students to review the usefulness of certain note-taking strategies, such as replacing certain words with symbols or using diagonal layout. The results of her questionnaire were encouraging, with students rating the usefulness of the strategies taught during interpreting training as either 9 or 10 on a 10 point scale. Subsequent analysis of students' notes, however, demonstrated that those same strategies were not actually used all that much (e.g. only 32 % of her participants used symbols in their notes).

This raises certain questions for the didactics of interpreting, such as how to teach and assess note-taking skills or, indeed, whether to teach them at all. Practitioners argue that although note-taking varies among interpreters, it nevertheless can and should be taught[13]. On the other hand, École Supérieure d'Interprètes et de Traducteurs "never thought much of note-taking as an underpinning of CI"[14]. Nevertheless, modern approaches to interpreting training include note-taking as a standard part of the curriculum[15].

10 including Dam, 2004, Chmiel, 2010, and Chen, 2017, 2020
11 Chen, 2017
12 Nai, 2020
13 see, e.g. Chmiel 2010, Jelec 2015, Janikowski 2015, Bartłomiejczyk and Stachowiak-Szymczak 2021.
14 ESIT, Paris, as cited in Ilg and Lambert 1996, p. 71.
15 see e.g. Ahrens and Orlando 2022 for a review.

2. Notes as a "semi-manufactured product"

Conference interpreting has been studied as a process and product. In this section we argue that there is a third approach, namely one that views notes for CI as the so-called "semi-manufactured product of interpreting"[16].

Research on CI as a process gives us a wealth of data regarding note-taking and note-reading. For instance, Andres[17] used video recording to measure the onset of writing in relation to source speech; Orlando[18] advocated for the use of the Livescribe Smartpen to study note-taking as part of teaching; Chen[19] used a combination of a digital pen and tablet to analyse the physical and temporal demands of various note-taking strategies. Mead[20] cautions that note-reading can be a constraint in CI, however. Depending on the methodology, such studies can be time and resource consuming, and, therefore, the scope of material and/or number of participants is limited. Chen suggests that the "lack of suitable research methods is an important reason for the lack of process research on consecutive note-taking".

Research focussing on the interpreting product (i.e. the target speech) has a longer tradition, but faces similar challenges. First, qualitative analysis of speeches is equally, if not more, labour-intensive as process analysis. There is also the issue of measuring speech quality. In order to study the target speech as a product of interpreting we have to agree on the criteria against which to judge it. Accuracy is one indicator of target speech quality, for instance, Chen (2020) divided the source speech into segments and looked for corresponding segments in the target speech to assess interpretation accuracy. Somewhat more controversially, Stachowiak-Szymczak and Korpal[21] considered the rendition of numbers, measured on a three-point scale, to be a good indicator of accuracy. Practitioners and interpreter trainers agree that the quality of the target speech does not depend solely on the accurate reproduction of facts and figures. Rather, it is a complex interplay of multiple variables, including, but not limited to

16 The term "półprodukt tłumaczenia" (semi-manufactured product of interpreting) has been proposed in the extensive volume on teaching conference interpreting by Chmiel and Janikowski (2015).

17 Andres, 2002

18 Orlando 2010

19 Chen 2020

20 Mead 2011

21 Stachowiak-Szymczak and Korpal 2019

target text accuracy, logical coherence, quality of target language, fluency and eye-contact.

In contrast to accuracy, research on interpreting quality revolves around subjectively perceived standards of interpreting. A number of researchers[22] found that interpreters considered target text delivery, logic, fluency, as well as pleasant voice and native accent to be markers of quality. Interestingly, when asked which markers were important for quality, interpreters prioritised different features than audiences[23]. This is why quality is often found too recipient-dependent to be deemed objective. Finally, Tryuk[24] comments that quality is complex, and its understanding evolves with the interpreting profession.

On the other hand, CI notes can be analysed according to measurable criteria, such as the use of symbols vs. words[25], abbreviations, visualisation, semantic use of empty space[26] and so on. In fact, Chen[27] argues that interpreters' notes serve as a window into the interpreting process. Although researchers such as Orlando[28] see notes for CI as an interpreting product, we would like to argue that they are rather a stage in the production of the final speech. Much like a builder mixes sand and water to produce cement should be: Much like a builder mixes cement, water, and sand to produce mortar in order to construct a concrete wall, the interpreter converts the source speech into notes, which then become the basis for the production of the target speech. In this way, notes are the *semi-manufactured product* of interpreting which is then used to deliver the finished speech. Therefore, the analysis of interpreting notes falls in the middle of the research spectrum, between product and process analysis. At the same time, analysing notes by hand is labour-intensive and time consuming.

Nevertheless, analysis of notes as semi-manufactured product was so far conducted largely through hand annotation[29]. The vast majority of interpreters use paper notepads and pens, while some resort to tablets, e-pens, drawing pads and even laptops. Mueller & Oppenheimer[30] report better effects generated by the

22 For instance, Bühler 1986, Kurz 1989, 1993, 2001 and Pöchhacker & Zwischenberger 2000.
23 Kurz 2001
24 Tryuk 2012, p. 46 ff.
25 Dam, 2004; Chen, 2020
26 Chmiel, 2010
27 Chen 2020
28 Orlando 2010
29 e.g. Chmiel, 2010; Dam, 2004
30 Mueller & Oppenheimer 2014

pen-and-paper method, at least in sighted individuals[31]. Generally, students are encouraged to use bound notebooks over loose sheets of paper[32]. For researchers interested in the process, this means either encouraging students to use a digital pen[33], combination of digital pen and tablet[34] or even recording the note-taking process on video[35].

Most researchers admit that the validity of insight would be increased by studying a larger or more diverse sample of participants, or more language pairs. In this paper, we propose to automatise the analysis of some aspects of notes as a semi-manufactured product of interpreting that is affected by didactic intervention in the interpreter training classroom.

3. Teaching note-taking

Considerable volume of literature has already been devoted to teaching both note-taking for CI[36] and teaching conference interpreting in general[37]. Teaching note-taking for CI is a challenge because not only do we introduce a semantically different system of writing, but also ask students to perform a manual task under challenging conditions (e.g. on a notepad, standing up) and under pressure. What is more, note-taking for CI requires the students to revise the assumptions they learned for writing in a linear, everyday fashion[38].

There is considerable individual variation in note-taking. So much so that even Matyssek[39], who urged his students to learn and use a pre-defined symbol system, admits that individual variation is to be expected at later stages of interpreter training. Janikowski[40] encourages didactics to take into account students' strengths, and allow students to gradually develop good note-taking habits rather than force them to conform to any particular set of rules.

31 Visually impaired interpreters rely on Braille note-taking devices, resign from notation altogether, or record the source text and replay it while producing their target text, the result being similar to SimConsec; Figiel, 2017.
32 Janikowski, 2015
33 Orlando, 2010
34 Chen, 2020
35 Andres, 2002
36 e.g. Rozan, 2002; Matyssek, 1989
37 e.g. Chmiel & Janikowski, 2015; Setton & Dawrant, 2016
38 Janikowski, 2015
39 Matyssek 1989
40 Janikowski 2015

Assessment has to take into account that learning note-taking is a gradual process with considerable variation in outcomes. It requires effort, particularly in the early stages of learning where students get overwhelmed by the need to coordinate listening, memorisation and note-taking. Students might also become discouraged by the lack of immediate results[41]. Measuring students' progress in note-taking is, therefore, not only useful for grading, but also an important way to encourage and direct learning.

3.1. Grading and tracking students' progress

Most universities and schools that train conference interpreters offer courses in note-taking, especially at the graduate and post-graduate level[42]. Teachers focus on e.g. writing down less (in favour of remembering), diagonal page layout and the use of symbols[43]. Nevertheless, to the best of our knowledge, few publications discuss the outcomes of notation training. Despite the existence of resources for interpreter training (such as the European-Commission-funded ORCIT), there are few tools for gauging interpreter's competence in note-taking. In other words, it remains unclear if teaching students to remember more and write down less, or to stay away from full sentences in favour of words and phrases makes them actually do so. We can only assume training works because the students' target speeches appear to improve over time.

Related studies may be divided into two streams. One focuses on the role of notes in performance, and the other on teaching notation strategies, and measuring the success of those strategies. The first stream starts with Gile[44] who investigated two groups of 7 students each, during consecutive interpreting training. One group was free to take any notes during listening, while the other was instructed to take selective notes including only numbers and names. The first group was less accurate when it comes to writing names. Gile concluded that taking rich notes required more attention management, which led to mistakes. Hsiao & Chang[45] investigated the effect of note-taking on English text comprehension, in Taiwanese students and learners of English. They concluded that note-taking could be used as a tool in teaching to support comprehension and listening skills. Somewhere in-between the two streams, Alexieva[46] observed that the quality of

41 e.g. Janikowski, 2015
42 Sanchez, 2018
43 Chen, 2017
44 Gile 1991
45 Hsiao & Chang 2014
46 Alexieva 1994, p. 200 ff.

interpreting drops after introducing notes to students. Students get excited about learning and using symbols, and tend to over-focus on that aspect of CI to the detriment of others. In other words, at the initial stage of teaching notation is a new, unautomated element of interpreting. The second stream is represented e.g. by Nai[47] who embarked on a study investigating a notation strategy she referred to as *focus-on-meaning*. The strategy revolved around learning to deverbalize, and proceeded in three (here simplified) steps: learning symbols, learning keywords and learning how to split attention between memory and notes. Nai[48] concluded that "students trained by this method pay more attention to the meaning of the speaker in the process of interpreting notes, instead of sticking to the speaker's wording, and learn *deverbalization*. From a slightly different perspective, Xu & Chai[49] asked trainees to self-report on difficulties in note-taking and observed e.g. that students who had difficulties with decoding their own notes and translating notes into successful target text formulation also tended to depend on notes too much, instead of using memory.

As new methods are introduced into research on consecutive interpreting[50], care should be taken to develop new paradigms also for studying notation. As it is, study designs frequently involve post-task questionnaires and retrospective protocols which, while informative, are subjective and difficult to generalise across populations. This lack of methods contributes to the lack of research on the process of note-taking (Chen, 2020, p. 118). Therefore, in the next section we propose an automated tool for the analysis of notes.

4. Differences in notes taken by trainees and professional interpreters

A quick comparison of notes produced by a student and a professional makes it clear that note-taking is a skill, and one that is honed throughout years of experience. While professional interpreters note down sequences of keywords and symbols, often arranged on a diagonal axis, novice note-takers tend to write down as much as possible, and write down full words or even entire sentences in long, uninterrupted horizontal sequences. The latter approach creates a set of problems, both for the first and second phases of CI. Focussing on writing

47 Nai 2020, p. 1094 ff.

48 Nai 2020, p. 1097

49 Xu & Chai 2008

50 see e.g. Chen, 2016 for a discussion on triangulating eye tracking, digital pen recording and voice recording

things down creates a listening/memory barrier in the novice interpreter. Mead[51] observes that notes can be perceived as a constraint in CI, which may indeed be the case if using notes is inefficient (e.g. by a trainee). Instead of actively listening for information, they devote energy to writing everything down. Not only does this result in notes that are practically illegible (cramped text, small font, hurried and misshapen letters), but also causes the interpreter to forget the source speech because they may have written it down but did not understand and/or process the information.

Untrained notes can be distinguished by the following features:

- use of complete words rather than abbreviations and symbols;
- too much information noted down;
- long, uninterrupted, horizontally-written sequences
- dense and poorly organised text.

This is why didactic intervention is crucial in the development of good note-taking habits and a cornerstone for the trainee interpreter's future success. Even though participants in interpreting courses are normally expected to be fluent in their working languages both in speech and in writing, they need to be separately trained in taking notes for CI, and clear differences are seen in their performance if compared to professionals.

4.1. Use of space

Space can be used for notation in CI in a variety of ways[52]. Interpreter training commonly uses Rozan's[53] principles: verticality and shift, a system which Janikowski calls "staircase notation". Kohn & Albl-Mikasa[54] describe such notes as structured in a "vertical, indented and terraced way".

Janikowski (2015) suggests that certain principles of notation appear to be universally helpful. For instance, spacing the symbols and words further apart improves legibility and allows for subsequent additions to the text. Condensation and generalisation depend on the use of space in note-taking. Interpreters note down from general to the specific, and from top left to bottom right. Chmiel (2010) describes this phenomenon as "use of space as a symbol". By leaving space on the left margin, or using principles of staircase notation, interpreters

51 Mead 2011

52 see e.g. mind mapping, linear notation, four-column notation, Gillies' 2005 SVO model.

53 Rozan 2002, p. 82–85

54 Kohn & Albl-Mikasa 2002, p. 262

assign meaning not only to words and symbols, but also to empty spaces. These note-taking strategies help interpreters tease apart and subsequently remember the structure of the source speech. Conscious use of space is what distinguishes professionals from trainees.

4.2. Text density

Most students show a tendency to "over-note"[55], in that they try to note down every word as it is spoken by the speaker. This is a problem for a variety of reasons. Giles[56] blames excessive notation for problems in comprehension. Students are much more likely to miss information because they are busy writing than they are to mishear the speaker. Unskilled note-taking causes overload where the student is unable to divide their attention successfully between understanding, remembering and writing.

Also, the denser the text, the less legible the notes. The effect of too densely written text has been investigated by Mead[57] who asked a group of students and professionals about the reasons behind pauses and hesitations in CI. Many students found it difficult to read what they have just written down. Therefore, an overarching goal for teaching note-taking is to show trainees how to write less and more efficiently, relying on memory while remaining supported with notes.

---

55 Sanchez, 2018

56 Giles 2005

57 Mead 2011

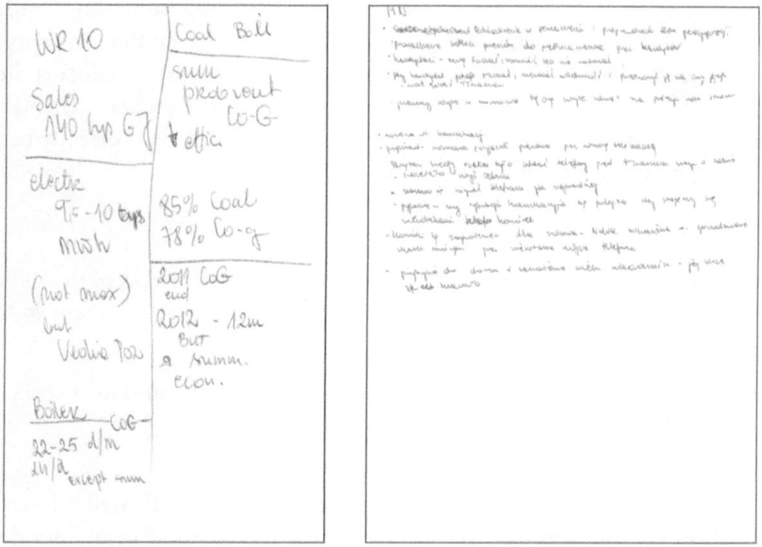

Figure 1. Differences in notes for consecutive interpreting taken by a student (right) and a professional (left). Professional's notes are spread across the page but the text is much less densely written. Student's notes show a tendency to use long, unstructured passages of text. Source: Data collected by the authors.

As we see in Figure 1, novice or untrained interpreters tend to write down entire sentences and phrases with little spacing; professional interpreters use diagonal notation, resulting in a more distributed structure of text.

5. Automatic analysis of notes for consecutive interpreting training

The goal of the didactic process is to train the novice interpreter to write down less, remember more, and structure notes in a way that will make them easy to read[58]. However, the students' success has so far been measured through their performance on target speeches rather than, as mentioned in Section 2 of this

58 see e.g. Rozan 2002, Chmiel & Jankowski 2015 or Romano 2018 on different aspects of student note-taking and their role in CI

paper, their notes as a semi-manufactured product. At the same time, students benefit from feedback on their note-taking skills separate from their interpreting performance. So far, this has been a challenge to provide, in no small part due to the individual variation in note-taking techniques and preferences. This is why our measure of successful didactic intervention in note-taking is directly related to *how* and *how much* trainees note down.

5.1. Hypotheses

We assumed that students' notes at the beginning and at the end of the didactic intervention, understood as a 1-semester course in notation for CI, are going to differ on the following scales:

- degree to which the interpreter writes down information and uses space as a semantic device (measured through their use of page);
- structure of their notes (measured through text density).

Page use. As the interpreter gains note-taking skills, they will write down less information (presumably storing the remaining information in memory and/or relying more on the use of space as a symbol). Hence, we expect the notes to cover less space on the page after instruction.

Text density. The notes' sentence-like horizontal layout that resembles a regular handwritten text (horizontally written sequences, one below another) will be replaced by a more spread out, concept-based diagonal structure.We expect the text to be less dense after training.

5.2. Participants

Data was collected from 49 students of conference interpreting at the beginning and at the end of the first semester of their programmes. Three instructors at three different academic institutions in Poland gathered the data. Samples of notes came from three groups of students:

- group X – 21 MA students of conference interpreting,
- group Y – 7 BA students of conference interpreting,
- group Z – 20 MA students specialising in translation whose curricula included a full consecutive interpreting course, including notation.

All students were fluent in their working languages (in this case: Polish as their A language and English as their B language). Students' proficiency in their B language varied, but in all instances was considered enough to successfully apply to an English language interpreting programme.

5.3. Method

Data was collected in two stages: at the start and end of the first semester of studies. In the X and Y groups, the course dedicated to strategies and note-taking for consecutive took place before a separate course in consecutive interpreting, while in the Z group note-taking was taught as an element of the consecutive interpreting course. In each group, the instructor collected two sets of notes from participants: one produced at the beginning, and another at the completion of the course. All participants took notes from the same speeches from the European Commission's DG SCIC Speech Repository 2.0. The speeches used were: "Kawa"[59], in Polish and "Communication"[60], in English. Speeches chosen for this study were of roughly equal length, prepared specifically for teaching purposes and classified as "pedagogical material" in the Speech Repository database.

5.4. Procedure

All instructors followed the same procedure for data collection. The procedure was written down and distributed to the instructors to ensure compliance across groups. In the first stage of the study (which we later call "no training") each student was given as many blank (unlined[61]) pages (A4 format[62]) as needed, and was informed that they were going to practise consecutive interpreting with notes.

The task was to listen to the speech, take notes and then interpret the speech from the notes. The students were informed that their notes will be collected after the exercise but not graded. The instructors encouraged trainees to use as much or as little of the page as they wanted. Before proceeding, the students were asked to sign their initials in the top right corner of the pages for coding purposes. Next, the instructor opened the Speech Repository 2.0 website and presented the students with the vocabulary relevant to the topic of the first speech (vocabulary is listed on the website under each video). The students

59 Feder, 2009

60 Campbell, 2007

61 Unlined pages introduce less noise in image processing, see section 5.5. for an explanation.

62 This is larger than what is normally recommended for note-taking (Jones 1998, Gillies 2005), therefore top-spiral notepads (most popular among professional interpreters) could be used to maximise ecological validity in future studies. However, as we used the same paper format at the beginning and the end of the course, it did not constitute a confounding variable.

discussed the vocabulary and found equivalents in their target language. This was done to ensure that the lexical difficulty of the speech was not a confounding variable. After the students took notes and interpreted the first speech in pairs, their notes were collected and 3–4 more blank pages issued. Next, students were familiarised with the vocabulary of the second speech and then asked to listen, take notes and interpret in pairs. Notes were collected after the exercise had been completed.

The second stage of the study (which we call "after training") took place at the end of the semester, approximately 5 months after the first stage. We repeated the same procedure. We decided to use the same two speeches in both stages of the study to compare results across conditions. This solution was also chosen (as opposed to using a new, therefore unknown, yet structurally and lexically different text), as interpreters rely mainly on working memory, while only a small share of content information is stored in the long-term memory – a phenomenon that is elsewhere referred to as the Zeigarnik Effect[63]. "Memory in interpreting only lasts for a short time. Once the interpreting assignment is over, the interpreter moves on to another one, often with different context, subject and speakers"[64]. The implications of the choice of stimuli are discussed further in the discussion section. The notes acquired were scanned, anonymised, and assigned a code. Then, notes were analysed.

5.5. Image processing

To measure page use and text density of the notes we used a computer programme developed for this purpose. After scanning, colour images were converted to greyscale pictures with values associated with each pixel in the range of 0 (black) to 255 (white). The greyscale image was then converted to a black and white (BW) image by applying an empirically selected threshold, i.e. a value between 0 and 255. If the value associated with the greyscale pixel is below the threshold, the pixel is mapped as black, otherwise it is mapped as white (empty). Choosing an appropriate value of this threshold is not trivial. Making it too low results in a noisy BW image, where the handwritten notes are indistinguishable from lines on paper or scanning imperfections. On the other hand, if the threshold is too high, some of the notes may be not visible in the BW picture. This is why we used unlined paper for the study. For our ensemble of notes the best choice of the threshold turned out to be 240. Finally, we applied a median filter of a

63 Ahrens 2017
64 Zhong 2003

small radius (3 pixels) to remove single pixel noise that appears as a side effect of the threshold-based greyscale to BW conversion. This filter scanned a small neighbourhood of each pixel and replaced the colour of a pixel with the most common pixel value in the neighbourhood. Both of these processes are standard in image processing.

Once the pre-processing was over, we were faced with the problem of selecting which areas of the page contained notes (i.e. how much of the page was used for note-taking vs. left blank). There are many approaches to this problem. In this case, we decided to apply a simple algorithm that identifies rectangular clusters of pixels, representing chunks of text on a page. This is because handwritten text (including symbols) is likely to be arranged in rectangular chunks. Our clustering algorithm uses one parameter referred to as padding[65] . Figure 2 illustrates the image analysis.

As a result, for each page of notes we established two values: the area covered in ink (i.e. handwritten chunks: words, abbreviations, symbols, arrows, lines etc.) and proportion of the page that was covered in handwritten chunks vs. left blank.

Figure 2. Figures illustrate the steps in image analysis. First, we scan the page, then we calculate page use and finally from that we learn text density.

65 Here, we assume that the paper is white and the text is black. Step 1: We find the smallest and the largest values of a pixel x-coordinate for a fixed y-coordinate marking the segment of pixels containing notes. Step 2: We find the smallest and the largest values of a pixel y-coordinate for a fixed x-coordinate marking the segment of pixels containing notes. Only pixels selected as both x and y segments are marked as a part of a cluster. We found that setting this parameter at 10 pixels was enough to obtain mostly uniform clusters of pixels for our BW images.

Page use. We identified clusters of pixels that represented chunks of handwriting on a page. Page use was calculated as the percentage of the entire page that was covered in chunks, which are defined as the handwriting and clusters of pixels around it (see Figure 3 below).

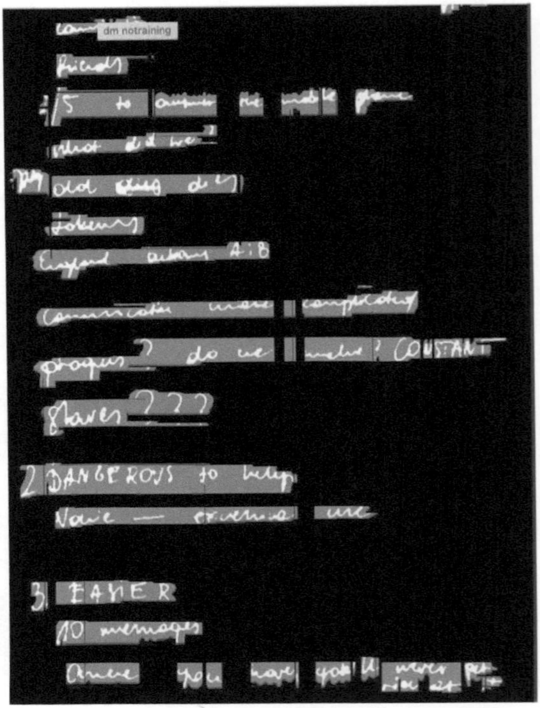

Figure 3. Handwriting and the cluster of pixels around it allow us to see how much of the page is covered in chunks (page use)..

This parameter itself is not indicative of the interpreter's progress. It allows is to monitor how much empty space the participant leaves on a page and serves to calculate our second parameter:

Text density. Text density is the ratio of handwriting (ink-covered area) vs. the area covered by the clusters identified above. To illustrate on two different writing styles, the notes of a participant writing in big letters will have low text density, while the notes of someone using smaller letters will be characterised by high text density. For example, in Figure 4, Participant A uses big letters and notes down 5 pieces of information:

Figure 4. An example of note-taking style with low text density (Participant A).

Because the area covered by text is around half the page, page use will be relatively high (the letters are large, hence the rectangle drawn around each chunk is relatively big). The area covered by the ink in comparison to the page use is, however, smaller than in Figure 5:

Figure 5. An example of note-taking styles with higher text density and low page use (Participants B and C, respectively)

Participants B and C use small letters, noting down 8 and 12 pieces of information, respectively. The area covered by text is around a quarter / third of the page. Page use will be relatively low (the letters are smaller, hence the rectangle drawn around each chunk is relatively small). Text density is, however, high, because the percentage of the area inside each chunk covered by ink is larger than in Participant A.

All participants use comparable pen sizes, therefore – the ink line width is comparable between the two. These measures (area on page covered by chunks, ink-covered space within each chunk) in conjunction translate into lower text density when the participants use larger letters. We assume that professional interpreters' take their notes like Participant A (who noted down 5 pieces of information spaced further apart), and beginners take notes like participant C (who noted down 12 pieces of information in close proximity).

6. Results

Overall, we collected 196 pages of notes in the "no training" condition and 179 pages of notes in the "after training" condition. Assorted examples are shown in Figure 6.

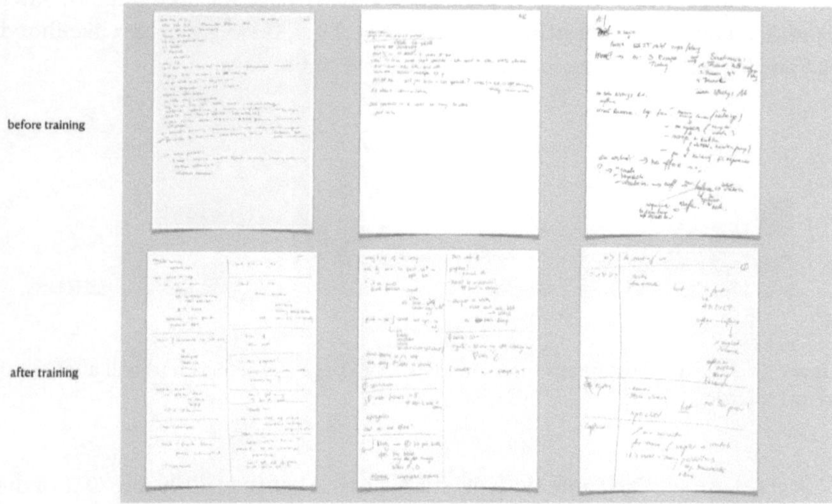

Figure 6. Comparison of the structure of notes taken by the same students before (top row) and after (bottom row) didactic intervention.

Data are organised into four groups describing (i) page use before training, (ii) page use after training, (iii) text density before training, and (iv) text density after training. For pairs (i)–(ii) and (iii)–(iv) we have conducted the t-test for two means with unknown standard deviations. For sets (i) and (iii) the number of pages analysed was 196, whereas for sets (ii) and (vi) we processed 179 pages.

Page use. We expected the notes to cover less space on the page after instruction.

For data sets (i)–(ii) the mean page use is 0.15 and 0.20, respectively (standard deviaiton is estimated as 0.18 and 0.27, respectively). Here, to perform a t-test for two means and unknown exact values standard deviations we applied the Welch-Satterthwaite's equation to estimate the number of degrees of freedom to be 309. This results in a p-value of 0.0442. Thus, the two means are significantly different at a p-value of 0.05 but do not seem to go completely in line with our hypothesis.

The p-value is a useful indicator of statistical significance. However, it does not tell the full story and while it's commonly used, its proper application should be limited to Gaussian-shaped probability distributions. Thus, to complete our analysis we refer to the relevant histograms, shown below.

In Figure 7, we see that untrained participants (left) are more-or-less equally likely to use between 10 and 30 percent of a blank page for taking notes. After training (right), two interesting things happen. First, there is a bigger likelihood that participants are going to use less than 10 % of the page.

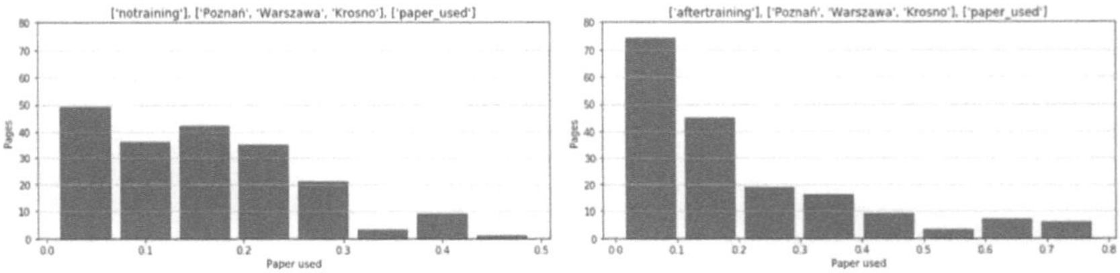

Figure 7. Page use. Histogram shows tendencies in page use before (left) and after (right) teaching.

Second, we see that some students started to use between 60 % and 70 % of the page. The former would suggest that after training students tend to write down much less, which is in line with our hypothesis. The latter could be because they learn to make much better use of a single page (see Figure 7).

Text density. We expected the text to be less dense after training.

For data sets (iii)-(iv) the mean text density is 0.22 and 0.18 and the estimated standard deviations are 0.23 and 0.19. Here, the estimated number of degrees of freedom is 370. This results in p-value of 0.0998. Thus, the two means are significantly different at a p-value of 0.10. These results are in line with our hypothesis.

Histogram in Figure 8 shows that after didactic intervention the average text density drops. Trained students are more likely to produce notes with 15–20 % text density, while untrained students' text density is higher.

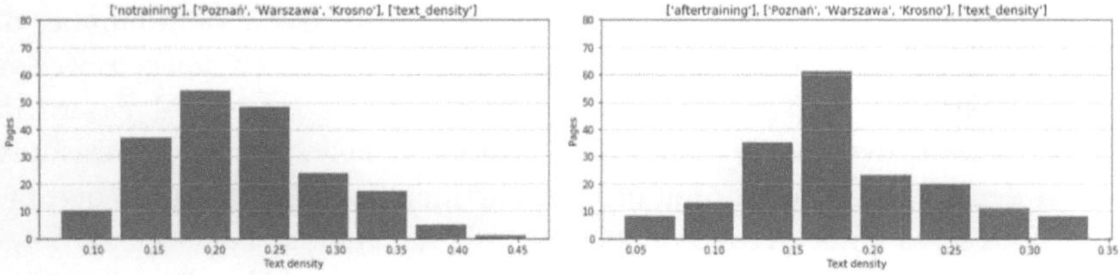

Figure 8. Text density before (left) and after (right) teaching.

7. Conclusions

This paper proposes a scalable method for the automatic analysis of notes for CI, focussing on two measurable features of notes, namely – the use of space and text density. By tracking how the use of space and text density changes over the course of learning, our method permits the assessment of progress in interpreter training. We show that participants learned to note-down less and improve their use of space as a semantic symbol, producing more legible notes for easier content retrieval. We observed changes in notation in samples gathered at three different teaching institutions (with slightly different programmes) which allows us to tentatively conclude that didactic interventions dedicated to note-taking translate into better notation.

In all schools, we consistently observe a decrease in the median of text density before and after didactic intervention: in Warsaw and Krosno about 5 %, whereas in Poznań this relative drop is twice as large. The final values of the median of text density in Poznań and Warsaw are identical, i.e. 0.18. In general, the statistical parameters obtained from Poznań and Warsaw are very similar, while Krosno exhibits some discrepancies. We attribute this to a smaller sample size and thus a more pronounced role of outliers in Krosno. The relative 5–10 % decrease of median of text density is the only phenomenon that is universal for all three schools. We may attribute that to different course organisation and/or stage of studies.

First, while the notation course precedes consecutive interpreting training in X, it takes place along consecutive practice in Z. This may suggest that a dedicated course in note-taking is an advantageous format for improvement in note-taking strategies in the space of one semester for students of conference interpreting. Second, while X and Z are postgraduate courses, the Y group was composed of undergraduates, suggesting students' maturity and educational stage might affect learning outcomes.

Teaching note-taking likely changes students' performance on a number of levels, including structure of text, amount of information noted down, as well as number of symbols used and language used in the notes. For practical reasons, in this paper we analyse two of these four indicators, namely structure as measured by text density and amount of information written down as measured by page use. More research is needed on the use of source/target language in note-taking, as well as automatic recognition of symbols. It would be also interesting to see whether notes that are "more advanced" in terms of our measurements translate to better interpreting performance. Further research will focus on the comparison of trainee and professional interpreters' notes.

We believe our results help in the assessment of note-taking in consecutive interpreting, specifically by tracking student progress and goal completion. Our method is particularly suited for remote teaching, or in larger classrooms because the parameters of notes are calculated automatically.

References

Ahrens, Sonke. (2017). How to Take Smart Notes: One Simple Technique to Boost Writing, Learning and Thinking. CreateSpace Independent Publishing Platform.

Ahrens, B. & Orlando, M., (2022), Note-taking for consecutive conference interpreting. In The Routledge handbook of conference interpreting. Albl-Mikasa, M. & Tiselius, E. (Eds.). Abingdon, Oxon: Routledge, Taylor and Francis Group, (pp. 34–48).

Alexieva, B. (1994). On teaching note-taking in consecutive interpreting. In C. Dollerup & A. Lindegaard (Eds.), *Teaching Translation and Interpreting 2: Insights, Aims, Visions* (pp. 199–206). John Benjamins.

Andres, D. (2002). *Konsekutivdolmetschen und notation* [Consecutive interpreting and note-taking]. Doctoral dissertation, Universität Wien.

Bartłomiejczyk, M. & Stachowiak-Szymczak, K. (2021). Modes of conference interpreting: Simultaneous and consecutive. In M. Albl-Mikasa and E. Tiselius (Eds.). *The Routledge Handbook of Conference Interpreting* (pp. 19–33).

Bühler, H. (1986). Linguistic (semantic) and extra-linguistic (pragmatic) criteria for the evaluation of conference interpretation and interpreters. *Multilingua* *5*(4), 231–235.

Campbell, H. (Speaker). (2007). *Communication* (EN-PL): https://webgate.ec.europa.eu/sr/speech/communication. Accessed June 15, 2010.

Chen, S. (2016). Note-taking in consecutive interpreting: A review with special focus on Chinese and English literature. *The Journal of Specialised Translation, 26*, 151–171.

Chen, S. (2017). Note-taking in consecutive interpreting: New data from pen recording. *The International Journal of Translation and Interpreting Research, 9*(1). https://doi.org/10.12807/ti.109201.2017.a02

Chen, S. (2020). The process of note-taking in consecutive interpreting: A digital pen recording approach. *Interpreting. International Journal of Research and Practice in Interpreting, 22*(1), 117–139. https://doi.org/10.1075/intp.00036.che

Chmiel, A., 2010. Interpreting Studies and psycholinguistics: A possible synergy effect. In Gile, D., Hansen, G., Pokorn, N., (Eds.), *Why Translation Studies Matter*. (pp 223–236). Benjamins.

Chmiel, A., & Janikowski, P. (2015). *Dydaktyka tłumaczenia ustnego*. Stowarzyszenie Inicjatyw Wydawniczych.

Dam, H. V. (2004). Interpreters' notes: On the choice of language. *Interpreting, 6*(1), 3–17. https://doi.org/10.1075/intp.6.1.03dam

Figiel, W. (2017). *Tożsamość i status tłumaczy z dysfunkcją wzroku [The identity and status of interpreters with sight impairment]* [PhD Thesis]. Z University.

Feder, M. (Speaker). 2009. *Kawa* (PL-EN): https://webgate.ec.europa.eu/sr/speech/kawa. Accessed June 15, 2020.

Gile, D. (1991) Prise de notes et attention en début d'apprentissage de l'interprétation consécutive – une expérience-démonstration de sensibilisation. *Meta* 36 (2), (pp. 431–439).

Gile, D. (2009). *Basic concepts and models for interpreter and translator training* (Rev. ed). John Benjamins.

Gillies, A. (2005). *Note-taking for consecutive interpreting: A short course*. St. Jerome.

Hsiao, S., & Chang, F.A. (2014). Teaching Consecutive Interpretation Note-Taking Strategies to Improve Taiwanese Senior High School Students' English Listening Comprehension. *Compilation and Translation Review*. 7: 2 (pp. 107–150).

Ilg, G., & Lambert, S. (1996). Teaching consecutive interpreting. *Interpreting, 1*(1), 69–99. https://doi.org/10.1075/intp.1.1.05ilg

Janikowski, P. (2015). Notowanie [Note-taking]. In P. Janikowski & A. Chmiel (Eds.), *Dydaktyka tłumaczenia ustnego* (pp. 141–166). Stowarzyszenie Inicjatyw Wydawniczych.

Jones, R. (1998). *Conference interpreting explained*. St. Jerome.

Jelec, A. (2015). Przetwarzanie w tłumaczeniu konsekutywnym [Processing in consecutive]. In P. Janikowski & A. Chmiel (Eds.), *Dydaktyka tłumaczenia ustnego* (pp. 167–184). Stowarzyszenie Inicjatyw Wydawniczych.

Kohn, K., & Albl-Mikasa, M. (2021). Note-taking in consecutive interpreting. On the reconstruction of an individualised language. *Linguistica Antverpiensia*, New Series – Themes in Translation Studies (pp 257–272).

Kurz, I. (1989). Conference interpreting – User expectations. In D. Hammond (Ed.), *Coming of Age: Proceedings of the 30th Annual Conference of the American Translators Association* (pp. 143–148). Learned Information.

Kurz, I. (1993). Conference interpretation: Expectations of different usergroups. *The Interpreters' Newsletter*, 5, 13–21.

Kurz, I. (2001). Conference interpreting: Quality in the ears of the user. *Meta: Translators' Journal, 46*(2), 394–409. doi: 10.7202/003364ar.

Matyssek, H. (1989). *Handbuch der Notizentechnik für Dolmetscher: Ein Weg zur sprachunabhängigen Notation* (2. ed.). Julius Groos.

Mead, P. (2011). Co-ordinating delivery in consecutive interpreting. *inTRAlinea. on- line translation journal, 13.* https://www.intralinea.org/specials/article/1666

Mueller, P., & Oppenheimer, D. (2014). The pen is mightier than the keyboard: Advantages of longhand over laptop note taking. *Psychological Science, 25*(6), 1159–1168.

Nai, R. 2020. Study on "Deverbalization" in Teaching Note-Taking in Consecutive Interpretation. *Proceedings of 4th International Conference on Culture, Education and Economic Development of Modern Society (ICCESE 2020).* Atlantis Press. (pp 1093–97).

Orlando, M. (2010). Digital pen technology and consecutive interpreting: Another dimension in note- taking training and assessment. *The Interpreters' Newsletter, 15,* 71–86.

Pöchhacker, F. (2006). *Introducing interpreting studies* (Reprint). Routledge.

Pöchhacker, F., & Zwischenberger, C. (2000). Survey on quality and role: Conference interpreters' expectations and self-perceptions. (http://aiic.net/p/3405) (date of access: 3 June 2020).

Romano, E. (2018). Teaching note-taking to beginners using a digital pen. Między Oryginałem a Przekładem 24 (42), (pp 9–16).

Rozan, J.-F. (2002). *Note-Taking in consecutive interpreting. Notatki w tlumaczeniu konsekutywnym.* Tertium.

Sanchez, M. (2018). (Over)Note-taking in consecutive interpreting. *International Journal of English Language & Translation Studies, 6*(3), 150–156.

Setton, R., & Dawrant, A. (2016). *Conference interpreting: A trainer's guide*. John Benjamins Publishing Company.

Stachowiak-Szymczak, K., & Korpal, P. (2019). Interpreting accuracy and visual processing of numbers in professional and student interpreters: An Eye-tracking Study. *Across Languages and Cultures*, 20(2).

Szabó, C. (2006). Language choice in note-taking for consecutive interpreting. *Interpreting, 8*(2), 129–147. DOI: 10.1075/intp.8.2.02sza.

Tryuk, M. (2012). *Ocena jakości w tłumaczeniu ustnym: konieczny etap kształcenia tłumaczy konferencyjnych* [The assessment of quality in interpretation: A necessary stage in the education of conference interpreters]. *Lingwistyka Stosowana/Applied Linguistics/Angewandte Linguistik, 6*, 45–55.

Xu, H. M. & Chai, M. J. (2008). Difficulties Perceived by Professional Trainee Interpreters and Non-Professional Interpreters in Note-Taking When Doing Consecutive Interpreting—An Empirical Inquiry through Simulated Recall. *Foreign Language Research*, 1 (pp 122–127).

Zhong, W. (2003). Memory Training in Interpreting. *Translation Journal* 7(3). http://accurapid.com/journal/25interpret.htm

Tomasz Korybski

Chapter 13 Hybrid and synchronous simultaneous interpreter training: Configurations, constraints, opportunities and perceptions

Abstract: The interpreting services market has experienced profound transformations due to recent technological advancements and the global pandemic, resulting in a notable transition from traditional on-site assignments to online (remote) jobs. Recent research (Bujan Collard 2021, Saina 2021) has highlighted the challenges accompanying this shift. In a post-pandemic reality, stakeholders, including clients, agencies, and service users, are increasingly leveraging Remote Simultaneous Interpretation (RSI) technology for its organizational benefits and cost-efficiency, but many types of assignments still require on-site presence. Moreover, the emergence of computer-assisted interpretation (CAI) technologies (Fantinuoli 2021, Prandi 2020, Frittella 2022) has further complicated the work environment for both current and future interpreters. This dynamic landscape necessitates a re-evaluation of interpreter training approaches, which is already underway.

This paper offers an analysis of the prevailing challenges and opportunities in interpreter training. Firstly, it investigates potential configurations for hybrid/blended interpreter training, encompassing both remote and on-site components, and the relevant technologies. Secondly, it explores the constraints inherent in the blended training model and provides recommendations for addressing these challenges. Thirdly, it explores the possibilities presented by hybrid interpreter training, emphasizing the integration of modern computer-assisted interpretation tools (CAI tools) and other innovative solutions. Lastly, it introduces a pragmatic and evidence-based human perspective by presenting the results of a longitudinal pilot study on advanced interpretation students' perceptions of blended interpreter training, with a focus on the perceived effectiveness of such training.

Keywords: hybrid interpreter training, synchronous interpreter training, simultaneous interpreting, computer assisted interpreting

1. Introduction

The recent disruptions in the interpreting services market, caused by both technological developments and the Covid-19 pandemic, have led to a significant shift from on-site jobs to on-line (remote) jobs with several associated challenges reported in recent studies (Collard and Bujan 2021; Saina 2021). As the pandemic is receding, there is a need to explore the composition of the market once again, but what seems to be apparent is the fact that the proportions of on-site to on-line jobs have shifted significantly. Clients, agencies, and services users are tapping into the flexibility of the RSI technology to achieve organisational advantage and cost-effectiveness, which in turn significantly impacts the profession. At the same time, some jobs can still only be performed on-site, or client preference is for interpreters to work in the event's location. What is adding to the complexity of the situation is a further development of computer-assisted interpretation (CAI) technologies (Fantinuoli 2019; Prandi 2020; Frittella 2022). This creates a mixed working environment for present-day and future interpreters. What should follow closely is a shift in the approach to interpreter training which we indeed are beginning to observe.

This chapter seeks to offer a magnifying-glass look at the existing challenges and opportunities for a hybrid (both remote and on-site) delivery of simultaneous interpreter training. Firstly, it explores the possible configurations of hybrid delivery of simultaneous interpreter training and the technologies that make these configurations possible. Secondly, it also looks at the constraints brought about by the blended mode of delivery, with suggestions on how to tackle them. Thirdly, the paper investigates the opportunities afforded by hybrid interpreter training, with an emphasis on the inclusion of modern computer-assisted interpretation tools (CAI tools) and other solutions in interpreter training in the blended mode. Finally, to include the human factor, the paper presents the results of a small longitudinal pilot study on how advanced students of interpretation perceive hybrid (on-site and on-line) delivery of interpreter training, with emphasis on the perceived effectiveness of hybrid interpreter training.

2. Hybrid live delivery of simultaneous interpreter training as a form of blended learning

Blended learning, in its broadest non-academic dictionary definition, is a 'a way of learning that combines traditional classroom lessons with lessons that use computer technology and may be given over the internet'[1]. This combination of learning methods has been available for a relatively long time now, with the term 'blended learning' in regular use since the late 1990s (e.g., Clark 2003: 23). The interpretation of the term and its exact definition has already been subject to academic analysis (for a detailed presentation of the relevant definitional nuances see Friesen 2011), but for the sake of this chapter I will focus on two possible aspects of blended learning that are important in the context of hybrid simultaneous interpreter training in the way I mean it here. The first aspect is the *synchronous nature* of training (i.e., I will only focus on *live* or *real-time* delivery of interpreter training), and the second aspect is the *location* of instruction – classroom-based, on-line, or a synchronous combination of the two in different configurations. Of course, there are other aspects of blended learning that are highly pertinent for the delivery of interpreter training, such as any application of Computer Assisted Interpreting (CAI) tools, Computer Assisted Interpreter Training (CAIT) tools, flipping the training, virtual training (Braun et al. 2011), or the use of on-line resources.[2] The focus of this paper is to explore in more detail the live and remote mode of delivery of interpreter training, in an attempt to provide an overview of the constraints, challenges, and opportunities it brings.

2.1. Interpreter work and training environments: The necessary overlap

As a matter of course, teaching, the design of instructional material as well as the selection of teaching delivery modes will be shaped and impacted by the subject matter being taught (Arbaugh et al. 2010: 39). In the case of remote interpreter training, an important driver of all decisions regarding the delivery of teaching is the actual work environment of an interpreter – or, to phrase it more precisely, the interpreter's multiple work environments. This factor was already complex enough before the pandemic, and with the growth of remote simultaneous interpreting (RSI) platforms and videoconferencing platforms used for interpreting, another layer of complexity has been added. It is therefore important to try to re-create the existing practical market demands in interpreter training to simulate a variety of work environments as well as the range of

---

1 Cambridge English Dictionary

2 For a comprehensive discussion of a broader set of aspects of blended learning in present-day interpreter training see Biernacka (2021), and for a technology-focused overview of solutions for blended learning in interpreter training see Kajzer-Wietrzny and Tymczyńska, 2014.

technological solutions applied in them. At the same time, it seems equally important to maintain the highly interactional character of interpreter training, with a strong focus on regular feedback making use of a variety of available feedback options. The assumption that all interpreter training can go back to its pre-pandemic mode seems to be flawed at the outset: the change in work environments and the accompanying rapid technological change appear to be irreversible and must be taken into account when designing effective interpreter training curricula for today and tomorrow. This section presents an overview of possible technological solutions, configurations, challenges, and opportunities in live blended simultaneous interpreter training.

2.2. The technology

There are many technological solutions and applications that are being used to deliver simultaneous interpreter training, but few have been *specifically* designed to deliver such training. Unlike training in consecutive interpreting which can be successfully delivered using any videoconferencing platform (Rodriguez Melchor et al. 2020), remote training in simultaneous interpreting has a much broader set of technical requirements for audio, video, and backchannel communication. Although every RSI platform is theoretically capable of delivering the basic functionalities necessary for simultaneous interpreter trainers (i.e., simulating an environment with the three key roles of interpreter(s), event moderator(s), and audience), the convenience and effectiveness of such training may be limited – for example, it can work well in the case of one-on-one or one-on-two classes, but such a set-up is a rare luxury in tertiary education. Furthermore, the main challenge associated with using a commercial version of an RSI platform is that it often requires the instructor to use multiple instances of the platform's application to be in the role of the event's moderator (manager) and audience at the same time. Additionally, for practical reasons RSI platforms do not offer an option to create multiple booths with the same language combination – which is precisely one of the requirements in simultaneous interpreter training. Other challenges include controlling a dual audio track at different volume levels (the source and the student's target) or facilitating recordings. These challenges have led some companies to develop bespoke interpreter training platforms, with notable examples being GreenTerp's[3] educational platform (created as a spin-off from GreenTerp's RSI platform and recognised for its functionality by the Conférence

3 www.gtmeeting.com, accessed 5 April 2023

Internationale Permanente D'instituts Universitaires De Traducteurs Et Interprètes, CIUTI)[4], and Sanako's language and interpreter education platform[5]. Both offer the instructor access to audio from multiple booths, AV share to multiple booths, as well as recording of targets and feedback functionalities. Of course, not all educational institutions have access to such tools, and for practical and economic reasons simultaneous interpreter training during the pandemic was very often delivered using 'regular' videoconferencing solutions available to universities through their licenses, such as Microsoft Teams, Google Meet, Webex, or Zoom. The latter has been more suitable for simultaneous interpreter training since the 2022 upgrade which has allowed interpreters to listen to their virtual boothmates during delivery – but it is still necessary to 'click through' to the right configuration to listen to the tandem partner, which may lead to loss of short fragments and the interpreter's inability to react. The obvious technological challenge is therefore to choose and then rehearse any solution that will be used for training in simultaneous interpretation. This aspect cannot be underestimated – otherwise it will cause additional strain for the instructor and render the curriculum less realistic. Typically, however, existing interpreter training curricula do not allow separate technological induction classes, and in the case of most applications, a few hours are needed to introduce and apply the technology, learn the interface, trouble-shoot, and test possible configurations.

2.2.1. *The configurations for remotely delivered simultaneous interpreter training and the challenges involved*

Live training of simultaneous interpreters delivered remotely can be implemented in many different configurations. It is important to consider them as an important variable before a course begins and, possibly, 'test-drive' at least some of these configurations during the technological induction component of the course.

Configuration 1: All students remote and on-line, instructor remote and on-line

This all-remote configuration was often imposed on higher education institutions by the realities of the pandemic. In simultaneous interpreter training, it is crucial for the instructor to put together a quick guide for the students that they need to read through prior to the technological induction. Typical issues in this configuration may include browser incompatibility and

4 www.sanako.com/connect, accessed 2 April 2023

5 www.ciuti.org, accessed 5 April 2023

connectivity / data throughput. Screenshots of the most important operations on the relevant application's interface provided to the students in advance may prove useful. During the delivery, the interactional component may be limited as, depending on the choice of the application, students may not be seen during their performance, and a separate feedback session with cameras switched on may be necessary. The instructor's role is to make sure the settings of the sessions are all in place and trouble-shoot 'on the go'. In the light of the research results presented later in this chapter, it may be prudent to opt for this configuration only after the class and the instructor have interacted on-site, and (possibly) after a dry run to check connectivity and give students time to resolve any technical issues on their side.

Configuration 2: Remote instructor, all students on-site

In this software-only configuration, access to a laboratory is required as students will be working individually or in tandems. However, they will not be using any on-site equipment apart from the booths which ensure soundproofing. A pre-requisite is reliable and stable internet access from inside the booths (preferably via an Ethernet cable), and a level of familiarisation with the platform or software suite to be used concurrently by the instructor and the student. For the instructor, an important consideration is how to take advantage from the on-site presence of the whole group of students (for example by designing peer feedback or group feedback tasks). This configuration may be particularly useful in the case of classes run by busy practitioners, for whom remote delivery can be more attractive than the necessity to turn up for on-site classes throughout the term.

Configuration 3: Instructor and most students on-site, one or more students on-line

This configuration can be planned ahead or become an ad-hoc necessity during the term, for example due to the student's quarantine or other health- or travel-related emergency. As contingencies do happen, it is reasonable to plan for this configuration and decide in advance whether the lab set-up allows for a mixed-mode delivery (both on-site delivery with booths, consoles and local lab equipment and software or platform-based delivery for remote participants), or whether a software-only delivery is preferred due to technical constraints. The former may be more complex to implement and requires a good audio-video set up in the room: the instructor will need to run an instance of the software/platform of their choice, with video input (ideally) provided by the voice- and motion-controlled camera in order for both the instructor and the peers to be visible to online participants. The latter, in turn, may be a simpler choice but will require the students to work from on-site booths connected to the Internet and without using the physical interpreter's consoles.

The three main configurations described above may be further complicated by adding an external speaker or speakers / audience who can be both on-site and remote. Such additional actors will also add to the instructor's class preparation workload and any required technical tests ahead of the session, which must be considered in curriculum development.

2.2.2. Computer Assisted Interpreting (CAI) tools and Computer Assisted Interpreter Training (CAIT) tools in live delivery of remote simultaneous interpreter training

Computers and, more broadly speaking, information and communication technologies have been present in interpreter education for at least a few decades now, stemming from Computer Assisted Language Learning (CALL) technologies. One of the first ways to integrate digital data storage for interpreter education was to establish the first speech banks, including probably the most widely recognised Speech Repository of the EU (Frittella 2021: 106). In the context of live delivery of simultaneous interpreting classes via videoconferencing and RSI solutions, both speech banks and preparation tools such as glossary extraction and management tools (e.g., the first iterations of Interpretbank, Fantinuoli 2016: 44) are still very relevant, but the recent technological developments have offered a new range of possibilities afforded predominantly by Automatic Speech Recognition (ASR) and Speech-to-Text (S2T) technologies. Recent research projects have started to explore how live provision of (elements) of automatically recognised speech transcript can impact the interpreter's performance. Based on a small-scale experiment focussing on the use of ASR for number recognition, Defrancq and Fantinuoli (2021: 1) report that 'ASR provision improves overall performance for almost all number types'. Another project taking a closer look at the integration of AI and ASR in an RSI platform is the SmartTerp project (as reported by Frittella and Rodriguez 2022). The project's objectives include finding out if ASR technology is capable of 'supporting interpreters in the rendition of common problem triggers, i.e., named entities, acronyms and specialised terms, and numbers' (Frittella and Rodriguez 2022: 142). Preliminary findings based on self-reports from the interpreters taking part in the project's experimental phase are promising for the use of ASR in live delivery of RSI assignments. A broader scope of application of ASR (not just problem triggers, but a full ASR transcript and its impact on interpreter performance) is being investigated in an ongoing project at the University of Surrey (Rodríguez González et al. 2022). Furthermore, Chmiel and Spinolo (2022) are investigating interpreter experience and performance in virtual booths and their findings will also shed more light on how interpreters interact with RSI technologies and assistive solutions. All in all, we should soon have enough empirical data to claim we know more about which solutions can work for interpreters delivering RSI assignments. It seems very likely that ASR technology is one of the potentially valuable additions, so a natural consequence would be to add it (on top of other CAI tools) to the range of tools used also in remote delivery of simultaneous interpreter training. This will undoubtedly add another layer of complexity to the training set-up presented above, as well as adding to the workload of the trainer – but such a level of complexity seems inevitable in the face of recent technological developments and the market reality for interpreters. Effective training must seek to re-create and use environments which are very similar to the real ones, or which at least contain most of the components that future interpreters can encounter in their real-life assignments.

2.3. Simultaneous interpreter training through blended learning: The human interaction aspect

Of course, the technological and configuration layers are not the only points to consider when designing a modern-day remote delivery of simultaneous interpreting classes. A crucially important element of this pedagogical set-up is the human interaction aspect. In the wake of the Covid-19 pandemic, researchers are increasingly looking at how many educational contexts have been impacted by the sudden shift to technology-dominated and predominantly remote settings. Although there are clear advantages of remote and blended learning, studies show that on-site human interaction can lead to more active engagement on many levels: behavioural, cognitive, and emotional (e.g., Hewett et al. 2019). Consequently, curriculum design for courses that will most likely benefit from a blended approach (and simultaneous interpreting is one such course given the post-pandemic market reality) need to be carefully designed to take the best out of the two worlds. Importantly, social competence dynamics and their impact on cognitive performance must be taken into account to facilitate an effective and reality-driven curriculum design.

Table 1 below presents the categories of challenges discussed above that add to the complexity of the interpreter trainer's tasks in the current technological, educational, and market reality. Importantly, while the list may still be expanded to add more details, even the components that it contains now go far beyond the 'traditional' instructor preparation workload in simultaneous interpreter training.

Table 1: Complexity of interpreter trainer's workload in hybrid delivery

Challenge area in hybrid training preparation and delivery	**Interpreter trainer's tasks**
Human and interaction layer	Course sessions sequence planning; Rapid interaction management during (fewer) onsite sessions; Understanding group dynamics with a view to facilitate future (on-line) sessions; Establishing social cohesion of the group on-site to aid a smoother on-line delivery.
Content development layer	Development of pre-course technical guidelines; Development of suitable course content – with speeches to match the mode of delivery; Adaptation of conventional on-site activities to the on-line context; Feedback session design for the two modes.
Technical and technological layer	Platform selection and testing; Liaising with technical support staff prior to lab use in hybrid mode; Selection, integration and testing of CAIT/CAI tools; Planning the configurations and considering their alignment with the curriculum; Self-training for a smooth delivery and troubleshooting through demo sessions with platform providers as well as rehearsals.

3. Building a case for a blended delivery of simultaneous interpreter training: Results of a pilot study

On top of the complexity-related challenges presented in the first part of this chapter, there are also important pragmatic considerations and questions stemming from actual hybrid (on-site and on-line) delivery of simultaneous interpreter training. The predominant question is: does it work well and are its effects satisfactory for both students and trainers? There are multiple approaches to answering such a question, and more research is needed to understand how effectively interpreter training can be delivered in remote and partially remote modes – in comparison to the traditional fully on-site delivery. Apart from investigating trainers' attitudes (as in Biernacka 2021), another possible approach to gauging the effectiveness of blended delivery of simultaneous interpreter training is to look at student assessments. In this section I will present the results of a small-scale longitudinal pilot study aimed at understanding the *perception* of blended learning in simultaneous interpreter training, with an emphasis on training effectiveness and the possible changes in the level of acceptance of remote training over time.

3.1. Study objectives and hypotheses

The objective of the pilot project was to gain an insight into how advanced students of simultaneous interpreting compare and assess the effectiveness of on-line and on-site training during a one-year long, full-time course of simultaneous interpreting. The hypotheses at the point of launching the study were that (1) a hybrid (on-site / face-to-face and on-line) delivery of simultaneous interpreter training is more likely to be assessed more positively than purely remote delivery, and that (2) perception of remote delivery is likely to be more positive if remote delivery is preceded by an on-site session at the beginning of the course.

3.2. Participants and timeframe of implementation

The study was performed over one full academic year (2021–2022) with students of the final year of Applied Linguistics (interpreting pathway) at Adam Mickiewicz University in Poznań. The group consisted of 13 students, but due to absences only nine filled in both questionnaires required for the study. It is important to note that the group of students already had a good understanding of the nature and limitations of remote learning as they had attended fully remote consecutive interpreting classes in the previous academic year (which was heavily affected by lockdowns during the most intense phase of the pandemic). As the academic year 2021–2022 was also partially affected by temporary university closures, it was an assumption before the course started that it would be delivered in a hybrid way: on-site when allowed by the instructor's schedule and by the pandemic, and on-line during any lockdown or health-related university premises closure. The initial plan was to carry out three on-site sessions, amounting to over a half of all teaching hours planned for the course (60 x 45 minutes), but eventually, due to a temporary shift to online classes caused by the pandemic at the beginning of 2022, a total of 28 hours of teaching were delivered on-site, while the remaining 32 hours were delivered on-line. The on-site sessions were more intensive and implemented over two on-site days of face-to-face workshops (6 hours + 8 hours), while the remote classes took place regularly in one- or two-week intervals, with two hours devoted to simultaneous interpreter training and two hours for training in consecutive interpreting. All of the remote classes were delivered via Zoom (the professional license with interpreting functionality). The size of the sample does not warrant statistical analysis and the conclusions drawn on the basis of the findings are of qualitative nature – however, groups of students of simultaneous interpreting are rarely larger than the one described here due to laboratory sizes at most universities, so even such a small group can render meaningful results, which is why the findings and conclusions are included in this chapter. Additionally, please note that the presentation of findings and conclusions in further sections only pertains to the simultaneous training component of the course in question – there was a separate section of the questionnaires on consecutive interpreter training which falls beyond the scope of this contribution.

3.3. Method and procedure

The students received two short questionnaires with questions regarding their on-line and on-site learning experiences. The first one was filled in on day two of the first on-site session, in October 2021, and the second and final questionnaire was filled in at the end of the final on-site session, in June 2022. As the questionnaires contained questions on the perceived effectiveness of training and were distributed by the instructor (the author), to avoid the risk of the respondents withholding some comments, all the questionnaires were anonymised using numbers rather than names and collected by the students themselves prior to handing over to the researcher. Additionally, the students were able to opt out of the study at any point in time during the academic year and up to three months after collecting the final questionnaire. One important challenge in the administration of the questionnaires was the fact that the researcher was also the respondents' trainer. To address this challenge, the pilot study was very clearly presented as separate from the course and as an activity that has no impact whatsoever on the grading of the students. Furthermore, no part of the questionnaire tested any interpretation ability, and the trainer's only contact with the students' handwriting was when he read the randomly numbered questionnaires, which made it impossible to match the students' names to the questionnaires.

3.4. Findings

This section presents the findings from the two questionnaires. Due to the conciseness of the questionnaires, I have decided to quote all the questions preceding the findings in full.

3.4.1. *Questionnaire 1*

This questionnaire was distributed at the end of the first on-site session of the course and consisted of four questions. Approximately 15–20 minutes were allotted for questionnaire completion. The students were asked to provide their answers across the two modes of delivery (on-site vs. on-line) given that all the other variables were stable (class duration, instructor, sources, and activities during the class). The table below presents both the questions and non-redundant answers across the nine respondents (direct quotes).

Table 2: Summary of findings from Questionnaire 1

Question / Task	Answer pertaining to on-site training (total, n=9)	Answer pertaining to on-line training (total, n=9)
How would you assess the **effectiveness** of simultaneous interpreting training depending on the mode of delivery? Please provide your answers on a scale from 1 to 5, where 1= very poor and 5= very good	44 (max=45)	38 (max=45)
In a perfect world, what do you think should be the **proportions** of on-site vs. on-line simultaneous interpreter training? Please use percentages totalling 100 %	73.33 % (mean)	26.67 % (mean)
Please provide 1–3 **advantages** of each delivery mode	real-life, real equipment, easier to focus, more effective learning, focus on tasks rather than solving technical issues, more efficient, booth practice	popular, learning new technologies, authentic challenge, learning new ways of interpreting, adapted to market reality, flexible, prepares for the reality of the profession, convenient
Please provide 1–3 **disadvantages** of each delivery mode.	less flexibility for class scheduling, lower level of health safety	sound quality, technical issues with data throughput and connectivity, time is sometimes wasted on tech issues, platform isn't perfect, switchover in a tandem can pose difficulties

As can be seen in Table 2 above, at the beginning of the course (following the first on-site session) the effectiveness score difference is in favour of on-site training. Furthermore, the respondents' 'perfect world' proportions of on-site vs. on-line training indicate a strong preference for on-site training, albeit with a recognition that there should be room for on-line training in the curriculum – according to the respondents, about one in four sessions should be on-line. A better explanation of these proportions can be found in the lists of advantages and disadvantages, with a more balanced picture in the case of advantages, and more disadvantages cited in relation to online delivery of simultaneous interpreting courses.

3.4.2. *Questionnaire 2*

To track any possible change between the beginning and the end points of the course, the respondents received a similar questionnaire that yielded the results summarised in Table 3 below. An additional element of Questionnaire 2 was a question on how the self-perceived level of acceptance of hybrid (on-site and on-line) delivery of simultaneous interpreting classes changed throughout the academic year.

Table 3: Summary of findings from Questionnaire 2

Question / Task	**Answer pertaining to on-site training (sum, n=9)**	**Answer pertaining to on-line training (sum, n=9), max=45**
How would you assess the **effectiveness** of simultaneous interpreting training depending on the mode of delivery? Please provide your answers on a scale from 1 to 5, where 1= very poor and 5= very good	40 (max=45)	41 (max=45)
In a perfect world, what do you think should be the **proportions** of on-site vs. on-line simultaneous interpreter training? Please use percentages totalling 100 %	66.11 % (mean)	33.89 % (mean)

(*Continued*)

Table 3: Continued

Question / Task	Answer pertaining to on-site training (sum, n=9)	Answer pertaining to on-line training (sum, n=9), max=45
Please provide 1–3 **advantages** of each delivery mode	more feedback and additional information, smoother cooperation with booth partners, physical equipment, more engaging, motivating, interpreting is more interesting on-site, preparation for on-site exams, easier to focus	flexibility, more concrete feedback, more speeches covered, learning how to work on-line, inconsistent quality of audio, reflecting the current market situation, intimacy, concurrent access to the internet, learning a new platform for service delivery, technical reliability, longer (cumulative) periods of actual delivery,
Please provide 1–3 **disadvantages** of each delivery mode	not enough space in booths when some booths are out of order, exhausting, classroom too small, some equipment of poor quality, acoustic problems	on-line classes are very tiring, lack of direct contact and interaction with teacher and peers, lower motivation, challenging cooperation with booth partner

The second questionnaire yielded some differences in both the scores and the quoted advantages and disadvantages. Importantly, unlike in the case of the first questionnaire, the effectiveness scores for on-site and on-line delivery were nearly equal (40 and 41, respectively), with a slight (one point) advantage for on-line delivery, which may come as a surprise after a much more pronounced difference in favour of on-site at the beginning of the academic year. The suggested proportions also reveal a more positive attitude to on-line than in the first questionnaire, although there is still a visible preference for more on-site classes (approximately two-thirds of on-site classes in the 'perfect world' scenario). The lists of advantages and disadvantages from the second round are more balanced than in the first questionnaire, with an apparent deeper insight into both the benefits and the challenges associated with each mode of delivery. Interestingly, the reported issues in the technical and technological area are not limited to on-line delivery – in fact, many students mention them with reference to on-site labs and physical booth equipment, too. The added element in the second questionnaire was a blank diagram with the vertical axis featuring three emoticons representing approximate levels of acceptance and satisfaction with hybrid delivery, and the horizontal axis representing the duration of the course split into months (see Fig. 1 below). The students were asked to draw a curve to show how their acceptance for the hybrid mode changed over time, and the curves from the nine respondents have been plotted into the chart below.

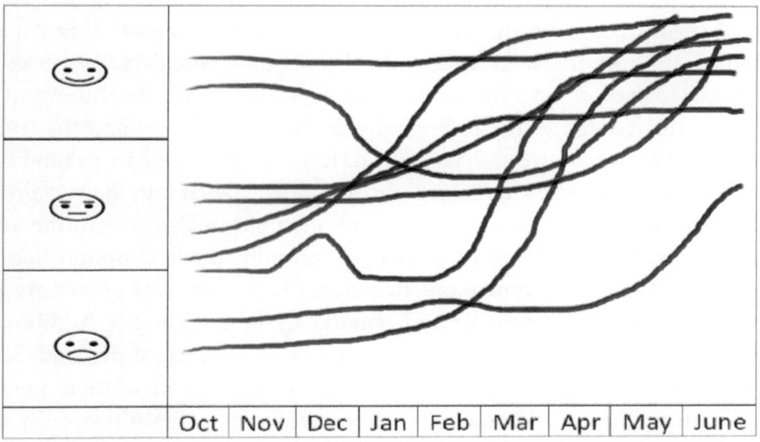

Fig. 1. Curves drawn by the nine respondents to represent their attitude to hybrid delivery of simultaneous training changing over time.

Table description in alternative text: The Figure shows a line chart. Along the vertical axis, there are three icons positioned from top to bottom: a smiley face, a neutral face, and a sad face. Horizontally, the axis is divided into sections for months, from October to June to represent the duration of the academic year. In the chart, there are nine lines representing the student's attitudes to hybrid delivery. All lines but two start in the 'sad face' and 'neutral face' sections of the horizontal axis, but then all of them climb to finish in the 'neutral face' or 'smiley face' sections, representing a more positive attitude at the end of the course. Some lines are flatter than the others and the upward curve is positioned at different moments of the academic year for individual students. One line has a spike in acceptance level, then a drop, then another spike. One line is nearly flat, starting and finishing in the 'smiley face' section of the vertical axis.

With one exception, the curves show a positive trend with a growing level of acceptance and satisfaction over time: apparently, as familiarity with the technology and blended delivery grows, so does the positivity towards a shift from on-site only simultaneous interpreting classes.

4. Conclusions and remarks on further research

Based on the results presented above, and with the caveat of the sample size, the two hypotheses formulated at the beginning of the research project can be confirmed. Firstly, the qualitative comments, the rating and the smiley chart all seem to confirm that the level of acceptance of remote simultaneous interpreter training increases over time. This is understandable because over time the elements of uncertainty that were present at the beginning of the course (mainly related to the technology, the pace of delivery and the level of commitment required), were all partially or fully resolved. Less focus (and time) invested in managing the technology meant it slowly faded into the background and became a facilitator, while more attention could be directed to the actual process of acquiring skills and knowledge. Secondly, the assumption that it is a good idea to begin the course on-site whenever possible was proven right by some of the students' comments and remarks in Tables 2 and 3. Additionally, it is becoming clear that the students' awareness of the current demands of the market is also shaping their attitudes to training: while some of them may not be too keen on distance learning and may openly admit that they prefer face-to-face training, they still recognise the importance of attending remote classes to learn the technologies and the workflow. Finally, it seems that we now also need to look at the on-line vs. on-site question through the lens of relative experiences: inconsistent on-site equipment performance, maintenance works, lab availability and other factors may effectively induce students into thinking that the on-line mode could better cater for their training needs. By the same token, poor platform choices and connectivity issues may result in an aversion to on-line training. Future research in the area must therefore take these variables into account to produce meaningful and generalisable results, as lab conditions and on-line training expertise vary across educational institutions.

All in all, to conclude this chapter, it seems fair to say that a shift in the approach to simultaneous interpreter training is imminent. Firstly, the market demands and the fact that practising interpreters are already doing much of their work remotely means that curricula will have to follow suit. Secondly, the role of the interpreter trainer has expanded to include more technology-related and preparation tasks than before (see Table 1). Future additions to RSI and bespoke training platforms such as ASR-based real-time speech recognition or even speech-to-text translation will further add to the complexity of the trainer's tasks: the presence of more technology will impact material development, feedback provision, and performance evaluation. Time will need to be allocated to purely technical tasks and connectivity checks, and overall preparation time will inevitably expand. On the other hand, hybrid live delivery of classes also opens opportunities such as easier access to experienced remote professionals who might not otherwise be interested in delivering training due to travel / commute time and cost. This may be especially valuable when instructors are needed for training in retour interpreting which is often a market requirement these days, in particular with regard to language combinations featuring English as B or C language. Thanks to on-line training, accessibility for students can also improve through greater flexibility, provided that the platforms and tools selected for teaching truly meet the needs of all student communities, including, for example, students with disabilities. It is also certain that more research is needed into the delivery and effectiveness of simultaneous and consecutive interpreter training in the new technological reality and in different sub-fields beyond 'typical' conference interpreting, such as community interpreting, healthcare interpreting and interpreting in emergencies, to name but a few. Ending on a positive note: learning new skills and new teaching modes with a significant technological component is a must for interpreter trainers, but since most of them are or have been practising interpreters, acquiring new knowledge, and rapidly adapting to a new work environment is second nature to them anyway. However, their increased workload must be noted and considered by professional and tertiary education institutions.

References

Arbaugh, J. B., Bangert, A., Cleveland-Innes, M. (2010). Subject matter effects and the Community of Inquiry (CoI) framework: An exploratory study. *Internet and Higher Education*, 13, pp. 37–44.

Biernacka, A. D. (2021). Towards a common blended learning model for conference and public service interpreting. A case study. In: Šveda, P. (ed.), *Changing Paradigms and Approaches in Interpreter Training: Perspectives from Central Europe*. Routledge.

Braun, S., Slater, C., Gittins, R., Ritsos, P., Roberts, J. C. (2011) Interpreting in Virtual Reality: Designing and developing a 3D virtual world to prepare interpreters and their clients for professional practice. In Kiraly, D., Hansen-Schirra, S., Maksymski, K. (eds,), *New Prospects and Perspectives for Educating Language Mediators* (pp. 93–120), Gunter Narr Verlag.

Chmiel, A., Spinolo, N. (2022). Testing the impact of remote interpreting settings on interpreter experience and performance. Methodological challenges inside the virtual booth. *Translation, Cognition & Behaviour,* 5(2) (2022), pp. 250–274.

Collard, C., Bujan, M. (2021) *ESIT Research Project on Remote Simultaneous Interpreting.* Paris: ESIT.

Clark, D. (2003). *Blended Learning: An EPIC White Paper.* Retrieved from http://www.scribd.com/doc/84278560/Clark-D-Blended-Learning, date of access: 20 February 2023.

Defrancq, B., Fantinuoli, C. (2021). Automatic speech recognition in the booth : Assessment of system performance, interpreters' performances and interactions in the context of numbers. *TARGET-International Journal of Translation Studies,* 33(1), pp. 73–102. https://doi.org/10.1075/target.19166.def

Fantinuoli, C. (2016). InterpretBank. Redefining computer-assisted interpreting tools. https://aclanthology.org/2016.tc-1.5.pdf, date of access: 20 February 2023.

Fantinuoli C. (2021). "Conference interpreting and new technologies". In: Michaela Albl-Mikasa and Elisabet Tiselius (eds), Routledge Handbook of Conference Interpreting. Routledge.

Frittella, F. M. (2021). Computer-assisted Conference Interpreter Training: Limitations and Future Directions. *Journal of Translation Studies vol. 02/2021,* pp. 103–142. https://doi.org/10.3726/JTS022021.6

Frittella, F. M., Rodriguez, S. (2022). Putting SmarTerp to Test: A tool for the challenges of remote interpreting. *INContext: Studies in Translation and Interculturalism Vol. 2 No. 2* (2022)

Friesen, N. (2011). *The Place of the Classroom and the Space of the Screen: Relational Pedagogy and Internet Technology.* New York: Peter Lang.

Hewett, S., Becker, K., Bish, A. (2019). Blended workplace learning: The value of human interaction. *Education and Training,* 61(1), pp. 2–16. https://doi.org/10.1108/ET-01-2017-0004

Kajzer-Wietrzny, M., Tymczynska, M. (2014) Integrating Technology into Interpreter Training Courses: A Blended Learning Approach. In: Intralinea Online Translation Journal, Special Issue: Challenges in Translation Pedagogy, https://www.intralinea.org/specials/article/integrating_technology_into_interpreter_training_courses

Prandi, B. (2020). The use of CAI tools in interpreter training: Where are we now and where do we go from here? *inTRAlinea* Vol. 1/2020.

Rodríguez González, E., Saeed, M. A., Braun, S., Davitti, E., Korybski, T. (2022). The new remoteness: Investigating the role of interface design and automatic speech recognition in supporting interpreters in cloud-based RSI. Conference presentation, 10th European Society for Translation Studies Congress. Retrieved from https://www.researchgate.net/publication/361641294_The_new_remoteness_Investigating_the_role_of_interface_design_and_automatic_speech_recognition_in_supporting_interpreters_in_cloud-based_RSI on 20 February 2023.

Rodríguez Melchor, M. D. Horváth, I., Ferguson K. (eds.). (2020). *The Role of Technology in Conference Interpreter Training*. Oxford, Bern, Berlin, Bruxelles, New York, Wien: Peter Lang.

Saina, F. (2021) Remote Interpreting: Platform Testing in a University Setting to Shape a Post-COVID Scenario. In: *ITA 2021 Conference: The new World – Translation in an Age of Uncertainty*. Israel Translators Association.

Ziegler, K., Gigliobianco, S. (2018). Present? Remote? Remotely present! New technological approaches to remote simultaneous conference interpreting. In: Fantinuoli, C. (ed.), *Interpreting and Technology* (pp. 119–139). Berlin: Language Science Press.

Wojciech Figiel

Chapter 14 Teaching simultaneous interpreting during the COVID-19 pandemic: Technology, society, access

Abstract: In this paper I explore my personal experience as a teacher of simultaneous interpreting during the first few months of the COVID-19 pandemic. To demonstrate its relevance in a wider social context I employ evocative autoethnography. I use Bourdieu's theory of capitals to highlight the ways in which me and my students were (not) able to use resources we had. The paper is focussed on technical issues related to the introduction of online simultaneous interpretation classes. It also deals with accessibility of adopted solutions. I conclude by stressing the importance of disability activism for my success as a teacher during the COVID-19 pandemic.

Keywords: accessibility, simultaneous interpreting, teaching, COVID-19, theory of capitals, autoethnography

1. Introduction

The COVID-19 pandemic caused an enormous upheaval for teachers and learners alike. This required a (group) effort to prepare and deliver classes which would result in the provision of best possible teaching practices.

On March 10th, 2020, the Rector of the University of Warsaw issued a regulation requiring an immediate stop to on-site classes[1]. Little did we know that for the next year and a half virtually all teaching would move online. As university teachers, we were given two weeks to prepare alternative forms of teaching adapted to the new circumstances.

Simultaneous interpreting proved to be one of the hardest subjects to teach online within the domain of humanities and social sciences, as recognised in

1 The full text in English of the Order no. 50 of March 10th, 2020, can be consulted at https://en.uw.edu.pl/wp-content/uploads/2020/03/order_uw_rector_on_prevention_of_the_spread_of_covid-19_virus_among_the_community_of_the_university_of_warsaw.pdf (accessed 20.03.2023).

April 2020 by the then University of Warsaw's Deputy Rector for Students' Affairs[2].

There had been very little, if any, prior experience with online teaching of simultaneous interpreting. Thus, teachers had to adapt quickly to the new reality. Students also expressed their concerns regarding the transition into what was dubbed as emergency remote teaching (ERT) (Hodgest et al., 2020). Even before the lockdown was implemented, a journalist from one of the opinion-making weekly magazines, "Polityka", interviewed several students of interpreting from the Institute of Applied Linguistics who expressed doubts that classes could take place online (Cel, 2020). They reported that it would be challenging to offer online courses in which students need to watch a video, interpret it in booths, and then provide feedback for their peers.

And yet, after only a few weeks of intense searching and collaborative learning, we were able to design ERT tools which ever since then have continued to be improved and are now part and parcel of the teaching process.

This paper aims at describing this journey from my individual perspective. A perspective that not only involves the technical preparation of platforms and materials, but is also related to accessibility of these tools for me as a visually impaired trainer. In this sense it is a rather unique contribution.

At the same time, I wish to emphasise that other trainers of simultaneous interpretation will have other stories to tell and I am absolutely convinced that valuable lessons can be drawn from these. Thus, I want to make it abundantly clear that I am not pretending to claim here (or anywhere else) that I am the only teacher of conference interpreting who has successfully managed the COVID-19 crisis.

2. Theoretical perspective

In the present analysis I am employing two major frameworks. The theory of capitals by Pierre Bourdieu (1986) and autoethnography (Kacperczyk, 2014; Adams et al., 2022).

Pierre Bourdieu's theory has had multiple applications within the field of translation studies (cf. Simeoni, 1998; Wolf & Fukari, 2007; Sela-Sheffy & Shlesinger, 2011; Voerderobermeier, 2014) and has been recognised as one of the cornerstones of the sociological (or social) turn in translation studies (Wolf, 2010). In this paper I am employing the concepts from the Bourdieusian theory

2 See https://youtu.be/ikV-PorUibM?t=4432 (accessed 20.03.2023).

of capitals, which help us understand what resources are at the agents' disposal and why they are (not) able to employ them.

Bourdieu defines capital as "accumulated labor (in its materialized form or its 'incorporated,' embodied form) which, when appropriated on a private, i.e., exclusive, basis by agents or groups of agents, enables them to appropriate social energy in the form of reified or living labor." (1986: 241). He posits that, apart from economic capital, there are other types of capital, notably cultural, social and symbolic capital. In addition, these forms of capitals can reveal themselves in several states.

The objectivised state of cultural capital are objects possessed by agents. These objects are transferrable. In the context of the present paper, objectified state of cultural capital is represented, for example, by fast internet connectivity or high-quality headsets. However, in order for the objectivised cultural capital to be effective, agents need to know how to use it, i.e. possess high volumes of embodied cultural capital. The latter is defined as the dispositions that agents acquire over their lifetime. Thus, the acquisition of cultural capital in its embodied state requires time and effort and cannot be delegated. In the context of this paper the embodied state of cultural capital are the competences acquired by teachers and students of simultaneous interpretation. The institutionalised state of cultural capital are the recognised titles or degrees that flow from possessing stocks of embodied and objectivised cultural capital. The social form of capital, in turn, is "the aggregate of the actual or potential resources which are linked to possession of a durable network of more or less institutionalised relationships of mutual acquaintance and recognition" (Bourdieu, 1986: 251). Finally, symbolic capital, which is a special form of capital, is defined by Bourdieu as "prestige, reputation, fame" (Bourdieu, 1991: 230). Bourdieu states that, under cetain conditions, it is possible to convert one from of capital into another, e.g. cultural capital in its objectivised state may be converted into economic capital.

The second concept, which underpins the analysis undertaken in this paper, is autoethnography. As suggested by Elllis et al. (2010: para. 5), "[a]s a method, autoethnography combines characteristics of autobiography and *ethnography*".

According to Adams et al. (2022: 3):

> "Autoethnography" consists of three characteristics or activities: the "auto," or self; the "ethno," or cul- ture; and the "graphy," or representation/writing/ story.

Thus, papers following this approach should present author's own account of a given event/process and place it in its cultural and/or social context. In addition, autoethnographical accounts differ from standard research publications, in that their aim is to evoke emotions and feelings in readers. Discussing the experience of writing such accounts, Elllis et al. (2010: para. 5) explain:

> When writing an autobiography, an author retroactively and selectively writes about past experiences. Usually, the author does not live through these experiences solely to make them part of a published document; rather, these experiences are assembled using hindsight(…). In writing, the author also may interview others as well as consult with texts like photographs, journals, and recordings to help with recall.

Pat Stikes (2022) argues that the roots of autoethnography go back to sociological imagination, a concept coined by Charles Wright Mills (1959/2000), in which he postulates that the goal of sociological research should be to understand the relationships between the personal troubles and public issues. Such research endevours should include biographical perspective which allows them to place an individual within a broader social structure Mills (1959/2000).

Kacperczyk (2014), in turn, suggests that autoethnography is, among other things, a technique for collecting data:

> authoethnography is conceived as an act of auto-narration based on the proces of introspection, in which the narrator analyses his own experiences, reflects on personal life experiences, while relating them to the social context in which they occurred. […] The essence […] is the mental process itself, the self-reflective and self-analytical activity set in motion by the subject, which is carried out in order to better understand himself in the surrounding world. (Kacperczak, 2014: 37, my translation)

Thus, on the one hand, I am providing an analysis of my own experiences as a trainer, and on the other hand, I try to place them in a broader social context of the pandemic and a need for access for all.

So far the method of autoethnographical research has found a limited echo within translation studies (Hokkanen & Koskinen, 2016; Hokkanen, 2017).

In this article I am employing evocative autoethnography. Papers inspired by this approach "… take the form of a narrative about how the views of their authors on a given topic have been shaped and clashed, and resemble a personal story about grappling with a topic, a story of writing a text, rather than a problem-oriented scholarly communication" (Kacperczyk, 2014: 50, my translation)[3]. This strategic choice determines the form of this paper, which is written in first person and is replete of my personal reflections.

---

3 … przybierają postać narracji o tym, jak kształtowały się i ścierały poglądy ich autorów na omawiany temat i przypominają raczej osobistą opowieść o zmaganiu z tematem, historię pisania tekstu niż uporządkowany pod kątem problemowym przekaz naukowy

The article is based on my own experiences as interpreter trainer at the Institute of Applied Linguistics, where I have been teaching conference interpreting (for students with Polish A, Spanish B/C and English B/C languages). Fittingly for an autoethnographic project, I rely on my own memories of the events described in this paper. I am supporting myself with e-mail correspondence between me and my students, as well as recorded materials from the classes. As there was a general sense of uncertainty as to the validation of the courses of simultaneous interpretation delivered online, after consulting with students, we decided to record every class. Hence, I am able to consult for the purposes of the present analysis an archive of all classes and mock conferences. All materials are anonymised.

3. The challenges of teaching simultaneous interpreting online

Immediately after March 10th, 2020, I started thinking what would be the ideal platform for the provision of simultaneous interpretation training. In thinking of this challenge, I had several priorities;

- classes needed to be synchronous. I rejected outright the idea of providing my students with materials to work asynchronously, as my overarching goal was to reproduce real-life conditions of simultaneous interpreters as faithfully as possible;
- in line with this goal, I was looking for a platform that could reproduce (or at least provide a modicum of experience of) booths;
- as I had been using many video materials (usually these were films available on YouTube), the platform had to offer video reproduction synchronised across all the devices;
- As I am visually impaired, I was forced to look only for such solutions that would be accessible. For example, I required high contrast functionalities and keyboard shortcuts to operate the most frequent activities;
- The platform needed to be free of charge, as at that time the university did not offer us any financial support.

It has to be stressed that right from the beginning I realised that all these priorities had to be met. Some compromises could be made, but, overall, the right solution(s) needed to comply with all the features mentioned above.

Trainers, and interpreter community in general (cf. Przepiórkowska, 2021), began to organise webinars and look for solutions[4]. As useful as those initiative were, no one had knowledge about accessible solutions for the purpose at hand.

4 See e.g. https://vimeo.com/399502353/f6e195082a (accessed 20.03.2023)

Hence, I needed to seek advice from elsewhere. I decided to draw expertise from the community of the blind. At that time, for over 12 years there had been a Polish podcast channel ran by and for the community of the blind[5]. In addition, in August 2019, that group of tech-savvy blind podcasters launched TyfloPrzegląd (TyphloReview) weekly show where listeners could call and ask for assistance. Those podcasters gave me many ideas I would implement in practice.

In terms of Bourdieu's theory of capitals, blind podcasters were part of my social capital, as they were available to assist me in my search of efficient and accessible videoconferencing tool(s).

It was from the members of this community that I learnt that Zoom was (and continues to be) an extremely accessible videoconferencing tool. They tested zoom for its accessibility and offered two hands-on shows on how to work with zoom using screen readers (TyfloPodcast, 2020a, 2020b). At the same time, the first edition of audiobook covering accessibility of zoom was published (Mosen, 2020).

The Basic version of Zoom, available for free in the education sector, had many features that could be used for the purpose of classes of simultaneous interpretation. First, it offered breakout rooms that served as virtual booths. Students would not only be able to work in pairs, but also to see each other. In the latter part of the 2020 summer semester I discovered that students left their cameras intentionally on. These served them to, for example, coordinate handover. That was surprising for me because, as a visually impaired person, I would never use camera for this purpose and would prefer to exchange chat (or voice) messages with my boothmate. Second, Zoom had (and continues to have) features that allow users to enjoy unprocessed sound of very high quality (the so-called "Original sound"). Before every class I would insist on students turning these features on, as they would help me with understanding them and preserve my sense of hearing intact.

The following is an excerpt from an e-mail sent to all students where I summarise my experiences:

> A few remarks that will allow us to use better the possibilities offered by zoom:
>
> 1. Please enter zoom settings and select Audio tab, then Advanced, and then tick the checkbox Show in-meeting option to "Enable original sound". Then, during the meeting, please make sure that the following is shown in the top-left corner: "Turn off original sound" and choose the microphone that you use (there is a little down arrow there). We will be able thus to better hear each other;

5 Tyflopodcast, www.tyflopodcast.net/ (accessed 20.03.2023)

2. For people who have poor internet connection, I suggest choosing the least possible film quality in the youtube settings in order to decrease traffic;
3. I strongly recommend learning a few keyboard shortcuts, e.g. "Alt+A" for turning on/off the microphone. This will make your work easier. Let me remind you that we can use chat and, if needed, cameras in the virtual booths (e-mail to students sent on 18.04.2020)[6].

It can thus be seen that I was sharing the experiences I gained through the contact with the community of blind podcasters (1) and some of my own experiences as a blind person working with zoom (3). Interestingly, I suggested decreasing video quality (2), which, although obvious from the perspective of blind people, might not have been the best choice for my sighted students.

Also, in parallel with instructions on working with zoom, I would always emphasise aspects related to occupational health of interpreters, notably the use of (more or less) professional headsets:

> In view of this exceptional situation, I appeal and urge you to get headsets and microphones which are better than earbuds. This will make your work much easier. I myself did not have such headset, but I have one now. :) In professional work, we usually use such over-ear headphones. Professionally, I would not use earbuds for interpreting assignments.[7]

Incidentally, some of my recommendations did not receive enthusiastic reactions from the students. One group, anonymously, wrote that they would not purchase any special equipment just for my classes. As will be demonstrated below, the

---

6 Kilka uwag, które lepiej pozwolą nam wykorzystać możliwości zooma:

1. Proszę wejść w ustawienia zooma i wybrać zakładkę Audio, a następnie Advanced, a następnie zaznaczyć pole Show in-meeting option to "Enable original sound". Następnie już podczas samego spotkania proszę upewnić się, że po lewej na górze jest napisane „Turn off original sound" i wybrać obok używany przez Państwa mikrofon (tam jest taka strzałka w dół). Wtedy lepiej będziemy się słyszeć;

2. Dla osób, które mają słabe łącze sugeruję, aby w ustawieniach filmu na youtubie wybrać najmniej obciążającą łączę jakość;

3. Bardzo sugeruję nauczyć się kilku skrótów, np. „Alt+A" do włączania/wyłączania mikrofonu. To ułatwi pracę. Przypominam też, iż mamy do dyspozycji chat oraz ew. kamery w wirtualnych kabinach.

7 W związku z naszą wyjątkową sytuacją apeluję i proszę Państwa o zaopatrzenie się w zestawy słuchawkowo-mikrofonowe z prawdziwszego niż „pchełki" do uszu zdarzenia. To bardzo ułatwi Państwu pracę. Ja sam nie miałem, ale już mam.:) W warunkach pracy zawodowej posługujemy się zwykle takimi nausznymi słuchawkami. Z „pchełek" ja zawodowo nie tłumaczyłbym.

very idea of conducting classes over Zoom was treated with a lot of skepticism by the students.

As a last point concerning Zoom, I should mention my attempts at creating amusing rituals around mundane activities, such as assignment of students into breakout rooms. It would always take a few minutes for interpreter tandems to emerge, which created a relaxed atmosphere around the activities.

Looking at this stage from the vantage point of Bourdieu's theory of capital, I managed to multiply, through social capital, my volumes of embodied and objectivised cultural capital. The former is represented by the ability to work with Zoom, while the latter by fast Internet connection and specialised headset. The same was true for my students: in order to fully benefit from my classes they needed to know how to work with Zoom and have access to broadband Internet connection, as well as suitable headphones. In hindsight, a category of particular relevance to autoethnography (cf. Ellis et al., 2010), I am aware that I demanded a lot from my students. It should therefore not be surprising that some expressed their resistance. The pandemic led to deepening of global digital divide (cf. Correia, 2020) between those who had access to digital technologies and those who did not. This divide was clearly visible during my classes and I made an effort to accommodate those (few) students who could not benefit from the state-of-the-art tools I was promoting.

4. Synchronous playback of videos (1)

However, the use of Zoom solved only one challenge, that of having an accessible platform with virtual booths. Students needed to watch videos they would interpret. And the use of screen sharing feature was not possible, because, as I explained in the e-mail sent to students, "where would I then write my comments [feedback] for you"(e-mail sent to students on 14.04.2020)[8]? That was, again, a by-product of me having a visual impairment, as I am always taking notes concerning student interpretation on my laptop. In addition, at that time Zoom did not offer simultaneous screen sharing to all breakout rooms.

Therefore, I needed to find another solution. The first attempt at solving this problem was to use the Sync Watch plugin for Google Chrome[9]. All students were asked to use Google Chrome and install the plugin on their devices. Although its use was problematic, as at times videos were not properly synchronised and

8 (…) gdzie ja wtedy pisałbym komentarze dla Państwa

9 https://chrome.google.com/webstore/detail/sync-watch/ggiafipgeeaaahnjamgpjcgkdpanhddg (accessed 20.03.2020)

students could (accidentally) pause video, nevertheless it allowed me to conduct first synchronous classes (starting in mid-April 2020).

As I grew confident in using the technical setup described above, I started training colleagues from the Institute. I organised several training sessions attended by teachers working with most of the languages that we offer at the Institute of Applied Linguistics. As described below, the method did gain traction among these teachers.

In light of Bourdieusian concepts, my cultural capital became my colleague's social capital, which they could mobilise for their benefit.

5. Synchronous playback of videos (2)…

However, it soon became clear that technical complications resulting from the use of Sync Watch made it very difficult for me to carry on working with this tool[10]. Therefore, as usual, I started looking for better solutions by referring to the resources offered by the community of blind podcasters. In mid-April 2020, they found out about BigBlueButton, an open source platform used for educational purposes. As reported in one of their shows (TyfloPodcast, 2020c), BigBlueButton was fully accessible.

In fact, the BigBlueButton developers are keenly aware of accessibility issues and have set up a whole page devoted to this subject[11]. On this page, they provide a step-by-step tutorial for content creators and any other interested users that discusses what is the exact purpose of the implementation of accessibility features. In addition, BigBlueButton has had annual accessibility audits, the latest of them performed a year ago (Berman, 2022). It has been used successfully in educational settings for inclusion of persons with sensory disabilities. It has also been used as a platform for cultural events, including film festivals, during the pandemic by the community of the blind (Albin & Figiel, 2022).

From my perspective it was important that BigBlueButton (BBB) offered synchronised watching of videos, where only the moderator would be able to play and pause the video. Thus, it solved the most acute issues arising from the use of Sync Watch. In addition, since BBB offers chat functionality, I was able to communicate with all students at the same time (even though they were in

10 It has to be pointed out, though, that my colleagues from the Institute of Applied Linguistics continued to use Sync Watch right until the end of the 2020 Summer semester.

11 https://docs.bigbluebutton.org/accessiblity/ (accessed 20.03.2023).

breakout rooms on Zoom). This, although creating its own complications, gave me much more control of the teaching process.

Analysing this development through the lenses of Bourdieu's theory, it can be posited that this is another case of a successful use my social capital resulting from my participation in the field of disability activists (podcasters).

6. … and mock conferences

I soon realised that, in absence of regular interpreter functionality available on basic version of Zoom, BBB was a suitable place for inviting speakers. Thus, BBB played a role of a meeting room while Zoom that of virtual booths. In late May and June 2020 I organised four mock conferences, three with Spanish-speaking guests and one, bigger, with a speaker addressing students in English. All speakers for these events were recruited through my personal contacts.

The following was the technical setup for the mock conferences. Both students and speakers were logged on two platforms: BBB and Zoom. On Zoom, students were divided into breakout rooms where they would work in pairs interpreting what they heard on BBB. The speaker would be assigned manually to different booths by the meeting moderator.

Students expressed positive opinions about these mock conferences. In particular, they were happy to provide a service for someone who had a genuine need to listen to their interpretation to be able to communicate. As for challenges, they found it difficult to work with two platforms running at the same time. In addition, there were several complaints about some feedback loops (during one event, a speaker did not turn off his microphone on Zoom).

The success of these mock conferences resulted from, to a large extent, the volumes of social and cultural capital. The former represented by the mobilisation of speakers and moderators for the events. While the latter resulting from mastery of the use of Zoom and BBB at the same time. It has to be stressed that these volumes of embodied cultural capital were acquired both by me and also, to some extent, by my students.

7. Feedback and assessment

In general, students appreciated the effort put in organising emergency remote teaching.

When it comes to the overall assessment of courses, some students stressed that their approach to synchronous classes changed over the course of the semester:

> At the beginning, no one in the group wanted to have a class through Zoom. And everyone was like, 'no, no, don't do that'. And yet, in retrospect, we appreciate it (student contribution to the class of 04.06.2020).[12]

In the same vein, another student expressed the following opinion:

> At first I was quite skeptical, because I liked the fact that I could record [materials delivered asynchronously] when I liked, and that if I wanted to, I could even record all three, because the maximum I had to do were three recordings a week, one after the other. In one day, say, on Sunday evening or something like that. And I thought it [synchronous classes] would totally confuse me [...] I suspect that you are aware of this, that your method spread around the institute. Thanks to which, despite the fact that I was skeptical about the German classes I had in this way, for example, it later turned out that they were much better than simply recording myself, and that it gave me more than I expected it could (student contribution to the class on 04.06.2020).[13]

As can be seen in the quote above, the suggested procedure did get traction among some of the other teachers teaching simultaneous interpreting at the Institute of Applied Linguistics.

Many students expressed their positive opinion about the adopted methods of teaching:

> I was very pleased that such classes were organized, so I really appreciate it[14] (student contribution to the class on 04.06.2020).
>
> I am really happy that at least one class was delivered live [synchronously]. Because I personally find that sending these recordings gives me absolutely nothing. Also, it's hard for me to get into it. And it seems that my performance is five times worse than if I were to do it in the class.[15]

---

12 Na początku nikt z grupy nie chciał mieć zajęć przez zooma. I wszyscy byli: 'nie, nie, tylko nie to'. A z perspektywy czasu jednak to doceniamy.

13 Na początku byłem taki dosyć sceptycznie nastawiony, bo podobało mi się, że mogę się nagrać wtedy, kiedy mi się podoba, i że jakbym chciał, to mógłbym nagrać nawet wszystkie trzy, bo w maksymalnym momencie miałem do zrobienia trzy nagrania w tygodniu, jedno po drugim. W ciągu jednego dnia, powiedzmy, w niedzielę wieczorem czy coś takiego. I myślałem, że to mi totalnie rozreguluje [...] Podejrzewam, że jest pan tego świadomy, że pana metoda rozeszła się po instytucie. Dzięki czemu mimo tego, że byłem sceptycznie nastawiony do zajęć, na przykład, z niemieckiego, które miałem w ten sposób, to potem się okazało, że one są znacznie lepsze niż te zwykłe nagrywanie się, i że to mi dało więcej niż spodziewałem się, że może.

14 No tak się ucieszyłam, że coś takiego zostało zorganizowane, więc doceniam to.

15 Bardzo się cieszę, że chociaż jedne zajęcia mieliśmy, właśnie, na żywo. Bo ja zuję osobiście, że przesyłanie tych nagrań nie daje mi absolutnie nic. Poza tym trudno mi się do tego zabrać. I, nie wiem, idzie mi pięć razy gorzej niżbym miała po prostu pójść na zajęcia.

In addition, one student offered suggestions for improving the procedure in the future:

> I would maybe not put so much emphasis on working in booths. Because, I don't know how others feel, but working in booths is kind of… I know that this is how you will work regularly, but the problem is that here, at least, working through Zoom, when you hear everything through one channel, and I, for example, hear everything through headphones now, both the speaker that we are interpreting and the person who is interpreting, that is, the boothmate, it's hard for me to give any help, because I hear everything at once. It's not like I hear one thing with one ear and the other with another ear. So, supporting [boothmate] is not at all that easy, and basically I don't do it, because I can't, I am not able to. (student contribution to the class on 04.06.2020) [16]

As suggested by the quotation above, despite difficult conditions, students were keenly aware of the fact that one of their task was to provide support for their boothmates.

8. Conclusions

The second quarter of 2020 forced us to learn quickly how to operate in the new circumstances. In Bourdieusian terms, we had to acquire sizeable volumes of cultural capital (both in its embodied and objectivised states). Teaching during lockdown required a lot of social capital, both for inviting speakers, as well as for acquiring the necessary knowledge to conduct classes.

The most important social capital I possessed was access and support offered by the community of blind podcasters. They were the ones who discovered most of the solutions to my problems. What is more, they dedicated their free time to test these solutions with me. This, together with other, more mainstream, support offered by a wider community of interpreters, allowed me to provide students with best possible teaching experience. In addition, I was able to teach other trainers, and in doing so I was part of their social capital and, at the same time, expanded their volumes of embodied and objectivised cultural capital.

16 Ja bym może nie nie kładł aż tak dużego nacisku na pracę w kabinach. Bo, nie wiem, jak inni, ale praca w kabinach jest jakby… W sensie wiadomo, że tak się będzie normlanie pracowało, ale problem polega na tym, że tutaj przynajmniej, pracując przez zooma, że jak się słyszy wszystko z jednego kanału, w sensie no ja na przykład przez słuchawki teraz, zarówno nagranie, które tłumaczymy, jak i osobę, która tłumaczy, w sensie konkabinę, to mi jest ciężko udzielić jakiejkolwiek pomocy, bo słyszę wszystko naraz. To nie jest tak, że mam jedno ucho tu, a drugie tam. Także udzielanie tej pomocy wcale nie jest takie proste i w zasadzie ja tego nie robię, bo nie mogę, bo nie potrafię.

Importantly, I had the opportunity to transfer capitals from the field of disability activism into teaching practice.

It was gratifying to see that both students and university authorities appreciated these efforts. In the following two years we were granted more resources and, gradually, emergency remote teaching became transformed into a genuine online teaching and now, into hybrid teaching. However, the volumes of culture capital I acquired over that first few months of online teaching continue to bear fruit.

References

Adams, T., Holman Jones, S., & Ellis, C. (2022). Introduction. Making sense and taking action: Creating a caring community of autoethnographers. In T. Adams, S. Holman Jones, & C. Ellis (Eds.), *Handbook of Autoethnography, 2nd edition* (pp. 1–22). New York: Routledge.

Berman, D. (2022). *Compliance Analysis and Opinion*. Available online at https://bigbluebutton.org/accessibility/ (accessed 20.04.2023).

Bourdieu, P. (1991). *Language and Symbolic Power*. Cambridge: Polity Press.

Bourdieu, P. (1986). The forms of Capital. In E. Richardson (Ed.), *Handbook of Theory and Research for the Sociology of Education* (pp. 241–258). Westport: Greenwood.

Cel, J. (2020). *Studenci wzięli szturmem BUW, zanim go zamknięto*. Available online at https://www.polityka.pl/tygodnikpolityka/spoleczenstwo/1945738,1,studenci-wzieli-szturmem-buw-zanim-go-zamknieto.read (accessed 20.03.2023).

Correia, A. (2020). Healing the digital divide during the COVID-19 pandemic. *Quarterly Review of Distance Education*, 21(1), pp. 13–21.

Ellis, C., Adams, T., & Bochner, A. (2010). Autoethnography: An overview [40 paragraphs]. *Forum Qualitative Sozialforschung / Forum: Qualitative Social Research*, 12(1), Art. 10, http://nbn-resolving.de/urn:nbn:de:0114-fqs1101108 (accessed 20.03.2023).

Figiel, W., & Albin, K. (2022). Receptor tools. In *The Routledge Handbook of Audio Description* (pp. 353–364). New York: Routledge.

Hodges, C., Moore, S., Lockee, B., Trust, T., & Bond, A. (2020). *The Difference between Emergency Remote Teaching and Online Learning*. Available online at https://er.educause.edu/articles/2020/3/the-difference-between-emergency-remote-teaching-and-online-learning (accessed 20.03.2023).

Hokkanen, S. (2017). Experiencing the interpreter's role emotions of involvement and detachment in simultaneous church interpreting. *Translation Spaces*, 6(1), pp. 62–68.

Hokkanen, S., & Koskinen, K. (2016). Affect as a Hinge: The translator's experiencing self as a sociocognitive interface. *Translation Spaces*, 5(1), pp. 78–96.

Kacperczyk, A. (2014). Autoetnografia – technika, metoda, nowy paradygmat? O metodologicznym statusie autoetnografii. *Przegląd Socjologii Jakościowej*, X(3), pp. 32–74.

Mills, C. W. (1959/2000). *The Sociological Imagination*. Oxford: Oxford University Press.

Mosen, J. (2020). My Zoom book, "Meet Me Accessibly", to be withdrawn on 30 September. Available online at https://mosen.org/my-zoom-book-meet-me-accessibly-to-be-withdrawn-on-30-september/ (accessed 20.03.2023).

Przepiórkowska, D. (2021). Adapt or perish: How forced transition to remote simultaneous interpreting during the COVID-19 pandemic affected interpreters' professional practices. *Między Oryginałem a Przekładem*, 27(4(54)), pp. 137–159.

Sela-Sheffy, R., & Shlesinger, M. (Eds.). (2011). *Identity and Status in the Translational Professions*. Amsterdam / Philadelphia: John Benjamins.

Simeoni, D. (1998). The pivotal status of translator's habitus. *Target*, 10(1), pp. 1–39.

Stikes, P. (2022). Introduction: Doing autoethnography. In T. Adams, S. Holman Jones, & C. Ellis (Eds.), *Handbook of Autoethnography, 2nd edition* (pp. 23–28). New York: Routledge.

TyfloPodcast. (2020a). *Zoom*. Available online at https://tyflopodcast.net/zoom-podcast/ (accessed 20.03.2023).

TyfloPodcast. (2020b). *Zaawansowane opcje platformy Zoom*. Available online at https://tyflopodcast.net/zaawansowane-opcje-platformy-zoom/ (accessed 20.03.2023).

TyfloPodcast. (2020c). *TyfloPrzegląd z dnia 21 kwietnia 2020*. Available online at https://tyflopodcast.net/tyfloprzeglad-z-21-kwietnia-2020/# (accessed 20.03.2023).

Vorderobermeier, G. (Ed.). (2014). *Remapping Habitus in Translation Studies*. Amsterdam / New York: Rodopi.

Wolf, M. (2010). Sociology of translation. In: Gambier Y., & van Doorslaer, L. (Eds.), *Handbook of Translation Studies Volume 1* (pp. 335–340). Amsterdam / Philadelphia: John Benjamins.

Wolf, M., & Fukari, A. (Eds.). (2007). *Constructing a Sociology of Translation*. Amsterdam / Philadelphia: John Benjamins.

Studies in Language, Culture and Society

Edited by Łucja Biel, Andrzej Kątny and Piotr Ruszkiewicz

The editors of this series invite books addressing the nexus between language, culture and society. Contrastive studies are welcome in particular, whether of a synchronic or diachronic orientation. Various perspectives on language/communication are of interest: grammatical, pragmatic, sociolinguistic, discursive and semiotic. A wide range of theoretical and methodological positions is accepted: cognitive/anthropological/corpus linguistics, as well as pragmatics, interactional sociolinguistics, (specialized) genre analysis, and critical discourse studies.

The cutting edge of the series is to publish innovative research elucidating the processes of *inter-* and *intra-*language variation and change, and – at the same time – relating them to flows *in* and *across* cognate categories of culture, community and society.

The series publishes monographs and edited volumes reporting on data-driven research that carries a potential for application in translation studies, language teaching, multilingual (multicultural) education, and interdisciplinary critical discourse studies.

The languages of publication are English and German, yet book proposals in other major languages will also be considered, if centrally contributive to the main aim of the series.

Vol. 1 Ewa Kucelman: Self-based Anaphora in Early Modern English. 2013.

Vol. 2 Łucja Biel: Lost in the Eurofog: The Textual Fit of Translated Law. 2014.

Vol. 3 Marek Kuźniak / Agnieszka Libura / Michał Szawerna (eds.): From Conceptual Metaphor Theory to Cognitive Ethnolinguistics. Patterns of Imagery in Language. 2014.

Vol. 4 Grzegorz Kowalski: Claim-making and Claim-challenging in English and Polish Linguistic Discourses. 2015.

Vol. 5 Małgorzata Tryuk: On Ethics and Interpreters. 2015.

Vol. 6 Anna Duszak / Grzegorz Kowalski (eds.): Academic (Inter)genres: between Texts, Contexts and Identities. 2015.

Vol. 7 Alicja Witalisz: English Loan Translations in Polish. Word-formation Patterns, Lexicalization, Idiomaticity and Institutionalization. 2015.

Vol. 8 Agnieszka Kampka / Katarzyna Molek-Kozakowska (eds.): Rhetoric, Knowledge and the Public Sphere. 2016.

Vol. 9 Maria Załęska / Urszula Okulska (eds.): Rhetoric, Discourse and Knowledge. 2016.

Vol. 10 Łucja Biel: Lost in the Eurofog: The Textual Fit of Translated Law. Second Revised Edition. 2017.

Vol. 11 Karolina Broś / Grzegorz Kowalski (eds.): Discourse Studies – Ways and Crossroads. Insights into Cultural, Diachronic and Genre Issues in the Discipline. 2017.

Vol. 12 Iga Lehman: Authorial Presence in English Academic Texts. A Comparative Study of Student Writing across Cultures and Disciplines. 2018.

Vol. 13 Katarzyna Stachowiak: Phonology Matters in Interpreting. 2018.

Vol. 14 Agnieszka Biernacka: Interpreter-Mediated Interactions of the Courtroom. A Naturally Occurring Data Based Study. 2019.

Vol. 15 Małgorzata Gaszyńska-Magiera: Reception of Translations of Spanish American Prose in Poland in 1945-2005 from the Perspective of Intercultural Communication. 2019.

Vol. 16 Dariusz Koźbiał: The Language of EU and Polish Judges. Investigating Textual Fit Through Corpus Methods. 2021.

Studies in Language, Culture and Society

Edited by Łucja Biel, Andrzej Kątny and Agnieszka Biernacka

Vol. 17 Katarzyna Wasilewska: Administrative Reports. A Corpus Study of the Genre in the EU and Polish National Settings. 2021.

Vol. 18 Agnieszka Biernacka / Wojciech Figiel (eds.): New Insights into Interpreting Studies. Technology, Society and Access. 2023.

www.peterlang.com

www.ingramcontent.com/pod-product-compliance
Ingram Content Group UK Ltd.
Pitfield, Milton Keynes, MK11 3LW, UK
UKHW041826100926
8556IPUK00002B/36

9 783631 884850